About the Authors

Sandra Hardin Gookin has jumped full force into the computer world with her husband, Dan. Her background in speech communications (an excellent degree from Oklahoma State University) has enabled her to join the writing style of Dan. She too can make difficult subjects, such as computers, easy to understand. Sandra's current list of titles include *Teach Yourself Windows 2000 in 24 Hours, How to Use Excel 2000,* and *Parenting For Dummies.*

Dan Gookin is as close to a household name as it gets in the computer book industry. Dan is not only a talented writer but also a computer "guru" whose job is to remind everyone that computers are not to be taken too seriously.

Dan has written over 70 books on computers, including the original "Dummies" book, *DOS For Dummies,* which started this whole *For Dummies* sensation. Dan's most recent titles include the best-selling *Buying a Computer For Dummies, PCs For Dummies,* 7th Edition, *Word 2000 For Windows For Dummies,* and *How to Use Excel 2000.* He holds a degree in communications/ visual arts (okay, let's be honest: Art!) from UCSD and lives with his wife and four sons in the rustic and untamed state known as Idaho.

More Gookin Titles

To find more titles written by Dan Gookin and Sandra Hardin Gookin, please visit their Title Page, at http://www.wambooli.com/titles/.

ABOUT IDG BOOKS WORLDWIDE

Welcome to the world of IDG Books Worldwide.

IDG Books Worldwide, Inc., is a subsidiary of International Data Group, the world's largest publisher of computer-related information and the leading global provider of information services on information technology. IDG was founded more than 30 years ago by Patrick J. McGovern and now employs more than 9,000 people worldwide. IDG publishes more than 290 computer publications in over 75 countries. More than 90 million people read one or more IDG publications each month.

Launched in 1990, IDG Books Worldwide is today the #1 publisher of best-selling computer books in the United States. We are proud to have received eight awards from the Computer Press Association in recognition of editorial excellence and three from Computer Currents' First Annual Readers' Choice Awards. Our best-selling ...For Dummies® series has more than 50 million copies in print with translations in 31 languages. IDG Books Worldwide, through a joint venture with IDG's Hi-Tech Beijing, became the first U.S. publisher to publish a computer book in the People's Republic of China. In record time, IDG Books Worldwide has become the first choice for millions of readers around the world who want to learn how to better manage their businesses.

Our mission is simple: Every one of our books is designed to bring extra value and skill-building instructions to the reader. Our books are written by experts who understand and care about our readers. The knowledge base of our editorial staff comes from years of experience in publishing, education, and journalism — experience we use to produce books to carry us into the new millennium. In short, we care about books, so we attract the best people. We devote special attention to details such as audience, interior design, use of icons, and illustrations. And because we use an efficient process of authoring, editing, and desktop publishing our books electronically, we can spend more time ensuring superior content and less time on the technicalities of making books.

You can count on our commitment to deliver high-quality books at competitive prices on topics you want to read about. At IDG Books Worldwide, we continue in the IDG tradition of delivering quality for more than 30 years. You'll find no better book on a subject than one from IDG Books Worldwide.

John Kilcullen
Chairman and CEO
IDG Books Worldwide, Inc.

Eighth Annual
Computer Press
Awards ≥1992

Ninth Annual
Computer Press
Awards ≥1993

Tenth Annual
Computer Press
Awards ≥1994

Eleventh Annual
Computer Press
Awards ≥1995

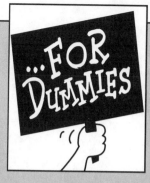

™

References for the Rest of Us!®

BESTSELLING BOOK SERIES

Are you intimidated and confused by computers? Do you find that traditional manuals are overloaded with technical details you'll never use? Do your friends and family always call you to fix simple problems on their PCs? Then the ...*For Dummies*® computer book series from IDG Books Worldwide is for you.

...*For Dummies* books are written for those frustrated computer users who know they aren't really dumb but find that PC hardware, software, and indeed the unique vocabulary of computing make them feel helpless. ...*For Dummies* books use a lighthearted approach, a down-to-earth style, and even cartoons and humorous icons to dispel computer novices' fears and build their confidence. Lighthearted but not lightweight, these books are a perfect survival guide for anyone forced to use a computer.

> "I like my copy so much I told friends; now they bought copies."
>
> — Irene C., Orwell, Ohio

> "Quick, concise, nontechnical, and humorous."
>
> — Jay A., Elburn, Illinois

> "Thanks, I needed this book. Now I can sleep at night."
>
> — Robin F., British Columbia, Canada

Already, millions of satisfied readers agree. They have made ...*For Dummies* books the #1 introductory level computer book series and have written asking for more. So, if you're looking for the most fun and easy way to learn about computers, look to ...*For Dummies* books to give you a helping hand.

1/99

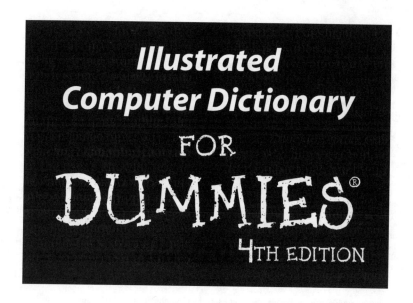

Illustrated
Computer Dictionary
FOR
DUMMIES®
4TH EDITION

by Sandra Hardin Gookin and Dan Gookin

IDG Books Worldwide, Inc.
An International Data Group Company

Foster City, CA ◆ Chicago, IL ◆ Indianapolis, IN ◆ New York, NY

Illustrated Computer Dictionary For Dummies,® 4th Edition

Published by
IDG Books Worldwide, Inc.
An International Data Group Company
919 E. Hillsdale Blvd.
Suite 400
Foster City, CA 94404
www.idgbooks.com (IDG Books Worldwide Web Site)
www.dummies.com (Dummies Press Web Site)

Library of Congress Control Number: 00-101530

ISBN: 0-7645-0732-X

Printed in the United States of America

10 9 8 7 6 5 4 3 2 1

4B/TR/QY/QQ/IN

Distributed in the United States by IDG Books Worldwide, Inc.

Distributed by CDG Books Canada Inc. for Canada; by Transworld Publishers Limited in the United Kingdom; by IDG Norge Books for Norway; by IDG Sweden Books for Sweden; by IDG Books Australia Publishing Corporation Pty. Ltd. for Australia and New Zealand; by TransQuest Publishers Pte Ltd. for Singapore, Malaysia, Thailand, Indonesia, and Hong Kong; by Gotop Information Inc. for Taiwan; by ICG Muse, Inc. for Japan; by Intersoft for South Africa; by Eyrolles for France; by International Thomson Publishing for Germany, Austria and Switzerland; by Distribuidora Cuspide for Argentina; by LR International for Brazil; by Galileo Libros for Chile; by Ediciones ZETA S.C.R. Ltda. for Peru; by WS Computer Publishing Corporation, Inc., for the Philippines; by Contemporanea de Ediciones for Venezuela; by Express Computer Distributors for the Caribbean and West Indies; by Micronesia Media Distributor, Inc. for Micronesia; by Chips Computadoras S.A. de C.V. for Mexico; by Editorial Norma de Panama S.A. for Panama; by American Bookshops for Finland.

For general information on IDG Books Worldwide's books in the U.S., please call our Consumer Customer Service department at 800-762-2974. For reseller information, including discounts and premium sales, please call our Reseller Customer Service department at 800-434-3422.

For information on where to purchase IDG Books Worldwide's books outside the U.S., please contact our International Sales department at 317-572-3993 or fax 317-572-4002.

For consumer information on foreign language translations, please contact our Customer Service department at 1-800-434-3422, fax 317-572-4002, or e-mail rights@idgbooks.com.

For information on licensing foreign or domestic rights, please phone +1-650-653-7098.

For sales inquiries and special prices for bulk quantities, please contact our Order Services department at 800-434-3422 or write to the address above.

For information on using IDG Books Worldwide's books in the classroom or for ordering examination copies, please contact our Educational Sales department at 800-434-2086 or fax 317-572-4005.

For press review copies, author interviews, or other publicity information, please contact our Public Relations department at 650-653-7000 or fax 650-653-7500.

For authorization to photocopy items for corporate, personal, or educational use, please contact Copyright Clearance Center, 222 Rosewood Drive, Danvers, MA 01923, or fax 978-750-4470.

Authors' Acknowledgments

We would like to extend special thanks to Jordan Gookin and Tyler Sherman for their hard work in looking up computer terms for us. It's a tedious, boring chore that they did without too much complaining, tears, or temper tantrums. Thanks also to all the other people who wrote computer dictionaries from which we stole words we never really use. And, as usual, thanks to the IDGB staff for doing such a blasted fine job with everything.

No one named "Webster" was involved with this project. No meat products (or meat by-products) were consumed while typing the text of this book.

Dan and Sandy Gookin

Publisher's Acknowledgments

We're proud of this book; please register your comments through our IDG Books Worldwide Online Registration Form located at http://my2cents.dummies.com.

Some of the people who helped bring this book to market include the following:

Acquisitions, Editorial, and Media Development

Project Editor: Rebecca Whitney

Acquisitions Editor: Ed Adams

Proof Editors: Teresa Artman, Dwight Ramsey

Technical Editor: Jeff Wiedenfeld

Editorial Manager: Mary C. Corder

Editorial Assistant: Sarah Shupert

Production

Project Coordinator: Maridee V. Ennis

Layout and Graphics: Elizabeth Brooks, Barry Offringa, Brian Torwelle

Proofreaders: Laura Albert, David Faust, Steven Jong, Susan Moritz

Special Help
Constance Carlisle

General and Administrative

IDG Books Worldwide, Inc.: John Kilcullen, CEO

IDG Books Technology Publishing Group: Richard Swadley, Senior Vice President and Publisher; Walter R. Bruce III, Vice President and Publisher; Joseph Wikert, Vice President and Publisher; Mary Bednarek, Vice President and Director, Product Development; Andy Cummings, Publishing Director, General User Group; Mary C. Corder, Editorial Director; Barry Pruett, Publishing Director

IDG Books Consumer Publishing Group: Roland Elgey, Senior Vice President and Publisher; Kathleen A. Welton, Vice President and Publisher; Kevin Thornton, Acquisitions Manager; Kristin A. Cocks, Editorial Director

IDG Books Internet Publishing Group: Brenda McLaughlin, Senior Vice President and Publisher; Sofia Marchant, Online Marketing Manager

IDG Books Production for Branded Press: Debbie Stailey, Director of Production; Cindy L. Phipps, Manager of Project Coordination, Production Proofreading, and Indexing; Tony Augsburger, Manager of Prepress, Reprints, and Systems; Shelley Lea, Supervisor of Graphics and Design; Debbie J. Gates, Production Systems Specialist; Steve Arany, Associate Automation Supervisor; Robert Springer, Supervisor of Proofreading; Trudy Coler, Page Layout Manager; Kathie Schutte, Senior Page Layout Supervisor; Janet Seib, Associate Page Layout Supervisor; Michael Sullivan, Production Supervisor

Packaging and Book Design: Patty Page, Manager, Promotions Marketing

◆

The publisher would like to give special thanks to Patrick J. McGovern,
without whom this book would not have been possible.

◆

Table of Contents

Introduction

Here it is, the *Illustrated Computer Dictionary For Dummies,* 4th Edition, your shield in the constant word battle that takes place between the nerds, geeks, technoweenies, and people like us who have to put up with the jargon. We've scoured the magazines and manuals. We've hung out at seminars and snuck into corporate BBQs. We've hunted down words in dark, programmers' dungeons and listened to taped conversations of bigwigs talking in acronym-speak. And we've been to Microsoft and read the bathroom stall walls. Okay, and we've even made up a few words ourselves. The result is this comprehensive, easy-to-understand approach to computer terms and — if you dare — figuring out how to incorporate such terms into your everyday conversation.

The Logical Approach

After long periods of careful thought, we decided to lay this book out in alphabetic format and, further, to alphabetize all the words for your referencing needs. Symbols ("@#$%^&*!") and numbers (0–9) are listed first in their own chapters. After that, it's A to Z — with all the letters in between in proper order. (And we're assuming that you know the alphabet here, sung to the tune of *Twinkle, Twinkle* in case you forgot; ask any 5-year-old.)

Each chapter starts off with a graphical depiction of the letter (or random things for the symbols). You'll see the letter and then boxes describing the letter: Nerd info, Braille, Alien alphabet, Semaphores, American Sign Language, and Morse code.

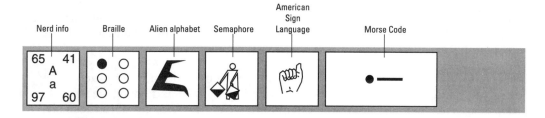

The Nerd info box contains the ASCII code values for each letter in the four corners: decimal values on the left and hexadecimal values on the right. Uppercase letters are shown at the top; lowercase on the bottom. This is for true computer nerds only, but we thought it looked cool, so we included it anyway.

The words are presented in the following format. First, we give you the word itself, and then a pronunciation guide, followed by the word's meaning or a definition and optional sample usage:

dictionary *(dik-shun-aer-ee)* A book that contains a list of words and their pronunciations and meanings. When you don't know what a word means, you look it up in a dictionary. When you want to be sure that you're using a word properly, you look it up in the dictionary. When you're losing an argument and need some random though professional-sounding source to quote, you use the dictionary. "My kid keeps asking me what words mean, so I tell him to 'look it up in the *dictionary*' because I'm too embarrassed to admit that I don't know what the words mean myself."

Icons Used in This Book

An Internet or online term.

A term having to do with the Windows operating system.

A Macintosh computer term, just to make those people happy.

Philosophical Stuff

Nothing is worse than reading a manual, book, or article and then coming across a word you don't know. So, you look the word up and are unable to understand the definition. You're still lost.

Our purpose behind this dictionary is to both enlighten and inform in such a way that you really understand the new term you just read. To add flavor, we've tossed in some entertainment value as well. Computers are always thought of as these big, frowning, cold, and serious devices of torment — like nuns in a Catholic school. The truth is, they aren't. And nuns really aren't big and frowning either! Instead, computers have a vast potential for humor and enjoyment, as we're sure nuns do too! This book presents technical information with that attitude in the hopes that you will understand it better. And if not that, then at least you'll be able to tolerate the terminology with a modicum of levity.

@ # $ % ^ & * ! 0 – 9

| Numbers and Symbols | | | | |

! *(exclamation point; bang)* 1. The exclamation point is used at the end of a sentence to denote excitement ("Your wife is here!") or maybe surprise ("My heart!"). In Spanish, a preceding exclamation point pre-alerts the reader to the excitement level of the sentence: "¡Su esposa esta aqui!" Y "¡Mi corazon!" 2. In the C programming language, the ! is used to mean "not," as in this example:

```
!TRUE = FALSE
```

 The preceding line means "Not true is the same thing as false" — almost a universal truth anywhere but in Washington, D.C. 3. In the old Usenet electronic-mail system, ! was called a bang. It's used in someone's electronic address — like a highly effective zip code, as shown in this example:

```
crash!dang
```

This line could be the electronic address of "dang" on the crash system. The address is "crash, bang, dang." (It's no longer a valid address on the Internet.)

Did you ever notice that all the sentences in *Mad* magazine end in either an exclamation point or a question mark?

!= *(not equal)* This symbol means "not equal." It's a combination of the ! (not) sign and the = (equal) sign, often used in making a mathematical comparison, such as in the C language. "Watching baseball on TV is just != to being at the ballpark." See also <>.

" *(double quotes)* This symbol is often used to "hug" text, in what's called a *string* of text. For example:

```
"The pastry was dry and the
coffee tasted like it had been
strained through a dirty gym
sock."
```

The text between the quotes is the string, but the quotes themselves are not.

(pound, number, or tic-tac-toe) 1. The pound symbol, located above the 3 key on American keyboards. This symbol is used in written language to represent numbers or items: "All right, Becky, you chose #3, Medical Instruments I've Found on the Beach." 2. In some versions of UNIX, the # is the system prompt:

```
# rm /usr/*
```

3. The # symbol also has appeal as a nice, solid character. Some people use it decoratively or to produce crude graphics:

@

```
######
#      #
# #  # #
#      #
# #### #
#  ##  #
#      #
######
```

4. On British keyboards, the # symbol is replaced by ₤, which really means "pound." (The # is called the "hash" character in English English.)

*(error message)* An error message in an Excel spreadsheet informing you that the numeric value entered in the cell is too wide to display within the cell. See the following table for more Excel error messages:

Message	Occurs When
#Value!	The wrong type of value for a calculation is used.
#DIV?0!	A formula divides by zero.
#Name?	Microsoft Excel doesn't recognize text in a formula.
#N/A	A value is not available to a function or a formula.
#REF!	A cell reference is not valid.
#NUM!	A problem occurs with a number in a formula or function.
#NULL!	You specify an intersection of two areas that do not intersect.

$ *(dollar sign; string; hex)* 1. The dollar sign is used in a number of ways, most of which really have to do with money. When followed by a number, as in $1,000,000, the dollar sign obviously means one million dollars, big bucks, moola. 2. In the BASIC programming language, a dollar sign is used to identify a *string,* or text variable. FIRST$ would be a variable named FIRST that holds a string value. It's pronounced "first-string," by the way; not "first-SS" or "first-dollar sign." 3. Some programming languages use the dollar sign to denote a *hexadecimal* (base 16) number. For example, $14 is the hexadecimal value 14 (20 decimal). $A1 is the hexadecimal value A1 (161 decimal). In this usage, the $ is pronounced "hex." $A1 is "hex-A-one." 4. In MS-DOS, the dollar sign is used as a meta character to insert exciting items into the DOS prompt:

```
prompt $p$g
```

In this example, the $p inserts the time into the DOS prompt and $g inserts the greater-than (>) character.

% *(percent sign)* 1. The percent sign sometimes actually represents a percentage value: 15% means 15 percent or 15 parts out of 100 or .15 or a value that's considered fairly good for weather forecasters and economists. The percent sign also plays numerous roles in various programming languages. 2. In BASIC, the percent sign denotes an integer variable: ITEM% is an integer variable named ITEM. You don't pronounce the %. 3. In the C programming language, the % is used as the *modulus* operator (which figures out the remainder when one number is divided

@

by another). The % is also used to format output with the printf function.

& *(am-per-sand)* 1. The character is correctly called an ampersand. *Ampers* comes from the ancient Vulcan for "this squiggly symbol means" and *and,* meaning "and." 2. Commonly used to represent *and,* as in "such & such" or, more accurately, "Sterling, Worbletyme & Grockmeister." Most purists reject this form, preferring to spell out the letters a-n-d. 3. In computer programming, & sometimes represents a "logical and." For example:

```
IF(NUMBER=1 & LETTER=A) THEN
"We're at the beginning."
```

4. In the C programming language, two ampersands are used to make a logical and operation: &&.

' *(apostrophe; tick; single quote)* 1. In English, marks the possessive: "Bill's deficit." 2. Pairs are used to double-quote text, often with the accent grave (the backward apostrophe, `):

```
``This is less serious than we
thought.´´
```

3. In the BASIC programming language, the apostrophe at the start of a line marks a comment.

( ) *(parentheses, parens)* 1. Parentheses are used in programming to group things together. Usually, this grouping happens in long mathematical operations; what appears between the parentheses is figured out first. 2. Most programming languages use parentheses to group together options and arguments for certain commands and keywords. 3. A single parenthesis is a

paren. When someone says "left paren," he's referring to the (character. The right paren is the). This comes in handy when reading computer typing instructions over the phone.

(C) *(copyright symbol)* 1. Many software packages use a big C in parentheses to represent the © (copyright) symbol because the © isn't on most keyboards. Likewise, you may see (TM) for a trademark. 2. In most Microsoft Office applications, you can produce the copyright symbol by pressing Ctrl+Alt+C on your keyboard; pressing Ctrl+Alt+T produces the trademark symbol.

 * *(asterisk; star; splat)* 1. In most computer programming languages and spreadsheets, the asterisk serves as the multiplication symbol. This is probably because the × symbol does not appear on the keyboard and a little X (x) just doesn't cut it. 2. In some operating systems, the asterisk serves as a wildcard character representing a group of letters in a filename. The asterisk is pronounced "star" in this case: *.* is "star-dot-star." 3. In e-mail and other plain-text communications, the asterisk is used in a decorative fashion. Occasionally, it may appear to add emphasis when italics and bold type aren't available:

```
I was so *embarrassed*.
```

4. The asterisk may be used as a form of self censorship while sending an e-mail message:

```
Eat **** and die!
```

5. Nathan Hale did not say "I regret that I have but one asterisk for my country."

@

6. Other names for * include "dingbat" and "splat." Splat is from the final result of dropping something mushy from a high altitude. The resulting spot would look like this:

Splat!

+ (plus) 1. The addition symbol. Be grateful that this symbol is on your keyboard, lest you be forced to use the letter *T* or something equally obnoxious to represent addition:

```
2 + 2 = 5
```

2. The plus sign may also be used to connect two items, as shown in this example:

```
COPY A.DOC+B.DOC AB.DOC
```

In DOS, this command glues the file B.DOC to the end of the file A.DOC, creating a new file AB.DOC. This gluing together is known as *concatenation,* which is literally translated as "sticking two cats together," though the more common "sticking two things together" is generally accepted. (See *concatenate* for the details as well as pronunciation.)

– (minus sign; hyphen) 1. The minus sign is used in various corners of computer mathdom, primarily as the minus sign:

```
4 - 2 = 2
```

It's also used to identify a negative number:

```
--5
```

2. The hyphen is the minus sign's evil twin, which is the same character but used with words, such as Mary-Francis. 3. Two hyphens can be used together in text to denote a clause or parenthetical element – – like this! 4. In typographical terms, there are hyphens, en dashes, and em dashes, which are each used in different circumstances. The hyphen is the smallest one of the three. An *en dash* is a dash character with the same width as the letter *n*. The *em dash* is a longer dash, the same width as the letter *m*. This is all typographical trivia that makes only finicky editors happy.

. (period, dot) 1. Used in text to mark the end of a sentence. 2. In math, the period is used to mark the decimal portion of a number: 3.141. In that case, it's pronounced "point," as in "three point one four one." 3. In some countries, the period is used to separate the hundreds from the thousands or the thousands from the ten-thousands: 1.000 is one thousand. (In these weird places, the comma is used as the decimal point. Strange.) 4. In some operating systems, the period is used to separate a filename from its extension. 5. In a hockey game, there are three periods: . . . 6. The period is used to separate elements in an Internet address. In this case, the period is pronounced "dot," as in

```
www.dummies.com
```

which is pronounced "Dub-ya dub-ya dub-ya dot duh-mees dot kom."

/ *(slash; division symbol)* 1. The forward slash character is used in text to separate items: on/off and up/down, for example. 2. In computer math, the / symbol is used for division. This is because the ÷ character isn't available on most keyboards. So 15/3 means "15 divided by 3." 3. This symbol has a host of names associated with it: In addition to *slash* and *division symbol,* you may find *forward slash, solidus, stroke, virgule, and the forward-pointing thing under the question mark key.* 4. Internet address dividing line, used like this:

```
http://www.wambooli.com/titles
```

: *(colon)* 1. In most PC operating systems, a colon is used after a disk drive letter, such as in the C: drive to refer to your hard drive, and after device names, such as in PRN: to refer to the printer. 2. In C programming, the colon is sometimes used, such as when you're declaring structure templates for bit fields. 3. Humans use the colon to digest food.

General Colin Powell.

 :-) *(smile; smiley)* Electronic-mail method of showing a smile. (Put your head on your left shoulder to see the smile.) It implies that the tone of the message is happy. This symbol is necessary in many cases when a tongue-in-cheek message could easily be misunderstood. "No, I don't think you're a geek. You have no fashion sense, but you're not a geek. :-)"

 :-(*(frown)* Electronic-mail method of showing a frown, as in sadness. The opposite of :-).

 :-* *(kiss)* Electronic-mail method of showing a kiss, as in physical contact, lips meeting. Do not use casually.

; *(semicolon)* Used in some Windows files as well as in DOS's CONFIG.SYS file, as a symbol to show that a line of text is a comment and not some command.

```
;This line will be ignored: The
computer is afraid of it!
```

 ;-) *(wink)* Electronic-mail method of showing a wink, as you would do in a verbal conversation. See also :-).

< *(less than)* 1. Used in most computer programming languages to compare two values, testing to see whether one is less than another. 2. Some operating systems use the less-than symbol to redirect input to a device.

<= *(less than or equal to)* The less-than symbol can be combined with the equal sign to compare two values in a test. The test passes if the first value is less than or equal to the second. For example:

```
9 <= 10 is true
10 <= 10 is true
10 <= 9 is false
Hollywood <= "real life" is
always true
```

<> *(not equal; angle brackets)* 1. In some programming languages, the <> symbol set is used to test whether two values are not equal to each other. It's

pronounced "not equal to." 2. Angle brackets are sometimes used when straight-edged people tire of parentheses. There is no rhyme, reason, or rule for when these symbols are used. 3. Angle brackets may also enclose emphasized text in e-mail: "Tomorrow I'm turning <gasp> 30 years old!"

= *(equal sign)* 1. Used to denote equality or that something is equal to something else. For example, CALORIES = TASTES GOOD. 2. In most programming languages, the equal sign is used when assigning a value to a variable.

How the equal sign equates two items.

== *(double equal sign; is equal to)* 1. Used in some instances to denote that two things are equal. 2. In the C programming language, the double equal sign is used when comparing two values.

> *(greater than; quote; redirected output)* 1. The greater-than symbol in math. For example:

```
Feelings > Honesty
```

2. Commonly used in electronic mail when quoting what someone had just written to you:

```
You wrote:
>Your mother dresses you funny.

And you wonder why I don't
write you any more?
```

Other characters can be used to quote text, though > is most common. 3. Used in some operating systems to redirect output to a file or some other device.

>> *(append)* 1. There is really no way to pronounce any of these symbols, though "ugh-ugh" is often used. Some say "double greater-than." Others may just say "append," which is what these characters do in DOS:

```
TYPE SIGNATUR.TXT >> LETTER.DOC
```

The preceding DOS command takes the information in the file SIGNATUR.TXT and sticks it to the end of the file LETTER.DOC. Note that this trick works only with text files, not with documents created with a word processor or other formatted documents. 2. The bit-wise shift-left command in the C language — something completely nerdy that needs no additional explanation here. 3. In some European languages, these characters are used as quotes, though they're doubled up:

```
>Jaques! The Quiche is ruined!
```

>= *(greater than or equal to)* Used to compare two values in a test (as in a database query, for example). The test passes if the first value is greater than or equal to the second value. For example:

```
10 >= 9 is true
10 >= 10 is true
10 >= 11 is false
good >= evil -- we hope is true
```

? *(question mark)* 1. The question mark sits at the end of a sentence when the sentence is a question? Sure it does! 2. Used in some operating systems as a wildcard character, a placeholder for other characters to be matched in a search. 3. In BASIC, the ? can be used as an abbreviation for the PRINT command.

@ *(at sign)* 1. An abbreviation for *at,* as in "Meet Jon @ 7 PM for secret rendezvous." 2. Used in Internet mail addresses to identify the domain, such as

```
dang@idgbooks.com
```

which is the address of *dang* (Dan Gookin) "at" *idgbooks* (dot) *com,* which is the domain. 3. Like the * and # symbols, the @ has a variety of other terms used to describe it. You may encounter *about, strudel, rose,* and *cabbage.*

[] *(square brackets; brackets)* 1. Parentheses who just never really caught on. Mostly you'll find square brackets used to describe options for a command. For example:

```
spin [/fast] [/backward]
```

The brackets mean that the items enclosed within them are optional. 2. Brackets are used in various programming languages in different ways. In C, they contain array element numbers; in Assembly, they reference memory locations; and so on.

**** *(backslash)* 1. The symbol used in MS-DOS to separate directories and filenames, such as C:\WINDOWS\SYSTEM or A:\PASCAL. Don't goof up the backslash key with the forward slash (/). 2. The backslash is used in various programming languages for various purposes too various to mention here.

^ *(caret; hat; control)* 1. The wee little symbol above the 6 key on most keyboards is known as the *caret.* It is used in foreign languages to accent certain letters, and it has a variety of computer purposes as well. 2. Used as an abbreviation for *control,* which refers to the ASCII control characters as well as to key combinations on your keyboard. So, Ctrl+S can also be written as ^S (pronounced "control-S"). You may even see ^S appear on a menu as a command's shortcut key. 3. Used in many programming languages for a variety of purposes. For example, ^ is used in some programming languages as a mathematical operator for "raising to the power of": 2^4 means 2 to the fourth power. In C, ^ is used as a bit-wise exclusive OR operator.

_ *(underline; underscore)* 1. The underline is often used as a replacement for a space when the space is not allowed. For example: FILE_NAME instead of FILE NAME. 2. Used to emphasize words in e-mail where text cannot be underlined:

```
Now you're _really_ fired!
```

3. Unlike with a typewriter, you cannot backspace and press the underline key to underline your text on a computer screen. It just doesn't work that way.

` *(accent grave)* 1. A backward apostrophe, most often used when simulating double quotes, as in

```
``Oui, oui. It is a sauce we
make from grease and flour.´´
```

Normal apostrophes end the quote, but the accent grave (found in the upper-left corner of your keyboard) starts the quote. 2. The hardest part about dealing with this doodad is how to pronounce it. Is it "grave," as in serious or a place where dead bodies go to relax? Or could it be gravé, as in the way a French person would say "gravy"? 3. Used to accent letters in some foreign languages.

{ } *(curly brackets; braces)* 1. An alternative form of parentheses, most often found in C language programs. The curly brackets are used to "hold" various items in the program — items that belong to certain parts of the program or that carry out specific functions. 2. Often used when someone gets tired of plain ol' parentheses.

| *(vertical bar; pipe)* 1. Many programming languages use the pipe symbol as the logical OR mathematical operator. It's pronounced "or," as in

```
SIX-OF-ONE | HALF-A-DOZEN-OF-
THE-OTHER
```

2. In the C programming language, the pipe is used as a bit-wise logical OR. Two pipe symbols, | |, are used as the logical OR for comparing two values. 3. In some operating systems, the pipe is used to send (or pipe) output through a filter, such as a sorting program. The filter modifies the output.

~ *(tilde)* Pronounced *till-duh* or *till-dee*. 1. Used as an accent character in some languages: For example, *año* means "year" in Spanish. To produce that character in a Microsoft Office application, press Ctrl+~ (which is Ctrl+Shift+`) and then the letter *n*. 2. Some programming languages may use the ~ to mean *not*. See also *!* (the exclamation point). 3. In the C language, the tilde is the 1's complement. 4. In Australia, the national anthem is "Waltzing Ma ~."

0 *(zeer-oh)* The symbol for the number zero, which isn't to be confused with a capital *O*; they may have been the same thing on old typewriter keyboards, but not in a computer. Sometimes the zero has a diagonal line through it, just to drive home that it is a zero and not a big *O*.

0.something micron technology A technology used to produce the very small circuits in a microprocessor. The *something* is replaced by a number. "Using 0.18 micron technology, a single chip can contain as many as 125 million transistors, roughly the number found in an entire PC or in Fred's brain."

101-key keyboard *(won-oh-won-kee kee-bord)* A keyboard that has four distinct parts: a typewriter keyboard, a cursor keypad, a numeric keypad, and a row of function keys. "Bob's the doubting type. He actually counted every little key on his keyboard and was, in fact, quite pleased to find 101 of them."

A 101-key keyboard.

104-key keyboard *(won-oh-for-key kee-bord)* A new, deluxe keyboard that contains 104 keys (up 3 keys from the popular 101-key keyboard). The 3 keys are nestled around the Spacebar: Two of them are Windows keys, and the third is a menu key.

10000 bug *(tin-thow-sund buhg)* A problem with computers in the year 10000 when they're forced to deal with the fact that programmers of the late 1990s fixed the 2000 bug but did not anticipate the rollover from the year 9999 to the year 10000. Also known as the Y10K bug. See also *Y2K*.

1-2-3 *(won-too-three)* A spreadsheet program. See *Lotus 1-2-3.*

16-bit *(siks-teen-bit)* Refers to something that works with computer information 16 bits at a time. Twice as efficient as 8-bit stuff, half as efficient as 32-bit thingies. "A 16-bit version of a 2-bit shave and a haircut would probably result in a trip to the infirmary."

2-bit *(too-bit)* 1. Something cheap, insignificant, or not worthy of attention, such as some people you may know. 2. Twenty-five cents. "Your opinion and 2 bits will get you an extra shot of espresso in your latté."

286 *(two-ay-tee-siks)* Nickname for the 80286 microprocessor, used in the IBM AT class of computers. Successor to the old 8088 PCs and supplanted by the 386 family of PCs.

3-D *(three-dee)* Abbreviation for three-dimensional. "Linus, it's hard to tell if the board enjoyed your 3-D presentation with half their faces buried in motion-sickness bags."

3-D mouse *(three-dee mowse)* A mouse (pointing device) that moves up and down in addition to back and forth and left to right. It's typically used with three-dimensional software.

3½ -inch floppy disk *(three-and-uh-haf-inch floppy disk)* The standard-size floppy disk used on PC and older Macintosh computers. The disk typically stores 1.44MB of stuff.

32-bit *(thur-tee-too-bit)* A computer-something-or-other that works with 32-bit chunks of information. Pentium-type PCs have 32-bit microprocessors. "A 32-bit computer is to a 16-bit computer as an 8-cylinder car is to a 4-cylinder model."

386 *(three-ay-tee-siks)* Abbreviation for the 80386 family of microprocessor, which includes the 80386, 80386DX, and so on. "Believe it or not, *386* computers were once thought of as so fast that only nerdy scientists would use them. Now, good luck trying to get a 7-year-old not to sneer at one."

 404 Error *(for-oh-for ayr-or)* A Web browser message telling you that the Web page you tried to load cannot be found. See also *World Wide Web* and *Web browser.*

486 *(for-ay-tee-siks)* Abbreviation for the 80486 family of microprocessors. Also known as the i486, 486DX, 486DX2, 486DX4, 486SL, 486SLC, and maybe even the 486SX. At one time, this all meant something. Today, it's something nerds debate over lunch.

4X *(for-eks)* See *quad-speed drive.*

56K modem *(fif-dee-siks-kay moh-dum)* The current "top" standard for traditional computer modems. This modem supposedly communicates 56,700 bits per second, which is about a page of text every second. It's currently the fastest standard allowed over plain old telephone lines.

@

640K limit *(siks-for-tee-kay lim-it)* The design limitation restriction on all IBM-compatible computers that restricts them to using a maximum of 640K of conventional memory. "In 1981, 640K was a ton of memory, so the 640K limit was thought to be unbreakable. Today, Windows breaks it with a wiggle of its pinky toe."

6502 *(siks-tee-fiev-oh-too)* The family of microprocessors used in the original Apple computers. Eventually, the 6502 was replaced by the 65C02 and then the 65C16 in the Apple IIgs computer, the last of the mighty Apple II line.

68000 *(siks-tee-ayt-thou-zend)* Refers to the family of microprocessors used in Macintosh computers. Motorola makes them.

680x0 *(siks-tee-ayt-oh-eks-oh)* Abbreviation indicating the Motorola 68000 family of processors, including the 68000, 68020, 68030, 68040, and whatever's next. "All Macintosh computers use the *680x0* processor. The bigger the number *x,* the more you paid for your Mac."

68881 *(siks-tee-ayt-ayt-ay-tee-one)* The math co-processor used with the 68000 processor.

6X *(siks-eks)* Six times as fast as the original CD-ROM drive speed. Used to impress a computer buyer with how fast his CD-ROM drive is.

8-bit *(ayt-bit)* Refers to a computer—something that works with information in 8-bit chunks. "Today, *8-bit* computers are about as impressive as the Yugo."

8-bit color *(ayt-bit cul-or)* A color depth of 8 bits, which enables the display of up to 256 colors.

80286 *(ay-tee-too-ay-tee-siks)* Numeric designation for the processor used in the IBM AT family of computers. "The *80286* isn't used in computers today, though some government devices, such as nuclear power plants and the space shuttle, still use them."

80386, 80386DX *(ay-tee-three-ay-tee-siks; -dee-eks)* The first 32-bit microprocessor used in IBM-compatible computers. 80386DX is the official designation, though most folks would say 80386 or just 386. "The minimum requirement to run Windows is a *80386* processor. Yeah, right. That's like saying the minimum requirement to get into Harvard is a spinal cord."

80386SX *(ay-tee-three-ay-tee-siks es-eks)* A low-cost and slower version of the 80386DX processor. Like the 80386DX, this processor can process 32 bits of data at any given time, but it can transfer only 16 bits of data at a time.

80387 *(ay-tee-three-ay-tee-sev-en)* The math co-processor designed to work with the 80386DX, 80386SX, and 80386SL processors. "Plugging a 80387 math co-processor into a 80386 computer is like strapping a calculator to its belt."

80486, 80486DX *(ay-tee-for-ay-tee-siks; -dee-eks)* Numeric designation for the processors used in many IBM-compatible computers, the successor to the 386 line. The 80486DX is its official name, though many people use 80486, 486, or i486 because they think that it makes them sound cool.

80486SX *(ay-tee-for-ay-tee-siks es-eks)* Low-cost and slower version of the 80486DX processor. The main difference is that this processor lacks the math co-processor capabilities of the 80486DX. Presently found only on cheap clones at the bottom of illegal landfills.

80586 *(ay-tee-fiev-ay-tee-siks)* The unofficial designation for the Pentium processor. The main reason Intel chose not to name this microprocessor the 80586 is that no one can trademark a number. So the company came up with a trademarkable name (Pentium) instead. "Even though it's officially called Pentium, you'll still hear the diehard geeks referring to the chip as a '586."

8086 *(ay-tee-ay-tee-siks)* A 16-bit processor used in some early IBM PC-compatible computers, most notably the first Compaqs.

8087 *(ay-tee-ay-tee-sev-en)* The math co-processor designed to work with the 8088 and the 8086 processors.

8088 *(ay-tee-ay-tee-ayt)* The first processor used in the IBM PC. Although this is a 16-bit processor, it can transfer only 8 bits of data at any given time, kind of like having only one door on a city bus instead of two. "Knowing that the first IBM PC used an *8088* microprocessor is as trivial as knowing the name of the guy who drives the Zamboni at a hockey game."

80x86 *(ay-tee-eks-ay-tee-siks)* An older designation referring to all the Intel family of microprocessors, from the ancient 8088 to the Pentium. Replaced by x86; see also *x86*. "Dave thinks he's being clever when he refers to all 80x86

processors as 6,880 processors." (Only those who know that 80 multiplied by 86 is 6,880 will get this.)

8.3 filename *(ayt dot three fiel-naem)* The old MS-DOS filename law: Filenames are restricted to eight characters followed by an optional period and up to three additional characters as an "extension."

83-key keyboard *(ay-tee-three-kee kee-bord)* The name of the original IBM PC keyboard, which had (ironically) 83 keys. Unlike today's 101-key keyboards, the numeric keypad was scrunched up next to the main typewriter keys, there were no separate cursor keys, and all the function keys (F1 through F10) were arranged in two columns on the left side of the keyboard. It made a nifty "clacky" sound.

84 Lumber *(ayt-ee-for lum-ber)* Has nothing to do with computers. It's the name of a lumber company in California. I just remembered it from my childhood.

8514 *(ay-tee-fiev-for-teen)* A graphics standard for the PC, similar to Super VGA. See also *Super VGA*.

86 *(ay-tee-siks)* Bar and restaurant lingo meaning that something is out of stock or no good. Can refer to any part or item that no longer serves a purpose or should be eliminated. "Whew! Those shellfish should be *86'd!*"

| 65 41
A
a
97 60 | ● ○
○ ○
○ ○ | | | | ●— | |

A: *(aye co-len)* The primary floppy disk drive. On a PC, the first disk checked for a copy of the operating system. Often pronounced without the "colon" part, as in "I looked on my *A* drive to see why the disk wouldn't go in and, lo and behold, there was already a disk in there."

A1 reference *(aye-won ref-ur-ens)* A style Microsoft Excel uses to label columns with letters (A through IV, meaning the letters *I* and *V,* for a total of 256 columns) and rows with numbers (1 through 65,536).

AA (auto answer) *(aye aye)* The ability of a modem to answer automatically. Used to label a light on an external modem to indicate that auto answer is activated.

aardvark *(ard-vark)* One of the first words listed in good dictionaries. Comes from the old Afrikaans phrase meaning "earth pig," which refers to a nocturnal mammal known to burrow its way through African

The "earth pig."

terrain, eating termites and dragging its big, floppy ears and long, ugly tongue and heavy tail. "The dictionary gods will curse you if you leave *aardvark* out of any dictionary you write."

abacus *(ab-a-kus)* A handheld tablet used for making mathematical computations. The abacus uses beads and your fingers to quickly figure out addition, multiplication, subtraction, and division. It does

The new, electronic abacus.

it quite accurately, faster than most people can use a calculator, and its batteries last a lifetime.

abandon *(uh-ban-dun)* To clear the work from your computer screen without saving it. Basically, the stuff is lost, never to return again.

abbreviation *(uh-bree-vee-ay-shun)* Popular Internet shorthand used in e-mail, chat rooms, and USENET for common ideas, thoughts, or expressions. Also known as acronyms (see *acronym* for a list of examples).

ABC *(aye bee see)* Abbreviation for Atanasoff-Berry Computer; a device that was a precursor to the ENIAC and, therefore, is sometimes considered to be the first electronic digital computer. Professor John Atanasoff and student Clifford Berry at Iowa State University created the ABC in the early 1940s.

A

A-B cable *(aye-bee kay-bul)* A USB cable with a fat end (A) and a larger, truncated square end (B). The A end is the "upstream" end, usually plugging into the computer or a USB hub. The B end plugs into a device, such as a printer or scanner.

A-B switch *(aye-bee switch)* A device that lets you connect two peripherals, such as two printers, to a single computer. The A-B switch lets you manually switch between the devices.

abort *(uh-bort)* To stop something before it's finished or completed, such as a program running out of control or a nuclear missile careening out of control. Popular methods include frantically hitting Esc, Ctrl+Alt+Delete, or the Break key.

Abort, Retry, Fail? *(uh-bort, ree-tri, fay-el)* The cryptic message DOS displays whenever an error has been made and the computer needs for you to decide what to do. Type A to cancel. If you can fix the problem, such as by placing a floppy disk in drive A, type R for Retry. Don't bother with Fail. (In some versions of DOS, the message is "Abort, Retry, Fail, Ignore?")

About box *(uh-bowt boks)* A tiny little window that appears in the middle of the screen, displaying the program's name, version number, and anything else the programmers thought the general public may want to know. For an example, click the Help button in Word. Then choose About Microsoft Word. There's that tiny box with Word information. "Ever wonder why the *About box*

never tells you what the program is supposed to accomplish? I suppose that should be the what's-it-all-about box."

abs *(abs)* 1. An abbreviation for *abs*olute value. 2. Abs is a command used in many programming languages and spreadsheet programs that calculates the absolute value of a number — never negative, always positive. "If your spreadsheet shows a tax balance of −$12,500, quickly calculate the *abs* value and you'll wind up with a refund instead of owing money."

absolute address *(ab-so-loot uh-dress)* See *address*.

absolute reference *(ab-so-loot ref-er-rens)* A term used in spreadsheets that tells a formula to use a specific cell or group of cells. If you copy or move the formula from one cell to another at a later date, the formula still uses the specific cell defined earlier. "An *absolute reference* is something you have to specifically demand if you want to make sure that your spreadsheet formulas don't get all screwed up."

absolute value *(ab-so-loot val-yoo)* See *abs*.

AC *(aye see)* Abbreviation for alternating current. The power that comes out of the wall socket is AC. Computers, and most other devices, use DC. A device called a transformer converts the two, keeping everyone happy.

AC-3 *(aye see three)* A Dolby Digital audio recording technology with surround sound. Used on DVD movie disks.

Accelerated Graphics Port *(ak-sel-ur-ay-ted graf-iks port)* A graphics standard for displaying 3-D images. Commonly known by its acronym, AGP, and often called an "AGP port," which of course means that the computer genius using that term is actually saying "Accelerated Graphics Port port."

accelerated video adapter *(ak-sel-ur-ay-ted vi-dee-oh ah-dap-ter)* A special piece of video hardware that makes graphics work faster.

accelerator *(ak-sel-ur-ay-tur)* 1. A piece of hardware or software that makes some other (typically slow and pokey) device in the computer work faster. 2. Another term for shortcut keys. An accelerator enables you to do the same function as a mouse, except using a key or a combination of keys.

accelerator board *(ak-sel-ur-ay-tur bord)* A special circuit board that plugs into a computer and makes it or one of its pieces parts run faster. Accelerator boards usually contain a faster processor that replaces or supplements the computer's existing processor. "Too bad they don't make *accelerator boards* for commercials on TV." See also *processor.*

accelerator key *(ak-sel-ur-ay-tur kee)* See *shortcut keys.*

acceptance test *(ak-sep-tens test)* A demonstration of a new software or hardware product that illustrates the product's capabilities and features. Dating is very similar to an *acceptance test.*

access *(ak-sess)* The ability to get into something, or to locate something. Access is used in respect to disks, records, files, and network entry procedures.

access arm *(ak-sess arm)* The arm that holds the head that reads and writes the information on the disk in a disk drive. "Oh, the

The access arm both reads and writes information.

read-write head is connected to the . . . access arm! And the access arm is connected to the . . . access shoulder! And that is the way of the Lord!"

access charge *(ak-sess charj)* The charge placed by a communication service or telephone company for the use of its network.

access code *(ak-sess kohd)* Also known as the username or ID and password on a network or online service. "The workers started gathering weapons in hopes that it would inspire Marcia to remember the *access code* for the payroll system."

access control *(ak-sess kon-troll)* The mechanisms for limiting access to certain items of information based on a user's identity. A system administrator uses access control to control a user's access to networks and directories. It's the Windows 2000 version of a controlling parent.

access denied *(ak-sess dee-nied)* A message given when your computer is unable to retrieve whatever you requested.

A

 access number *(ak-sess num-bur)* The telephone number used by an online subscriber to get into their service.

access privileges *(ak-sess priv-e-liges)* The extent of a user's capability to use and modify directories, files, and programs located on other computers on a computer system or network. They are typically used as a safety device so that not everyone on a network can get into all the files and mess with them.

access time *(ak-sess tiem)* The way a hard drive's speed is measured. Each hard drive has a different access time, measured in milliseconds (ms). The fewer the milliseconds, the faster the hard drive. "A good, fast hard disk has an *access time* of 12 milliseconds. Steve, on the other hand, has an *access time* of about 48 hours."

accessory *(ak-sess-oh-ree)* The little extra doohickeys used with your computer. See also *peripheral.* "I want to do my whole computer lab in pink *accessories*." Also an abbreviation for *desk accessory*; see *desk accessory.*

account *(uh-cownt)* Your presence on a computer system. Typically, everyone at a large corporation, university, or secret evil government installation will have their own account on the computer system. If you subscribe to an Internet Service Provider, you have an account on its system. "Matt has no social life; his computer *account* is overdrawn."

account lockout *(uh-cownt lock-out)* A Windows 2000 security feature that locks a user's account if the user tries to log on and fails too many times in a specified amount of time.

accounting package *(uh-cown-teen pak-adj)* Software that keeps track of business expenses and other accounting nonsense.

accumulator *(uh-kyoom-yoo-lay-tor)* 1. A microprocessor register, typically the A or AX register, that holds values or results of some operation. 2. One who accumulates. "Bill is an *accumulator* for money."

ACK *(ack,* like you're choking) 1. Abbreviation for acknowledge, ASCII code 6, produced by the Ctrl+F keyboard combination. 2. In some areas of computer communications, the ACK code is sent by one computer to acknowledge the proper receipt of information from another computer. See also *ASCII, NAK.*

acknowledgment message *(ack-nol-edge-ment mess-age)* A notice that the message you sent arrived or was retrieved by the person you sent it to. Or, the acknowledgment message could be that an error occurred before the message could be retrieved. Also called an "ack" by the monosyllabic.

acoustic coupler *(ah-koo-stik cup-ler)* An old-style modem device that works by shoving the handset of a telephone into two rubber cups. This was necessary in the old days, before the breakup of

Old-style acoustic coupler modem.

AT&T, when phones were directly wired into the wall and you really didn't have a phone jack into which a modem could plug. Accoustic couplers are still widely used in foreign countries and for laptops when access to a phone jack is restricted. Hollywood loves them as well because they're more obvious than dull, old modem boxes ("Look, Shirley! The computer is 'talking' on the phone!"). "Did you hear? Madonna's gone high tech. She's replaced her cone bra with a pair of *acoustic couplers.*"

acoustical sound enclosure *(ah-koo-stick-ahl sownd in-klow-shur)* An insulated cabinet for noisy impact printers that reduces the noise those printers make.

ACPI *(aye see pee eye)* Acronym for Advanced Configuration and Power Interface. A way to manage power consumption in a computer system as well as in household devices and office equipment. On a computer, ACPI allows you to turn off some devices while keeping the rest of the computer running. "Marge must have her *ACPI* on; she's talking, but I think her brain is asleep."

 Acrobat files *(ak-ro-bat fi-els)* A type of file format commonly used to store documents on the Internet. Acrobat (the program) works a like an online fax machine. The files look the same on both the viewer's screen and the sender's screen. You need to obtain the Acrobat reader to view the files.

acronym *(ak-ro-nim)* A word created by taking letters from two or more words to create a new word. Examples are BASIC, FORTRAN, and DOS. Acronyms are also used in e-mail messages and chat rooms.

Common E-Mail Acronyms

Acronym	Meaning
AAMOF	As a matter of fact
AFAICT	As far as I can tell
AFAIK	As far as I know
AFK	Away from keyboard
B4	Before
BAK	Back at keyboard
BBIAF	Be back in a few (understood to mean minutes)
BBL	Be back later
BSF	But seriously folks
BTDT	Been there, done that
CUL	See you later
CUL8R	(same)
DIIK	Damned if I know
EG	Evil grin
<G>	Grin (as in you're smiling)
F2F	Face to face
FAQ	Frequently Asked Questions list
FOC	Free of charge
FWIW	For what it's worth
FYI	For your information
GMTA	Great minds think alike
IMHO	In my humble (or honest) opinion
IMNSHO	In my not-so-humble opinion
KISS	Keep it simple, stupid
L8R	Later
LOL	Laughing out loud
RE:	Regarding
ROFL	Rolling on the floor laughing
TIA	Thanks in advance
TTFN	Ta-ta for now
TTYL	Talk to you later

Act! *(akt)* A contact-management program from Symantec that enables the user to develop customer and client databases. This program is very popular among sales representatives.

active *(ak-tiv)* A common computer word that refers to something that has the current focus of attention.

active area *(ak-tiv ayr-ee-uh)* A region of the screen or window that is accepting input or some other type of stimulation (but not singing) from the user.

active cell *(ak-tiv sell)* The cell in a spreadsheet that is selected or highlighted.

active configuration *(ak-tiv con-fig-yoor-aye-shun)* 1. The current configuration, typically when several different types of configurations are available. 2. The factory configuration. See also *default.*

active content *(ak-tiv con-tent)* Information, such as a weather map, news, or a stock market ticker, that changes as it is updated for the Web.

Active Desktop *(ak-tiv desk-tohp)* A feature first introduced with Windows 95 that allows an application, such as a Web browser, to take over the desktop; the application appears as the desktop instead of as some background pattern or graphic. In addition, for users permanently attached to the Internet, Active Desktop can continually update Web pages.

Active Directory *(ak-tiv dir-ek-tor-ee)* See *current directory.*

active file *(ak-tiv fi-el)* The file or document being created, edited, or manipulated somehow by the operating system or a specific application.

active light *(ak-tiv lite)* A teensy light on some computer device that lets you know something is alive and ticking (or dead and annoying).

active matrix *(ak-tiv may-triks)* A type of color display found on many laptops. An active matrix display uses transistors to control the screen. If you were an engineer, you'd be impressed by this and nod your head accordingly. "My new KneeCap 150 laptop uses the superior *active matrix* display, so I can see crisp color graphics of a parrot at 39,000 feet."

active window *(ak-tiv win-doe)* The window on the screen that's currently in use. If two or more windows appear on the screen, the active window usually appears brighter around the edges. "It's the goal of every window on the screen to become the *active window*." See also *window.*

Active X *(ak-tiv ex)* A set of technologies that permits programs and software to play together well over a network, no matter which programming language was used. Developed by Microsoft, promoted by Microsoft flacks, and is the Microsoft answer to Java.

actuator *(ak-choo-ay-tor)* A mechanism that causes a device to be turned on or off, adjusted, or moved. The element that moves the head assembly on a disk drive or an arm of a robot is an *actuator*.

Ada *(ay-duh)* 1. A structured programming language that was supposed to be the standard language for all defense-related programming work. Naturally, hardly anyone uses it, although U.S. tax-payers supported all its development. 2. Ada Byron, the Countess of Lovelace, who is generally credited with writing the first computer program for a mechanical loom machine that Charles Babbage designed. She was Lord Byron's niece. Ada (the programming language) is named after her. "I'm sure the Countess of Lovelace would be pleased with the fact that a program written in her name is used to fire Exocet missiles from nuclear-powered aircraft carriers."

Adam West *(ad-um west)* The star of the "Batman" TV series that appeared during the 1960s. "There just is no other Batman than *Adam West.*"

adapter *(uh-dap-ter)* 1. Another name for an expansion card. Typically, a piece of hardware that plugs into your computer's innards (into an expansion slot). Unlike an expansion card, which may just expand the computer's features, an adapter is used to communicate with an external device, like a hard drive, monitor, or some other doohickey. 2. A simple connector, designed to hook up two plugs of different types. "Earl is convinced he can use his computer to help him garden. He's currently looking for a weed-whacker *adapter.*"

ADB *(aye dee bee)* Acronym for the Apple Desktop Bus. The Macintosh communications port for keyboards, mice, trackballs, graphics, and other input devices. Replaced by the USB on newer-model Macs.

A/D converter *(aye-dee con-ver-ter)* Stands for Analog-to-Digital Converter. A device that converts analog signals into binary code for the computer. For example, a thermometer hooked to your computer would use an A/D converter to change the information into information your computer could use.

adder *(add-urh)* A computer circuit that adds two numbers together.

add-on *(add-on)* 1. Anything added to a computer to enhance or increase its capabilities. 2. Costs money.

add-on program *(add-on pro-gram)* A program that works with and enhances the features of another program. "The original Lotus 1-2-3 was terribly popular despite its somewhat limited abilities. To fill in the gaps, enterprising individuals created *add-on* programs to boost 1-2-3's features."

 address *(uh-dress)* 1. A memory location. The value is often displayed in hexadecimal (base 16), mostly just to keep anyone but official PC postal employees from finding anything in memory. Everything stored in your computer's memory has a specific *address.* 2. The location of an item in a spreadsheet. Cells in a spreadsheet have a row-and-column address. "The *address* of the first cell in a spreadsheet is A1. That's also the name of my favorite steak sauce." 3. The location of something on the Internet. This could be an electronic-mail address or a Web

A

page address. "You want my *address?* Which one do you want? You have about three to choose from: e-mail, Web page, or my *address* in the IRS computer's memory banks."

 address book *(uh-dress book)* A place to store your electronic-mail names and addresses. "My *address book* is filled with all the most popular geeks, thanks to online dating."

admin *(add-min)* Abbreviation for administrator. See also *administrator*.

administrator *(add-min-iss-tray-tor)* The computer account for the person or people who actually run the computer system. The administrator is responsible for setting up and managing the local computers and their users and groups. "When you need to complain, send mail to the *administrator*. Include a bribe and you'll get help faster."

 Adobe *(uh-doe-bee)* Adobe Systems, Inc. A graphics and desktop publishing software company. A popular product is Adobe Illustrator.

Adobe Illustrator *(uh-doe-bee il-uh-stray-tor)* A powerful computer drawing and illustration program, available for the Macintosh, Windows, and other computing platforms.

ADSL *(aye dee ess el)* Acronym for Asymmetric Digital Subscriber Line, a new type of fast online communications that allows top speeds without new wiring. Designed to replace ISDN. ADSL is one of the xDSL family of Internet connections. Subscribers must live within a certain distance of the main telephone exchange office, and they must pay a surcharge for using the service.

 AFE *(aye eff ee)* Acronym for Apple File Exchange. A Macintosh utility that converts files between the Mac and PC disks.

 AFK *(aye eff kay)* Acronym for away from keyboard. Used during Internet chat groups when someone leaves the computer.

```
OK Jon, we'll meet in Hawaii
for that secret rendezvous
(afk)
Sorry, I had to go put some
more medicine on this huge
fever blister I have on my lip.
```

agent *(ay-jent)* An automated program. A program or utility that carries out specific tasks at specific times or when certain conditions are met. For example, an agent may inform you that your disk drive is getting perilously full. "I have an *agent* that doesn't tell me anything. It must be a secret agent."

AGP *(aye jee pee)* Acronym for Accelerated Graphics Port. See also *Accelerated Graphics Port*.

AI *(aye eye)* See *artificial intelligence*.

 AIFF file *(aye eye eff eff file)* Acronym for Audio Interchange File Format.

AIM *(aye eye em)* AOL Instant Messaging, a method of chatting with an online individual by sending messages back and forth — like instant e-mail.

air vents *(ayer ventz)* Holes or slits on the console panel of your computer. Like any other motor, your computer has to breathe.

alarm *(uh-larm)* 1. An audible or visual warning that something has gone wrong. 2. A reminder found in calendar programs.

alarm filtering *(uh-larm fill-ter-ing)* The ability to pinpoint the device that has failed in a network-management situation.

alert box *(uh-lert boks)* A graphical box or window that displays a message or warning.

ALGOL *(al-gall)* 1. Acronym for *algorithmic language.* ALGOL was one of the first programming languages to encourage structured programming. Pascal is a direct descendent of ALGOL. 2. Has nothing to do with Al Gore. "When Betty told her parents that she programmed *ALGOL,* they thought that she was working for the Clinton administration."

algorithm *(al-gor-rithm)* 1. A step-by-step set of instructions that accomplishes

Has he got rhythm, or is he just A-flat?

some common programming task in a simple, yet dignified, manner. 2. The pace at which Al Gore does the macarena.

alias *(ay-lee-ess)* 1. A code or symbol representing something else. 2. A reference to a file that may look like it's right there in front of you, but could be anywhere. This makes it easy to find common files, but doesn't require all the disk space a full-on copy would. Think of alias files as Elvis impersonators that can appear everywhere you look. "The FBI is having trouble finding its word processing documents. Experts assume that the files are using *aliases* and, once known, should be easy to locate."

aliasing *(ay-lee-ess-ing)* The ugly-looking jagged or stair-stepped appearance of diagonal lines in computer graphics images. Sometimes referred to as *the jaggies.* "Trying to draw diagonal lines on a computer is about as easy as drawing circles on an Etch-A-Sketch. Because whenever you draw a diagonal line, you get *aliasing,* which makes your straight line look like the kind of staircase a 7-year-old would build."

alignment *(uh-lien-mint)* 1. A hard disk's drive head's ability to read and write information without error. 2. The relationship of text to the left and right margins, as in centered or left justified, for example. "Shirley is so cute. She tried to adjust the *alignment* of text in her word processor by tilting the monitor." 3. The arrangement of graphics; how the graphics line up to each other: centered, to the left, right, top, bottom.

allocate *(al-oh-kayt)* The process of dividing a computer's resources. "In the Bible, Matthew 14:15 describes how Jesus *allocated* two fish and five loaves of bread between more than 5,000 people. Now if he could only come back and allocate our two PCs and one laser printer between ten people in the office."

allocation unit *(al-oh-kay-shun yoo-nit)* Same as cluster, which is the minimum unit of storage on a disk.

alpha geek *(al-fuh geek)* The lead nerd at your company. The guy who usually makes all the computer decisions, whether that's really his job or not. Could also be a she. *He* is used here because it's the third person gender neutral in English. I'm not trying to make some kind of sexist statement. To wit: "Mary is our *alpha geek.* Tell her about the toast in the CD-ROM drive."

A typical alpha geek.

alpha test *(al-fuh test)* The initial testing of a new program, usually conducted by the programmers and their trusted friends. Alpha test programs usually don't work correctly. "Before Microsoft released Windows 95, the company ran it through an *alpha* test of their own employees. Once they found the first few bugs, they released the program into a beta test so that everyone else could find those same mistakes too."

alphanumeric characters *(al-fuh-noo-mayr-ik kar-ik-ters)* Letters and numbers. Not symbols. Not punctuation marks, diacriticals, or dingbats. And something like "*&^%$#@" is way-out.

Altair *(all-tayr,* not *al-tar)* 1. The name of one of the first personal computers. 2. A star in the constellation Aquila. (See the command joke in the Alt key definition.) 3. Home of the Krell.

AltaVista *(al-tuh vis-ta)* 1. One of the many search engines on the Internet. It's foreign: *Vista* means to see, and *Alta* is a contraction of the Italian *Alotta.* 2. www.altavista.com.

alternating current *(al-ter-nay-ting kur-ent)* The type of electricity used in America. Often abbreviated as AC. Alternating current changes polarity a given number of times a second, referred to as *hertz.* It sounds screwy, but it allows electricity to flow farther than direct current (DC). Your computer, and most electronic devices, must convert AC power to DC to run properly.

Alt key *(alt;* like "halt" without the *h)* A special type of shift key on computer keyboards. Often used in combination with other keys to give commands to the computer. A common command is Alt+Tab to switch between programs. "In some programs, you press *Alt*+R to redo something. In other programs, you press *Alt*+R to replace. And in outer space, *Altair* is a star in the constellation Aquila."

ALU *(aye ell you)* Acronym for arithmetic-logic unit. The portion of the central processing unit (CPU) that makes all the decisions for the microprocessor. In a way, it's the microprocessor's wife.

AM *(aye em)* Abbreviation for amplitude modulation.

Amazon.com *(am-uh-zon-dot-com)* The first Internet megastore (you can find it at www.amazon.com). You can buy books, toys, videos, electronics, and almost anything except concrete (which is too expensive to ship).

AMD *(aye em dee)* Advanced Micro Devices, a hardware manufacturer that creates Intel-compatible microprocessors for PCs and other devices.

Amdahl *(am-doll)* A computer manufacturer founded by Gene Amdahl, just like Thomas J. Ibm founded IBM. Oh, wait. The second part of that might not be true.

 America Online *(uh-mayr-ik-uh on-lien)* A national dial-in computer service (abbreviated AOL), where you, your computer, and a modem can do all sorts of interesting things. America Online is quite popular and a nifty way to try out the Internet without a huge investment in software. "If *America Online* went to Europe, would it still be *America Online,* or would it be called Europe Online? Or maybe America in Europe Online?"

Amiga *(uh-mee-ga)* The name of the most technologically advanced, inexpensive personal computer on the market from Amiga International. Of course, it flopped. Commodore introduced the Amiga in 1985.

amp *(amp)* 1. Abbreviation for *amp*ere, a unit for measuring electric current. "Volts, smolts. It's the *amps* that will kill you." 2. A device connected to your computer speakers that allows everyone in the neighborhood to know when you're zapping aliens with your turbo thruster rifle.

ampersand *(am-per-sand)* The way you pronounce &. See also &.

amplitude *(am-pleh-tood)* The strength of a signal measured in decibels. "Lois doesn't say much, but when she does, it's with amplitude."

analog *(an-uh-log)* The opposite of digital. Analog values are not absolute values; they are immeasurable or constantly changing. For example, an analog clock has a dial and hands that "sweep 'round." A digital clock displays numbers and changes only on the minute. (See also *digital.*) "Computers are *digital,* which means that they understand On and Off and Yes and No. People are analog because they understand Yes, No, I dunno, Who cares?, Why are you asking me this?, Maybe, and We'll see."

analog modem *(an-uh-log mo-dum)* The traditional type of modem. Modems are analog because they take digital information from the computer and convert it into sounds that can travel over phone lines. Of course, today the phone company takes the sounds and converts them into digital information to make the transfer more efficient. See also *digital modem.*

analog monitor *(an-uh-log mon-uh-tor)* Another term for any VGA or standard computer monitor used today. Older, RGB monitors and newer, flat-screen monitors are digital.

analog-to-digital port *(an-uh-log to di-ji-tul)* Also known as "A-to-D port," it's another term for the computers' joystick port. It's the way the computer reads movement of the joystick. "I suppose that they called it *analog-to-digital port* because scientists in white lab coats would look silly working on a joystick port."

A

anchor cell *(ayn-core sell)* In a spreadsheet program, the cell in a range where the cursor is pointed.

AND *(and)* 1. A logical operation comparing two bits. The result of the operation is based on the value of the two bits; in this case, whether they are the same or different (see chart). If both bits are the same (both 1 or both 0), the result is TRUE, or 1. Otherwise, the result is FALSE, or 0. 2. The programming command that performs the logical AND operation.

AND

1 AND 1	=	1
1 AND 0	=	0
0 AND 1	=	0
0 AND 0	=	1

How the AND operation works.

andama *(end-um-ah)* A fill-in word when you're trying to think of something else to say or really don't have anything of importance to say. From the vulgar Latin *etama,* which means exactly the same thing. "This girl in my school has this really big mole on her lip, *andama* I, uh, can't seem to keep from staring at it during class, *andama,* and now all the other kids keep looking at it too."

angle bracket *(an-gul bra-ket)* The less-than (<) or greater-than (>) characters, found on your keyboard.

angstrom *(anj-strum)* A unit of measurement equal to approximately $\frac{1}{250}$ millionth of an inch. It is used to measure the doodlies in a chip.

animated cursor *(an-uh-may-ted ker-ser)* A mouse pointer that changes to various images, and sometimes moves or is animated in some way; for those who would rather click on icons using a fluttering wasp than a boring old arrow.

animation *(an-uh-may-shen)* To use your $2,000 computer to create Saturday-morning-style animated cartoons. Creating the appearance of movement of drawn objects. (See also *Mickey Mouse.*) "Our spreadsheet uses *animation* to help illustrate the declining sales of our competitors. Alas, we don't have the sound hooked up, so when the graph slams into zero, George will make an audible thud noise."

annotation *(an-oh-tay-shen)* A note inserted into a document, used mostly when two or more people are working on the same thing and need to exchange notes. Annotations don't print with the rest of the text and are usually visible only by using special commands.

 anonymity *(an-o-nim-i-tee)* The concealment of the identity of a person posting a message in a newsgroup. The ability to post a message or send e-mail without the recipient's knowing who sent it. "It's much easier to have an outrageous opinion when you have *anonymity.*"

ANSI *(an-zee)* 1. Abbreviation for American National Standards Institute, an organization that defines standards for different industries that most people ignore anyway. 2. Specific rules that govern the way programming languages are supposed to work. 3. Commands that control how information is displayed on a computer screen (largely ignored). 4. A type of graphics used by text-based BBS systems. 5. How kids get when they've been riding in the car too long. ("Kids get ANSI.")

ANSI bomb *(an-zee bom)* A devious sequence of ANSI commands that actually types a deadly DOS command on your computer. This can be done in a number of ways, none of which I'd like to write about in any detail here. Leave it to say that when such a string of ANSI commands appears on your screen, there's little you can do to stop it except for immediately shutting off your computer.

ANSI C *(an-zee cee or Aunt C C)* A standard definition for the C programming language as defined by the American National Standards Institute. Nearly every C compiler tries to follow the ANSI C standard as closely as possible, and then they add enhancements that pretty much destroy the whole purpose of a standard in the first place.

ANSI character set *(an-zee kar-ak-ter set)* A standard set of characters used by a computer. The ANSI character set includes ordinary letters and numbers plus strange little symbols, such as foreign language symbols, smiley faces, and lines and boxes. "Linda is a collector. All she needs is the evil Dr. Modulus statuette and her *ANSI character set* will be complete."

ANSI graphics *(an-zee gra-fiks)* Special characters that create simple graphics, such as lines, boxes, and colors. Often used by text-only BBSs; see also *BBS*. "Earl spent months working with *ANSI graphics* to make his screen look colorful and exciting. Alas, we weren't impressed."

ANSI screen control codes *(an-zee skreen kon-troll kohdz)* Yet another standard that specifies a series of characters that clear computer screens. This was done through the ANSI.SYS device driver in the CONFIG.SYS file under DOS. Windows has rendered this item moot. "Using *ANSI screen control codes* today is about as common as finding a vertical hold knob on a TV set."

ANSI.SYS *(an-zee-dot-sis)* In MS-DOS, a configuration file that has instructions needed to display ANSI graphics and to control cursor locations, line wrapping, and the behavior of the keyboard.

ANSI terminal *(an-zee ter-muh-nol)* A terminal capable of carrying out ANSI commands. See also *dumb terminal.*

answer mode *(an-ser moed)* The state of a modem when it's ready to receive calls from other computers. In this mode, the modem picks up the phone whenever it rings. Normally, modems are not in this mode; they're in originate mode; see also *originate mode.* "At the start of the press conference, the senator will read a brief statement, and then he will switch into *answer mode.*"

answer-only modem *(an-sir-own-lee mo-dum)* A modem that can answer calls, but not initiate them.

answer/originate modem *(an-sir or-idj-uh-nayt mo-dum)* A modem that can answer and initiate calls. Most modems are answer/originate, which makes the term about as useful as "round car tire."

anti-aliasing *(an-tee-ay-lee-us-ing)* A software technique designed to remove the jagged edge along curved and angled objects. The jagged edge illustrates the best representation of the curve using the monitor's neatly arranged pixels. Anti-aliasing software uses various shading tricks to fool the eye into seeing a more proper rendition of the shape.

A

A

antiglare screen *(an-tee-glayr skreen)* A device to put over your computer monitor that cuts the glare from indoor lighting or from the outside sun. Basically, it keeps you from squinting and getting eyestrain. Most anti-glare gizmos are nothing more than a rack containing a stretched piece of nylon; beige or black, no taupe.

antistatic mat *(an-tee-stat-ick mat)* A mat or pad under or near a computer device that absorbs static electricity. The mat keeps your computer safe from the evils of random static discharge.

antivirus *(an-tee-vy-rus)* A type of program (utility software) that scans your system and detects virus or other evil programs. Antivirus software may also remove the infection, deleting it from your hard drive, and may also actively protect your PC from infection. It all depends on how much you want to be bothered by antivirus software and how much you put your PC at risk. "It's a good idea to run *antivirus* software on your computer, especially if you're using lots of diskettes others use or if you download software from questionable sources."

any key *(an-ee kee)* Any key on your keyboard. Programmers use the term *any key* to try to make things easier on you when they actually want you to use the Enter key or the Spacebar. In their twisted little minds, they think, "Hey, I'll just tell them they can press *any key* to continue, which allows them the freedom to press any key they like." In practice, it leads to frustration and eternal hunting for a key labeled Any.

AOL *(aye-oh-ell)* 1. Acronym for America Online. See also *America Online*. 2. Often followed by "disconnected me" or "is busy."

Apache *(uh-pach-ee)* Web server software that powers more than half the world's Web sites.

API *(aye pee eye)* Acronym for Application Program Interface, which is yet another way that's supposed to make computers easier than they really are. API defines a standard way that programs work with pull-down menus, dialog boxes, and windows. Microsoft Windows, OS/2, and the Macintosh are examples of API in action.

APL *(aye pee el)* Acronym for A Programming Language. A scientific programming language used to develop mathematical models. It is noted for its brevity and use of weird characters.

APM *(aye pee em)* Acronym for Advanced Power Management. The ability of a computer to shut down various components to save electricity.

app *(app)* Slang for application.

append *(ap-end)* To stick one thing on to the end of another thing. When you append a file, you stick one file on the end of the other, making one large file. "Bertha almost gave our system administrator a heart attack. He asked her to *append* one file to another, explained what it meant, and then later caught her gluing two disks together."

Apple II *(ap-ol too)* One of the first personal computers that actually did something useful. After introducing the Apple II, Apple released enhanced models named Apple IIe, Apple IIc, and Apple IIgs. Finally, Apple decided to drop the whole Apple II family and focus on selling Macintoshes. "I asked Wayne why he looked so pale. He said he saw the same *Apple IIe* he bought in 1983 for $2,500 at a garage sale, and they were asking $20 for it."

Apple III *(ap-ol three)* A computer that was supposed to replace the Apple II but wound up being ignored by the general public. After turning into a public embarrassment to Apple, the Apple III quietly disappeared and can now be found in landfills all across America. "Betcha didn't know that Apple will not name any product with a 'three' in it. This is because of the bad luck associated with the old *Apple III* computer."

 Apple Computer, Inc. *(ap-ol kom-pyoo-ter ink)* The makers of the Apple II series, the Macintosh series, and several other products. Based in Cupertino, California. Steve Jobs and Steve Wozniak, who had been teenage friends, founded the company in a family garage in Silicon Valley. Eventually, Apple Computer grew into a billion-dollar empire but never realized that it was selling *software* and not *hardware,* so it eventually lost its status as a computer pioneer.

 Apple desktop bus *(ap-ol desk-top buss)* Sometimes abbreviated as ADB, it defines an interface

Lots of things can be connected to the Apple desktop bus.

standard for connecting keyboards, mice, trackballs, and other input devices to Apple Macintosh computers.

Apple Desktop Interface (ADI) *(ap-ol desk-top in-tur-fase)* A set of guidelines developed by Apple Computer to ensure that the appearance and operation of all Macintosh applications are similar.

Apple Extended Keyboard *(ap-ol eks-ten-ded kee-bord)* A 105-key keyboard that works with the Macintosh SE Macintosh II and Apple IIgs computers.

Apple File Exchange *(ap-ol fiel ex-chanj)* A program that enables Macs equipped with suitable floppy disk drives to exchange data with IBM PC-compatible computers. It is the Macintosh's attempt at playing well with others.

Apple key *(ap-ol kee)* A key on an Apple keyboard that has the outline of the Apple logo. Also known as the Command key.

The Apple key.

A

Apple menu *(ap-ol men-yoo)* The tiny little apple (with a bite taken out of it) that appears in the far left corner of the menu bar on Macintosh computers. Clicking on the Apple menu displays desk accessories and other programs. "Herb was crushed not to find any cobbler on the *Apple menu*."

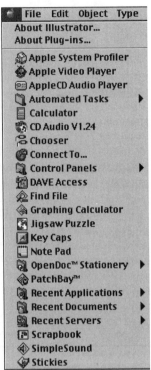

The Apple menu: No cobbler today.

 AppleScript *(ap-ol skript)* A shell programming language for the Macintosh, similar to HyperTalk.

 applet *(ap-let)* 1. A mini-application; typically, those that come with Windows, such as Paint or WordPad. 2. Any small program designed to do a specific task (hence *applet* as opposed to *application*). 3. A small Java program that Java-happy Web browsers can run on the Internet.

 AppleTalk *(ap-ol-tok)* A Local Area Network standard developed by Apple to hook Macintosh and IBM PC computers together. Every Macintosh computer has an AppleTalk port built-in (the same can't be said for IBM computers). AppleTalk is an inexpensive way to create a network, but it tends to be slower than other types of networks. See also *network*.

application *(ap-li-kay-shen)* Another name for a program, such as a word processor, spreadsheet, or database. *Application* implies work getting done or using something to meet an end. The word *program* is too robotic for most people.

application developer *(ap-li-ka-shen dee-vel-oh-pur)* The person or company that creates and publishes a computer program.

 application icon *(ap-li-kay-shen eye-con)* A tiny graphics symbol that represents a program. Opening the icon by double-clicking the mouse on the symbol runs the program.

ARC *(ark)* The name of a once-popular data-compression program that smashes multiple files into a single, smaller one. Once used heavily on IBM computers, the ARC file standard has been replaced by the ZIP standard.

arcade game *(ar-kayd gaym)* A type of computer game that relies more on quick actions and reflexes as opposed to real-world, simulation, or strategy games. Named after the popular coin-operated games of the early 1980s, such as PacMan, Asteriods, Defender, and Space Invaders.

 Archie *(ar-chee)* A text-based program designed to find files (archives) on the Internet. Although Archie can still be accessed, various search engines on the World

Wide Web have replaced it. See also *search engine.* Archie is now somewhat obsolete and has been replaced by Web-based services, such as Shareware.com; see also *shareware.*

architecture *(ar-kuh-tek-chur)* 1. The particular (and arbitrary) way computer equipment is designed. Similar computers, such as IBM PCs and clones, are said to have the same architecture. 2. Refers to the design of a communication system, as in "network architecture." See also *open architecture.* "Paul is taking a class on computer architecture. They're starting with the early cage look and moving up into the neo-classic, fawn-white structures."

archive *(ar-kiev)*: A place where important files are stored. Often this place is where you can never find the files again.

archive attribute *(ar-kiev att-ree-byoot)* A file attribute that indicates whether the file has been updated since the last backup. Similar to the archive bit.

archive bit *(ar-kiev bit)* A bit that is used by a backup program to determine whether the file has been backed up.

archive site *(ar-kiev siet)* An Internet-accessible computer that serves as a holding place for a collection of data, such as all messages from a mailing list or newsgroup.

ARCNET *(ark-net)* Acronym for *a*ttached *r*esource *c*omputer *net*work. The first Local Area Network, introduced in 1968 by Datapoint Corporation.

areal density *(air-ee-uhl den-sih-tee)* The tightness with which data can be packed on a hard disk or floppy disk; expressed in megabits per square inch

(Mb/in^2). "The *areal density* of those jeans Becky is wearing must be pretty high. How does she move in those things?"

argument *(ar-gyoo-mint)* A value given to a program. Most often used in programming. "The main program needs to give two arguments to the subprogram so that it can work properly. After the subprogram gets these two *arguments,* it can plot the next most likely sighting of Elvis, Bigfoot, and the Loch Ness monster."

argument separator *(ar-gyoo-mint sep-pur-aye-tor)* In spreadsheet programs and programming languages, a comma or other punctuation symbol that sets off one argument from another in a command.

 ARP *(aye ar pee)* Acronym for Address Resolution Protocol, the method by which Internet addresses are found. Techy stuff. ARP translates a cryptic-looking number into a Web page somewhere in the known universe.

 ARPANET *(ar-puh-net)* Acronym for Advanced Research Projects Agency Network, the nationwide computer network created by the Department of Defense in 1969 to link research institutions and universities together. ARPANET was merged with several other networks to create the Internet.

array *(uh-ray)* A collection of similar information, such as list of numbers, codes, text, or other items. All the items are usually of the same type. Each item in the array is an element. For example, an array may contain a list of blow-gun poisons used by various Amazon tribes.

A

The array could be called the *sting-array,* and each item in the array would be referenced by a unique element number.

arrow keys *(ayr-oh keez)* Special keys on the keyboard that move the cursor up, down, left, or right. Not surprisingly, the arrow keys have little arrows on them. Also referred to as *cursor keys.* "Bill just quit tech support. He told a lady to press the up-arrow key, and she shot back at him that there were 12 arrows on her keyboard, 5 of which pointed up."

artificial intelligence *(ar-tuh-fish-al in-tel-uh-jentz)* The fascinating science of making computers as smart as human beings (which may be a step backward, in some cases). Recently, the art of inserting artificial intelligence into computers is nothing more than making a program do what you want it to do. "Bob's been working on that *artificial intelligence* program for years. Soon, he says, he'll make computers just as smart as he is. Still, this worries me since I just saw him back his car over a fire hydrant."

artificial life *(ar-tuh-fish-al lief)* A research area devoted to the creation and study of computer simulations of living organisms. "After meeting her boss, Molly wondered how far the study of artificial life had gone."

ascender *(uh-sen-der)* The part of a lowercase letter that extends upward and rises above x-height. The letters *b, d, f, h, k, l,* and *t* have ascenders. The letters *s, u,* and *n* do not. "Letters with *ascenders* go to heaven when they're deleted; letters with descenders suffer an eternity in word processing purgatory."

ascending order *(uh-sen-ding or-der)* To arrange information from lowest to highest. "Hopefully, the air traffic controller will arrange the airplanes to take off in *ascending order.*"

ASCII *(ass-kee;* not *ask-too)* 1. An acronym that stands for American Standard Code for Information Interchange. ASCII defines a standard way of representing characters on computers. It is handy because computers that recognize ASCII can share files that contain only ASCII characters. See also *Unicode.* 2. A plain, boring text file. ASCII files contain no formatting or other information, just letters, numbers, and punctuation symbols. "A file composed of *ASCII* characters is about as exciting as gum without any flavor." 3. Character codes 0 through 127. See also *ASCII codes.*

ASCII codes *(ass-kee kohdz)* Code numbers from 0 through 127 that are assigned to characters and to special codes. The codes are divided into four types: control codes, symbols, uppercase letters, and lowercase letters.

A

Code	Character	Keyboard	Name
0	^@	Ctrl+@	NULL
1	^A	Ctrl+A	SOH, start of header
2	^B	Ctrl+B	STX, start of text
3	^C	Ctrl+C	ETX, end of text
4	^D	Ctrl+D	EOT, end of transmission
5	^E	Ctrl+E	ENQ, enquire, or "Here is . . ."
6	^F	Ctrl+F	ACK, acknowledge
7	^G	Ctrl+G	BELL (goes "ding")
8	^H	Ctrl+H, Backspace	BS, backspace
9	^I	Ctrl+I, Tab	TAB, tab key
10	^J	Ctrl+J	LF, line feed
11	^K	Ctrl+K	VT, vertical tab key
12	^L	Ctrl+L	FF, form feed
13	^M	Ctrl+M, Enter	CR, carriage return
14	^N	Ctrl+N	SO, shift out
15	^O	Ctrl+O	SI, shift in
16	^P	Ctrl+P	DLE, data link escape
17	^Q	Ctrl+Q	DC1, device control one
18	^R	Ctrl+R	DC2, device control two
19	^S	Ctrl+S	DC3, device control three
20	^T	Ctrl+T	DC4, device control four
21	^U	Ctrl+U	NAK, negative acknowledge
22	^V	Ctrl+V	SYN, synchronize
23	^W	Ctrl+W	ETB, end transmission block
24	^X	Ctrl+X	CAN, cancel
25	^Y	Ctrl+Y	EM, end message
26	^Z	Ctrl+Z	SUB, substitute
27	^[	Ctrl+[, Esc	ESC, escape
28	^\	Ctrl+\	FS, form separator
29	^]	Ctrl+]	GS, group separator
30	^^	Ctrl+^	RS, record separator
31	^_	Ctrl+_	VS, version separator

A

Code	Character	Code	Character	Code	Character
32	[space]	64	@	96	`
33	!	65	A	97	a
34	"	66	B	98	b
35	#	67	C	99	c
36	$	68	D	100	d
37	%	69	E	101	e
38	&	70	F	102	f
39	'	71	G	103	g
40	(	72	H	104	h
41	)	73	I	105	i
42	*	74	J	106	j
43	+	75	K	107	k
44	,	76	L	108	l
45	-	77	M	109	m
46	.	78	N	110	n
47	/	79	O	111	o
48	0	80	P	112	p
49	1	81	Q	113	q
50	2	82	R	114	r
51	3	83	S	115	s
52	4	84	T	116	t
53	5	85	U	117	u
54	6	86	V	118	v
55	7	87	W	119	w
56	8	88	X	120	x
57	9	89	Y	121	y
58	:	90	Z	122	z
59	;	91	[	123	{
60	<	92	\	124		
61	=	93	]	125	}
62	>	94	^	126	~
63	?	95	_	127	[delete]

ASCII file *(ass-kee fiel)* 1. A file that contains only ASCII characters. Often used when exchanging information between two word processors that don't read each other's formats. Also, some system files, such as CONFIG.SYS, must be in the ASCII (or plain text) format. 2. Another term for any of the following: DOS text file, plain text file, text file, text-only, unformatted document.

Ashton-Tate *(ash-ton tayt)* The company that developed the dBASE series of programs. See also *dBASE*. At one time, it was one of the Big Three software developers; back in the early 1980s, it was VisiCorp, who did the VisiCalc spreadsheet; MicroPro, who did WordStar; and Ashton-Tate, with dBASE. Today its building in Silicon Valley is a waterbed store. The founder was Charles Tate. Ashton was the name of the parrot in the lobby.

A-size paper *(aye-size pay-pur)* A page that is 8.5 by 11 inches in size.

ASM *(aye ess em)* The MS-DOS filename extension usually attached to a file containing assembly language source codes.

aspect ratio *(ass-pekt ray-shee-oh)* The ratio of the horizontal dimension of an object to its vertical dimension. A term used in graphics. When changing the size of a graphic, maintaining the width-to-height ratio is important to avoid distortions. "Movie buffs will tell you that most films are shot with a 3x4 *aspect ratio*."

The image is distorted because the aspect ratio was not maintained. Plus, it's just a goofy picture.

assembler *(ah-sem-bler)* A special program used to convert programs written in assembly language into machine code that the computer can understand. Not to be confused with assembly language, which is the type of programming language an assembler assembles.

assembly language *(ah-sem-blee lang-gwij)* A type of programming language that directly manipulates the computer's microprocessor. Assembly language programs are usually longer and harder to read than programs written in C or BASIC. On the other hand, assembly language programs run faster and take up less disk space than similar programs written in other languages.

```
HELLO WORLD for Assembly
    Org 100h
Start:
    mov ah,9h
    mov dx,string
    int 21h
Exit:
    int 20h
string:
    db "Hello,
world!",0dh,0ah,'$'
```

assign *(uh-sien)* To give a value to a named variable.

 assigned number *(uh-sined num-bur)* On the Internet, a value associated with a specific protocol that is controlled by the Internet Assigned Numbers Authority (IANA). An example of an assigned number is the port number assigned to a specific network service, such as USENET or Internet Relay Chat (IRC).

A

Association for Computer Machinery (ACM) The world's first educational and scientific computer society, now more than 80,000 members strong. ACM was founded in 1947 and sponsors conferences, journals, and book publishing. To find out more, connect to its Web site at `www.acm.org/`.

Association for Systems Management (ASM) The association for information systems professionals, focusing on the management of information systems and information technology. To find out more about ASM, connect to its Web site at `www.4w.com/asm/in/`.

Association for Women in Computing (AWC) Founded in 1978, this organization's purpose is to provide opportunities for professional growth through networking and programs on technical and career-oriented topics. For more information about AWC, you can read about its history or annual conferences, at `www.awc-hq.org/`.

asterisk *(ass-ter-isk)* The * symbol on the keyboard. See also *.

asynchronous *(ay-sink-ron-us)* 1. Any process that isn't synchronized. Often used when sending or receiving data through a phone line. Most likely a term you'll never use in your life, but it can make you sound knowledgeable around other computer geeks. 2. The opposite of *synchronous*. See also *synchronous*.

asynchronous communication *(ay-sink-ron-us com-myoo-nee-kay-shun)* A method of data communication in which the transmission of bits of data isn't synchronized by a clock signal, but rather by sending the bits one after another, with a start bit and a stop bit to mark the beginning and end or each data unit. Good examples are telephone lines, which can be used for asynchronous communication.

AT *(aye-tee)* 1. An acronym (like you were expecting somebody's initials?) for advanced technology. "In the computer biz, it's risky naming anything new *AT* because all advanced technology is outdated in 18 months anyway." 2. A type of computer compatible with the original IBM PC AT. Though that computer sported an 80286 microprocessor, most of today's systems are said to use the same design (or *architecture*) as the original AT. 3. The name of a set of modem commands originated on the Hayes micromodem. They used to call them Hayes-compatible modems, but now they claim them to be AT-command-compatible. The AT is short for "attention!"

AT&T *(aye tee and tee)* 1. An acronym that stands for American Telephone and Telegraph. Once a feared competitor of IBM's, AT&T never really hit it big selling computer hardware. Today, AT&T concentrates on communications systems and offers the national Internet service AT&T WorldNet. 2. The original developers of the UNIX operating system.

ATA *(aye tee aye)* Acronym for Advanced Technology Attachment. A disk drive interface. See also *IDE*.

ATA-2 See *IDE*.

ATA-3 *(aye tee aye three)* An experimental standard for attaching many different recording media, such as disk drives and tape drives, to a PC.

AT bus *(aye tee bus)* Refers to the 16-bit bus introduced with the IBM AT. Also known as the ISA bus.

AT keyboard *(aye tee kee-bord)* An 84-key keyboard introduced with the IBM PC AT. The AT keyboard is not up to current standards because now most computers are equipped with a 101-key keyboard.

ATM *(aye tee em)* 1. Acronym for asynchronous transfer mode, a method of sending audio, visual, and computer data over one line without getting anything confused or melting any telephone poles. 2. An acronym for a friendly robot that dispenses money. In this instance, the acronym stands for automated teller machine.

attach file *(uh-tatch fiel)* To send a file through e-mail or post a file to a newsgroup. Text files are attached as text. Binary files (programs, sound files, images, and so on) are converted into a special text format using a file encoder. The e-mail program is generally responsible for encoding and decoding the files.

attachment *(uh-tach-ment)* In e-mail, a binary file, such as a program or a compressed word processing document, that has been attached to an e-mail message. The content of the file does not appear in the e-mail message, but is a separate document you must open.

attachment encoding *(uh-tach-ment en-coe-ding)* The encoding format used to attach a binary file to an e-mail message.

attenuation *(at-ten-you-way-shun)* The loss of signal strength because the network cables are too long. "Warning, Will Robinson. Attenuation has not allowed successful data communications. Did you need help?"

attrib *(ah-trib)* An MS-DOS command that displays or changes file attributes.

attribute *(ah-trih-byoot)* 1. Various descriptions of a file, such as its date, time, read-only, archive, system, hidden, or other settings. These are the file attributes. 2. Character emphasis in word processing, such as **bold,** *italics,* or underline. Also refers to font style and type size, such as Courier at 12 points.

audible click *(aw-dee-bul clik)* See *audible feedback.*

audible feedback *(aw-dee-bul feed-bak)* The capacity of a keyboard to generate sounds each time a key is pressed. Also known as an audible click.

audio *(aw-dee-oh)* 1. Relating to sound. "A computer with *audio* capability can annoy your ears as well as your eyes." 2. Sound technology. A computer component that deals with sound.

audio jack *(aw-dee-oh jak)* A connector on a computer or peripheral that lets you attach sound-producing or -recording devices. Also known as RCA or mini-din connector.

audiovisual *(aw-dee-o-viz-yoo-al)* Relating to both sight and sound.

audit *(aw-dit)* A tracking process that shows the activities of users by recording selected types of events in the security log of a server or workstation. "Molly knew that Vanessa wasn't working because of the network audit. FreeCell isn't a company activity."

authentication *(aw-thin-tih-kay-shun)* The process by which a computer system validates a user's logon information. Many systems, such as Windows 2000, require users to log on to their computer network. The workstation performs an authentication to verify that the user is approved to work on the system.

authoring *(aw-thor-ing)* In multimedia, the process of preparing a presentation that involves not only the written part of the presentation but also the sound, graphics, and video components.

authoring language *(aw-thor-ing lan-gwij)* A computer-assisted instruction application that provides tools for creating instructional or presentation software. The authoring language in HyperCard is named HyperTalk.

authoritative restore *(aw-thor-uh-tay-tiv ree-store)* A type of backup-and-restore operation in Windows 2000 that automatically replaces all existing copies of objects that have been treated as authoritative; information in an Active Directory, for example.

AutoCad *(aw-to kad)* A popular computer-assisted design (CAD) program used by architectural and engineering companies. AutoCad was designed by Autodesk.

auto-dial/auto-answer modem *(aw-to di-el / aw-to an-ser moh-dem)* A modem that can dial out and receive incoming calls. Most modems available today are auto-dial/auto-answer. You may find an answer-only or manual-dial modem at a garage sale — if you look hard enough.

auto disconnect *(aw-toe dis-kuh-nekt)* The ability to remove a user after a period of inactivity. Usually done by online services to ensure that someone doesn't walk away from the computer and forget to hang up. The auto disconnect makes that line available for another user.

AUTOEXEC.BAT *(aw-toe-eks-ek-dot-bat)* A file containing commands that run each time DOS or Windows starts. See also *batch file*. Short for *auto-exe*cutable *bat*ch file. No longer required beginning with Windows 95, though included for compatibility reasons.

auto-logon *(aw-toe log-on)* A feature of communications programs that enables you to automate the process of logging on to a BBS or online service.

automatic backup *(aw-toe-mat-ick bak-up)* A program feature that saves a document automatically at a period the user specifies, such as every 10 to 15 minutes. This feature can help you avoid a extensive work loss in the case of a power outage or system crash. Also called Autosave.

automatic emulation switching *(aw-toe-mat-ick em-yoo-lay-shun swich-ing)* The ability that printers have to change printer control languages without human intervention.

automatic font downloading *(aw-toe-mat-ick font down-lo-ding)* The transfer of fonts from the hard disk to the printer as the fonts are needed to complete a printing job.

automatic recalculation *(aw-toe-mat-ick ree-cal-cyoo-lay-shun)* In a spreadsheet, the ability of the cell value to be recalculated every time any cell in the worksheet changes.

AutoPC *(aw-toe pee-see)* Designed by Clarion, the first car computer that recognizes verbal commands. The AutoPC has more than 1,200 words in its vocabulary and understands commands to change radio stations, provide turn-by-turn directions based on its Global Positions System (GPS) navigation unit, and read e-mail subject lines.

autoresponder *(ah-toe-ree-spon-der)* An e-mail address that sends a canned response to any e-mail it receives. Also known as autoreply, mailbot, and e-mailbot. "The White House uses autoresponders to people who send them e-mail. Basically, their autoresponder says "Thanks for writing, but we're not going to read your message.""

AUX *(awks)* The first serial port on a PC, also known as COM1. AUX is short for *aux*iliary port. "Old farmer Vern gave up computing altogether. The toll-free phone support guy told him to plug his modem into the *AUX* port. Darn beast nearly hooved him to death."

Avogadro's number *(ah-vo-god-rowz num-ber)* 1. 6.0225×10^{23}. 2. A very large number. 3. A constant value used by scientists that represents something so important that they decided to name it after the guy who discovered it. "I'm tired of calling up girls for dates who turn me down. Give me *Avogadro's Number* and maybe I can talk physics to him or something." 4. Rumor has it that if you dial Avogadro's number backward, you can hear demonic messages.

awk *(awk)* Scripting language.

axis *(ack-siss)* An imaginary line drawn through the center of something. In computer graphics, the X-axis runs horizontally, from left to right. The Y-axis runs vertically, up and down. "The world tilts on its *axis,* about 23 degrees."

A

A

B

B: *(bee co-len)* The drive letter given to the (optional) second floppy disk drive on a PC.

backbone *(bak-bohn)* The main item or central location for something. The backbone of the Internet consists of the main computers to which many other computers are connected.

 Back button *(bak but-en)* 1. A graphical button in Web browser software used to return to the previously visited Web page. 2. A place on your back where you have your spouse press and it makes you go "Ahhh!"

Atlas

Axis

Back Button

Lumbar region

Sacroiliac

The Back button in use.

back door *(bak dor)* A secret way, such as a password, of getting into a program. Usually, only the original programmer knows about it. It sounds sneaky, but it allows programmers to update software with a minimum of hassle. It is not a bug or virus.

back end *(bak end)* Something that takes place without the user's knowing about it, usually the final step in some procedure. Has nothing to do with *rear end*.

background *(bak-grownd)* 1. A multitasking term; when a program runs a program (or task) that you're not currently working with or have visible on the screen. See also *active window, multitasking*. "Though you can run two or more programs at the same time, you can use only one program at a time. All other programs run in the background, like extras in a Godzilla movie." 2. Another term for desktop wallpaper, the graphic design or image you see while using an operating system like Windows. See also *wallpaper*.

background application *(bak-grownd ap-lee-kay-shun)* Any application that is inactive when running more than one application.

background noise *(bak-grownd noyz)* Any interference on a telephone line, usually electrical static. Often causes random or "garbage" characters to appear and can disconnect you if the noise is loud enough.

backlight *(bak-lyt)* To illuminate a screen with additional lighting from behind. Used to highlight LCD screens. "Harry is so cheap. He saved himself $50 by not getting a *backlit* laptop, thinking he could just hold a flashlight behind the lid to accomplish the same thing."

back panel *(bak pan-el)* The panel at the rear of the computer. Most of the connections to the power and the peripherals are made at the back panel. "Yup, those guys who design computers are smart. They put all the cable connections on the *back panel* so that they'd be inconvenient to everyone."

back quote *(bak kwoht)* The ` character. Also called a back tick. See also ` (accent grave).

backslash key *(bak-slash kee)* The key with the \ symbol on it, often found above the Enter key on most keyboards. See also \ (backslash). Over the phone, you might say 'Type CD *backslash* DOS and press the Enter key.' But the person you're talking to types this:

```
Seedy back slash doss and press
the inner key
```

backspace *(bak-spays)* 1. The key on the keyboard that has the word *Backspace* on it. There may also be a left-pointing arrow on the key. 2. The act of pressing the Backspace key, which deletes something. In a word processor, the Backspace key erases the character to the left of the cursor (like a little PacMan). "Too bad they don't have a *Backspace* key to take back things you shouldn't have said."

backtracking *(bak-trak-ing)* A system to try to find a problem in a program. You try one solution and if it doesn't work, go back and try another one.

backup *(bak-up)* 1. A safety copy of a file made in case the original file is unintentionally changed or destroyed. "Hey, Jefferson! Houser just erased our

Christmas bonus file. Where's that *backup* you made yesterday? You did make a *backup,* didn't you? Jefferson, how come you don't look so good?" 2. The copy of the file itself. 3. The process of creating a backup file or a backup of every file in the computer system. 4. The MS-DOS command that performed the backup operation. The name of any program that backs up files.

backup media pool *(bak-up mee-dea puel)* A collection of data-storage media that has been reserved for use by Windows 2000 Backup.

Backup Operator *(bak-up op-er-ay-tor)* A member of this group can back up and restore files and folders regardless of any ownership or permissions of the files and folders.

backup set *(bak-up set)* A collection of files and folders (and any other data) that have been backed up and stored on a file or tape.

backward compatible *(bak-werd cum-pat-uh-bul)* When software written for an earlier version of a microprocessor works on a later model. Can also refer to files for a specific application. If the program can still read files generated by an older version, it's said to be backward compatible.

backward search *(bak-werd surch)* A search that starts at the cursor and works backward through either a database or a document.

bad *(bad)* A prefix used to refer to something as no longer good or unable to perform its job. For example, the phrase "bad sectors" on a disk drive refers to an area so damaged by meteor showers as to be unable to store any information. It does not refer to the moral disposition of any software or hardware.

bad break *(bad brayk)* 1. An improperly hyphenated line break. 2. When things don't go well.

bad sector *(bad sek-tor)* An area on a floppy or hard disk that doesn't reliably record data. Not to worry, the operating system does not use the bad sector, though having too many bad sectors on a disk indicates impending doom.

BAK *(bak)* A three-letter file extension given to backup files, especially the ones created automatically by some applications (such as some word processors). The backup file name looks like this: memo.BAK.

balloon help *(buh-loon help)* Starting with System 7 on the Macintosh, Apple introduced balloon help, which provides little windows of helpful information on the screen. Balloon help gets its name because the windows it displays look like the speaking balloons in comic strips,

Balloon help for Excel.

although some balloons look more like boxes. "*Balloon help* just displays a little bit of help, unlike the normal help menu, which displays gobs of information you can't use or understand."

banana problem *(buh-nah-nuh problem)* Something that tends to grow and grow without stopping. An out-of-control project. From the old saying "I know how to spell *banana,* but I don't know where to stop."

bandwidth *(band-width)* 1. A measurement of a signal, typically done in hertz. For example, the speed at which the information is sent from the computer to the monitor. 2. A disparaging term in e-mail or on newsgroups referring to a useless message or a message with little information as a "waste of *bandwidth.*" 3. Bandwidth is not how much space a musical group takes up while on stage.

bang *(bang)* A common slang term for an exclamation point (!). Most often used in programming.

banking online *(bane-king online)* The ability to work with your personal financing through the Internet. Many financial institutions (such as banks) now offer the services of paying bills and checking account status through the Internet.

bank switching *(bank switch-ing)* 1. A way of quickly switching between two different groups of memory chips, giving the illusion that it's all the same memory. Bank switching is used to overcome built-in hardware limitations. For example, PCs in the 1980s used bank switching to provide more memory. See also *expanded memory.* 2. What Wells Fargo is trying to get BankAmerica customers to do and vice versa.

banner *(ban-nur)* A box running across a Web page that is used for advertisement.

Banyan vines *(ban-yan vienz)* A type of network marketed by the Banyan company. Banyans are trees that have long vines and multiple roots, a nifty metaphor for a computer network.

bar *(bar)* The suffix of foobar, a common term used by UNIX hackers and programmers. See also *fubar.*

bar chart *(bar chart)* A chart that illustrates comparisons among individual items. Categories are organized vertically; values, horizontally.

bar code *(bar kohd)* A pattern of narrow and wide black-and-white strips. The strips represent numbers or codes, which are read by a scanning device. This provides a much faster method of product and inventory identification than relying on hourly employees with optional reading skills.

bar code reader *(bar kohd ree-dur)* A device that scans bar codes and then converts the bar code into digital information for the computer's digestion.

bar graph *(bar graf)* A graph that plots data using horizontal bars. The X-axis is the vertical axis, and the Y-axis is the horizontal axis.

base *(bays)* The number of digits used in a counting system. Base ten uses 10 digits, base two (binary) uses 2, and base sixteen (hexadecimal) uses 16. "Most people use *base* 10 because we have five fingers on each hand. My cat only has four toes on each paw, so he must count using *base* 8 (or *base* sixteen if he uses his back paws too)."

baseband transmission *(bays-band trans-mih-shun)* A type of digital data transmission in which each wire carries only one signal or channel at a time. See also *broadband.*

base font *(bays font)* The default font for a document. Unless you specify a font in a word processing document, the program uses the base font.

Bash *(bash)* The *Bourne-again sh*ell. A command-line environment for Linux that allows extensive editing, history listing, and other tricks. Built about the Bourne shell.

BASIC *(bay-sik)* 1. Acronym for Beginners All-purpose Symbolic Instruction Code, a programming language specifically designed to make programming easier. Developed at Dartmouth in the late 1960s and early 1970s. Early PCs and versions of DOS came with a version of the BASIC programming language. That was because most early PC buyers would write their own programs for the thing — kind of like carving your own set of golf clubs before playing each day. 2. Used disparagingly; although BASIC is easy to use, many programmers look down on it as a "toy" language. Early versions of BASIC lacked the ability to create cool programs that would wipe out your hard disk or blow up your modem. Newer versions of BASIC now offer such features, but BASIC no longer has the popularity it once did because it has been replaced by the C programming language.

B

Basic Input/Output System. See *BIOS*.

BAT *(bat)* The file extension identifying batch files. See also *batch file,* which just happens to be the next term defined.

batch file *(batch fiel)* 1. A special text file that contains lists of operating system commands and special instructions. Running the batch file causes the computer to follow all the instructions. 2. In DOS, any file that ends with the BAT extension. Batch files are essentially text files, though the text in the files are DOS commands and special batch file programming instructions. "I'm sorry you misunderstood me. I said that *Hillary* should be a *batch file*."

batch processing *(batch praw-sess-ing)* When the computer executes program instructions, one after the other, without user intervention.

batch program *(batch pro-gram)* A text file that contains one or more operating system commands. A batch program's filename has a .cmd or .bat extension. See also *extension*.

Batman *(bat-man)* A popular comic book character who dresses like a bat and goes around doing good deeds in crime-ridden Gotham City. "I like *Batman* because he's the only superhero who isn't radiated or mutated in some way. He just has a lot of nifty gadgets."

battery backup *(bat-er-ee bak-up)* 1. A battery that's ready to supply electricity the moment a power outage occurs. See also *UPS*. 2. The battery inside your PC that keeps track of the current time and other configuration information even when Mr. Computer is unplugged.

battery pack *(bat-er-ee pak)* A rechargeable battery that supplies power to a computer, usually a portable or laptop computer.

baud *(bod)* 1. The rate of signal changes when transmitting data, such as over a modem. Named after French engineer J. M. E. Baudot. Commonly, and incorrectly, confused with bits per second (bps) when measuring modem speed. See also *bits per second.* 2. Because it rhymes with "bod" (short for body), it is often the source of much lame computer humor: "Peter tried to pick up that cute girl in the computer science class using his modem. She slapped him, though, after he asked her what her baud rate was."

baud rate *(bod raet)* The maximum number of changes that can occur per second in the electrical state of a communications circuit. Commonly confused with bits per second (bps). See also *bits per second.*

bay *(bay)* 1. A compartment, inside the computer console, designed for system expansion. 2. The compartment inside a computer console into which you place a disk drive.

BBS *(bee bee ess)* Acronym for bulletin board system, a computer and modem that others can dial into and copy files, leave messages, and share information. Most are privately run, though many major developers and manufacturers have their own BBSs for users who want technical information or updates. The World Wide Web is quickly replacing the BBS for this type of information exchange. "Most *BBS* systems have more BS than B."

B

BBSs *(bee bee ess ess)* Plural of BBS; bulletin board systems.

BCC *(bee see see)* See *blind carbon copy.*

BCD *(bee see dee)* Acronym for Binary Coded Decimal, a technique that programs use to ensure accuracy for financial calculations. "Most spreadsheets use *BCD* so that rounding errors won't mess up your calculations. My accountant should try *BCD* sometime. . . ."

 beach ball pointer *(beech bal poyn-ter)* A mouse pointer that appears to let you know that the computer is actually doing something, although

Beach ball pointer.

nothing seems to be happening. The symbol looks like a beach ball, spinning around — hence its name. The beach ball pointer is the Mac counterpart to the Windows hourglass. "My Mac shows the beach ball pointer so much that small people in swimsuits have appeared to play with it."

bed *(bed)* 1. The background music for multimedia presentations. 2. Somewhere that you won't find computer programmers at 2:30 a.m.

bells and whistles *(bels and wis-els)* 1. A slang term to describe the multitude of extra features a program offers. 2. Fancy features not particularly useful but mostly required to outdo the competition.

Bemer, Bob *(bahb bee-mer)* The IBM programmer who created, among other things: the escape sequence, the function behind the Escape key; the concept behind eight bits in a byte; the

backslash character; the name COBOL; he also had a hand in designing the ASCII character codes.

benchmark *(bench-mark)* 1. A performance test. 2. The rating given to a specific piece of equipment. "This monitor benchmarks at 30. And for $400 more, it can benchmark at 15 (faster)." When you are testing software, tasks such as sorts or searches are timed and used for comparisons between products. 3. To perform the performance test; the act of setting benchmarks.

Berkeley *(bur-klee)* 1. Refers to the version of UNIX developed and perfected by the computer scientists at the University of California at Berkeley. 2. One of any of a number of amazing things that comes from UC Berkeley.

Bernoulli box *(ber-noo-lee boks)* A mass storage system using removable cartridges that work on the Bernoulli principle. Named after a Swiss scientist who predicted the dynamics of a rapidly spinning, flexible disk around a fixed object and decided that his college education hadn't been a waste of time after all. Zip drives are a type of Bernoulli box. "Don's a little slow. He brought a *Bernoulli box* for lunch, figuring that it contained some type of Italian meal."

Bernoulli, Daniel *(ber-noo-lee dan-yell)* The Swiss scientist who is credited for the Bernoulli box. Born February 8, 1700, in Groningen, The Netherlands; died March 17, 1782, in Basel, Switzerland.

Daniel Bernoulli of the Bernoulli box.

berserk *(ber-zerk)* 1. A fit of rage that Vikings often went into during the heat of battle. 2. A fit of rage computer users go into when their computer fails to work the way they thought it would. "Watch out for Fred. He's been trying to print sideways in WordPerfect, and I think he's about to go *berserk* on us again."

beta software *(bay-ta soft-wayr)* The preliminary version of new software.

beta test *(bay-ta test)* The second stage of testing (alpha test is the first) of a program before releasing it to the general public. "*Beta test* programs are sometimes called Version 1.0 by companies that want to rush their program on to the market before it's ready."

beta tester *(bay-ta tes-ter)* A person who uses a beta test program. "Before Microsoft released Windows, they gave it to 50,000 *beta testers* around the country. After they discovered it to be full of bugs, Microsoft sold it to the rest of us."

Bézier curve *(Bez-ee-ay kurv)* A mathematically generated line for displaying irregularly shaped curves. To create Bézier curves in most computer graphics programs, you plot a straight line and then manipulate two points, called control handles, somewhere in the middle. Moving these control handles in different directions twists the line into a Bézier curve.

 BG *(bee gee)* 1. One of the Brothers Gibb. 2. Abbreviation for background. See also *background*. 3. Acronym used in e-mail for "big grin." The intent is to show expression in your mail because the person receiving your messages can't see you sitting there with a big grin on your face.

```
Thanks for the 8 Gig hard drive
for Father's day! BG
```

bible (the) *(bie-bol;* not capitalized) Another name for the book *The C Programming Language,* by Kernighan and Ritchie. See also *K&R.* "Phil just can't program unless he has the bible handy."

bidirectional *(bi-duh-rek-shun-al)* Something that works both ways, sending and receiving information.

bidirectional printing *(bi-duh-rek-shun-al print-ing)* When a printer has the ability to print both from left to right and from right to left. This speeds up printing on non-laser printers.

big iron *(big ie-ron)* Slang term for a mainframe computer. "Your *big iron* costs millions of dollars, takes up half a room, and performs as much work as a $2,000 personal computer of today."

big red switch *(beeg red switch)* 1. A computer's On–Off switch. 2. The On–Off switch on anything. "The original IBM PC's On–Off switch was big and red, which is why *big red switch* is used to describe a computer's On–Off switch today."

BIN *(ben)* 1. A binary file. 2. A three-letter file extension to identify files containing binary data. "To identify his files more easily, Benjamin renamed all his BIN files to BEN. Now he wonders why his programs don't work." 3. The name of a directory on UNIX systems that contains program files.

binary *(bie-nayr-ee)* 1. Base two. 2. A counting system that uses two digits, 0 and 1. 3. Can also describe other systems that offer only two choices, such as the Republican and Democratic parties. 4. A star system with two suns.

binary coded decimal (BCD) *(bie-nayr-ee coe-ded des-ee-mul)* A method of coding long decimal numbers so that they can be processed by a computer with greater precision.

binary digit *(bie-nayr-ee di-jit)* The smallest unit of information handled by a computer. Either a one or a zero. See also *bit.*

binary file *(bie-nayr-ee fiel)* 1. Not a text file. Binary files contain information that only a computer (or a computer geek) would understand. 2. A file with the three-letter BIN file extension.

 binary newsgroup *(bie-nayr-ee nooz-groop)* A newsgroup whose messages are primarily encoded files as opposed to text messages. Binary newsgroups contain program files, sound files, graphics, and other non-text information.

binary numbers *(bie-nayr-ee num-burs)* A number system with a base of two. Most people use a number system that has a base of ten.

BIND *(biend)* Acronym for Berkeley Internet Name Domain. BIND is the most widely used DNS implementation on the Internet. Better look up DNS to see what that means.

binding offset *(bine-ding off-set)* The gap left on one side of a printed page to allow room for the document to be placed in a binder.

 binhex *(ben-heks)* A type of encoding that allows binary files to be sent along with text in an e-mail or newsgroup message. Primarily used by the Macintosh, though PCs with the proper software can also decode the files.

biological feedback device *(by-oh-loj-ee-kul feed-bak dee-vys)* A device that translates eye, body, and brain movements into computer input.

BIOS *(by-oss)* 1. Acronym for Basic Input/Output System. The BIOS is a set of instructions that tells the computer how to act, like a personality chip. Most computers have the BIOS built in as a chip plugged into the computer. 2. Another term for ROM or firmware.

bit *(bit)* 1. Contraction of *binary digit.* A binary digit can be either zero or one, on or off, true or false, or any other pair of opposite states, such as Florida and New York. 2. Bits are often used to measure the capability of a microprocessor to process data, such as 16-bit or 32-bit. "Believe it or not: 8 *bits* make up a byte, and 4 *bits* make up a nibble (often spelled *nybble*)."

bit depth *(bit depth)* Describes the richness of colors available for monitors, scanners, and other color input or output devices. The higher the value, the better the colors can be reproduced.

bitmap *(bit-map)* 1. A graphic image composed of pixels, or tiny dots. This contrasts with other types of images that may be represented by vectors or other mathematical algorithms too boring to explain here. 2. Slang for a bitmapped image; see also *bitmapped image.*

bitmapped font *(bit-mapt fawnt)* A type-face style stored as a matrix of tiny dots. When you enlarge the size of a bitmapped font, the font tends to look jagged. Bitmapped fonts gobble up lots of memory.

bitmapped image *(bit-mapd im-ij)* An image created from a bitmap. Most paint programs — such as MacPaint, PC Paintbrush, and the Windows 95 Paint program — create bitmapped images. They can be difficult to modify because you have to change pixels one at a time.

BITNET *(bit-net)* Acronym for *Because It's Time Network.* 2. An early international computer network that began in the early 1980s. Bitnet is incompatible with the Internet, which is slowly replacing it.

bits per inch *(bits pur inch)* A measurement of resolution, usually horizontal bit density. Abbreviated as bpi.

bits per second *(bits pur sek-ond)* 1. The speed of a modem. Refers to how many bits per second the modem can transmit or receive. Common values are 2400, 9600, 14.4K, 28.8K, 33.6K, and 57.6K. (K means either 1,000 or kilobits per second.) The faster the modem, the higher the bits-per-second value; at a bps speed of 28.8K (average), you can transmit approximately 2,880 words in a single second. 2. Not the baud rate; see also *baud.* Bits per second is often confused with baud. Earlier modems were measured with a baud rate, which was more-or-less equal to the bps value.

However, faster modems do not have corresponding bps and baud rates.

bit twiddler *(bit twid-ler)* Slang term for someone who is so nerdy that they like to spend all their time programming in assembly language. "Hi, my name is Norman, and I'm a *bit twiddler.*" Group: "Hi, Norman."

bit width *(bit width)* The number of bits a microprocessor can process at a time. The wider the bit width, the more powerful the microprocessor. Common bit widths are 8, 16, 32, and 64. "Since Virgil was from Oklahoma, he thought that a *bit width* had something to do with a horse's harness. He laughed at me when I told him it was related to computer terms."

bitwise *(bit-wiez)* Anything related to bits. "Don't be bitwise and byte foolish."

black box *(blahk boks)* A complex doodad that performs some specific function. Can be either hardware or software. "You stuff all these numbers into one end of the *black box,* and out the other end comes a balanced budget."

blank *(blangk)* 1. A term used to describe what you get when you press the Spacebar key. 2. A text box or other fill-in item that's empty. 3. Nothing. "My life is like the Spacebar key; it's a complete *blank.*"

blank cell *(blangk sell)* A cell that contains no values or formatting. "My Excel worksheet was full of blank cells. It appeared as though I wasn't doing my job."

B

bleed *(bleed)* When a page design element, such as a photo or text, extends to the extreme edge of the page.

bleed capability *(bleed cape-uh-bil-eh-tee)* The ability of a printer to print bleeds. Laser printers do not have a bleed capability because they need at least a ⅛-inch strip around the side of the page.

 blessed folder *(bless-ed fohl-der)* The folder containing the System and Finder files in a Macintosh. The system refers to the blessed folder when it cannot find a file. See also *path*.

blind carbon copy (BCC) *(blind car-bohn cop-ee; bee see see)* A copy of an e-mail message send to someone who does not appear on the original recipient's list. The recipient knows who sent the message and sees others that it was sent to or carbon-copied to, but does not see anyone on the BCC list.

bloat *(bloht)* The tendancy of programs to expand and fill all of memory and consume all system resources. Most programs bloat because they can; PCs have lots of resources. Other programs bloat when the programmer gets bored and adds new features "just because."

block *(blok)* 1. A collection of information lumped together for convenience. 2. A 512-byte chunk of information on disk. 3. The size of the chunks of information sent between two computers over a modem. "Leon asked maintenance to make a bigger hole in his office wall for his phone line. Seems he's having trouble with his modem's not being able to send big enough *blocks*." 4. A selected chunk of text in a word processing document.

blurb *(blurb)* A brief description of something. "Don't go into great detail about the meeting. Just type me up a quick blurb highlighting the important parts."

BMP *(bee em pee)* A file extension identifying a bitmap graphics file. "I couldn't figure out what Connie meant by 'bumpy' files until I explained that *BMPs* are bitmap graphic files, not bumpy files."

BNC connector *(bee en see kon-eck-tor)* 1. A metal jobbie at the end of a cable that twists to connect the cable to the back of your computer or to another cable. 2. Must stand for Big Nobby Connector.

A Big Nobby Connector.

boat anchor *(boht ang-kor)* Slang for something so useless it may as well be tied to a chain and used for dead weight to keep boats from drifting away. "You have a PC*jr?* May as well be a *boat anchor!*"

body type *(boh-dee type)* The font used when writing paragraphs of text, which is usually different from the headings and captions. Body type is typically set at 10–12 points. Some use 8 points, but that seems way too small.

bogus *(boe-gus)* 1. Something that's phony. 2. A fake item of data used when testing software. "The boss loved my report, but I didn't have the heart to tell him it was a sample filled with *bogus* data."

bogus newsgroup *(boe-gus news-groop)* A newsgroup that doesn't correspond to USENET's approved newsgroups.

boilerplate *(boy-ler-playt)* A prewritten slab of text used over and over. For example, the bio at the front of this book is a boilerplate used in all our *...For Dummies* books. Common uses for boilerplate documents are form letters, legal documents, or love letters to multiple partners. "Bob is such a womanizer. He has this *boilerplate* document he uses to swoon them, and then another *boilerplate* he uses when they break up."

bold *(bohld)* **1. A dark or heavy text style, just like you're reading now.** 2. To apply the bold style to text. 3. Something daring, like proposing a beginner's computer book and calling it *DOS For Dummies.* "***Bold*** need not be fearless and confident. It only need look darker than the other text." Also known as *boldface.*

 bomb *(bahm)* 1. A program designed to do something sneaky at a specified time. Many disgruntled programmers write bombs in their programs so that if they get fired, the bomb will go off on its own and wreck the company's program. 2. An icon, primarily on the Macintosh, that lets you know you're screwed.

bookmark *(buk-mark)* The act of remembering (marking) a page on the World Wide Web, making it easier to revisit that page later. Internet Explorer refers to bookmarks as favorites. See also *favorites.* "Sandy is so out of touch, she was watching TV and asked me to bookmark her favorite commercials."

Boole, George *(bool jorj)* Born November 2, 1815, in Lincoln, Lincolnshire, England. Died December 8, 1864, in Ballintemple, County Cork, Ireland. Mr. Boole invented a type of logical algebra. See also *Boolean.*

Boolean *(boo-lee-on)* A logical operation, involving OR, AND, XOR (exclusive OR), and other comparisons. Typically, programmers perform these operations on bytes and bits to somehow prevent nuclear reactors from blowing up. Named for the British mathematician George Boole.

boot *(boot)* 1. To start a computer. Derived from the idea that the computer has to "pull itself up by its bootstraps" or from the feeling that the only way to get a computer to work is to threaten to kick it with a boot. 2. To

George Boole; see Boolean.

load a specific operating system. "I can't get Linux to boot!" 3. Canadian: Used to refer to something at or around something else, "The cows are a-*boot* to come home."

boot disk *(boot disk)* The disk you use to start your computer. Most often a hard drive, though a floppy disk with the proper operating system installed can also boot a computer.

boot sector *(boot sector)* The area on a disk that is reserved for the operating system. The computer looks in the boot sector for the operating system when the computer first starts up.

bootstrap *(boot-strap)* 1. To help yourself without the aid of others, such as "pulling yourself up by the bootstraps. 2. Another, longer term for boot. Often used to refer to some specific part of the computer start-up process. "The *bootstrap* loader can't distinguish your hard drive from a pizza."

boot virus *(boot vie-rus)* A computer virus that infects the boot sector of a disk so that it is loaded into the computer's memory at the beginning of every operating session. A boot virus subsequently infects any additional disks inserted into the system.

Borland C++ *(bohr-land see-plus-plus)* The C++ language compiler available from Borland International. See also *C++*.

Borland International *(bore-land in-tur-nash-in-ul)* A company that provides programming and database tools. It was founded in 1983 and is headquartered in Scotts Valley, California.

 bounce *(bowns)* Something sent electronically that is immediately sent back to you. For example, if you send someone e-mail and the message is returned as undeliverable, it's said to have bounced.

Bourne, S.R. *(born)* The Bell Labs scientist who developed for UNIX a command-line interpreter or shell called the Bourne shell.

bozo *(boh-zoh)* Someone with no clue to what he's doing but with enough authority to keep others from ignoring him completely. "My boss is such a *bozo*. He thought that backing up a computer meant pushing it up against the wall."

bpi *(bee pee eye)* Acronym for bytes per inch. The number of bytes that fit into an inch of space on a disk or tape.

bps *(bee pee ess)* Acronym for bits per second. See also *bits per second*.

brace *(brays)* The left or right curvy bracket: { }.

bracket *(brah-ket)* The left or right straight character: [ ].

brain damaged *(brayn dam-ajd)* 1. Something that looks okay from the outside but internally is hobbled or limited. Something that does not or cannot live up to its potential. Often done on purpose: "We *brain-damaged* version 1 so that we could get all the bucks when people upgrade to version 2." 2. The 80286 microprocessor. 3. The 80486SX microprocessor. 4. Microsoft Office 95.

branch *(branch)* 1. When the computer follows a series of instructions and then suddenly starts following a completely different set of instructions. Often used by programmers to describe the logic of their programs. 2. A directory and all its subdirectories on a hard

An out-of-control directory branch.

drive. This follows the "tree" metaphor most people use to describe the way directories (or folders) are arranged on a hard drive.

break *(brayk)* To stop the computer from doing whatever it happens to be doing at the moment. To "break" the computer's concentration. "Ever wonder why the stop key on a computer is named *Break* and not Brake?"

Break key *(brayk kee)* 1. A key, like, named Break, on your keyboard. Like, duh! Often the Break key lives with the Pause key on your keyboard, just like a Siamese twin. 2. The Break key on a PC must be pressed with the Control key. In DOS, this is the same as pressing Ctrl+C to cancel some operation. "Velma was afraid to use the *Break key* in Windows. She didn't want to pick up all that glass."

breakpoint *(brayk-poynt)* A programming term for a place in a program where the computer temporarily stops running. Programmers use breakpoints to see how the program is behaving up to a certain point.

bridge *(brij)* A device that connects two Local Area Networks (LANs) or two segments of the same LAN. The two LANs being connected can be alike or different.

bridgeware *(brij-wayr)* A term for hardware or software designed to convert programs to a form that can be used by a different computer.

 broadband *(brod-band)* The holy grail of online communications. A single method of transmitting lots of information, voice, video, audio, and data.

broadcast message *(brod-cast mess-idj)* A message to all network system users that appears when you log on to the system.

 broken link *(broh-ken leenk)* Refers to a resource, such as a Web page, that has been moved or deleted. See also *404 Error.*

 broken picture *(broh-ken pik-chur)* When a picture isn't available on the Web, a broken picture icon appears in its place. "Someone just robbed `www.louvre.fr` — all the pictures are broken!"

brownout *(brown-owt)* 1. A power condition where juice is flowing, but not enough of it to power certain electronic devices or motors. When this happens, you may notice that the lights work but none of the computers (or the fridge) works. 2. A tamer version of a blackout.

 browse *(browz)* 1. To look for something, specifically a file on your hard drive. 2. A button that opens a window or dialog box allowing you to peruse disk drives and folders in a vain quest for some file you probably don't have in the first place. 3. To look for something on the World Wide Web. 4. Often used with the word *eye* to refer to those hairy strips (or single strip) on the forehead.

 browser *(browz-er)* See *Web browser.*

browser wars *(browz-er wars)* The battle between Microsoft Internet Explorer and Netscape Navigator to see which would be the preferred Web browser among PC users. Microsoft won that battle.

B

brute force *(broot fors)* To get something to work without regard to appearance, elegance, or finesse. "My program has a command that's supposed to move the paper in my printer up one sheet. Rather than use this command, I just use *brute force* and pull the paper out of the printer myself."

B-size paper *(bee-siez pay-pur)* Paper that measures 11 x 17 inches. See also *A-size paper.*

BTW *(by-the-way)* Acronym for *by the way*. Used online.

bubble jet printer *(bub-ohl jet prin-tur)* A type of ink-jet printer developed by Canon. The bubble jet printer uses special heating elements to prepare the ink for printing, as opposed to other ink-jet printers that use piezoelectric crystals.

bubble memory *(bub-ohl mem-or-ee)* A type of memory that retains its contents even after the power has gone off. Bubble memory was expensive and slow and is rarely used today. "Joan's PC was getting low on *bubble memory*, so she kindly poured some Mr. Bubble into the disk drive."

Buddy List *(buh-dee list)* A group of folks on the Internet, specifically AOL. When someone on your buddy list comes on-line, you're alerted to that fact so that you can send an instant message or otherwise annoy them. A list of friends.

buffer *(buf-er)* 1. A storage place in the computer's memory, created by software. For example, a program may set aside a chunk of memory for text you type at the keyboard — a buffer.

2. Memory in a peripheral, such as the buffer in a printer, that holds information until the printer is ready to print.

bug *(bug)* A problem that prevents a program from working properly. Typically unexpected, a bug is something nearly every program has. The plural is *bugs.* "There are more *bugs* in this program than there are bicycles in China!"

built-in pointing device *(bilt-in poyn-ting dee-vies)* A trackball that's built into a computer's case. Laptop computers have built-in pointing devices.

bulk storage *(bulk stor-idj)* A magnetic media that can store data. A disk drive. Or a place for storing bulks.

bulletin board *(bul-et-in bord)* A place on the Web where you leave a message (like a message board in a laundry room). Others can read your message and respond personally to you, or they can post their message on the bulleting board. "I met my girlfriend by posting messages on the *Babylon 5 bulletin board.* That's because my wife hates *Babylon 5.*"

bulletproof *(bul-it-proof)* 1. A type of software that anticipates potential mistakes a user may make and does its best to ensure that nothing goes wrong. "This program is *bulletproof.* No matter what you try to do, it still works perfectly." 2. A common myth. 3. Foolproof.

bundled software *(bun-dold soft-waer)* 1. Software that comes free (supposedly) when you buy a computer. Usually, bundled software is stuff you need anyway (like MS-DOS) or programs that aren't selling well, so the publisher's trying to give it away just to clean out its warehouse. "Most computers offer *bundled software,* such as Microsoft Office. The idea is that you pay half as much for twice as much software, two-thirds of which you don't need anyway." 2. Several different programs that come together as one package, such as Microsoft Works or Lotus Works or whatever it is they're calling the thing WordPerfect comes in now. See also *integrated software,* which isn't the same thing but could be if they tried hard enough.

burn in *(bern in)* 1. The process of testing electronic equipment to make sure that it works. Sometimes they do this at the shop, though you can do it yourself: Whenever you get a new computer, you should leave it on for 48 hours straight. If anything will go wrong, it will likely go wrong during this burn-in period. 2. An image that appears on a computer monitor even when the monitor is turned off. See also *phosphor burn-in.*

burn out *(bern owt)* 1. What happens when you stare at your computer screen for long periods of time, such as when you're typing a long list of computer terms for publication in a computer dictionary. 2. A tired, sluggish feeling that makes you want to collapse on the nearest flat surface that can support your weight. "Working on my computer really makes me feel *burned out.* After eight hours of staring at a computer screen, I can't wait to go home and stare at my TV for the rest of the night to unwind."

bus *(buhs)* 1. An electronic transportation system for sending electrons around. "Unlike a normal city bus system, a computer bus actually runs efficiently and gets electrons to the correct destination on time. 2. The electronic pathway on which information travels between the microprocessor and other important computer pieces parts. 3. Another term for the set of expansion slots in a PC.

Business Software Alliance (BSA)
A group of software publishers who have banded together to fight software piracy. It promotes laws against software theft, educates consumers, and brings software scofflaws to justice.

bus mouse *(buhs mowse)* A mouse that plugs into the computer's system bus as opposed to a serial port. The connection can be made directly or through an expansion card. "Janet lives in the city, so she got her computer a *bus mouse.*"

 busy thing *(biz-ee theeng)* An image or icon Web browser software displays when it's waiting for information. "When I see the *busy thing,* it means that I stop being busy and wait."

button *(but-en)* 1. Something you push to get something done. 2. A key on the keyboard. 3. A switch on your computer console or monitor. 4. A graphical representation of a button you activate by clicking on it with your mouse. "The Amish don't have *buttons* on their version of Windows 95; they use hooks instead."

byte *(biet)* 1. The basic unit of storage in a computer. Typically, 1 byte holds one character of information, like a letter, number or symbol. The word *ishkabibble* requires 11 bytes of computer storage. See also *gigabyte, kilobyte, megabyte.* 2. Eight bits. However, on some larger and antique computers, a byte is 7 bits long. Some weirder computers may use weirder sizes as well. The point is that a byte is not rigorously defined as being 8 bits in size.

B

C

C *(see)* A programming language developed at Bell Laboratories back in the 1970s when disco was popular. C is a general-purpose language, like BASIC and Pascal, but with the ability to manipulate the internal guts of a computer, like assembly language. C has been used to write many popular programs, including the UNIX operating system, Lotus 1-2-3, and Microsoft Excel. "Only wimps use BASIC or Pascal. Cool programmers code in *C* so that they don't have to write the same program over again to run on different computers."

Sample C program:

```
#include <stdio.h>
main ()
{
   printf ("Only wimps use BASIC
or Pascal.\n");
   printf ("Bitchen programmers
always use C.");
}
```

C++ *(see plus plus)* An improved version of the C language that adds object-oriented extensions. C++ has become popular because it's easy for C programmers to learn, provides object-oriented features to make programming large projects easier, and it sells lots of computer books. Like C, C++ is fast, portable, and confusing to learn and understand. "Only wimps use C. Cool programmers code in *C++* so that they can write bigger programs without losing their mind."

Sample program:

```
#include <iostream.h>
main
{
   cout << "Only wimps use C.\n";
   cout << "Bitchen programmers
always use C++.";
}
```

C: *(see koh-lan)* 1. The name given to the first hard drive in a PC. This is always true, whether or not the PC sports a drive B (B:). 2. Not a medical term. Not even room for a medical-related joke.

cable *(kay-bol)* 1. A connector, typically one that has electronic signals flowing through it, hither and thither. Cables connect different parts so that they actually do something useful. Cables can be either internal or external to the computer box. 2. The cable that connects your monitor to your computer plugs into your computer's video card. 3. The cable that connects your computer to your printer, called a printer cable, plugs into a parallel or serial port. "Gordon couldn't get his printer to work because the salesman forgot to sell him a printer *cable*. Then he sold Gordon a printer *cable* that wouldn't fit his computer's parallel port. Now Gordon's serving five to seven for aggravated assault." 4. The cable that connects your computer to your modem, called a serial cable, plugs into a serial port.

cable modem *(kay-bol mow-dum)* A modem designed to operate over cable TV lines. The coaxial cable used by cable TV provides greater bandwidth, which means that it's faster and makes non-cable-modem users severely jealous.

cable connector *(kay-bol con-ek-tor)* The doojabbies on both ends of the cable. See also *cable*.

cache *(kash)* 1. A place in memory where the computer can temporarily store data. Often called a RAM cache. 2. A software program that increases access to the disk drives. 3. A chip on a controller or inside the microprocessor itself, which helps improve operating speed.

cache memory *(kash mem-o-ree)* The specific memory chips or portion of memory used as a cache to make a computer run faster.

CAD *(kad)* Acronym for Computer-Aided Design, which substitutes a computer's graphics capabilities for drawing with paper and pencil. Computers running CAD programs often require huge amounts of hard disk space, high-resolution video displays, and a fast microprocessor. CAD has been responsible for designing the most recent engineering achievements, including the gas tank for the 1972 Ford Pinto, the nuclear reactors for Three Mile Island, and the focal lens for the *Hubble* space telescope. "Allan can't even draw a straight line with a pencil, but he designed his own car using *CAD*. Of course, it blew up when he turned the ignition key, but that's beside the point."

CAD/CAM *(kad-kam)* A combination acronym that stands for Computer-Aided Design and Computer-Aided Manufacturing. CAM means letting computers actually make the stuff that somebody designed using CAD or pencil and paper.

caddy *(kad-ee)* 1. A container that holds the CD-ROM. "I asked Dan to buy me a *caddy*. He came home with a young man to carry my golf clubs for me. That's not what I meant, but it still was a nice gift!" 2. A box used to hold floppy disks when not in use.

calculator *(kal-cyou-lay-tor)* 1. A small (usually handheld) computer that performs math calculations. 2. A program on the computer that does simple math calculations. Both Windows and the Macintosh have a calculator.

call *(kahl)* A programming term that means to transfer control to another part of the program and then return.

callback modem *(kahl-bak moh-dum)* A type of modem that requires an outside caller to call the modem, enter a code, and then hang up. The modem checks the code for verification and then calls the outside caller back. It is used when data must be protected from intruders.

Caller ID *(kahl-ur eye-dee)* 1. A telephone systems option that identifies who is calling you. "Aren't you going to answer the phone? No. I can see by the Caller ID that it's a phone solicitor. Why bother?" 2. A feature of some modems.

callout *(kahl-owt)* Names of items in an illustration. Computer books typically have several callouts to better define what the author is writing about.

call waiting *(kahl wayt-ing)* A telephone feature that lets you know when someone is calling even when you're already using the phone. This feature is of importance to computer modem users because the call-waiting signal disconnects a modem connection. You can usually turn the code on and off by using the code *70. "You should disable *call waiting* before you dial out using your modem."

CAM *(kam)* Acronym for Computer-Aided Manufacturing, when computers are used in manufacturing. "Thanks to *CAM,* people are becoming less and less necessary in the manufacturing world."

camera-ready *(kam-er-ah red-dee)* A photograph, drawing, or document that is ready to be printed and mass produced. Publishers using desktop publishing software often use this term. "When professional photographers take pictures of bikini-clad models frolicking on exotic beaches, they produce *camera-ready* pictures for the *Sports Illustrated* annual swimsuit issue. When I take pictures of Uncle Fred in his bathrobe with my Kodak Instamatic, I can't produce *camera-ready* pictures of anything at all."

cancel *(kan-sel)* 1. To take back or reverse an action. When you give the Cancel command, you're essentially telling your computer, "Oops, forget that I did that, and make everything like it was before." 2. A button in a dialog box that tells the computer to ignore what-

ever you've done in a dialog box. "I typed FORMAT C: and almost erased my entire hard disk. Luckily, when DOS asked me "Proceed with format (Y/N)?," I typed N to *cancel* that command."

 Cancel Moose *(kan-sel moos)* An anonymous group of people who watch the newsgroups for identical, large postings. If they find a post that has been sent to several newsgroups, the moose issues forged cancel notices to all the newsgroups to wipe the postings out. "The *Cancel Moose* is illegal, but since no one has been caught, they still do it."

capacitor *(kuh-pas-eh-tor)* An electronic device that can store electrical charge. The basis of a dynamic RAM cell.

Caps Lock *(kaps lok)* The key on every computer keyboard that lets you type capital (or uppercase) letters without having to press the Shift key each time. Most computers have a little light in the upper-right corner of the keyboard that lights up when you have pressed the Caps Lock key once. If you press the Caps Lock key again, the light goes off. Unlike with typewriters, pressing the Caps Lock key on a computer produces only uppercase letters. If you want to print ! or @ or any other symbol, you still have to hold down the Shift key first. "Sometimes my fingers slip and I press the *Caps Lock* key BY MISTAKE, AND THEN ALL MY TYPING LOOKS LIKE I'M SHOUTING."

caption *(kap-shun)* The name given with an image to better define what the image is supposed to be.

C

capture *(kap-shoor)* To store a screen image to a file on disk. Often used with desktop publishing and telecommunications. "Mary loves to *capture* screen images on her computer. She even has a little jail built in her office where she keeps them and, as the mood hits her, occasionally taunts them."

carbon copy *(kar-bun kop-ee)* A copy of an e-mail message sent to someone in addition to the main recipient. Abbreviated as *cc.* "No, Joyce, sending an e-mail *carbon copy* will not stain your fingers." See also *blind carbon copy.*

card *(kard)* 1. A punched card used in old computer programming. 2. A circuit board. See also *expansion card.*

caret *(kayr-et)* The name of the ^ symbol. See ^ (caret).

carpal tunnel syndrome *(kar-pul tun-ul sin-drome)* A form of repetitive strain injury (RSI) that occurs in the wrists. Symptoms are numbness or burning in the fingers or wrists. This injury can cause permanent damage if not taken care of. "I thought my daughter would get carpal tunnel syndrome from dialing the telephone so often."

carriage return *(kayr-edj ree-tern)* 1. The character produced by the Enter or Return key. Used to mark the end of input or the end of a paragraph in a word processor or as a substitute for the OK button in a dialog box. 2. The character produced by pressing the Enter or Return key. ASCII code 13. Named after the carriage return bar on a typewriter, which moved the platen from one side of the typewriter to another.

carrier *(kayr-ee-er)* A signal used by modems to detect the presence of another modem. Whenever one modem calls another modem, the two modems send carrier signals to each other. One carrier is the answer, and the other is the originate. "Admiral Davis could tell that the Yorktown had been sunk. He dialed up the ship's BBS with his modem and couldn't get a *carrier.*"

carrier detect *(kayr-ee-er dee-tekt)* The state that exists when one modem is actively communicating with another modem. External modems have a carrier detect light that clues you into this state. Otherwise, no one would care.

carrier frequency *(kayr-ee-er free-kwen-see)* The radio signal used to transmit information, such as with modems and the network.

carrot *(kayr-et)* The vegetable that parents claim will improve your vision. The favorite snack of Bugs Bunny. "While flying on American Airlines, the flight attendant told me to eat all my carrots because passengers were starving on Air India."

The favorite snack of Bugs Bunny.

cathode ray tube (CRT) The technology used in TV and computer screens. A CRT works by sweeping an electron beam back and forth across the inside of the screen. Each time

The ever-important cathode ray tube.

the beam makes a pass across the screen, it lights up phosphor dots on the inside of the glass tube, causing an illumination of the active portions of the screen.

cartridge *(kart-ridj)* 1. A self-contained, removable part of a computer or printer that is usually plastic, expensive, and hard to find when you need it. "My laser printer couldn't print any fonts until I plugged in a font *cartridge*." 2. A device that supplies ink to a printer, or a container for either a printer's ribbon or toner powder in a laser printer.

cascade *(kas-kayd)* 1. Several items, one after the other, arranged in a nifty pattern. 2. To arrange several windows neatly on a computer screen so that you can still see the title bar and upper-left corner of each one. "Until I had my computer *cascade* all my windows, some of my windows had been completely hidden from view. I still can't find anything I need, but at least the cascaded windows make me look nice and organized." 3. A set of interrupts in the IBM PC AT. You know, technical mumbo-jumbo.

case *(kays)* 1. In text-formatting terms, the style of letters, either UPPERCASE or lowercase. 2. (caps) In programming terms, a special command that lets the computer choose two or more possible options. 3. (caps) In technodweeb talk, an acronym that means Computer-Aided Software Engineering. "As a computer science major, my *CASE* courses in school taught me that I could use the *CASE* command in Pascal to replace multiple IF-THEN statements. To make programs easier to read, my teachers told me that the case of my typing would matter too. That's why I dropped out and became a cab driver instead."

case sensitive *(kays sens-uh-tiv)* The distinction made between UPPER- and lowercase letters. Some programs or systems require that certain commands be in either uppercase or lowercase. UNIX is a good example. Modems can be fussy in that way, too. "Bob is so *case sensitive.* He thinks that 'Hello' and 'HELLO' are two completely different words."

cassette tape *(kah-set tayp)* A reel of magnetic strip that can store information. Ancient computers used cassette tapes to store programs. Today, everyone uses floppy disks or hard disks. See also *tape, tape drive.* "I bought an old Timex/Sinclair computer that uses programs stored on *cassette tape.* I really screwed up my computer when I gave it a Led Zeppelin cassette tape by mistake."

cat *(kat)* A UNIX command that displays the contents of a file, hopefully one containing only text. It's from the word *concatenate,* which doesn't mean anything to us presently. "I typed *cat* on my keyboard, and the computer suddenly started purring."

catatonic *(kat-a-ton-ik)* A state of nearly total paralysis, usually brought on by staring at a computer screen too long. "At first I thought Gene was catatonic, but he was just waiting for Windows 95 to start on his computer."

catatonic cocktail *(kat-a-ton-ik kok-tale)* Also known as the "Downy cocktail." Diluted fabric softener sprayed on computer room carpets to prevent static electricity from being built up by feet shuffling on carpet.

C

cc *(see-see)* 1. Acronym for carbon copy. See *carbon copy.* 2. Used by management types who are just in too much of a hurry to tell you they've carbon-copied something in e-mail (or had their secretaries do it for them).

CCD *(see see dee)* Acronym for Charge Coupled Device. A semiconductor technology used to build light-sensitive electronic devices, such as cameras and image scanners. These devices detect in either color or black-and-white. "I wish there was a CCD that not only scanned my image in color but also scanned my image *thinner!*"

CD *(see dee)* 1. Acronym for the change directory command, CHDIR. 2. Compact disc, as in the favorite digital audio storage devices. See also *CD-ROM.* "Call a doctor! Janice has lapsed into a primal state! She's trying to configure her *CD* drive in MS-DOS, and all she can say is '*CD. CD* run. Run, *CD,* run.'"

A shiny new CD (compact disc).

CD-R *(see dee ar)* 1. Acronym for Compact Disc-Recordable. Using the proper equipment, you can use a CD-R to record your own CD. The information can be recorded only once and typically must be recorded all in one stretch, not a bit a time.

CD-ROM *(see dee rahm,* not *rome)* 1. Acronym for Compact Disc/Read-Only Memory. 2. A disk that contains megabytes of information. The information cannot be changed, and you cannot save new information to the disk (hence, read-only). A CD-ROM disk is round, silver and flat and looks like a UFO if you toss it in the air and use an out-of-focus camera to take its picture 3. The device that reads a CD-ROM disk. "My new *CD-ROM* drive lets me display entire encyclopedias, classical novels, maps from every country in the world, travelogues, and interactive X-rated films. Now I have no reason to leave the house."

CD-RW *(see-dee-ar-dub-ol-yoo)* Acronym for Compact Disc/Recordable-Writable. Like a CD-R, but with the ability to read and write information, just like a regular hard drive.

cell *(sel)* The intersection of rows and columns in a spreadsheet used to store text, numbers, and formulas. "My financial spreadsheet uses 300 *cells* to store all my vital business information. And there's a prison up the road that uses 300 *cells* to store various businessmen who keep such information from the IRS."

center *(sen-tur)* 1. To align text in the middle of the page. "It's always neat looking to *center* the title of your book in the center of the page." 2. To align graphics along their center axes.

central processing unit *(sen-tral praw-ses-ing yoo-nit)* The computer's microprocessor, abbreviated CPU. The little chip in personal computers that controls everything. A central processing unit looks like a thin wafer or a headless cockroach. See also *microprocessor.* "After you upgrade your computer's *central processing unit,* you can turn the old one into jewelry for a loved one."

Centronics port *(sen-tron-iks port)* A computer's printer port. Originally used to connect computers to Centronics printers. See also *parallel port, printer port.* "Ray's a real old-timer. He always calls the printer port a

Centronics port. Heck, he's been around so long, he remembers when computers used to need cranks to start."

CGA *(see jee ay)* Acronym for Color Graphics Adapter, the original color graphics standard for IBM and compatible personal computers. Replaced by EGA and then by VGA and SVGA. See also *EGA, SVGA, VGA.* "*CGA* graphics are as outmoded as platform disco shoes."

 CGI *(see jee ie)* Acronym for Common Gateway Interface, a way of dealing with information typed on a form on a Web page. Also how some Web pages can be customized and created on-the-fly. "Nothing beats *CGI* from a DNS saved to a DVD. Don't you just love TLAs?" See also *DNS, DVD,* and *TLA.*

CGM *(see jee em)* Acronym for Computer Graphics Metafile, a type of graphics file format standard used by programmers. "We drove to Detroit so that we could *CGM.*"

character *(kar-ak-ter)* 1. Any symbol you can type from the keyboard. Letters are characters, numbers are characters, and even $, @, _, ^, and ~ are considered characters. "Larry ran a word count in his word processor, and it told him that he has 4,128 *characters* in his document. 'Not bad for a budding novelist,' he beamed."

character code *(kar-ak-ter kohd)* 1. A particular character's ASCII code value. See also *ASCII.* 2. Any set of values assigned to specific characters in a computer. For example, some British computers use a character-coding scheme that's different from the standard ASCII. The ancient and seldom-

used EBCDIC standard is another type of character code. "Ralph is so into computers that he uses *character codes* to speak."

character graphics *(kar-act-er graf-iks)* Graphics created with specific characters, lines, or blocks. Early computers that lacked graphics ability used those chunky characters to simulate graphics. It was lame. "My computer doesn't display graphics, but with *character graphics* I can still draw little boxes on my screen, just like on an Etch-A-Sketch."

character printer *(kar-act-er prin-ter)* A printer that prints one character at a time. The ancient daisy-wheel printer is a good example of a character printer.

character set *(kar-act-er set)* A group of characters and symbols, organized into groups for different purposes. Because a byte has 256 different bit patterns in a PC, there are typically 256 characters in a character set. The standard ASCII characters appear as codes 0 through 127. Character codes 128 through 255 are different for each character set. For example, one character set may contain graphics characters, another may contain symbols used in foreign languages, and another may contain financial symbols.

chassis *(cha-see)* The metal frame where electronic components, such as circuit boards and power supplies, are mounted.

chat *(chat)* 1. To type at another human being, either over a network or on your modem. This crude form of communication makes you infinitely thankful for the gift of speech. 2. The title of a great cybernovel by Nan McCarthy. The story follows the plot line of two people who correspond by e-mail. "Reading *CHAT* is like peeking in on someone else's e-mail."

 chat group *(chat groop)* A gathering of people at a specific spot on the Internet who come together to chat about a specific topic. Guest speakers are often invited to these chat groups to talk (or chat). "Madonna is going to be at next week's chat group to talk about her newfound skill of mothering, specifically on how to nurse through a cone-shaped bra."

c

 chat room *(chat room)* Another term for a chat group. See also *chat group.*

CHDIR *(chaynj-dur)* Operating system command to change a directory. See also *CD.*

cheap *(cheep)* An adjective that denotes poor quality no matter what the actual cost may be. "If our company wasn't so *cheap,* it'd buy us new computers rather than force us to use these manual typewriters."

check boxes *(chek boks-es)* An on–off option typically found in a dialog box. When the check box is empty, the option has not been chosen. When the check box is marked, the option has been chosen. Two or more check boxes can be checked at the same time.

Here are some sample check boxes:

Why do you hate computers?

☐   Don't work the way you want

☒   Too expensive for what they offer

☐   Too complicated

☒   Not easy to use

checksum *(chek-sum)* A number calculated to verify the accuracy of data. You'll typically find it used on information transmitted through a modem. The sending computer tags a checksum on to the end of information it sends. The receiving computer calculates its own checksum. If the two match, then the data was received okey-doke. If the checksums don't match, the information is re-sent. "Carol really wants to make sure that her relationship with Steve lasts. She's checked their astrological signs, scoured the family history, consulted with an oracle, and performed a *checksum* on their bank accounts."

Chicklet keyboard *(chik-let kee-bord)* 1. A keyboard that consists of tiny buttons instead of keys. The buttons resemble candy Chicklets. Chicklet keys are usually too tiny to type on comfortably. 2. The IBM PC*jr* keyboard. The idea was to make it unattractive for business use. They succeeded to the extent that nobody bought the IBM PC*jr.* "IBM was obviously not in its right mind when it designed the PC*jr*'s *chicklet keyboard.*"

child process *(chie-old prah-ses)* A second program started by some program on your computer. They can do that, you know. When WordPerfect spell checks a document, it runs another program, the Spell Checker. WordPerfect is the "parent" program; the spell checker is the "child." Sadly, child processes are eventually killed by their parents' processes because computer programs are greedy and must maintain control. It's kind of a Greek tragedy type of thing. "Many *child processes* run away from home."

child record *(chie-old rek-ord)* A record that is lower in the hierarchical tree than a parent record.

chip *(chip)* 1. A thinly sliced potato, fried and crispy. 2. An integrated circuit inside a computer. Any of a number of flat, buglike things that make Mr. PC go.

A computer chip.

Christensen protocol *(chris-chen-sen proh-toh-kol)* See *XMODEM.*

CHKDSK *(chek-disk)* DOS's disk-checking program. CHKDSK doesn't really check the disk as much as it checks the disk's FAT (File Allocation Table). Any problems it finds are reported, but not immediately fixed. CHKDSK also returns the amount of disk space used and other disk trivia. See also *FAT, ScanDisk.*

Chooser *(choo-zer)* A Macintosh desktop accessory (DA) that lets you select which printer to use, whether to turn AppleTalk on or off, and whether to use the serial or parallel port. The Chooser always appears on the Apple menu, located at the far left side of the menu bar. "Using the Mac *Chooser* makes sense only if you have a number of things to choose from."

cipher *(sie-fur)* 1. In computer cryptography, the key or code used to identify or decode a message. Of course, this code may not be correct; you really don't want the correct information getting into the hands of the enemy, do you? 2. A prefix or suffix applied to various things dealing with cryptography.

CI$ *(see-ie-es)* Acronym for CompuServe Information Services. The dollar sign ($) replaces the *S* to let people know that using this service will cost them lots of money. See also *CompuServe.* "New subscribers call it CIS. Only after you get your first bill will you know it as *CI$.*"

circuit board *(sir-kut bord)* The piece of insulated material (typically fiberglass) on which the electronic components are mounted and connected to form a circuit. See also *expansion card, motherboard.* "The new engineer wanted to cut costs, so he decided to eliminate the *circuit board* from the computer."

circuit breaker *(sir-kut brayk-er)* A device that monitors the flow of electricity and cuts it off if it exceeds a certain level. The circuit breaker prevents the overloading, short-circuiting, or death or destruction of massive amounts of personal property. "Gus decided to plug in his computer, monitor, printer, microwave, electric car, and high-powered, antisatellite laser into one electric outlet. Good thing his *circuit breaker* worked, or else he might have blown the power grid for half the state."

CIS *(see eye ess)* Acronym for CompuServe Information Service. See *CompuServe.*

C

CISC *(sisk)* Acronym for Complex Instruction Set Computing, a type of microprocessor that uses complex instructions rather than simple instructions (which is what a RISC processor uses). The trade-off is that the microprocessor can do more, but takes more time to do it. A RISC processor can do less, but does it quickly. (Don't worry if this stuff makes no sense: No one in the computer industry understands it either.) See also *RISC.* "There are those who claim that RISC will rule the world, but until then *CISC* is king. And then there are those of us who'd rather make a living and watch an occasional video."

Class A / Class B *(klas ay / klas bee)* Two similar, confusing ratings given to electronic devices by the Federal Communications Commission (FCC). See also *FCC.* The rating is determined by the strength of electronic signals ("noise") escaping from a computer case. The Class A label means that the computer has been approved for use in an office. The Class B label is stricter and means that the computer has been approved for both the home and office. Ideally, you want a computer with a Class B label. If you put a computer with a Class A label in your home, the computer could interfere with your radio and TV reception.

clear key *(kleer kee)* A key found on some keyboards that serves the same function as the Delete key.

click *(klik)* 1. To press and release the mouse button. On a multibutton mouse, it's the leftmost button (the one your index finger rests on). 2. To point the mouse pointer at an object on the screen and then press and release the

button. 3. To activate an option, command, or button. "No, no! You keep the mouse on the mousepad when you *click* its buttons. Don't point it at the computer like a TV remote."

client *(klie-yent)* 1. A Local Area Network term that describes a computer that can request information, such as an application, from a file server, and can also perform independently from the network server when using a client application. "Not only is Bob's computer president of the Hair Club For Men Network, it's also a *client.*" 2. A Windows program that receives data through DDE. See also *DDE.* 3. Actually, no one really knows what it means, other than being a terrific buzzword.

client application *(klie-yent ap-luh-kay-shun)* A program that works on only one computer on a network. The program lives on that computer's hard drive and doesn't "see" any other computers on the network. On most networks, one big computer usually contains all the programs that everyone else uses. See also *file server.* If that one computer fails, none of the other computers can do anything. Because client applications run only on one computer and cannot be accessed by other computers in the network, a failure in one part of the network doesn't affect a client application (unless, of course, the part of the network that fails is the one computer holding the client application). Client applications cannot be used by anyone else in a network. 2. A Windows program with documents that can accept linked or embedded objects. See also *OLE.*

C

client/server net-work *(klie-yent sur-ver net-werk)* Networks where some programs and files are shared in one big computer, and each computer connected to the network can also run on its own. "We have a *client/server network* that lets everyone share the same database program and files with each other but gives all users the freedom to use whatever word processor they want on their own computer."

A lame clip art example.

clip art *(klip art)* Ready-made art, images, or pictures that you can freely copy and use. Often used for desktop publishing. "Clip art comes in handy when your own drawing resembles primitive cave scratching."

  clipboard *(klip-bord)* A temporary storage area for items cut or copied. Using the Paste command places a copy of the item on the clipboard into the current application. The clipboard can hold text or graphics or other objects. It can hold only one item at a time. Any new items that are copied or cut replace the current item on the clipboard. "No, Lois, you don't need to worry about pinching your thumb in the computer *clipboard.* It's all electronic."

clipboard computer *(klip-bord com-pyoo-ter)* A type of portable computer that resembles a clipboard. It has a flat display and uses a pen, rather than a keyboard, for input. "Everyone thought that Virgil was such a hard worker because he always seemed to be work-ing on his *clipboard computer.* Come to find out, he was playing FreeCell."

Clipper chip *(klip-er chip)* A special chip designed to encrypt and decode information sent by a computer. Sounds nice, but the chip was designed by the U.S. government and — through various laws, taxes, and whatnot — it's trying to get one installed on every computer as the de facto method for encrypting files. The catch is that the government would also be able to decode the files. Sure, it claims that it wouldn't do it without the cooperation of two bureaucratic organizations. And, if you believe that, the post office really means it when it says "Two-day mail," "The Pentagon is truly efficient," and "The IRS is gentle and for-giving." "Hopefully, the *Clipper chip* will never be a standard and we can encrypt our secret files and send money off-shore without the government's ever knowing about it because, frankly, it isn't any of their business anyway."

clock *(klohk)* 1. Something that keeps track of the time. 2. A device, inside every computer, that keeps track of time. Often supplied with battery power so that the time stays more or less cur-rent. If not, the time must be set when-ever the computer is first turned on. "Old PCs without a *clock* always assumed that the date was 1/1/80. Quite a lot of work got done on January 1, 1980."

clock tick *(klohk tik)* The computer's heartbeat. A special chip controls the clock ticks. Other devices inside the computer use each clock tick to time certain events or do certain things. A PC has 18-point-something clock ticks per second. Count them all!

C

clone *(klohn)* 1. Any piece of hardware or software that imitates a more successful (or pricier) version. 2. Any computer that runs the same software or is compatible with the same hardware as the original IBM PC or PC AT computers. Today, that's just about any computer that runs Windows or DOS. 3. A derogatory term for a cheap PC. The term "compatible" is preferred today. See also *compatible*. 4. Some sheep in Scotland.

close *(klohz)* 1. To remove a window from the screen in a graphical operating system. 2. To finish working on a document, removing it from the screen and optionally saving it to disk. 3. To quit a program. "The tech support guy told me to *close* my word processor's window, and I told him that it was 15 degrees outside and I'd be nuts to have the window open in the first place." 4. To manually shut a disk drive door or sliding caddy. 5. A programming command to finish working on an open file, saving the last bits of the file to disk and freeing up the file handle.

close box *(klohz boks)* A graphical gizmo that, when clicked, removes a window from the screen. Do not confuse with *clothes box,* which is where you throw your dirty laundry.

closed architecture *(klohzd ar-kuh-tek-chur)* 1. Equipment specifically designed to work with only the accessories made by the same company, usually the most expensive and least reliable equipment around. 2. Non-expandable, or limited expansion. 3. Nondocumented material, which is done primarily to prevent others from copying it. 4. The death knell for any computer. See also *open architecture*.

 clover key *(kloh-vur key)* The Macintosh key with the cloverleaf design on the top. The Macintosh's equivalent of an Alt key. See also *Command key*.

cluster *(klus-ter)* A chunk of disk space. The minimum amount of storage space given to a file on disk. For exam-

The ever-so-lovely clover design.

ple, if a hard drive sports 2K clusters, an 8K file would be stored in 8 clusters. The operating system handles this detail, but occasionally you may see some type of cluster error, which is why it's documented here.

CMOS *(see-mahs)* 1. Acronym for Complementary Metal-Oxide Semiconductor, a specially designed circuit that consumes very little power. CMOS circuits are often used in devices such as wristwatches, pocket calculators, and laptop computers. 2. A special chip in a PC that keeps track of system setup information, date, time, and so on. "When the salesguy told Maureen that her computer contained the latest *CMOS* processor, she replied positively. After all, old sea moss probably smells terrible."

coaxial cable *(koh-aks-ee-ul kay-bul)* A cable consisting of an insulating shield wrapped around a conductor. Coaxial cables are used for Local Area Networks because they carry more data than ordinary telephone wires. TVs use a type of coaxial cable. "We chose *coaxial cables* to connect our computers together — not because they're networked, but just because they won't fall that far when someone tosses them out a window."

C

COBOL *(koh-bahl)* 1. Acronym for COmmon Business-Oriented Language, a language used primarily for business applications for large mainframe computers. Developed in the 1960s by several computer companies and the U.S. Department of Defense, the language shows the influence that the drug-crazed, free-love era had on technology. COBOL programs tend to resemble plain-English sentences. Unfortunately, the plain-English sentences usually resemble those uttered by politicians or lawyers. "Verily I say unto you, *COBOL* is the Latin of computer languages: dead but still used in crusty, non-growing environments." 2. The programming language responsible for screwing up your bank accounts and phone bills. Recently, COBOL programmers were in great demand because they had to fix the 2000 bug. See also *Year 2000 bug.*

 cobweb site *(kob-web-siet)* A Web site that hasn't been updated for a long time.

code *(kohd)* 1. Programming instructions. 2. The art of creating programming instructions. "Amateurs write programs; hackers *code.*" 3. A secret number or password required in order to translate encrypted information.

coding *(koh-deeng)* To actually write a program using a specific programming language, such as C, BASIC, or Pascal. "I tried *coding* in COBOL until I switched to C. Now it takes me half as long to code with only twice as many mistakes."

cold boot *(kohld boot)* To restart equipment that has been turned off. Also known as a cold start. See also *warm boot.* "Sometimes, when the computer crashes, pushing its reset button doesn't even work. In these cases, you have to

cold boot your computer by turning it off, waiting for ten seconds, and then turning it on again."

cold fault *(kohld fahlt)* When an error occurs right after you start the computer. This occasionally happens because the computer is cold. "I once had a hard drive that wouldn't start when the office was cold. The tech said that it was a *cold fault,* so I set my coffee on top of the console for a few minutes and tried it again."

 cold fusion *(kohld fyoo-shun)* A derogatory term for fake science. Something that is foolhardy or trivial, often taken up by many people with sincerity. Named after the men from Utah who claimed that they could induce nuclear fusion at room temperature. (Their experiments could never be duplicated.) "Why don't you take your ideas to the *cold fusion* newsgroup, where they belong?"

ColdFusion *(kohld fyoo-shun)* A program used for developing a Web database.

cold start *(kohld start)* See *cold boot.*

color monitor *(kul-er mon-uh-ter)* A computer's visual interface, specifically one that displays images in color and not in monochrome. The term is rather redundant today because most monitors are color. You have to specifically request a monochrome model.

color printer *(kul-er prin-ter)* A computer peripheral capable of generating color hard copy. Any printer that can print in full color in addition to black. "My manager told me to get rid of the new *color printer.* He said that he was tired of seeing little red hearts in all the margins of my reports."

C

Colossus *(koh-la-sus)* The name of the United States' nuclear defense computer in the film *Colossus: The Forbin Project.*

Colossus: The Forbin Project *(koh-la-sus the for-bin prah-jekt)* A 1969 film in which the United States designs Colossus, a supercomputer to run all nuclear defenses. But after being turned on, Colossus finds that it has a Soviet counterpart, Guardian. The two computers eventually link up and become a single computer against which both nations must fight to regain control of humanity — you know, the old computer-versus-man theme that Hollywood loves. See also *supercomputer.*

column *(kahl-um)* 1. A vertical strip of text that appears on a page. Newsletters commonly display two, three, or four columns side by side. "Lola decided that her report on ancient Greece would look best with Corinthian *columns.*" 2. A vertical row of cells in a spreadsheet.

com *(kahm)* The Internet domain name for a commercial organization, though it's often applied to just about any Web site, whether it's run by a company, an individual, or a group.

COM *(kahm)* 1. A *com*munications port. A PC can have as many as four, numbered COM1 through COM4. Most PCs come with two COM ports: COM1 and COM2. An internal modem is typically found on COM2. "Bill is a staunch Republican. He never refers to his modem port as *COM*1 because he thinks that *COM* stands for communist." 2. The file extension for DOS programs. COM stands for *com*mand file.

COMDEX *(kahm-deks)* Acronym for *com*puter *d*ealers *ex*position. Usually held twice a year — once in winter and once in spring. The winter COMDEX in Las Vegas is one of the largest trade shows on earth. It can take up to 90 minutes to get a cab, yet no one gambles the entire week. "I went to Las Vegas *COMDEX* to see the latest computer equipment and software displayed. Then I decided that it didn't make a difference in my life after all, so I went out to Binions and played craps with some Taiwanese gentlemen."

 command box *(kom-and boks)* 1. An area of the screen in which you type instructions or directions. 2. The place where you type a URL in a Web browser. See also *URL.* "Dennis sat with his hands trembling as he began to type the address of his favorite Web page in the *command box.* He knew the importance of typing it correctly, or else he wouldn't get to see the updated issue of the Moscow University's college women."

command driven *(kom-and dri-ven)* Software controlled by typing commands or instructions. The opposite of menu-driven software, when your options are all displayed and you must choose one. Command-driven software is the most difficult to use, but it gives you more flexibility and control than menu-driven software. "It took me forever to learn my *command-driven* software. But ever since I got all the commands down, I'm a real speed demon on it."

 Command key *(kom-and kee)* The cloverleaf key on the Macintosh keyboard. Often used with other keys to perform commands. Similar to, though not the same as, the Ctrl key on a PC keyboard. "I'm glad they call it the *Command key.* I'm tired of telling people 'that key with the little cloverleaf-like thing on it.'"

command line *(kom-and liyen)* 1. The line of text typed at the DOS prompt. 2. A series of commands and other text typed at a prompt to get the computer to do something. "Hear about that new Broadway musical put on by the military? It's called *Command Line.*"

COMMAND.COM *(kom-and dot kahm)* The MS-DOS command processor. Essentially, this program is DOS, displaying the DOS prompt and acting on various DOS commands. "Deleting your *COMMAND.COM* file is a bonehead thing to do, but everyone does it at least once."

comment *(kaw-ment)* A brief note of explanation inserted into programs to describe what the program is supposed to do. Programmers use comments in their programs so that other programmers (and themselves) can understand what the program does and how it works. "It's good programming practice to insert plenty of *comments* in your programs, explaining what the program does and how it works, any assumptions you may have made, and nasty remarks about the project leader."

communications *(ka-myoo-nuh-kay-shens)* A shortened version of telecommunications or data communications. Often used to describe the transferring of information from one computer to another through a modem or a network. "Our department is looking for a new

communications director. The person must be nearsighted and cannot speak English."

communications link *(ka-myoo-nuh-kay-shens lingk)* The connection between computers that enables them to transfer data. "The *communications link* never did work, so I wasn't able to fax the picture I took of O.J. hiding the knife. Oh, well!"

communications program *(ka-myoo-nuh-kay-shens proh-gram)* Software that enables two computers to talk to each other and exchange information. "Our new *communications program* allows our two computers to talk to each other, but I think all they do is gossip."

compatibility *(kom-pat-uh-bil-uh-tee)* The capability of software or hardware to work with other software or hardware. "The salesguy claims that my new computer and printer have so much *compatibility* that if I take one out of the room, the other one will actually start to cry."

compatible *(kom-pat-uh-bil)* Any computer that can run the same software or use the same hardware as the original IBM equipment. Today, that applies to any PC that can run either DOS or Windows. It was more of an issue in the early days, when systems may not have been 100 percent compatible and, therefore, could not run off-the-shelf IBM or Microsoft software. See also *clone.*

compile *(kom-piel)* 1. To convert a program written in a programming language (BASIC, C, or Pascal, for example) into a language the computer can understand (machine code). A term that only

C

programmers care to know about. "Normally, the steps to writing a program are code, *compile,* and run. But with John's programming, the steps are code, *compile,* fix bugs, re*compile,* fix more bugs, etc." 2. A stack of modems in the desert.

compiler *(kom-piel-er)* A special program that converts text written in a programming language (C, BASIC, or Pascal, for example) into something the computer can understand (machine code). "The *compiler* works great at taking the grunts and squawks of a programming language and turning them into something the computer can understand. Now we need a *compiler* to translate what the programmer wrote in the manual into plain English."

Component Object Model (COM) *(kom-pow-nent ob-jekt ma-dul)* A programming method for communicating between applications. See also *OLE.*

composite video *(kom-poz-it vi-dee-oh)* A video signal used by TV sets, usually transmitted by one wire. By contrast, the signal used by your computer's monitor is an RGB signal, which uses separate wires for red, green, and blue. "If you really want to go blind or get a headache, use *composite video* to display computer information on your TV set."

compression *(kom-pres-shun)* To smash a file (or squish it) so that it takes up less space. This is done by complex mathematical algorithms so that the file can be decompressed back to its original state with only a few teeth missing. "Using that new *compression* program, we were able to save 50 megabytes of storage on our

hard drive. Now if they could only *compress* Frank into a small size, we'd save money on wicker furniture."

CompuServe *(kom-pyoo-serv)* A subscription-based online service that charges you lots of money for every second you're connected to it. In return, CompuServe provides files to copy, games to play, and services to use, such as making your own airline reservations or searching for information in newspaper articles. Absorbed by AOL in the late 1990s. "I needed to spend more money on my computer habit, so I bought a modem and a subscription to *CompuServe.*"

compute *(kom-pyoot)* 1. To calculate an answer using a variety of problem-solving techniques, including mathematics, heuristics, and looking over someone else's shoulder. 2. The task one undertakes when using a computer. "I *compute,* therefore IBM." 3. To make sense. Often used in the opposite: "That does not *compute.*"

computer *(kom-pyoo-ter)* 1. Any calculating device that processes data according to a series of instructions, costs lots of money, doesn't work the way that you think it should, frustrates you more than it brings you pleasure, and becomes obsolete three days after you buy it. "I bought a *computer* to simplify my life." 2. A microcomputer, such as a PC. 3. That smart girl in the back of your high school math class who looks a heck of a lot cuter as the years go by.

computer club *(kum-pyoo-ter klub)* See *user group.*

Computer Graphics Metafile *(kom-pyoo-ter graf-iks met-uh-fi-el)* See *CGM*.

computer art *(kom-pyoo-ter art)*
1. Images generated by a computer.
2. Images created on a computer.
3. Verbum. 4. Smashing a computer and selling it to a rich liberal who wouldn't know real art from the engine under the hood of their Volvo.

computer graphics *(kom-pyoo-ter graf-iks)* Anything that isn't text on a computer: pictures, business charts and diagrams, and art. "Give me *computer graphics!* I don't care if it's good; I just have to justify all this technology."

computer literate *(kom-pyoo-ter lit-er-et)* The ability to operate a computerized device, such as a money machine. It does not mean that you have to know how to program a computer or physically take one apart and put it back together again. "Am I *computer literate?* Sure am! I can get money out of my local ATM."

computer name *(kom-pyoo-ter naym)*
1. The name you give your computer, much like you would give a pet a name.
2. Used in computer networking so that each user can identify the computers. "My two computer names are Sybil and Sally. They're sisters."

computer science *(kom-pyoo-ter sie-ens)* The study of computers that incorporates engineering, mathematics, electronics, logic, information theory, and human behavior. "In many ways, calling this discipline *computer science* is like calling drama *theatre science* or calling art *painting science.*"

computer security *(kom-pyoo-ter see-kyoor-uh-tee)* The method or steps used to protect a computer and the information it contains. Examples include backing up your system or using passwords. "Our *computer security* is so good that even I can't get into my system."

con *(kahn)* 1. Short for console. 2. The keyboard and monitor, where you sit down and use the computer. 3. (cap.) The console device for an operating system, which supplies input and output. "When Captain Picard is done using the Enterprise's computer, he says, 'Mr. Riker, you have the *CON.*'"

concatenate *(kon-kat-en-ayt)* 1. To join two character strings together, such as "ABC" + "DEF" = "ABCDEF." 2. To join two files together. The term comes from the late Latin that literally means "to stick two cats together." "Jerry refused to *concatenate* two files into one because he claimed that he didn't have moral authority as a priest."

concurrent processing *(kon-kur-ent prah-ses-eeng)* The appearance of running two or more programs at the same time but in reality running only one. Because the computer shifts between the two programs quickly, it does appear that they're both running at the same time. "That new Snazzle PC offers *concurrent processing.* Now you can do twice as much half as fast."

confidence factor *(kahn-fi-dens fak-ter)* A term used by expert systems to place an abstract numerical value on an answer. Often used as an educated way of saying "I don't have the slightest idea, but here's my best guess." "The used-car salesman had a *confidence factor* of

c

99 that the car he was selling would work perfectly. Because used-car salesmen tend to lie as much as lawyers and politicians, I had a *confidence factor* of only 10 that he was telling me the truth."

CONFIG.SYS *(kon-fig dot sis)* A configuration file that sets various options for disk drives and loads special programs, called device drivers, into memory. One of the most important files and also the least understood. "The idea of dealing with a *CONFIG.SYS* file is so scary that Apple uses the mere threat of editing one to try and sell people on the Macintosh."

configure *(kon-feeg-yoor)* To prepare or customize hardware or software a certain way. Whenever you add a new piece of equipment or program to your computer, you have to configure it so that it will work properly. This process involves diddling with the hardware as well as setting up software. "Don't let Craig *configure* your computer. At his old office, they used to call him can-crash-it Craig."

connector *(kon-eck-tor)* The part of a cable that plugs into a port or interface to connect one device to another. Can also be the hole into which the cable plugs. A nice, technical yet generic term.

Three types of connectors.

console *(kon-sohl)* 1. The main computer box. The thing that all the other parts of your computer plug into. The console is either a flat slab sitting under your monitor or the tower model, which sits next to the monitor or on the floor. "The tech support guy wanted to know what kind of *console* Debra had. She said that she had lots of hugs and shoulders to cry on. Needless to say, the tech support guy didn't get it." 2. The main terminal for a large computer system, where the chief programmer or system operator sits and wreaks havoc.

console device *(kon-sohl dee-vies)* Another term for the computer monitor and keyboard. See also *CON.* "We must all console Tammy for accidentally spilling her coffee into her *console device.*"

constant *(kon-stant)* A value that never changes. "There are three *constants* in the universe: Death, taxes, and the fact that any computer you buy today is already obsolete."

context menu *(kon-tekst men-yoo)* A popup list of options or commands, typically relating directly to the item selected or clicked on. In Windows 9x, you can see context menus by pointing the mouse at something and pressing the right mouse button. See also *right-click.*

context-sensitive help *(kon-tekst sen-suh-tiv help)* Help that a program provides that changes according to what you're doing at the time. If you've chosen the Print command, context-sensitive help provides help about printing. If you've chosen the File Save command, context-sensitive help provides help for saving a file. If you're confused, context-sensitive help confuses you even more. "Our programmers were having trouble writing *context-sensitive help* in their program, so we told them all to grow beards, wear cardigan sweaters and sandals, and write poetry."

contiguous *(kon-teeg-yoo-us)* In one piece. Often used when describing files stored on a disk or data stored in a file. A noncontinuguous file is said to be fragmented. "If Marty doesn't pluck his eyebrows, they will become *contiguous*."

continuous-form paper *(kon-tin-yoo-us form pay-per)* Computer paper where the sheets are all connected but are perforated for easy separation.

control code *(kon-trol kohd)*
1. Character codes 0 through 31 in the ASCII code set. 2. Any key, A through Z plus a few misfits, pressed in combination with the Control key. 3. Special codes formerly used to control aspects of a teletype terminal, but now mostly used for trivial purposes in text-based programs. The following table shows how some of the keys are used on your keyboard and in DOS. 4. Codes (not specifically character codes 0 through 31) used to control something, such as the printer. "That 'burp' of text you often see at the top of a badly printed document is just some stray *control codes* that got into the mix."

control-clicking *(kon-trol klik-eeng)* The process of holding down the control key on the keyboard while at the same time clicking the mouse.

Control key *(kon-trol kee)* A special shift key, abbreviated Ctrl on some keyboards. The Control key works with other keys to give commands to a program. "They had to label the *control key* as Ctrl on most computers. No sense in giving the user any reason to believe they're ever in control."

 Control Panel *(kon-trohl pan-el)* A utility program that lists options for modifying various aspects of the system. "In the middle of a static snow storm, facing hurling electrons, Dr. Bitmap and his companion, Nancy Neutrino, finally reach the *Control Panel*. In seconds, they should wrest the computer from the clutches of the evil Dr. Modulus and his horde of evil, virus-crazed, proto-drones."

controller *(kon-trol-er)* As silly as it sounds, something that controls something else. Typically hardware, though a software controller is also possible. For example, a hard disk controller is the circuitry that controls the hard drive, connecting it to the computer. A video controller (more commonly, video adapter) controls your monitor and connects it to the computer's motherboard. "The problem with Laverne is that her mouth lacks a *controller*."

conventional memory *(kon-ven-shun-al mem-oh-ree)* The first 640 kilobytes of memory (RAM) in any IBM-compatible computer. This wouldn't mean anything, were there not the expanded and extended memory standards as well. No, a PC has no such thing as plain old memory. It all has to have a name. To drive this point home, see also *expanded memory, extended memory, upper*

C

memory. "In the era of multimegabyte computers, it's a severe drag that we still have to put up with the *conventional memory* limitation."

conversion *(kon-ver-shun)* To change from one format to another. There are different types of conversions: software, hardware, system, file, data, and media. "Wendy would like for everyone to call her Walter after her *conversion.*"

converter *(kon-vert-er)* Hardware or software that changes one item into another, such as an AC-to-DC power converter or a WordPerfect-to-Microsoft Word document file converter. "Tim's too stubborn to buy WordPerfect, so I had to use a special file *converter* so that he could use my WordPerfect files in WordStar."

cookbook *(kook-book)* A book of small code segments that the reader can use to do things in programs. For example, the cookbook may contain a routine for sorting information, which a program would steal — uh, borrow.

cookie *(koo-kee)* 1. A thin, baked piece of flavored dough that tastes great and contains nearly every chemical and substance known to man that causes heart disease, cancer, and tooth decay. 2. A special message you may see when you start your computer. See also *fortune cookie.* 3. A tidbit of information saved to your hard drive by a Web page. The information can be anything, which freaks some people out, although most often the information is something that helps you use the Web page the next time you visit. "We must get Claudia to

stop looking in the CD-ROM drive for *cookies* sent by the World Wide Web."

coordinate *(koh-or-din-ayts)* A location on a grid. Typically, one coordinate gives a horizontal (left and right) location, and another coordinate gives the vertical (up and down). The horizontal location is also referred to as X; the vertical is Y. Also used on *Star Trek* for giving locations for beaming people from or to a planet's surface. "Mr. Spock would always give his beam-up *coordinates* to Scotty exactly. That way, he was sure that he would beam up and not be melded with a rock, tree, or other nearby object, especially Captain Kirk."

coprocessor *(koh-pros-ess-er)* 1. A separate computer chip designed to do specific tasks and take some of the work off the main processor. The result is that the computer runs faster. 2. A math coprocessor, which aids the microprocessor in doing complex math, mostly because the microprocessor slept through algebra. 3. A graphics coprocessor that takes care of displaying images on the screen, resulting in faster, more colorful, and more detailed images. "Donna needs a *coprocessor* for her typing."

copy *(kop-ee)* 1. To make an exact duplicate of an item. 2. To create a duplicate of a file. "Whew! Your job is saved. You didn't delete the Christmas bonus file — you merely zapped a *copy.*" 3. To duplicate a chunk of text or graphics image to be pasted elsewhere. 4. The command that performs the copy operation.

copyleft *(cop-ee-left)* A play on the term *copyright;* used by the Free Software Foundation to grant you the right to use and reproduce software at your whim as long as you maintain the copyleft on your own modifications. It's kind of an "everyone share" type of philosophy.

copy protection (kop-ee proh-tek-shun) A way to prevent a computer from copying one or more files or an entire program. This feeble attempt at protecting profits resulted in lots of software developers going bankrupt; no one likes making using a computer any more difficult. Today, most copy protection schemes are no longer used.

CorelDraw (kor-el drah) A popular PC drawing and illustration program, made by foreigners in Canada.

corruption (kor-up-shun) When data in memory or on disk has been changed or perverted. "It has been rumored that the true definition of the word *corruption* is The Clinton Administration."

country code (kon-tree kohd) A two-letter suffix applied to an Internet address that identifies the country of origin. For example, fr is France, ag is Argentina, and va is the Vatican.

CP/M (see pee em) 1. Acronym for Control Program for Microcomputers. An operating system predating DOS that was popular on microcomputers back in the late 1970s and early '80s. 2. A type of computer that ran the CP/M operating system. "Lee keeps his old *CP/M* computer around for his own, strange sentimental reasons."

cps (see pee ess) Acronym for characters per second. Used to rate the printing speed of certain types of printers. "I was impressed with the daisy-wheel printer's 18 *cps* speed, until I realized that I could type faster than that."

CPU (see pee yoo) 1. Acronym for central processing unit. See *central processing unit*. "No, Madam, the computer doesn't have a fan because the *CPU* stinks." 2. C3PO's brother.

CR/LF (kayr-edj ree-turn lien-feed) Abbreviation for carriage return–line feed, the character or characters that end a line of text. CR is a carriage return, moving the print head to the start of the line; LF is a line feed, advancing the paper down one line in the printer.

crack (krak) 1. To break into a computer system. 2. To break the copy protection on a game. See also *hack*. 3. What you see when the plumber looks under the sink. 4. An illegal drug that stupid people use.

crash (krash) When the computer or a network suddenly stops working. Comes from the actual gruesome sound of the hard disk drive heads banging into the disk drive. "See the network *crash. Crash, crash, crash.* Watch the workers weep. Weep, weep, weep."

Cray (kray) The first supercomputer. The Cray-1 was different from all other mainframes of the day in that it used basic computer components but wired them tightly together. The shorter distances meant that information traveled quickly in the Cray, making it one fast computer. The Cray-XMP was the first computer to be used exclusively by the motion picture industry (which is the MP part of Cray-XMP). The movie *Starfighter* was done mostly on a Cray-XMP. Named after Seymour Cray, who designed the system. See also *mainframe*.

C

CRC *(see ar see)* Acronym for *c*yclical *r*edundancy *c*heck, an error-detection technique used to verify the accuracy of data. A CRC is often used when transmitting a file over a modem. That way, it ensures that the file received is an exact copy of the one sent. Disk drives also use a CRC to verify that information is correctly read from disk.

crippleware *(krip-ohl-wayer)* Software designed to be lacking certain features, such as the ability to print or save information to disk. Crippleware is built for demonstration purposes. If you like the product, you can buy the full version or disable the crippling features. Not a very nice term, but who are we to judge? See also *shareware*.

crisp *(krisps)* British term for a potato chip. See also *chip*. (They do not call a chip inside a computer a crisp, however.)

crosshairs *(krahs-hayers)* A type of cursor, designed for drawing or painting programs, that allows for precise placement of the cursor when drawing squares, circles, or lines. "So I gots me this drawing of an elk, ya see. And I gots it in my Paint program. So I go to draw me a bead, and the cursor turns into *crosshairs.* Blam! I click the mouse. Heh, heh. It's elk meat this Christmas!"

 cross posting *(kros post-ing)* The sending of a message to multiple newsgroups at the same time. "John keeps cross posting his 'The King is really dead!' message to all the Elvis groups."

CRT *(see ar tee)* Acronym for *c*athode *r*ay *t*ube. CRTs appear in computer monitors and TV screens. "Ralph is so nerdy, he even calls the TV set a *CRT.*"

cruise virus *(krooz vie-rus)* A type of computer virus that infects and searches other computers for specific data to either steal or sabotage. The military is rumored to be developing cruise viruses that will infect enemy computers and steal important data without being detected.

csh *(see-ess-aytch* or *see-shel)* One of many command environment programs for the UNIX operating system. It's similar to COMMAND.COM for DOS, displaying a prompt and allowing you to type various commands and whatnot. See also *sh*. "Paul is so lonely for UNIX that he's dressed up MS-DOS to look a lot like *csh.*"

Ctrl *(kon-trol,* not *sit-rel)* The keycap abbreviation for the Control key. See also *Control key.*

Ctrl+Alt+Del *(kon-trohl alt duh-leet)* 1. A keyboard combination that resets MS-DOS or brings up a special Shutdown dialog box in Windows. See also *Vulcan nerve pinch*. 2. A warm boot. See also *warm boot.*

CUA *(see yoo ay)* Acronym for Common User Access, a set of guidelines developed by IBM to provide a standard user interface for computer programs. "Though computer manufacturers are really pleased with the *CUA* guidelines, they tend not to follow them."

 CUL *(see yoo ell)* Acronym for "see you later." Used by those who correspond by e-mail but are too lazy to type "See you later." See also *CULA*. Not used in verbal conversation.

Thanks for helping me to embez-
zle all that money from the
company. CUL, Tom.

 CULA *(see-yoo-el-ay)* See you later, alligator. See also *CUL.*

current directory *(kur-ent di-rek-tor-ee)* 1. The active directory or folder, the one containing the files or programs you're currently working on. Any directory on a hard or floppy disk can be the current directory, but only one directory can be the current directory at any given time. "The tech support guy asked me which directory I was logged to, and I told him the *current directory*." 2. In UNIX, the *pwd* command displays the current directory. In DOS, the *cd* command is used.

cursor *(kurs-er)* 1. The annoying little blinking line that appears on the screen to let you know where your next typed character will appear. 2. The blinking underline or block in text mode. 3. Another term for the mouse pointer. 4. Another term for the insertion pointer used in graphical operating systems when editing text. "*Cursor* comes from the Latin word for *runner.* It has nothing to do with foul language."

cursor keys *(kur-ser kees)* The keys on the keyboard that let you move the cursor around. On IBM keyboards, the cursor keys double up as the numeric keypad. (What a stupid engineering design!) The eight cursor keys are the the up and down arrows, the right and left arrows, the Home and End keys, and the PgUp and PgDn keys. Many new keyboards have separate arrow keys available as well. See also *101-key keyboard.* "You won't believe this: I just pressed one of the *cursor keys,* and my PC uttered a foul word at me."

cut *(kut)* 1. To remove text or graphics from the screen. You can use the Paste comand to retrieve the most recent text or graphics that you cut. 2. Another term for a move operation; the first step is to cut, and the second is to paste. "The difference between the Copy and *Cut* commands is that Copy makes a duplicate and *Cut* (and Paste) is used to move something from one place to *another.*" 3. (cap.) The command that cuts text.

cut and paste *(kut and payst)* 1. To move text, graphics, or files from one spot to another. 2. Something that's easy. Computer designers attempt to draw on our beloved experiences of kindergarten by using fun, friendly terms for complex and scary operations. "I thought that Phillip was speedy on the computer, until I learned that he just used *cut and paste* to produce this week's report."

cut on *(kut on)* To turn something on. Chiefly used in the mid-Atlantic states. Mostly likely the opposite of "cut off," which means to turn off. "*Cut on* some lights in yer computer room. It looks like a cave."

cyber- *(sy-bur)* A prefix used to designate something as electronic in origin. For example, cyberpunk would be punk-style music done electronically. Cybersex is sex that takes place through an electronic media (as opposed to any physical contact). Steve Austin (the Six Million Dollar Man) was a cyborg, which means *cyb*ernetic *org*anism. "Josh finally broke down and bought a modem. He hated being a *cybervirgin.*"

C

cybernetics *(sy-bur-net-icks)* A form of study in the area of discovering what mechanisms control systems and how systems regulate themselves. Cybernetics used to be interested only in the study of biological and artificial control systems until it got bored and had to expand its horizons.

 cyberspace *(sy-bur-spays)* 1. The electronic ether where online communications takes place. Coined by William Gibson in his novel *Neuromancer,* it's the mental locale where folks with modems meet, somewhere out there in the nether world. 2. A nickname for the Internet. "I met my wife in *cyberspace.* I just hope that she looks as good as she writes because I've never met her face to face."

Cyrix *(sie-riks)* A company that manufactures microprocessors and other chips. "Some *Cyrix* chips compatible with Intel microprocessors are found in the guts of many desktop PCs."

C

D: *(dee koh-lin)* The drive letter designation for the first drive after your PC's first hard drive. This can be a CD-ROM drive, a second hard drive, a removable drive, a RAM drive, a Sunday drive, a 530-yard drive on a par 5, or any of a number of various drives available on the PC.

 DA *(dee ay)* Acronym for desk accessory. See *desk accessory.*

DAC *(dee ay see)* Acronym for *d*igital-to-*a*nalog *c*onverter. A gizmo that translates digital information into voltage, which is one way that audio or visual images are produced on a computer.

daemon *(day-mon* or *dee-mon)* A program that runs in the background, waiting for some condition. The daemon takes over when that event occurs, controlling some operation or executing special instructions. Daemons are a UNIX (and Linux) thing, usually running to control various network operations. The word is a pun-play on "demon," though; in typical UNIX style, they reworked it to stand for *d*isk *a*nd *e*xecution *mon*itor.

daisy chain *(day-zee chayn)* 1. To link several items together, one after another. 2. In word processing, to print several documents one after another. "Elaine was disappointed with her word processor. She thought that the *daisy chain* printing feature would help her decorate her Christmas tree." 3. To connect a series of peripherals together, one after the other, such as with a SCSI interface. So you may have a scanner, connected to a CD-ROM drive, connected to a tape backup, and then connected to your computer. They're all daisy chained.

Daisy-chaining SCSI devices to the PC.

daisy wheel *(day-zee wee-el)* A type of printer that used a plastic disk to print characters. The disk had spokes, and on each spoke was the imprint of a character. Daisy wheels were used in old-fashioned printers (unimaginatively enough, called *daisy-wheel printers* because the wheels look like daisy petals). Whenever the printer needed to print a character, it spun the daisy wheel around until the correct character appeared. Then it struck the daisy wheel spoke so that it smacked against an inked ribbon, printing the character on the page. (Sounds like lots of trouble to go through, simply to print a single character, doesn't it?) "Pages printed on a *daisy wheel* printer look like they came out of an ordinary typewriter. So who's *that* gonna impress?"

darnthing *(darn-thing)* 1. A phrase commonly uttered by novices and experts alike when confronted by a problem that the computer refuses to solve. (Actually, there are lots of other more common phrases, but this is a family dictionary.) 2. *&^%$!!. "This *darnthing* won't let me delete this word. I hate computers. I hate computers. I hate computers."

DAT *(dee ay tee)* Acronym for *d*igital *a*udiotape, a high-capacity type of tape used on computers primarily for backing up data. Can also refer to the type of drive that reads the tape. "Well, I'm sorry! I thought that you were being cute when you said *DAT* tape drive."

data *(day-tuh,* not *dah-tuh)* 1. Information that people think is important and useful to save. 2. The android character on *Star Trek: The Next Generation.* "They call Mr. *Data* by that name because he stores lots of information. By the same reckoning, they should call Barney the dinosaur, Mr. Stuff."

database *(day-tuh-bays)* An organized collection of information. "The DMV has scoured its *database* and cannot locate you. Therefore, you must not exist. Next!"

database administrator *(day-tuh-bays add-men-eh-stray-tor)* The human responsible for the design and management of the database.

database management system *(day-tuh-bays man-ej-ment sis-tem)* Several programs that massage, sort, and report on a single database.

data bits *(day-tuh bits)* The number of bits a computer uses to represent a character of data. The PC and the Macintosh use 8 data bits, commonly known as 8 bits in a byte.

data bus *(day-tuh bus)* The connection between the computer's microprocessor, memory, and peripherals. The data inside your computer is moved around on the data bus. Weird but true.

data compression *(day-tuh kom-pres-shun)* The process of making files smaller so that they take up less space. Often used for transmitting files through a modem (thereby reducing the time spent on the phone) and for storing files on a hard disk so that they take up less space. Files must be decompressed before you can use them. "Using *data compression* helps you store more information in less space. They need something like that in the airport for people's carry-on bags."

 data detector *(day-tuh dee-tek-ter)* An Apple tool that scans selected text in a document and then performs some action with the information it gathers.

data dictionary *(day-tuh dik-shun-ayr-ee)* A list of the information in database files. Also known as "data data."

Data Encryption Standard *(day-tuh en-krip-shin stan-dard)* Often abbreviated as DES, a government specification for encoding files using a password. The longer the password, the more difficult it is to decode the data. A supposedly secure specification that no one can crack except maybe the government, though recently a group of 14,000 users pooled their computing resources on the Internet and actually cracked the code. "The *Data Encryption Standard* can scramble text so badly that no one can read it without the right password. I believe that this is the process the government tax forms go through before we get them."

data entry form *(day-tuh in-tree form)* An onscreen fill-in-the-blanks thing. This form, of course, makes entering and editing data easier.

 data fork *(day-tuh fork)* The part of the file that contains information. On the Macintosh, all files have two parts to them: a resource fork and a data fork. The data fork usually contains information (the actual data) that the program needs to run. The resource fork usually contains the instructions for running a program or other needed resource information, such as fonts, icons, and menus. "No, Naomi, this little one is your *data fork*. The one you're holding in your left hand is your salad fork."

data glove *(day-tuh gluv)* A device that translates hand and arm movements into computer input.

data mining *(day-tuh min-ing)* A method for analyzing information in a database without knowledge of the meaning of the data.

data modem *(day-tuh mo-dum)* Not a fax modem. See *modem.*

data structures *(day-tuh struk-shoors)* A term programmers use to describe various ways to organize information within a program. Some common data structures include arrays, records, trees, linked lists, and anything else the programmer cares to invent. See also *algorithm.* "Your *data structures* must have been designed by someone with a crooked T-square."

data-transfer rate *(day-tuh-trans-fur rayt)* A measure of a CD-ROM drive's speed. It refers to the number of kilobytes the drive can read per second. The higher the speed, the better the performance. "Stan told Buffy how fast his *data transfer rate* was, and she fell asleep. I guess it wasn't fast enough."

data word format *(dah-tuh wurd format)* The word length, parity, and number of stop bits used to encode each byte transmitted through a serial port. This format was formerly something you had to configure, and there were several options to confuse yourself with. Today, most serial ports are configured by the operating system automatically. The most common data word format is 8-N-1, which stands for 8 bits of word length, no parity, and 1 stop bit. There was also 7-E-1, which was a 7-bit word length, even parity, and 1 stop bit. "Your android's *data word format* does not contain any contractions."

date *(dayt)* 1. What Melvyn will never get as long as he spends too much time with his computer. "Steve is desperate. He typed DATE at the DOS prompt and fully expected a gorgeous redhead to unfurl from his printer." 2. An operating system command (in MS-DOS and OS/2) that displays or changes the computer system's date. DATE gives you the chance to type the correct date, if necessary. 3. The current date, as kept by the computer system. 4. The year, month, and day that a file was created or last modified.

datum *(day-tum)* The singular of *data,* seldom used except by extremely socially backward programmers who wish to impress others with their useless technical knowledge. See also *data.* "Maybe Data, the android in *Star Trek: The Next Generation,* should have been named *Datum* because there's only one of him."

daughterboard *(dawh-ter-bord)* A circuit board that plugs into the motherboard. Get it? See also *expansion card, motherboard.* "It's the aspiration of every *daughterboard* to grow up and not be like her motherboard."

dBASE *(dee-bays)* 1. A database program produced by Ashton-Tate. dBASE is the copyrighted name of one of the first, most popular database programs ever, first on ancient CP/M computers and then on early DOS machines. It began its life called *Vulcan.* (Yes, it was named after Mr. Spock because he was full of information.) Then it became dBASE II and then dBASE III and then dBASE IV and then . . . Ashton-Tate went out of business. 2. Any database program. 3. The programming language used by the database program. 4. The type of files produced by a database program. See also *xBase.* "You think the DOS prompt is cryptic? The old *dBASE* prompt was just a dot on the screen!"

DCA *(dee see ay)* Acronym for Document Content Architecture. Yet another standard everyone ignores, this time for sending text files between alien computers on a network. Pushed by IBM.

DDE *(dee dee ee)* Acronym for *Dynamic Data Exchange,* the ability of several documents to share the same information.

Used with Microsoft Windows and OS/2, DDE lets two programs share data, such as numbers stored in a spreadsheet and a word processor report. "If it weren't for *DDE,* I'd have to type these numbers twice in my word processor report and spreadsheet. With *DDE,* I simply type the numbers in my spreadsheet and they magically appear in my word processor. Every time I change the numbers in the spreadsheet, the numbers automatically change in my word processor report."

DDT *(dee dee tee)* A pesticide used in the 1960s and '70s to wipe out insects, crops, small animals, and people wherever it appeared. "*DDT* keeps bugs out of my garden, so I sprayed some on my computer, hoping that it might get rid of the bugs in WordPerfect." 2. The name of the debugger that came with the old CP/M operating system. Get it? DDT? No more bugs? (Well, they didn't laugh at the user group meeting, either.)

debug *(dee-bug)* To eliminate problems in a program. The problems are called bugs, though often the "bugs" are due to the programmer not fully thinking about the problem at hand. Programmers try to debug a program while they are developing it, but often they miss things. See also *bug.* "Some programmers claim that they don't really program; they *debug.*"

debugger *(dee-bug-er)* A special program with the sole purpose in life to help programmers track down and eliminate bugs in a program. "Art thought that he was an excellent programmer until he ran some of his stuff through a *debugger* and his computer exploded."

decimal *(des-im-al)* Counting base 10. The normal way humans count rather than in hexadecimal or binary or some strange computer way to count. See also *binary, hexadecimal, octal.* "The officer didn't think that it was funny when Gary asked whether he should count backward from 100 using *decimal* numbers."

decimal number *(des-im-al num-ber)* A number that uses the digits 0, 1, 2, 3, 4, 5, 6, 7, 8, and 9 in ordinary base 10 notation.

decimal tab *(des-im-al tab)* A tab stop that aligns on the period (the decimal point); used in a word processor to line up values in an even column.

 decoder *(dee-kohd-er)* Special software that translates enco-ded messages back to real text the normal person can understand. Binary newsgroups usually use encoded files. See also *binary newsgroups.*

decrement *(deh-kre-ment)* To decrease a value or variable. Typically, a decrement is the same as "minus 1" or subtracting 1 from a number. In the C and C++ programming languages, the double minus sign (–) is used as the decrement operator.

decryption *(dee-krip-shun)* The process of converting indecipherable gibberish into plain English that everyone can understand. You need a key to be able to decrypt. See also *encryption.* "Every-thing that computer people write sounds like it has been encrypted by the CIA. But reading *DOS For Dummies* seemed like reading the *decryption* of all the normal computer terms."

dedicated *(ded-uh-kay-ted)* A piece of equipment that performs one specific function. For example, one computer in the office may be a dedicated word processor, used only for that purpose and definitely not for playing games or abusing e-mail. Many people will get a dedicated phone line so that they don't have to worry about someone picking up the phone and disconnecting them from the modem. "Well, I wouldn't know whether my computer has a *dedicated* FAX/modem. I mean, it's fond of the computer, but I don't know if it's grown that attached."

Deep Blue *(deep bloo)* An IBM computer designed specifically to defeat world champion chess player Garry Kasparov. Deep Blue wasn't smart or anything, and it knew chess only as well as its programmers. But it had the advantage of *speed,* being able to think through 200 million chess board positions in three minutes whereas Mr. Kasparov could manage only 340, give or take. With that advantage, Deep Blue went on to defeat Mr. Kasparov in their second matchup in 1997. "Garry Kasparov got paid $400,000 for losing a chess match to *Deep Blue.* If I could only arrange that kind of deal, I'd play him too!"

default *(dee-fawlt)* What would happen otherwise. If you don't make a choice, the computer makes an assumption, referred to as "the default." Truly a horrid word and one that should be eliminated from all manuals and computer books. Rather than say "The default choice is to turn color off," they should write "Color is turned off unless you desire otherwise." No, I'm not sticky on the point, but it's really time that we removed this awful definition of the word. (Look up *default* in a real dictionary to see what it really means.) "Floyd nearly had a heart attack when his computer said that it would choose the *default* option for his home mortgage program."

default directory *(dee-falt die-rek-tor-ee)* The directory on a hard disk that the computer uses to perform commands if it isn't given specific instructions to use another directory. See also *default drive, directory.* "The *default directory* is where unpaid mortgage files go."

default drive *(dee-falt driev)* The disk drive the computer looks for if it isn't given specific instructions to look elsewhere. "Eric was going to take his computer back as defective, until I told him that the *default drive* means C: for most computers."

default folder *(dee-falt fold-er)* The "user-friendly" term for a *default directory.*

default font *(dee-falt font)* The text type and size a program chooses for you unless you choose something else.

defragment program *(dee-frag-ment proh-gram)* A utility that removes disk fragments from a drive, ensuring that all files are contiguous. Running a defragment program every so often improves file access and makes for happier computer-using people.

DEL *(dell)* The DOS command used to delete files. See also *delete, erase.*

Del key *(dell kee)* The Delete key. Some keys are so tiny that they have room for only the first three letters of the word

delete. "In some programs, pressing the *Del key* erases the character to the left of the cursor. In other programs, pressing the *Del key* erases the character to the right. This is like driving one car where the accelerator pedal is on the right and driving your other car where the brake pedal is on the right."

delete *(duh-leet)* 1. To remove a file from a disk; to erase or kill the file. See also *erase.* 2. To remove a character or selected block from a document. To remove a cell's contents from a spreadsheet. 3. The DOS command that removes files from disk. 4. The name of a keyboard key that is often used to delete text.

delimited file *(dee-lim-uh-ted fiel)* A text file that contains information for a database, such as items separated by commas. The delimited file provides a common way of transferring information between different applications. In a delimited file, records appear one to a line. Fields are separated by tabs, spaces, or, most commonly, commas. The first line of the file contains the field names; for example:

```
NAME,FOOD GROUP,CALORIES
Oreos,Sugar,35 ea.
Ice cream,Dairy,1025 pint.
Jolt,Caffiene,600 can.
```

"Since no one here can get our word processor and database program to talk, we've created a *delimited file* of the people we hate the most."

delphi *(dell-fie)* 1. (cap.) A programming language developed by Borland, one that looks surprisingly similar to its once-popular Turbo Pascal product. 2. An oracle or wise person who lived in the city of Delphi in ancient Greece. Ancient Greeks would go visit the Oracle at Delphi to hear about their future, discover their past, or get this week's lottery numbers.

demo *(deh-mo)* 1. A preview of a program or an animated presentation describing a product or program. 2. To show a program before it's released to the general public. 3. A sample program written to showcase an idea or demonstrate a programmer's ability.

demodulation *(dee-mod-yoo-lay-shun)* Unmodulating, which is the process of receiving an analog signal and transforming it into a digital equivalent. See also *modem*.

demon dialer *(dee-mon di-uh-ler)* A modem program that dials numbers from 555-0000, for example, through 555-9999, logging each to disk and marking when it finds another modem. This is one way a hacker would find the numbers to other systems. Of course, once another modem answers, the hacker still has to break into the system. Also known as a war dialer. "I could use a *demon dialer* to find out which computers answer the phone in my prefix. Instead, I'll rewrite it so that it calls my ex-wife every five minutes for the rest of her life."

density *(dens-uh-tee)* The amount of information that can be put into a specific yiblette of disk space. Floppy disks are measured in single, double, high, and extended densities. "George McFly looked into her eyes and said, 'You are my *density.*'"

dependent worksheet *(dee-pen-dent wurk-sheet)* In Microsoft Excel, a worksheet that contains a link or reference formula to another Excel worksheet.

DES *(dee ee ess)* Acronym for Data Encryption Standard; see *Data Encryption Standard.*

descender *(dee-send-er)* The part of a letter that falls below the imaginary line on which the letter rests. For example, the letters *p, y,* and *q* have descenders, but the letters *t, u,* and *o* do not. See also *ascender.* "You used to judge a dot matrix printer by how it handled *descenders.* Some cheesy printers just shifted those letters up a tad, which looked utterly dorky."

descriptor *(dee-skrip-tor)* A smaller unit of measurement used to represent something else; for example, a descriptor that represents a chunk of memory located somewhere inside the computer. A file descriptor may be an integer value that represents a specific file. Yes, this is one of those nerdy programming things.

deselect *(dee-sel-ekt)* To remove selection. To change your mind after selecting an item, such as by unhighlighting an item or by removing the X in an option box. See also *select.* "Would George Bush have won the 1992 election had he *deselected* Dan Quayle as his running mate?"

 desk accessory *(desk ak-ses-oh-ree)* A simple utility program, such as a calculator or notepad, that runs while another program is running. Desk accessories are tiny, useful programs that most Mac users can't live without.

desktop *(desk-top)* The background that appears in graphical operating systems. See also *graphical user interface, wallpaper.* "So the guy said to 'double-click on my *desktop*,' and I said that the mouse was already on the desktop, so what was his point. I just don't think I get this computer nonsense."

A Windows 2000 computer desktop. Ummm, coffee!

desktop PC *(desk-top pee-see)* A computer that sits on top of your desk. A larger model. One that isn't a laptop and doesn't sit on the floor, like a tower PC. Contrast with *portable, laptop, notebook.* "The guy who designed this *desktop PC* must have had an awfully big desk."

desktop printer *(desk-top printer)* An icon that represents a printer on the desktop. This icon can be especially effective if you do a fair amount of printing.

desktop publishing *(desk-top publishing)* The process of combining text and graphics in a document; software used to create neat-looking newsletters, books, or brochures. See also *DTP.* "Those campy images of underground rebels churning out propaganda on mimeograph machines are rapidly being replaced by the reality of three nerds sitting around a computer using a *desktop publishing* program and arguing over picas, pitches, and points."

destination *(deh-stih-nay-shun)* The place where information is headed. Information comes from the source and heads to the destination, which can be a place in memory or a disk, folder, or file.

developer *(dee-vel-up-er)* More official than a mere programmer; the entire outfit that produces software. Although a guy named Bill may write the program, EvilSoftwareSoft is the program's developer.

device *(dee-vies)* 1. Any type of equipment — such as a printer, modem, monitor, disk drive, or mouse — that can send or receive data. "You know that you're hard-core when you call your printer a hard copy *device*." 2. A command in a PC's CONFIG.SYS file that loads software to control a certain device. (See the next entry.)

device driver *(dee-vies driev-er)* A program that controls a device. Device drivers are required in order to control some devices (a mouse, tape backup, or CD-ROM drive, for example) because the computer itself is too lame to do it. "When Grandma Margaret was a little girl, they called the *device driver* for their car a chauffeur.'"

Device Manager *(dee-vies man-eh-jur)* A Windows utility that displays a list of the computer's hardware. It allows you to troubleshoot and configure the hardware to keep Windows happy.

device name *(dee-vies naym)* An abbreviation that refers to a device connected to the computer. "Why MS-DOS couldn't just call the printer PRINTER and had to use a cryptic *device name* like PRN is beyond me."

dev/null *(dev nul)* 1. A directory (though technically a device) on a UNIX computer that does nothing, produces nothing, and can swallow anything as input and not care. 2. A place where people are told to go or to stick their useless ideas or complaints. Because the dev/null directory goes nowhere and does nothing, telling someone to send comments to dev/null is the polite equivalent of telling them to go "bug off." "Please send all flames to *dev/null.*"

diagnostic *(di-ag-nos-tik)* 1. Someone who doubts the existence of two gods. 2. To diagnose or analyze something for errors or its current operating condition.

diagnostic mode *(di-ag-nos-tik mohd)* An operating state where the computer or device is configured to report errors or its general operating condition. "In diagnostic mode, the computer spews out a bunch of error messages and other information, similar to what it does whenever I run Windows 2000."

diagnostic program *(di-ag-nos-tik proh-gram)* Software that tests computer hardware and software to decide whether they're operating appropriately.

diagnostic software *(di-ag-nos-tik soft-wayr)* Special programs that tell you what's in your computer or what's wrong with your computer or both. "I used *diagnostic software* to find out what was wrong with my computer. Come to find out it wasn't my computer at all. It was just me not knowing how to work Windows 98."

 dialer program *(di-al-er proh-gram)* A program used to dial up the Internet. You can't get on the

Internet without one. "I thought that a dialer program was like the Home Shopping Network, where you could order junk that you don't need and that costs too much in the first place."

dialog box *(di-uh-log boks)* A window that pops up to prompt for or display information. It's a dialogue between you and your software. "Why is it that most of my program's *dialog boxes* talk at me and not with me?"

Dial-up access *(dij-uh-tal ak-sess)* A means of connecting to another computer or the Internet, usually through a modem (as opposed to a direct connection).

 dial-up connection *(di-al-up kon-ek-shun)* Using a computer and modem to phone into an Internet Service Provider to connect to the Internet. This type of connection contrasts with a direct connection, in which your computer is wired directly into the Internet (you don't need to dial the phone first). See also *PPP.*

DIB *(dib)* Acronym for *d*evice-*i*ndependent *b*itmap, a type of graphics file format. A DIB graphics file supposedly carries information that allows it to be displayed on any computer, no matter which type of graphics it's using. A nice idea, if it ever worked. "John and I could never get our collection of post-modern dryer-lint art to display on our computers. Then we started using *DIB* files."

dictation software *(dik-tay-shun soft-wayr)* A program that allows you to speak to the computer and have those words translated into text on the screen. "Even with today's fast computers, dictation software can be slow and unreliable."

D

diddle *(dih-dl)* To tinker with or modify something because you have nothing better to do. See also *dinking*.

digital *(dij-uh-tal)* A way of representing objects using two distinct states such as On or Off, Low or High, Good or Bad, or Republican or Democrat. All computers are digital computers because they consist of millions of On and Off switches. See also *analog, binary.* "If in the future all clocks are *digital*, how we will ever teach our children about clockwise and counterclockwise?"

digital audio *(dij-uh-tal ah-dee-oh)* A sound that's been examined by a computer, translated into a string of numbers, and stored to disk. "Did you know that the sound on your CD is actually *digital audio*? Bet ya didn't know that, did ya?"

digital camera *(dij-uh-tal kam-uh-ra)* A handheld scanner or visual input device that creates graphics. The images must be downloaded to a computer or graphics printer.

digital modem *(dij-uh-tal moh-dum)* A modem that sends non-analog signals. Most modems are analog. A digital modem is used on specific digital networks.

digital monitor *(dij-uh-tal mon-uh-ter)* Not an analog monitor. I know, dumb definition. Most monitors today are digital. TV sets are analog. See also *analog monitor,* which probably has a better explanation for all this, anyway.

Digital Research *(dij-uh-tal ree-surch)* A company that produced the first "microcomputer" operating system,

CP/M. The company was trounced on in the 1980s by Microsoft and MS-DOS, and then it produced DR DOS. But DR DOS was eventually bought by Novell. See also *CP/M.* "*Digital Research* was one of the 'unstoppable' computer companies of the early 1980s, along with VisiCorp, which made the VisiCalc spreadsheet; MicroPro, which made WordStar; and Ashton-Tate, which made dBASE — none of whom is around today. This just goes to show you the volatile nature of the computer biz."

digital signal processor *(dij-uh-tal seeg-nal prah-ses-er)* A high-speed chip, like a microprocessor, that deals specifically with sound. A DSP is often used in a computer to speed up the audio and enhance communications, graphics, or other similar applications.

digital versatile disk *(dij-uh-tal vers-uh-tal disk)* The latest whiz-bang storage unit for a PC. See also *DVD.*

digitizer pad *(dij-uh-tiez-er pad)* 1. A flat input device used to read in sophisticated drawings. A device called a puck (like a mouse) is used to take readings from the pad, which are translated into digital information and stored in the computer. 2. Where the digitizer lived his reckless youth.

DIMM *(dim)* Acronym for Dual In-line Memory Module. This tiny expansion card adds more memory to your computer. Similar to a SIMM, though a DIMM allows for the wider (and faster) transfer of data.

dimmed *(dimd)* 1. An unavailable option or command, usually appearing on the screen in a soft, fuzzy color that's easy to overlook. 2. A temporarily unavailable option or command. "Richard tried to create a romantic mood, so he *dimmed* the lights. But then Sherry said, 'That option is not available!'"

dingbat *(deeng-bat)* 1. (plural) A font consisting of bizarre characters made up of bullets, Greek and Egyptian hieroglyphics, and geometric figures. 2. What Archie Bunker called his wife on the 1970s hit show *All in the Family.* "Martha never understood why her husband got her a T-shirt with a ❖ on the front." 3. A style of apartment found in Southern California.

dinking *(deen-keeng)* 1. To mess with your computer with no real production value in mind. 2. To goof around with an option. "Windows has three purposes: getting work done, playing, and *dinking.*"

DIP switch *(dip switch)* Tiny little switches, almost impossible to find or use properly. DIP is an acronym for *Dual-Inline Package* (as though that clarifies matters any). Mostly, you use DIP switches with modems or printers. The switches select options for output. Printed circuit boards can have them, too. "I think that they should call them teeny switches and reserve the term *DIP switch* for when Melvin in the next cubicle is replaced by a guy named Poindexter."

DIR *(dur)* 1. An operating system command that displays a directory listing — a catalog of files on a disk or in a directory. "I typed DIR at the DOS prompt and, lo, discovered that my disk was full of stuff I didn't know existed." 2. A directory file.

Direct Memory Access *(dur-ekt mem-oh-ree ak-ses)* See *DMA.*

DirectX *(deer-ekt-eks)* A set of routines that Microsoft implores game developers to use when programming for Windows 95 and later. Game developers (and players) want fast action games. Windows 95, on the other hand, gets in the way. So game developers write their software to circumvent Windows 95. Because of how much Microsoft hates being circumvented, it designed the DirectX standard for accessing the screen, keyboard, and joystick. Most game developers ignore DirectX.

directory *(deer-ek-toh-ree)* 1. A list of files on a disk. 2. Separate parts of the disk where other files are stored. Every disk has at least one directory called the *root directory.* You can create other directories and label them to keep your files that relate to different programs, data, and projects separated. See also *subdirectory.* "Most people know to create a bunch of *directories* to organize their files, but few follow through on it."

directory list box *(dur-ek-toh-ree list boks)* A list of directories, one or more of which can be selected to sate the lusty desires of some command. You use these boxes in Windows and OS/2 programs. "Whenever I press the Save command in my word processor, the program pops up a *directory list box* so that I can choose which directory to save the file in."

disc *(disk)* Another term for a disk, mostly used when referring to a CD-ROM disk. Probably British. (Yeah, it's them Brits with their spelling from the 14th century again.) See also *disk,* which is the way God spells it.

disconnect dialog box *(dis-kon-ekt di-al-log boks)* A tiny window announcing that you've had enough time on the Internet and now it's time to get back to the real world. If you want to stay on longer, click on the Don't Hang Up button. If you agree that you've been on long enough, click on the Disconnect button. "Just when I find something really juicy on the Internet, the *disconnect dialog box* pops up. I wonder if my mom is connected to this somehow."

disk *(disk)* 1. A magnetic storage device shaped like a pizza and encased in plastic. 2. A floppy disk. 3. A hard disk. 4. A CD-ROM disk or any other type of media you may slide into a computer somewhere. 5. The place where you save files, and the place where you open files that you think you once saved. "Although you can put the entire Encyclopedia Britannica on a CD-ROM disk, the Encyclopedia Britannica salesguy still weighs about 180 pounds and wears an ugly blue suit."

disk cache *(disk cash)* 1. What you can win in the PC Super Sweepstakes! 2. A portion of memory used to speed up disk access. The disk cache contains information frequently read from disk. By copying information from the floppy or hard disk and storing it in a disk cache, the computer can access the information faster at a later time. Some computers have a built-in disk cache. Some utility programs create a disk cache out of the computer's main memory. Generally, the larger the disk cache, the faster the computer runs. "The guy at the store told me that I could use a *disk cache* to speed up my hard drive. I thought that he was

referring to something like the Disney Dollars you use at Disneyland, but I was wrong."

disk capacity *(disk ka-pass-uh-tee)* The absolute maximum amount of information or data that a disk or other storage medium is capable of holding.

disk controller *(disk kon-trohl-er)* The hardware that controls the reading and writing of information from and to a disk. It doesn't do the actual reading and writing because all disk drives are members of the union, but it tells other gadgets what to do.

disk drive *(disk driev)* A mechanical device that reads disks. The drives are named A–Z in a PC. On a Macintosh, they're given names like Filbert and Ambidextrous. "Matt is so into golf that when I started talking about my *disk drive* giving me problems, he suggested that I use a 9-iron instead."

Disk drives shown in the My Computer window.

disk drive tongue depressor *(disk driev tung dee-pres-er)* A square piece of cardboard or plastic that is stuck in your disk drive during shipping. Rarely used anymore.

diskette *(disk-et)* Another term for disk, usually a floppy disk. "No George, a *diskette* is not a really small disk to be used with really small computers."

disk hog *(disk hawg)* A program that bloats and bloats until it takes up a considerable amount of hard disk space in relation to what it does. This is one of the side effects of having lots of disk storage in a computer; programs will bloat until they take up way too much disk space. Developers don't seem concerned about this. The feeling you get is that if they did, they could find a way to make their programs take up less space. But they don't, so the world now has disk hogs. "Excel is one *disk hog,* let me tell ya."

disk memory *(disk mem-oh-ree)* A misguided term that refers to storage on a disk. It should be merely "disk storage," which avoids confusion between disk and memory (RAM).

disk operating system *(disk op-er-ay-ting sis-tim)* 1. An older name for an operating system. In the early days of the microcomputer, it didn't come with disk drives. So when you upgraded to disk drives and needed a program to run the computer, you bought a disk operating system. Because most computers come with disk drives today, the "disk" part is dropped. See also *operating system.* 2. The long name for DOS. See also *DOS.*

disk partition *(disk par-ti-shun)* One section of a hard disk. A single hard drive can be partitioned into several different hard drives (as seen by the operating system). Each hard drive lives in its own partition. "Actually, a program is used to create *disk partitions.* Did a guy named Moses create this?" See also *partition.*

display *(dis-play)* The monitor or computer screen, specifically the information shown there. It's what you watch when you go a-computin'. See also *monitor.* "I called tech support to complain that my *display* looked like rubbish. Then they shyly admitted that it was their new, improved interface. I'm just happy that the people who design computer programs don't redesign the highway."

display adapter *(dis-play uh-dap-ter)* The hardware inside the computer that controls (or "drives") the display. The display adapter could be an expansion card or circuitry built into the motherboard.

dithering *(dith-er-ing)* Although it sounds like something drunk people might mumble in their sleep, dithering is the blending of two or more colors to get another color to display on the screen. This is done for low-resolution monitors and some displays that can't show every dang color in the universe. "Honey, roll over. You're *dithering* in your sleep again."

DLL *(dee el el)* 1. Acronym for *Dynamic Link Library,* an on-the-fly program that other programs may bring in to complete themselves or add a certain look and feel. DLL files contain commonly used routines that two or more programs can share. "The error message said '*DLL* file missing.' It's sad that when a program can't share, it has to act all stubborn like that." 2. The file extension for a DLL file.

DMA *(dee em ay)* Acronym for Direct Memory Access, a technique whereby information is transferred in a computer without assistance from the microprocessor. For example, it's possible to

D

transfer information between memory and an "intelligent" device, such as a hard drive, by simply telling a DMA chip, "Look, here, move this data from memory here to disk drive there." The information is moved without slowing down the microprocessor. "Our computer is really slow because our cable service doesn't offer the *DMA* channel."

 DNS *(dee en es)* Acronym for Domain Name Service, software that runs on an Internet computer that converts Internet names and addresses into actual locations on the Internet. The DNS server is a computer (or a program running on that computer) that translates weird Internet stuff you type into the real (and cryptic) addresses.

DOC *(dok)* 1. An abbreviation for *document*. 2. A file extension for document files, often used by word processors. "I asked Ellen if she could bring over some *DOC* files, and 40 minutes later she called to say that her physician wouldn't let her copy anything from his computer."

docking base *(dok-ing bays)* See *docking station*.

docking station *(dok-ing stay-shun)* A "home" for your laptop computer. Typically, a larger thing into which you plug your laptop computer, often by sliding your laptop all the way into the docking station. This extends your laptop's hardware, allowing you to use a larger screen and keyboard and other desktop features. "I save time and money by using a laptop on the road and then plugging it into my *docking station* back at the office."

document *(dok-yoo-mint)* A file created by a word processor or desktop publisher, containing words or pictures. See also *file*. "Cliff gave me all his *documents* on disk. Now I just need to figure out which word processor he used to create them all."

documentation *(dok-yoo-men-tay-shun)* The fat instruction manuals that everyone pays money for but no one bothers to read. Usually full of instructions that don't work, don't make sense, or are just plain wrong. "The project manager said that our *documentation* was too thick, so we just cut out every third word to get it down to size."

dogpile *(dawg pi-ol)* 1. A series of responses to a newsgroup posting. Usually negative responses. Usually short. Usually quite a few. 2. The name of a popular Internet search engine.

doinky *(doyn-kee)* Small, tiny. "Golly, those DIP switches are sure *doinky*."

 domain *(doh-mayn)* 1. A grouping of computers. 2. An organizational strategy in a database. 3. A method of identifying what type of organization you belong to when you access the Internet. There are several popular domains:

Domain	Type of Computer System
com	Company, business, commercial organization
edu	Educational institution
gov	The government (but not the military, because. . . .)
mil	Military institutions only

| org | Organizations (not in the preceding categories) |
| net | Networks, network resources |

See also *Internet address*. "Millie was happy to have a Net address that ended with the `mil` *domain*, until we told her that it was just because she worked for the Navy." 4. The name of your Internet Service Provider, such as `aol.com` or `idgbooks.com`.

dongle *(don-gal)* 1. A device that connects to the rear of your computer, often used as a copy-protection scheme. You cannot use a particular piece of software unless the proper dongle is installed. 2. Any device that connects to the back of your computer system that somehow enhances the computer's abilities. For example, a dongle may attach to your printer port, giving your PC the ability to capture video images but without interfering with your printer.

DOS *(daws)* 1. Acronym for *disk operating system.* 2. Another term for MS-DOS or PC-DOS, the operating system for nearly every PC in the world. (By the way, if you have Windows, you still have DOS.) See also *disk operating system.* "*DOS* is boss."

DOS prompt *(daws prompt)* The symbol, set of symbols, or words after which you type a DOS command. The DOS prompt essentially says "This is the computer. What do you want me to do?" Typical DOS prompts look like these:

```
C:\>
C:
C:\WINDOWS\SYSTEM>
.
```

See also *$* (dollar sign*).* "No, Phyllis, the *DOS prompt* has nothing to do with being on time."

 dot *(daht)* The way the period is pronounced in an Internet address. This pronunciation saves time over using the word *period,* which consists of three syllables. "You pronounce `www.dummies.com` as 'double-U double-U double-U dot dummies dot com,' not 'double-U double-U double-U period dummies period com.'"

dot com *(daht kahm)* A company that exists on the Internet and not in the real world. From the `.com` that follows a web address.

dot matrix *(daht may-triks)* 1. A grid on which characters are displayed or printed. 2. A type of printer or printout that creates letters and graphics by using lots of tiny dots. The more dots used, the sharper the image. The fewer the dots used, the more the printing looks like a cheap printer printed it. "D*ot matrix* printers are good for waking up the neighbors during the small hours."

dot pitch *(daht pitch)* 1. The smallest-size dot that a monitor can display, usually measured in millimeters (mm). Typical dot pitches for monitors are .41mm, .31mm, and .28mm. The smaller the dot pitch, the sharper the resolution on the monitor. 2. The distance between two color dots of the same color on a color monitor. "When I asked the salesman about his monitor's *dot pitch,* he replied that his dots were the best in town and that I'd be a fool to go elsewhere for them."

dots per inch *(dahts per ench)* Sometimes abbreviated as DPI, describes the quality of a printed image. The more dots per inch, the sharper the image. "My laser printer has a maximum resolution of 300 *dots per inch,* which is similar to the population density of Dhaka."

dotted quad *(daw-ted kwad)* The official name for the 192.168.0.1 type of Internet address. It's four numbers, none of which can be greater than 255 (that's the quad), separated by dots (that's the dots).

double-click *(duh-bol-klik)* To press the mouse button twice in rapid succession without moving the mouse between clicks. Click, click. See also *click.* "'*Double-click,*' said the manual. 'Click, click' went the mouse. Run, run did the program."

double-density disk *(duh-bol-den-si-tee disk)* A floppy disk that stores twice as much information in the same amount of space as a single-density disk. Double-density disks are abbreviated as DD. See also *high density.* "No, Blaine, *double-density disks* aren't any heavier than regular density disks."

DoubleSpace *(duh-bol-spays)* Another name for the Microsoft DriveSpace program. See also *DriveSpace.* "Grandma parks her car as though every space were a *doublespace.*"

down *(down)* When a piece of computer equipment temporarily stops working. "Our network's been *down* so often that it must be in China by now."

download *(down-lohd)* To copy files through a modem from a distant computer to the one you're working on. See also *upload.* "It helps you to remember *download* if you imagine that every online system you call sits on top of a hill. The files roll 'down' toward you."

downloaded font *(down-lohd-ed fawnt)* A font sent from the computer to the printer. Not a resident font.

downward compatible *(down-word kom-pat-uh-bohl)* The compatibility of software or hardware to work with earlier versions of the same software or hardware. See also *backward compatible.* "WordPerfect 7.0 is *downward compatible* with WordPerfect 5.1. This means that any files we created with WordPerfect 5.1 can still be used with WordPerfect 7.0. This is good news only if you plan on using WordPerfect until you die."

dpi *(dee pee eye)* Acronym for *dots per inch.* See *dots per inch.*

DPMI *(dee pee em eye)* Acronym for DOS Protected Mode Interface, a standard by which DOS programs can run under Windows. See also *protected mode, real mode.* "Boy, without this *DPMI,* I couldn't use my DOS programs in Windows. Of course, that makes you wonder why I have Windows in the first place if I'm still running DOS programs."

DPMS *(dee pee em ess)* Acronym for Display Power Management Signaling, a standard that reduces power to computer monitors when they're not in use. See also *Energy Star.* "My monitor uses *DPMS,* so if I don't touch the keyboard or mouse after a few minutes, the computer reduces the power to my monitor, thereby reducing my electricity bill. Bob's monitor doesn't use DPMS, so his computer wastes electricity, and the company takes this extra cost out of Bob's paycheck every week."

DR DOS *(dee ar daws;* not *dok-tor daws)* An alternative to MS-DOS that was released way too late by Digital Research and later bought by Novell. DR DOS showed lots of promise, but wasn't widely available. It's version 5.0, which was the first version of DOS to offer true memory management. It got Microsoft off its duff to produce the wildly successful MS-DOS 5.0. (For this we can thank DR DOS, but not for much else.) "Brad hates Microsoft so much that he uses only *DR DOS* and other non-Microsoft products."

drag *(drayg)* To move an onscreen object with the mouse. First, you have to highlight (select) the object you want by pointing to it with the mouse. Then hold down the mouse button and move the mouse. This drags the object around. "Moving things around on the screen with a mouse is such a *drag.*"

drag and drop *(drayg and drop)* Moving an object across the screen as a command. For example, you use a mouse to drag a document into a printer icon. This action prints the document. "My teacher asked whether my computer has *drag and drop.* I said yes; when I don't like the computer, I drag it across the table and drop it out the window."

DRAM *(dee-ram)* Acronym for *Dynamic Random-Access Memory.* Computers can use two types of RAM chips: DRAM and SRAM. DRAM chips are less expensive because the computer periodically has

to put the information back into the DRAM chips or else the DRAM chips forget. See also *RAM.* "The older humans get, the more their brain cells must be replaced with *DRAM* chips."

draw program *(draw proh-gram)* Software that lets you create graphical objects on the screen, such as lines, boxes, and circles. This differs from a Paint program, which doesn't draw objects but rather paints a picture, as you would do with crayons. With a draw program, you can go back and alter objects after they're done and not disturb other parts of the drawing. "I use a *draw program* to illustrate advanced technical journals, but all my trees still look like lollipops."

DRDRAM *(dee-ar-dram)* Acronym for Direct Rambus DRAM.

Drive A *(driev ay)* The personal computer's first floppy disk drive.

3½ Floppy (A:)
There goes Drive A.

Drive C *(driev see)* Your personal computer's main hard disk drive. Your computer may also have other drives, such as a drive D.

(C:)
Drive C.

drive list box *(driev list boks)* A list that shows disk drives on the computer. Often seen in a dialog box, where cruising between various disk drives is optional. The drive list box lets you decide on which drive to save a file. "My *drive list box* contains all drive letters A through Z plus four-wheel drive."

driver *(dry-ver)* A program that gives a device (such as a printer or disk drive, for example)

D

direction on how to work. The driver, as well as the peripheral, must be activated within the Extensions folder.

DriveSpace *(driev-spays)* A disk compression program developed by Microsoft, available on MS-DOS Versions 6.22 or later and Windows 95. Originally called DoubleSpace, but changed because of bad press, DriveSpace allows you to store more information on a hard drive. It does this by compressing files as they're saved to disk and then decompressing files as they're read from disk. The result isn't known to you, though your computer moves slower and you can store more information on a disk. It's a solution, though not the best one, for someone who's running out of disk space. "The best advice is to avoid *DriveSpace* and just buy a larger hard drive instead."

drop-down list box *(drawp-down list boks)* A dialog box gadget that contains a list of items as well as an input box in which you can type your own item. "Og like use *drop-down list box.* It give Og option of typing name or choosing from list. Og happy."

Drop Folder *(drop fohl-der)* A shared network folder in which users can place files or folders. The only people allowed inside are those with access privileges.

drum *(drum)* 1. An old type of computer storage, shaped like a drum with magnetic information read from and written to the outside of the drum. 2. The toner container on a laser printer.

DS/DD *(dee ess dee dee)* Abbreviation for double-sided/double-density, a popular standard for the old 5¼-inch disks. See also *double-density disk, HD.* "DS/DD

disks are the Geritol of computer disk formats."

D-shell connectors *(dee-shel kon-ek-toors)* A cable attachment that can be plugged in only one way. D-shell connectors are shaped like the letter *D,* flat but with one side longer than the other. "You have to match up the short and long sides of the *D-shell connectors* with their plug."

DSL *(dee ess el)* Acronym for Digital Subscriber Line, one of several high-speed methods of Internet access. It requires a special DSL modem, connection to the local phone office. and, of course, money.

DSP *(dee ess pee)* Acronym for digital signal processor. See *digital signal processor.*

DTE *(dee tee ee)* Acronym for data terminal equipment, which includes terminals, computers, modems, and other stuff.

DTP *(dee tee pee)* Acronym for desktop publishing; see *desktop publishing.*

DTR *(dee tee ar)* 1. Acronym for *Data Terminal Ready,* a signal used by a computer to tell its modem that it's ready to start receiving information. "It's definitely not true that female computers take longer to turn on their *DTR* light." 2. The light representing the DTR signal on an external modem.

dual boot *(doo-ahl boot).* A computer configuration that can start two different operating systems. See also *multiple boot.*

dumb terminal *(dum ter-min-al)* A unit consisting of a keyboard and a video display connected to another computer via a network cable. Dumb terminals don't have disk drives or their own processors, so they can't store files or do anything else on their own. Personal computers, on the other hand, can act as autonomous units that can be networked together. "Ray thought that putting the pointed cap on his PC would make it into a *dumb terminal.*"

dump *(dump)* 1. To copy information from one location to another without regard for its appearance or format. Often used for printing information that is temporarily useful. "I told my wife that I was in the middle of a screen *dump,* and she reminded me to wipe afterward." 2. What a larger computer does after a crash. This type of dump (also called a core dump) allows the system engineers to review the computer's contents to help look for bugs — which they never do.

duplex *(doo-pleks)* Telecommunications describing how signals are sent and how characters appear on the screen when you're communicating with a modem. *Full duplex* means that you send characters to the other computer, and everything you see on the screen comes from the other computer. This process is also know as *no echo. Half duplex* means that the characters you type appear on your screen directly, also known as *local echo.* "When you don't see the stuff you're typing, switch on half *duplex.* Or turn on your monitor, if you're *really* new at this."

duplicate *(doo-plee-kayt)* To make an exact copy of a folder or file that is already in existence. This process can be performed only if the original software is found within the computer or in any of the peripherals that are connected.

dust cover *(dust kuh-ver)* A plastic gown that fits snugly over your computer to keep the dust off. Used typically by people who don't use their computer often or those who are anal about dust. P.S. Don't ever use a dust cover while your computer is on. It'll get way too hot in there. "My wife was so worried about keeping the house clean that she put a *dust cover* on the computer, all our furniture, and even our cat. I'm encouraging her to go to counseling."

DVD *(dee vee dee)* 1. Acronym for *d*igital *v*ersatile *d*isk. A high-speed type of CD-ROM that holds lots of information — more than 4 gigabytes as opposed to the 600 megabytes of a traditional CD. Some versions of DVD may eventually hold 17 megabytes of information. 2. An acronym for digital video disk, which is essentially the same thing as a *d*igital *v*ersatile *d*isk, but used in the home as a replacement for the VCR. You can watch movies on computers that have DVD drives, although not much software is available on DVD. Some computers use DVD-RAM drives for backup (see the next entry).

DVD-RAM *(dee-vee-dee ram)* A version of the DVD drive and disk that can be both read from and written to. DVD-RAMs can store 2.6 gigabytes of information, or 5.2 gigabytes on a double-sided disk.

Dvorak keyboard *(duh-vor-ak kee-bord)* A specially designed keyboard that organizes keys for maximum typing efficiency. Although they're known to be more efficient than current keyboards, hardly anyone uses them, which isn't very efficient. (See also *keyboard, QWERTY.*) "The *Dvorak keyboard* is the Esperanto of computer keyboards."

D

dweeb *(dweeb)* A person who may be technically competent but is socially a jerk whom no one wants to hang around with after work. "Bob would make a great manager if he wasn't such a *dweeb*."

DWIM *(dwim;* rhymes with *swim)* Acronym for "*do w*hat *I m*ean" (not what I say). Often used when people want the computer to read their minds and ignore the commands they're typing. "I saw a father using *DWIM* on his daughter when he told her not to smoke, while he was puffing on a cigar and blowing smoke in her face."

DXF *(dee eks ef)* Acronym for Drawing Interchange Format, a graphics file format for exchanging files between different programs. Originally developed for use with the AutoCAD drawing program. "If only Ralph would save his stuff in *DXF* format, we all could see his cool outer space drawings."

dynamic *(die-nam-ik)* Something that is flexible as opposed to something that cannot be moved or relocated (which is static). "Bob is so *dynamic* that he should be carved out of marble."

dynamic allocation *(die-nam-ik owl-oh-kay-shun)* The storage of information in the computer's memory (the *heap*) while the program is running. Unless you plan on writing your own programs, you can safely ignore this definition. See also *static*. "The desk clerk told the three televangelists to go into halls A, B, and C. This I call *dynamic allocation* for salvation."

 dynamic IP address *(die-nam-ik ie-pee uh-dress)* A different Internet address assigned each time you call your Internet Service Provider. This configuration option for many dialer programs allows the Internet provider to give you a unique ID each time you call, as opposed to the same ID (which is known as a static address).

dynamic RAM *(die-nam-ik ram)* Dynamic random access memory. See *DRAM*.

E

e *(ee)* A prefix used to indicate anything of an electronic nature or some type of Internet activity. For example, *e-mail* is *electronic* mail.

E: *(ee koh-lon)* A drive letter designation for any of a number of different types of disk drives in a PC system. It could be a hard drive, CD-ROM drive, removable drive, RAM drive, scenic drive, sex drive, or any of a number of various drives available on the PC.

 e-bay See *eBay*.

 eBay *(ee-bay)* The name of the largest and most popular auction site on the Internet. It's at www.ebay.com. We're not sure where they got the name eBay, though it began as a resource for Internet users to trade Pez dispensers.

eBay in action!

EBCDIC *(ee bee see dee eye see)* Acronym for Extended Binary Coded Decimal Interchange Code. A way of representing characters on a computer. Some mainframes use EBCDIC. Most microcomputers use ASCII. See also *ASCII.* "IBM tried to get everyone to follow the *EBCDIC* standard, but everyone else followed the ASCII standard instead. In the computer biz, 'standard' should refer to a flag."

 e-business *(ee biz-nes)* The electronic economy. Any company on the Internet is said to be in e-business.

echo *(ek-oh)* 1. A command used in online communications that determines whether your software displays the characters you type. If you can't see what you're typing, echo is said to be off; turning echo on allows you to see your typing. If you see double words, such as *tthhiiss,* you have to turn echo off. See also *duplex.* 2. An operating system command that displays text on the screen. The ECHO OFF command in a DOS batch file keeps the computer from displaying commands on the screen.) "Do I hear an *echo* hear an *echo* hear an *echo*?"

ECP/EPP *(ee-see-pee ee-pee-pee)* Acronym for Enhanced Capabilities Port/Enhanced Parallel Port. It's a type of super printer port. Whoop-tee-doo. "My new computer came with an *ECP/EPP,* and it can do many wondrous and amazing things, though I only use it to plug in my printer."

ED *(ee dee)* 1. Nickname for any of a number of popular text editor programs. 2. Acronym for *extended density,* a type of disk drive standard that never really caught on. A 3½-inch ED disk can store 2.88 megabytes of information. "Joel uses his *ED* disks as coasters. They certainly serve him better as a conversation piece than they ever did in any disk drive."

EDI See *Electronic Data Interchange.*

edit *(ed-it)* 1. To modify, change, or update data. The stuff that's edited can be text, graphics, a program's source code, or any computer information. "Jeff's idea of a good *edit* is to run the spell checker on his stuff." 2. The name of any of a number of popular text-editing programs.

edit menu *(ed-it men-yoo)* A menu that lists a program's editing commands (such as copy, cut, and paste).

editor *(ed-it-er)* A program specifically designed for modifying, changing, or updating files. The two types of editors are line editors and full-screen editors. A *line editor* lets you change one line at a time, such as DOS's old EDLIN or UNIX's ed. A *full-screen editor* lets you change multiple lines that appear on the screen, such as the PC-DOS E editor or the Notepad editor in Windows. Word processors, such as WordPerfect and Word for Windows, are much more sophisticated than simple editors. But sometimes an editor is all you need, especially if you are using it to edit programming code. "I have several *editors* on my computer, but QEdit is my editor-in-chief."

EDLIN *(ed-lin)* 1. A line editor that came with MS-DOS Versions 5.0 and earlier. EDLIN was pretty much a useless program that nobody except the most nerdy people used. MS-DOS Version 6.0 and later no longer include EDLIN. "With MS-DOS Version 6.2, *EDLIN* is finally dead(lin)." 2. Used for comparison with any silly or stupid program. "Jenkins, your new modem program is a dumb as *EDLIN.*"

EDO RAM *(ee-doh ram)* 1. Acronym for Extended Data Out Random Access Memory, a type of memory that's much faster, lowfat, low cholesterol, and just plain better than normal RAM, especially on Pentium computers. 2. A ruminant from ancient Tokyo. In this instance, it would be pronounced "ed-oh ram."

educational software *(ed-yoo-kay-shun-al soft-waer)* One of many kinds of software programs designed to teach, train, or instruct. Most people figure that educational software is geared toward children; however, some educational programs are designed to teach adults; for example, typing tutors, musical trainers, and foreign language software. "It's always recommended that you check software reviews before buying *educational software* because a lot of it is really stupid."

edutainment *(ed-yoo-tayn-ment)* A combination of *edu*cation and enter*tainment.* Often refers to software programs. Edutainment has grown out of trying to meet two different needs. Software needs to be entertaining, or else the kids won't like it. It also needs to be educational, or else the parents won't like it. See also *infotainment,* which is another attempt to concatenate two unrelated words. And see *concatenate* while you're at it.

EEPROM *(ee-prom)* Acronym for Electronically Erasable Programmable Read-Only Memory, a special computer chip that can be reprogrammed through electrical signals. EEPROM chips are like ROM chips in that they contain instructions for the computer. And they're like RAM chips in that their contents can be changed; unlike RAM chips, though, EEPROMS don't lose information when the power goes off. See also *PROM.* "Computer guys take their high school gals to the *EEPROM* every May."

EGA *(ee jee ay)* Acronym for Enhanced Graphics Adapter, a graphics standard once used for IBM computers and now remembered solely by trivia buffs. EGA followed the initial CGA standard and was eventually replaced by the VGA and SVGA standards. See also *CGA, SVGA, VGA.* "*EGA* graphics were 'hot stuff' when Ronald Reagan was President."

egrep *(ee-grep)* The *extended grep* command, found on many UNIX systems. See also *grep.*

EIEIO *(ee ie ee ie oh)* 1. Nonsensical but rhythmic phrase used by farmers when they forget the rest of the words to a song. "Old McDonald had a farm, *EIEIO!*" 2. Probably an acronym for something.

EISA *(ee-suh)* Acronym for *Extended Industry Standard Architecture.* EISA was an attempt to expand on the ISA standard while competing with the MCA (MicroChannel) standard. Today, both EISA and MCA are dead, and the ancient ISA standard remains — a triumph for antique technology! See also *bus, ISA, MCA.* "I don't care if it's an *EISA* bus, does it go to Altoona?"

eject *(ee-jekt)* 1. To remove a disk from a disk drive. "He's looking for the data. No. No. No! It can't be found! That disk is out of here. *Eject! Eject! Eject!*" 2. The command that ejects a disk from a disk drive.

Electronic Data Interchange *(ee-lek-tron-ik day-tuh in-ter-chanj)* A method by which businesses exchange standardized documents. This way, different companies can exchange documents without having to use complex and unusual file formats.

 electronic mail *(ee-lek-tron-ik mayel)* 1. Messages created, sent, and read completely on computers without ever being printed on paper. Electronic mail usually involves sending messages to other users on some kind of network, either a local network or the Internet. "With rising postal rates, it's cheaper to use a computer to send *e-mail* than to use an envelope and a stamp. Of course, you have to buy a computer first." 2. The program that is used to create electronic mail.

electronic signatures *(ee-lek-tron-ik sig-nah-choors)* See *signature.*

electrostatic discharge *(ee-lek-troh-stat-ik dis-charj)* Also known as ESD, a small burst of electricity. For example, when you generate your own static electricity, touching a grounded piece of metal produces an electrostatic discharge. ESD can be deadly to RAM chips, for example. All computer equipment, however, is designed to deal with a certain amount of ESD. Anything over that amount could damage the computer's innards.

E

elevator box *(el-uh-vay-ter boks)* See *scroll box.*

elite *(ee-leet)* Typefaces that print as 12 characters per inch. Left over from the typewriter days, elite often appears on printers as one of many choices to make for printing documents. (On a computer, the Courier font at 10 points tall approximates the old typewriter elite.) See also *pica.* "There is no such thing as an *elite* font on a computer. If you want to use characters that tiny, select a font at 10 points."

ELIZA *(ee-lie-za)* A famous artificial intelligence program that mimicked a psychotherapist. Users typed their problems into the computer, and ELIZA parroted back empty phrases to give the appearance of deep thought (and then billed them $200 an hour). See also *artificial intelligence.* "Whenever Sondra is feeling down, she just loads *ELIZA* on her computer and talks to it. Right now, her biggest problem is that she talks only to her computer instead of to people."

ellipsis *(ee-lips-eez)* Three tiny dots (. . .) that appear next to commands on pull-down menus. When an ellipsis appears next to a command, you know that the program will ask for more information or display a dialog box. "When I finally told Paul what the *ellipsis* means on a pull-down menu, he was relieved. He originally thought that the program wasn't finished and that they'd fill in the rest later."

em dash *(em dash)* A long hyphen. The em-dash is a character used in typesetting that is as wide as the letter *M.* This character is used to add emphasis in

text. The em dash can be approximated by typing two hyphens (such as - -) See also *en dash.* "Here is an example of an *em dash:* 'Don't touch that — oh, well, you have another hand anyway.'"

eMachines *(ee-mah-sheens)* A company that makes computers designed to inexpensively connect to the Internet.

Emacs *(ee-max)* A full-screen text editor common to UNIX and Linux. It stands for Extensible MACro System.

 e-mail *(ee-mayel)* Short for electronic mail. Also spelled with a capital: E-mail. See also *electronic mail.*

 email *(ee-mayel)* Another way to write e-mail or E-mail. Oh, heck, just see *electronic mail.*

 e-mail address *(ee-mayel address)* A person's location in the electronic ether. A name (or sometimes number or code) assigned to a person for receiving e-mail. "Once, I typed the wrong *e-mail address* and sent a love letter to my ex-wife."

embedded object *(em-bed-ed ob-jekt)* A document from one program included in another document, such as an Excel spreadsheet living in the midst of a Word document.

emergency boot disk *(em-ur-jen-see boot disk)* A special disk, usually a floppy, that can be used to start the computer when the hard drive fails to respond. This disk is created by Windows during installation or can be created using a special system program. Usually contains some diagnostic programs to help recover from an emergency.

EMM *(ee em em)* Acronym for *Expanded Memory Manager,* a utility program that creates expanded memory for those few DOS programs that need it. "Our service guy said that *EMM* memory was a white elephant on our PCs. I suppose that EMM stands for Elephant Memory Management."

emoticon *(ee-moht-uh-kon)* A combination of characters inserted into e-mail or newsgroup postings that represent feelings or moods not properly expressed in the message. There are lots of them. There's a whole book full of them, in fact, so we don't go through the pain of repeating them all here (especially the cows). See also :-) (a smiley). "Laurie always puts tons of *emoticons* in her messages, which makes me think that she's utterly manic when she goes online."

EMS *(ee em es)* Acronym for *Expanded Memory Specification,* which is actually short for LIM-EMS, the Lotus-Intel-Microsoft Expanded Memory Specification. EMS defines a specific way for older PCs to use more than 640K of memory. Originally developed for Lotus 1-2-3 users so that they could load huge spreadsheets into memory. See also *expanded memory.*

emulation *(em-yoo-lay-shun)* To mimic the appearance and functionality of a specific piece of hardware or software. Emulation allows cheapie stuff to behave just like the real thing. For example, a no-name printer may offer Epson or Hewlett-Packard LaserJet emulation. Most modems offer Hayes emulation. "David's running Macintosh *emulation* on his IBM PC, which is then running an IBM *emulation* program. Nobody can waste time in a high-tech way like David."

emulator *(em-yoo-lay-ter)* A piece of hardware that performs emulation. Hardware emulators are the cheapest and worst way to tweak the performance of one computer or another. "Don't buy a cheap piece of hardware with an *emulator* on it and expect it to get the work done."

en dash *(en dash)* A hyphen that is the width of the letter *N.* En dashes are used to represent *through,* such as pages 64–98. See also *em dash.* "Here is an example of how to use an *en dash:* 'I stuck my leaf collection between pages 56–64 because that's the only use I could find for my MS-DOS user manual.'"

enable *(en-ay-bol)* 1. To activate a command or piece of hardware. 2. A command that is available for use, as opposed to a disabled or dimmed command.

Encapsulated PostScript file See *EPS.*

encryption *(en-krip-shun)* 1. The scrambling of information with a code or password so that other people can't read it. Often used to protect sensitive files, electronic mail, or legal documents so that the general public can't understand what they really mean. See also *Data Encryption Standard.* "Sorry, Josh, most of the laws in the state constitution are not written with *encryption;* that's just the way lawyers talk." 2. Available on OS9, keeps your files and information safe when transferring them over the Internet.

E

End key *(end kee)* The key on the keyboard with *End* printed on it. (What a remarkable coincidence!) It is often a neighbor of the Delete key or living with the number 1. "The *End key* usually moves the cursor to the end of the line. It does not "end" online communications or stop any program."

end user *(end yoo-zer)* 1. You! 2. The person who winds up using a computer or program that someone else designed. See also *programmer.* "The person who ends up reading this book is not called the *end user.* He or she is called the reader."

end-of-file *(end-of-fiel)* Sometimes abbreviated as *EOF,* this special character marks the end of a file. In MS-DOS, Control-Z is the end-of-file character. Usually, the marker is placed automatically by whatever software created the file. "The *end-of-file* marker is like the caboose on the train: It's the last thing in the file."

endless loop *(end-less loop)* 1. A set of instructions in a program that repeats over and over without any chance of ever stopping. 2. See definition 1. See also *infinite loop, loop.* "I think I'm stuck in an *endless loop.* I think I'm stuck in an *endless loop.* I think I'm stuck in an *endless loop.* I think I'm stuck in an *endless loop.* I think I'm stuck in an *endless loop.*"

Energy Saver *(en-ur-jee say-vur)* A function that lets the user schedule sleep or a shutdown whenever the computer is idle for half an hour or more. A startup and separate display sleep option are also given.

Energy Star *(en-ur-jee star)* A standard developed by the Environmental Protection Agency to designate computer equipment that will reduce

The Energy Star logo.

power when not being used. For example, an Energy Star monitor requires less electricity if the user doesn't touch the mouse or keyboard after a certain length of time. Energy Star monitors must consume less than 30 watts of power when not in use. See also *ACPI.* "Besides eating vegetables and refraining from hurting helpless animals, I buy only *Energy Star* equipment so that my computer doesn't waste electricity."

enhanced IDE *(en-hanst eye dee ee)* See *IDE.*

enhanced keyboard *(en-hanst kee-bord)* See *101-key keyboard.*

Enhanced Small Device Interface See *ESDI.*

ENIAC *(ee-nee-ak)* Acronym for *Electronic Numerical Integrator And Calculator,* the name of an early computer built from vacuum tubes in the 1940s. Its job was to calculate artillery ballistic tables for World War II and after. See also *ABC, vacuum tube.* "In the computer museum, we saw a model of the *ENIAC* that took up a whole room and did as much useful work as those freebie solar-powered calculators the bank gives away."

E-notation *(ee noh-tay-shun)* Short for exponential notation, a way that scientists express large and small numbers without burdening the computer's zero key. For example, 1.0E6 is E-notation for one million, and 1.0E100 is E-notation for a googolplex. "*E-notation* is the kind of weird stuff that makes you thankful that you only have to put up with WordPerfect."

Enter key *(en-ter kee)* 1. A keyboard key named Enter. 2. Often used to signal the computer that you're done typing a command; only after you press the Enter key is your text sent to the computer for rumination. 3. Used to end a line of text in a text editor. 4. Ends a paragraph of text in a word processor. 5. Also called the *Return key.* "The *Enter key* comes from the computer's calculator past. The Return key comes from the computer's typewriter past."

enum See *enumeration.*

enumeration *(ee-noo-mer-ay-shun)* Counting or listing one by one.

environment *(en-vie-ron-ment)* A storage place where the operating system keeps track of various system and user settings. Items are placed into the environment using special startup commands. The operating system then examines the items in the environment to configure the computer, customizing it for the user and any special hardware. The environment is used on UNIX, Linux, DOS, OS/2, and Windows computers.

environment variable *(en-vie-ron-ment var-ee-uh-bol)* An item in the computer's environment. The variable identifies an item in the environment, and the variable's contents determine how the computer configures itself. For example, the TEMP variable may indicate the location of temporary files on disk.

EOF *(ee oh ef)* See *end-of-file.*

EOL *(ee oh el)* 1. Abbreviation for *end-of-line,* as in the end of a line of text on the screen. 2. The EOL character, usually produced by pressing the Enter or Return key. "Okay, buddy. It's the *EOL* for you." (Quote overheard between two computer nerds, fighting for control of the only working computer left in the office.)

EOR *(ee oh ar)* An abbreviation for the logical exclusive OR operation. See *XOR.*

EPA *(ee pee ay)* Acronym for Environmental Protection Agency, a government agency dedicated to protecting us from ourselves. The EPA guards the country from the predatory nature of other government agencies and their allies. "New orders from the *EPA:* Have Paul Bunyan brought in and shot."

epoch *(ep-ik)* The exact date a computer's time clock uses as 0. The time clock then starts counting seconds from that date. For example, a Macintosh's epoch begins on January 1, 1904. That's date-and-time zero as far as the Mac is concerned.

EPROM *(ee-prom)* Acronym for *Erasable Programmable Read-Only Memory,* a type of chip that can be erased by ultraviolet lights. An EPROM is like a ROM chip in that it contains instructions for the computer. Like a RAM chip, an EPROM can be written to; however, you need an ultraviolet light to erase an EPROM chip. See also *EEPROM, PROM.*

EPS *(ee pee es)* Acronym for *Encapsulated PostScript,* a graphics image stored using instructions written in the PostScript page-description language. EPS graphics files are actually long, complex text files. The text contains instructions on how to draw the

E

image. Most expensive desktop publishing and illustration programs can handle EPS files. Unfortunately, most people can't afford these expensive programs and wind up storing files in other formats instead. See also *PostScript.* "Brian stored all his graphics as *EPS* files. Now he's desperately searching for a PostScript laser printer or a typesetting machine so that he can print them."

erase *(ee-rays)* 1. To remove a file from a disk. 2. An operating system command that removes files. See also *delete.* "Make sure that you don't *erase* your files, unless you're sure that you don't need them anymore."

ergonomics *(urg-oh-nom-iks)* The science of designing equipment for maximum human comfort and minimal possibility of lawsuits in the future. Some people get *carpal tunnel syndrome* or *RSI* (repetitive strain injury) from improper positioning of their wrists when they type or from working at computers too long without breaks. Ergonomics involves the study of how to prevent these (and other) problems from poorly designed equipment in the workplace. So tell your boss that you need a better chair and more breaks! "My whole computer desk uses *ergonomics* to hold the monitor at the optimum height and distance from my eyes. Because I liked it so much, I replaced my computer with a TV, and now I just vegetate in comfort at my desk."

Error-free protocol *(ayr-or-free proh-toe-kal)* A method of confirming that information received is identical to what was sent. For example, the receiver of a chunk of info sends a special summarized bit of info back to the sender to confirm that the chunk matches. If not, the chunk is re-sent until it's received

properly. Some examples are the early XMODEM and ZMODEM file transfer utilities used on the Internet.

error message *(ayr-or mes-idj)* A cryptic note that the computer displays to let you know that the program isn't working right or that you've really screwed up. If you're lucky, the manual will tell you what on earth the message means, and, if you're really lucky, the computer won't beep rudely at you. "I think I've seen every *error message* this computer can display."

Esc *(es-kayp)* 1. Abbreviation for Escape, often found on the Escape key. 2. The Esc key is often used to cancel a command. Pressing the key is the same as choosing a Cancel button in a dialog box. "I wonder whether the Air Force has an *Esc* key for launching nuclear missiles?" 3. In some instances, pressing the Esc key changes editing modes. 4. ASCII code 27. See *ASCII.*

ESDI *(ee es dee ie; ez-dee)* Acronym for *Enhanced Small Device Interface,* once an interface standard for hard disks. See also *IDE.*

etc *(et-see;* not *et-set-uh-rah)* A directory on a UNIX computer where various and sundry files are kept. "Jerry had all the UNIX gurus fooled until he slipped up and called the *etc* directory 'et cetera.'"

Ethernet *(ee-ther-net)* A Local Area Network standard that uses radio frequency signals carried by coaxial cables or twisted-pair cable. Developed primarily by Xerox. See also *LAN.* "Our computers are connected through an *Ethernet.* That doesn't mean that we know what we're doing — it just means that we have the lingo down pat."

E

e-ticket *(ee tik-et)* An electronic ticket, one that exists only in the computer and not in the real world. For example, getting an e-ticket to fly on an airplane requires that you merely purchase the ticket; no paper ticket is ever issued. Showing up at the airport, you get a boarding pass, but never a true ticket, for the flight. "I'm a big fan of e-tickets, but I still keep a paper receipt. I don't trust computers *that* much."

 etiquette *(et-uh-kit)* The rules and regulations of proper behavior. E-mail has rules of etiquette for proper written behavior to keep everyone in line. "Kristin didn't know that typing everything LIKE THIS MADE IT APPEAR THAT SHE WAS YELLING. She needed a lesson in e-mail *etiquette*."

EULA *(yoo-lah)* Acronym for *end-user license agreement*, the secret legal code, included with every software product, that tells you that anything bad which happens is not the developer's fault and that you don't really own the software — you're merely using it. This is somewhat of a contradiction because the owner should always be responsible. But attorneys have shown us over time that, in fact, it's the person with the most money who's ultimately responsible in the end.

event *(ee-vent)* Something that happens in the computer. Some activity or action that takes place, which a program can act on. For example: a keypress, a certain time, and a click of the mouse are all types of events.

event-driven programming *(ee-vent-driv-en pro-gram-ing)* A style of writing programs that waits for the user to press a key or a mouse button before doing anything else. When the user presses a key or mouse, it's called an *event*. "You could say that CNN has *event-driven programming*."

Excite! *(eks-iet)* A Web portal that contains news, weather, sports, stocks, a search engine, and other customizable content. The address is www.excite.com.

exclusive OR *(eks-kloo-siv or)* A logical operation performed on the bit values of two different bytes. Often used when displaying graphics on the screen. See also *XOR*. "No, I'm sorry, sir; you're just a regular OR, and this club is for the *exclusive OR* only."

EXE *(ee eks ee)* A file extension identifying a program *(executable)* file for some operating systems. See also *BIN, COM, DOC, extension.*

execute *(eks-uh-kyoot)* 1. To start a program. 2. Performing a task. 3. To put to death, which is what some people would like to do to Windows 95.

exit *(eks-it)* The command that quits a program. The civilized way to end a program; this command makes it quietly go away until the next time you need it. Contrast with *Ctrl+Alt+Del*. See also *quit*. "To quit some programs, you have to choose the *Exit* command. To *exit* other programs, you have to choose the Quit command. And to *exit* still other programs, you must first go through detox."

expand *(eks-pand)* To decompress previously compressed files so that the computer can use them. On IBM computers, most files are compressed using the PKZIP program. On Macintosh computers, most files are compressed using the StuffIt program. See also *compression, data compression, explode, ZIP.*

E

WinZip is becoming the compression/decompression tool of choice in the Wintel world. "I told Amanda to *expand* her files, so she put them on a high-fat diet."

expanded memory *(eks-pan-ded mem-oh-ree)* Extra memory available to older DOS programs. Expanded memory was DOS memory available in addition to the basic 640K. Sometimes called EMS or LIM-EMS. Expanded memory is not memory "above" the 1MB mark on a PC. It's more like "beside" it because data is swapped quickly into and out of a small region of memory in the computer. See also *EMS, extended memory, XMS.* "Lotus helped develop *expanded memory* so that people could load large 1-2-3 spreadsheets into memory."

expansion bus *(eks-pan-shun bus)* The part of the computer's bus that enables you to plug in boards to give your computer more features. Nearly every computer sold these days has an expansion bus. See also *bus, expansion card, expansion slot.* "The *expansion bus* didn't make the turn and knocked down a fireplug."

expansion card *(eks-pan-shun kard)* A circuit board designed to plug into a computer's expansion bus. Expansion cards usually give a computer more memory, an internal modem, or some other whiz-bang capability that the computer didn't naturally come with by itself. See also *expansion bus, expansion slot.* "I just can't keep my poker face when I'm dealt a fancy new *expansion card.*"

expansion slot *(eks-pan-shun slot)* The physical opening in a computer's expansion bus into which expansion cards plug. "When you go to Las Vegas, be

sure to play the *expansion slot.* Maybe you'll win a new Dodge Viper."

Expedia *(eks-pee-dee-uh)* An online travel site, www.expedia.com.

expert system *(eks-pert sis-tum)* A program that mimics the intelligence of a human expert in a specific field of knowledge, such as mining or medicine. The expert system includes a knowledge base of information that has been gathered from an expert along with a set of rules for processing the information. Expert systems ask users questions and reach conclusions that are hopefully similar in quality to those that a human expert may reach. See also *artificial intelligence.* "Hey, honey, why don't we let the *expert system* choose our wine for dinner tonight?"

explode *(eks-plohd)* 1. Another term for decompressing previously compressed files. Rather than tell you that they are expanding a file, some programs tell you that they're exploding them. See also *compression, data compression, expand, ZIP.* "Some compressed files are packed in so tight that you must *explode* them to get the data out. Please wear the proper safety attire before attempting this on your own computer." 2. What any number of computers used to do in 1960s TV shows, specifically those produced by Irwin Allen.

 Explorer *(eks-plor-er)* 1. Short for Microsoft Explorer, the file-management program starting with Windows 95. 2. Short for Internet Explorer, the Microsoft Web browser software. See also *Internet Explorer.*

exponential notation *(eks-poh-nen-shal noh-tay-shun)* See *e-notation.*

extended ASCII *(eks-ten-ded ass-kee)*
Character codes 128 through 255.
Normal ASCII codes only characters 0
through 127. However, a byte on a PC
has 255 possible bit combinations,
which makes room for 128 more characters than the standard ASCII set. To fill
in the remaining 128 characters, someone dreamt up extended ASCII codes.
The extended codes include the normal
128 ASCII character codes plus foreign
language, mathematical, and block
graphic characters. Another improvement of a "standard" that defeats the
meaning of having standards in the first
place.

extended memory *(eks-ten-ded mem-oh-
ree)* Memory above the 1-megabyte
mark. This includes all memory on an
Intel 80286 or later miroprocessor.
Extended memory can be used only by
high-power programs or by operating
systems, such as Windows, OS/2, or
UNIX. See also *XMS.* "My PC has 976MB
of *extended memory,* barely enough to
run Windows 95."

extended memory specification *(eks-
ten-ded mem-oh-ree spes-if-uh-kay-shun)*
Sometimes abbreviated as XMS, a set of
rules for programs to access extended
memory. See also *XMS.* "You think that
they could have come up with a name
other than *extended memory specification.* See how close it sounds to expanded memory specification? But who
would expect logic from the computer
industry?"

extended partition *(eks-ten-ded par-ti-
shun)* Under DOS and Windows, a hard
disk partition that is not the primary
(bootable) partition. Most extended partitions are divvied up into drives
D, E, F, and on up. In some cases, the

extended partitions may contain other
operating systems.

extension *(eks-ten-shun)* An optional
addition to an MS-DOS filename, consisting of a period and as many as three
other characters. The extension often
identifies the type of file and which program created it. A Pascal file usually has
the .PAS file extension, a BASIC file has
the .BAS file extension, and backup files
have the .BAK file extension. See also
BIN, COM, DOC, EXE. "My income tax file
needs an *extension.*"

Extensions *(eks-ten-shuns)* Files
that enhance your computer's
capabilities. Extensions must
remain in the Extensions folder within
the System folder for them to work
properly.

Extensions Manager *(eks-ten-
shuns mahn-eh-jur)* Used to turn
software extensions on or off, a
major factor in your computer's performance. When running an application,
see to it that the extension for the
selected program is on. If the extension
is off, a warning appears, indicating that
the application cannot be used.

external hard drive
*(eks-turn-al hard
driev)* A hard drive
that lives outside the
computer box. The
hard drive has its own
little house, with a
cable connecting it to the computer and
a power cable plugging it into the wall.
Oh, and a blinking light. Very important,
those blinking lights. External hard
drives are most often SCSI hard drives,
though USB, FireWire, and other types
of drives also exist. They're more

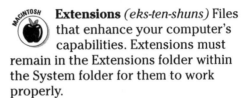

*The lonely external
hard drive.*

E

expensive than internal drives because, in addition to the drive, you pay for the drive's house and power supply.

external modem *(eks-turn-al moh-dum)* A modem that lives in its own box and is physically located outside your computer, as opposed to an internal modem located inside your computer. See also *internal modem.* External modems typically cost more than internal modems because you have to pay for the plastic doohickey the modem sits in. They also junk up your desk with more cables. "It is the desire of all internal modems to one day break free and become *external modems.*"

eyeball frazzle *(ie-bawl fraz-zul)* 1. The unofficial term given to those who read too much information on the World Wide Web. "It was a gruesome sight. Ed had sat at his computer for nine hours straight, reading trivia on the Web. When he finished, he had (gasp!) *eyeball frazzle* (loud scream)!" 2. The condition produced by viewing an ancient CGA display on a PC. Though, unlike the Web, it takes only two-and-a-half minutes to get eyeball frazzle with CGA.

eyeball search *(ie-bawl surch)* To find something merely by looking for it, as opposed to using the computer to search.

e-zine *(ee-zeen)* Any publication distributed in digital form, as in the World Wide Web or electronic mail.

E

F

F: *(ef koh-lon)* A drive letter designation for any of a number of different types of disk drives on a PC system. It could be a hard drive, CD-ROM drive, network drive, removable drive, test drive, RAM drive, overdrive mode, or any of a number of various drives available on the PC.

F-keys *(ef-kees)* See *function keys*.

facing pages *(fay-sing pay-jez)* 1. Two pages of a bound document that face each other when the document is open. Usually the even-numbered page appears on the left; the odd-numbered page appears on the right. "Many cookbooks show the recipe on one side and a picture of what you're supposed to be cooking on the other side. These *facing pages* show you that some of the best fiction writers today are writing cookbooks." 2. The command in desktop publishing and word processing programs that lets you see how two pages look side by side.

factorial *(fak-tor-ee-al)* All the numbers from *1* to a specific number multiplied together. So the factorial of 4 is 4 x 3 x 2 x 1 = 24. The factorial of a number is abbreviated with the exclamation point, such as 4! "The *factorial* of 4 is 24. The *factorial* of 3 is 6. Truly, this must be the most useful bit of information you've read so far."

fail *(fayl)* When something no longer works the way it's supposed to. See also *Abort, Retry, Fail?* "John decided to name his three computers Abort, Retry, and *Fail*."

fail safe *(fayl sayf)* When something is so well designed that it's impossible for anything to go wrong, go wrong, go wrong. . . . "Our computer is absolutely *fail safe*. But that's only because we never bother turning it on."

failure *(fayl-yoor)* When something goes wrong, it's usually something labeled as fail safe. See also *fail, fail safe*. "We had a hard disk *failure* that wiped out all the company's data. I swear that this had nothing to do with my employment hearing."

 fair use *(fayr yoos)* A legal term relating to copyrighted material. You can use copyrighted material for your own personal use, but you can't use it in anything that will be sold or used for advertising. This term specifically applies to Web pages on the Internet. "To my children, *fair use* means being able to grab any toy from any other child."

fanfold paper *(fan-fohld pay-per)* Paper connected together with perforations and folded neatly in a stack, usually designed for tractor-feed printers. Also called *continuous paper*. "*Fanfold paper* looks a lot like toilet paper but with holes along the sides as well. But don't use it as toilet paper because it's not nearly as soft and cushy as the real thing."

 FAQ *(fak)* 1. Acronym for Frequently Asked Questions. This moniker is used in USENET newsgroups. Often times, people ask the same questions over and over. To satisfy them without repeating lots of information and boring the old-timers, the questions and answers are put into either a FAQ file or a FAQ area of the newsgroup. 2. The actual file or Web page containing the list of frequently asked questions. "Having a *FAQ* allows USENET users to be rude and patronizing toward new members by saying 'It's in the FAQ, you moron!' instead of answering a question."

FAT *(fat)* Acronym for File Allocation Table, a map showing the operating system where files are located on disk. "When the repair guy told Gail, 'Something's corrupted your *FAT*,' she blamed the Chinese Fat-Burning Tea."

 FAT32 *(fat thur-tee-too)* A newer, better, faster, and, yes, fatter version of the original DOS and Windows File Allocation Table; see also *FAT*. The FAT32, introduced with Windows 98, optimizes disk access, improves file storage, and allows for direct access to hard disks with a capacity over 2GB. Most newer Windows 98 computers come with FAT32-formatted hard drives. Older systems must be converted (which is not recommended).

fault tolerance *(fawlt tall-ur-ens)* The ability of hardware or software to continue working despite the fact that all

hell is breaking loose around it. This is accomplished by having backups, multiple copies of information, or several separate systems designed to take over in an emergency.

favorites *(fayv-ohr-its)* The term Microsoft Internet Explorer uses for bookmarks. This term isn't as useful as bookmarks because you may add a Web page to your list of favorites that's more useful or necessary than it is favored. See *bookmark*. "Jason found it odd, adding the humorous recipe for Banana Slug Pie to his list of *favorites*."

fatal error *(fay-tel ayr-or)* A problem that causes a program or computer to halt completely. See *crash*. "No, sticking your tongue into the expansion slot of an active computer would be a *fatal error* for you, not for the computer."

 fatbits *(fat-bits)* Individual pixels greatly magnified on the screen. Most paint programs (including MacPaint) enable you to zoom in on a picture so that you can edit individual pixels, called FatBits because they look so huge. See also *pixel*. "Susan was disgusted when she found out that her MacPaint rendering of a low-cal dinner still had *fatbits*."

fax *(faks)* 1. Short for facsimile copy machine, a device that sends a printed page through the phone lines to another machine that prints a copy. 2. The document received and printed by a fax machine. "Walt has a *fax* machine, call forwarding, call waiting, a beeper, a cellular phone, and an answering machine. And then he spends an extra $100 a year so that he can have an unlisted phone number."

F

fax modem *(faks moh-dum)* A modem that also has the circuitry to send and receive faxes like a fax machine. That's just about any modem today. You need special software to run the modem in fax mode. "For heaven's sake, don't try using the Windows 95 *fax modem* software!"

FCB *(ef see bee)* See *file control block.*

FCC *(ef see see)* Acronym for Federal Communications Commission, a U.S. government agency that regulates all equipment (including computers) that produces radio-frequency signals. See also *Class A/Class B.* "My computer has an *FCC* Class B rating, which means that it doesn't interfere with radio signals, but it sure interferes with my mental signals."

FDISK *(ef-disk)* The program that prepares and partitions a PC's hard drive. FDISK, or a similar program, is required to configure a hard drive before it can be formatted and an operating system installed.

featuritis *(fee-choor-ie-tus)* The steady increase of program features that 90 percent of the people in the world will never use. Software companies often get carried away and brag about features their programs offer that no other programs have. Naturally, these same companies never stop to question whether anyone really needs these features that they're advertising. "I stopped buying WordPerfect, Microsoft Word, and Lotus 1-2-3 because they had creeping *featuritis.* Now I'm back to using a pad of paper, a pencil, and an adding machine."

feed *(feed)* To shove paper into a printer. "*Feed* the paper into the printer. Just make sure that you don't *feed* your tie into the printer at the same time."

feed line *(feed line)* 1. Connects the antenna to the receiver in a wireless communications system. 2. The mob of people waiting for the cafeteria to dish up some yummy lunch slop.

female connector *(fee-mayel kon-ek-tor)* A type of plug that consists of one or more holes that a corresponding male connector plugs in to. See also *male connector.* "Yup, with this new *female connector* and *male connector* cable set up, we could put on one heck of a show for the engineering staff."

ferric oxide *(fayr-ik oks-ied)* The magnetic coating that gives hard disks, floppy disks, and tape cassettes their recording capabilities. "If you touch the surface of a floppy disk, you may rub the *ferric oxide* off. Then the disk is ruined, and your fingertips will have a subtle magnetic taste."

 fiber exhaust *(fie-bur eg-zawst)* A term to describe the possibility that the amount of traffic on the Internet may exhaust the amount of bandwidth available to transmit all this information. See also *bandwidth.*

fiber optics *(fie-bur op-tiks)* Thin yiblettes of glass used to carry light signals for communication purposes. One fiber optic cable can replace huge copper cables. Not only do fiber optics take up less space, but they also can carry more information. Fiber optics are very popular for modern LANs because

F

they are less susceptible to radioactivity and other types of interference. Fiber optics also has the potential for providing various types of interactive information services. See also *cable, LAN.* "The phone company wants to replace its copper cables with *fiber optics.* That way, they can send more data faster and hike up the rates."

Fibonacci numbers *(Fib-oh-na-chi numbers)* Some sort of mathematical pattern where the third number is the sum of the previous two numbers: 4, 8, 12, 20, 32, and so on. These are used in some computer programs to speed up sorting and to quickly locate information. Named after Leonardo Fibonacci, a fully employed Italian mathematician from the 13th century.

field *(feeld)* Space reserved for storing specific information in a database program. A fill-in-the-blanks blank. Fields may contain a person's name, address, phone number, age, Social Security number, sex, zip code, or anything else you want, as long as all items in a given field have a similar structure. A group of related fields make up a database record. See also *database, record.* "The database instructions told Ed to put his name into a *field,* so he hopped on the harvester and mowed a giant ED into the corn."

FIFO *(fee-foh)* Acronym for First In, First Out. A term used by programmers to describe a data structure where the first item stored is also the first item retrieved. Unless you plan to write your own programs, you can safely ignore this term. See *LIFO, queue, stack.* "Lines at movie theaters or stadiums all use *FIFO.* The first person in line is the first

person to get in. Unless, of course, everyone charges forward and uses the English soccer fan approach."

fifth-generation computers *(fifth-jen-er-ay-shun kom-pyoo-ters)* A new class of computers that manipulate data more efficiently (with massively parallel processing) and understand written and spoken human language. In 1981, the Japanese announced that they wanted to be the world leaders in building fifth-generation computers. More than 15 years later, the only major Japanese contribution to computers has been Nintendo. See *artificial intelligence.* "*Fifth-generation computers* will be just as smart and unruly as your other employees."

file *(fiel)* 1. The basic chunk of information stored on a computer disk. Files can be programs, text, raw data, or graphics. Text files consist solely of ASCII characters. Binary files consist of data stored in a proprietary manner, such as Lotus 1-2-3 .WK3 files or dBASE IV .DBF files. See also *data.* "I wish that they would have called the information stored on disk 'drawers' rather than *files.* It opens the door to lots more double entendres." 2. A menu listing commands that manipulate files.

file attribute *(fiel at-ri-byoot)* Detailed information about a file used by the operating system. File attributes may make a file hidden or prevent you from deleting it or indicate whether the file has been backed up. Changing a file's attributes does not affect the file's contents but may affect the computer's ability to modify or view the file. See also *file.* "No, Wendy, there is no 'cute' *file attribute.*"

F

file compression *(fiel kom-pres-shun)* To smash (or squish) a file into something smaller so that it takes up less disk space (or less time to transmit). "*File compression* comes in handy if you're running out of disk space or if you're just too lame to erase files you haven't needed since 1981."

file control block *(fiel kon-trol blok)* Often abbreviated as FCB, it's a chunk of memory that contains information about a file used by the operating system or by a programmer — you know, people who would seriously care about such things. "Sid was quickly ditched at the cocktail party when he started asking questions such as 'Then give me a proper reason why the *FCB* shouldn't be located at offset 1A-hex in the PSP header?'"

file conversion *(fiel kon-ver-shun)* To translate one file format into another. See also *import.* "I use Word, but Frank uses WordPerfect. So my documents are useless to Frank until I use a *file conversion* program that translates all my Word files into WordPerfect files."

File Exchange *(fiel ex-chanj)* A software program that opens most DOS and Windows files on a Macintosh. The program MacLink Plus does a better job.

file handle *(fiel han-del)* A number used to identify a file inside a program. Because programmers love numbers, the file handle serves as an open file's ID for reading and writing and eventually closing the file inside the program. Nerdy stuff. "No wonder you keep losing your files! The *file handle* is broken!"

file list box *(fiel list boks)* A display of available files, typically inside a dialog box, from which a specific file can be chosen. "Mildred's *file list box* broke, and now she has files all over her desk."

File menu *(fiel men-yu)* A menu that contains various file settings, such as Open, Save, and Print. The Quit or Exit command is also found there.

The File menu for a Word document.

filename extension *(fiel-naym eks-ten-shun)* The last part of a filename, which is used by Windows to identify the type of file. For example, .BMP means that the file is a Paint graphics image. .DOC indicates a document created in Word. "No, Bob, that *filename extension* you're wearing looks completely natural."

file server *(fiel serv-her)* The big cheese computer on the network. The computer that stores all the users' programs and data files on its own hard disk. Most large networks have at least one file server. File servers are particularly useful for acting as post offices for electronic-mail messages or other applications where users need to share files or send them back and forth. Because the file server spends its time running the network, nobody can use the file server computer to do anything else. See also *electronic mail, network*. "Hi. I'm an IBM 499 TXL, and I will be your *file server* this evening. This is Tad. He's my printer."

file sharing *(fiel shayr-ing)* The ability of more than one computer to access information in a file. File sharing prevents the information from being altered by different computers at one time. If that happens, you have to wait until the file is no longer "busy." Without file sharing, many people could modify the same file at once with potentially disastrous results. "My name is Billy Cartwright, and this is my file, OOBADOOB.DBF. Please, everyone pass it around and take a look at it, but only one of you may make modifications at a time, in accordance with the rules of good *file sharing*."

file size *(fiel siez)* The amount of disk space a file requires for its existence, usually measured in bytes. "You can't copy that file to that disk because the *file size* is 451,092 bytes and the disk has only 46,782 bytes free."

file system *(fiel sis-tem)* The way files are organized on a disk. In Windows, it's the system of storing files in folders, but beneath that it includes all the programming and mechanics of how the files are stored and accessed by the operating system and various programs. The Macintosh also has its own, unique file

system utterly different from Windows. Linux, UNIX, and Novell Netware also have their own file systems.

fill *(fil)* 1. A command used by paint and draw programs that mimics spilling a bucket of paint inside a closed shape, such as a circle or rectangle. If you want to create a black circle, you would first draw an empty circle and then use the Fill command to fill the circle with black. 2. The color used by the Fill command. 3. The spreadsheet that copies values or formats to a group of cells. "Phyl's favorite PC command is *Fill*."

filter *(fil-ter)* 1. A special program that modifies standard output, such as the output of an operating system command. MS-DOS has three filters: MORE, FIND, and SORT. MORE scrolls long output screen by screen, FIND searches for text, and SORT sorts ASCII files. Unless you're a diehard operating system nut, you'll probably never need to know about this type of filter. 2. A method for displaying only certain types of records in a database. For example, displaying only those people who sent you Christmas cards last year. "John, dear boy! Come on in! I was using this new *filter* I bought. It removes all the worthless junk from a file and distills it down to the bare essentials — only the important stuff. Problem is, I ran your documents through the filter, and nothing came out the other end."

find *(fined)* 1. To locate something, such as a bit of text in a document or a file on a disk drive. *Find* is replacing *search* as the word of choice for commands and functions that locate stuff in Windows. See also *search*. 2. The command that finds things. See also *find dialog box*.

find and replace *(fiend and ree-plays)*
A command that locates a bit of data and
changes it to something else. The newfangled term for what everyone used to
call "search and replace." Every word
processor offers a find-and-replace command so that you can quickly change
multiple words or phrases at the touch
of a button. "When Margaret Mitchell
wrote *Gone with the Wind,* she originally
named her heroine Pansy O'Hara. At the
last moment, she changed it to Scarlett
O'Hara. If she had used a word processor, she could have just used the *find
and replace* feature to make the changes
instantly. Instead, some poor editor had
to manually go through each page and
change it all by hand."

find dialog box *(fiend die-a-log boks)*
A special window used to help you
locate text or files. Displayed by the
Find command.

 Finder *(fiend-er)* The part of the
Apple Macintosh operating
system that provides cute little
icons, menus, and windows for copying,
moving, and deleting files. Most
Macintosh programs require a certain
version of the Finder, such as Version
6.02 or Version 7.01, before they will
work. "If it weren't for the *Finder,* the
Macintosh would be as clumsy to use as
MS-DOS. In fact, Microsoft Windows
mimics the Finder, which is why IBM-
compatible computers are finally getting
easier to use."

 Finger *(fin-ger)* 1. A UNIX program that would strive to find
someone through e-mail. The
only problem was that you had to know
which computer system they were using

or their domain. 2. To find someone
using the Finger program. "I fingered
you on the Internet using the *Finger*
command. Isn't that romantic?"

firewall *(fiyer-wal)* A protective barrier
(provided by software) that prevents
others on the Internet from gaining
access to sensitive parts of your computer. The term *fire* may be overkill, but
it stresses the importance of the device.
"They should call the *firewall* a brick
wall, and it should leave a lump on the
head of anyone who tries to break
through."

 FireWire *(fiyer-wiyer)* A super
cable to which you can connect
as many as 63 devices, by daisy-
chaining them together. FireWire, also
known as IEEE 1394, allows for many
peripherals to attach to a single computer, all of which can operate at relatively high speeds. In the future, devices
such as external hard drives, CD-R/RW
drives, DVD and DVD-RAM drives, scanners, digital cameras, videocameras,
and more will use the fast FireWire standard. See *SCSI, serial port, USB.*

firmware *(firm-wayr)* Software embedded into a chip as opposed to being
stored on disk and loaded into memory.
See *ROM.* "Every computer has *firmware*
that tells the computer how to start
itself up. Too bad every person doesn't
have firmware to tell him or her how to
use a computer."

fixed disk *(fiksd disk)* A hard disk. You
can't remove the disk from the computer, hence the name *fixed.* "My hard
drive just came back from the shop, so
now I know it's a *fixed disk.*"

F

fixed pitch *(fiksd pich)* A typeface where all characters are the same width. Computer screens, typewriters, and cheap dot-matrix printers display type using fixed pitch. See *monospacing, proportional pitch.* "Ron came out of the bullpen in the seventh inning to show the hometown his *fixed pitch.*"

fixed-point number *(fiksd-poynt number)* A number where the decimal point displays a specific number of digits to the right. In comparison, floating-point numbers display to the right of the decimal point the number of digits that are needed. "Currency values are usually represented by a *fixed-point number* where only two digits appear to the right of the decimal point, except during times of high inflation."

flag *(flag)* 1. An on–off switch in a program. Used by programmers to check some condition. For example, a flag may be used to keep track of whether certain input has been received from a user and, if it has been received, to display an error message. 2. A bit in the microprocessor's flags register, which reports the results of certain microprocessor operations. "Dorothy wrote a program that she feels is very patriotic: All it does is to raise all the microprocessor's *flags.* Now if she could only program the modem to whistle a salute."

flame *(flaym)* An angry, often nasty, brutal, and unsportsmanlike letter found only in electronic-mail messages. "Ignore any online *flame* that links you to the Nazis or compares you with Adolf Hitler."

flamebait *(flaym bate)* A very strong or opinionated post to a newsgroup or Internet bulletin board with the intention to elicit extreme responses (or flames). "Oh, I see that Steve's posted his weekly *flamebait,* just so he can sit back and laugh while everyone starts yelling."

flame wars *(flaym wars)* An exchange of angry electronic-mail messages, usually between two people who sincerely hope that the other person gets run over by a train as soon as possible. "The first time I got a flame, I ignored it. But the guy pestered me so much that I got into a *flame war* with him. Trust me — it's worse than paintball."

flash memory *(flash mem-oh-ree)* A ROM chip that can be changed through software, without having to replace the entire chip. Also known as *flash programmable BIOS.* "I always thought that *flash memory* was those red spots you see after someone takes a picture of you."

flat-file database *(flat-fiel day-ta-bays)* Information stored in files, records, and fields. This database is more powerful than a freeform database, but the information has to be fairly organized for it to work. See also *relational database.* "I used the *flat-file database* to find a girl who was 5 foot 9 inches tall, curvaceous, from Oklahoma, and a speech major. It worked, and now she's my wife."

flatbed scanner *(flat-bed skan-er)* A device that reads photographs or anything on a sheet of paper and translates it into a graphical file stored inside the computer.

A typical scanner.

Flatbed scanners look like photocopying

machines, but are much slower. "I use my *flatbed scanner* to translate pictures of my goat into files I can post on the Internet."

floating head *(floh-ting hed)* Another term for the mechanism that reads or writes information from a disk. See *head.* "When Johnson told me about my hard drive's *floating head,* I immediately thought of the movie *Zardoz.*"

floating-point coprocessor *(floh-ting poynt ko-pros-es-or)* See *math coprocessor.*

floating-point operation *(flow-ting poynt op-er-ay-shun)* A speed test that measures how fast a computer can do math. "You know that you need a life when you start comparing your *floating-point operation* results with your friends."

floating-point unit *(floh-ting poynt yoo-nit)* Another name for a math coprocessor. Specifically, it's a math coprocessor that's built into a microprocessor, which is what you find in a 486DX or Pentium. See also *math coprocessor.*

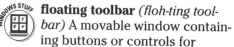 **floating toolbar** *(floh-ting tool-bar)* A movable window containing buttons or controls for manipulating stuff in a program. They "float" over the text, always remaining in front of what you're doing and generally getting in the way. "Vern did a screen dump, and all his *floating toolbars* washed away."

floppy disk *(flah-pee disk)* A removable disk, typically 3½ inches square. The original floppy disk was 8 inches square and truly had a flop to it. Later 5¼-inch models were also slightly floppy, but 3½-inch disks aren't floppy at all, though

they're still called floppy disks. The 3½-inch, high-density 1.44-megabyte floppy disk is the standard for all PCs. "Kay detested her floppy disks being so floppy, so she sprayed them with starch."

A floppy disk. Wow.

floppy drive *(flop-pee driev)* The type of disk drive that eats floppy disks. Drive A on a PC is the floppy drive. Early Macintoshes also

The front of a floppy drive.

sported a floppy drive, though it's now an external option on nearly all Macs.

floptical *(flop-tik-ol)* A trademarked name for a type of disk that uses both magnetic and optical techniques for storing information. Floptical describes both the disk drive and the 3½-inch disk that fits into it. The disk can store megabytes of information, yet it looks similar to the standard, 3½-inch disk. The floptical drive can also read and write to standard 3½-inch disks. See *magneto-optical disk.* "Amazing Marvin has a *floptical* disk. Now he has many more megabytes to store his junk."

flowchart *(floh-chart)* A diagram consisting of lines and boxes that programmers use to represent the way their programs are supposed to work. Programmers who spend their time creating flowcharts have an unusually high propensity for writing fiction, telling fairy tales, and working as double agents for the CIA. "Before you start writing your program, decide how it's going to work by drawing a *flowchart* first. Then, as you write your program,

F

you can modify your *flowchart* so that it matches the way your program really does work."

flow control *(floh kon-trol)* An option specifying whether the XON and XOFF characters (Ctrl+S and Ctrl+Q) can be used to pause and resume the transmission of information. This is one of those options you'll find deeply buried on some communication program's setup menu.

flush *(flush)* 1. To empty out the contents of a data structure or buffer. 2. To align text either flush left or flush right:

```
This is                     This is
an example             an example
of flush                   of flush
left.                           right.
```

See also *justify*. "Kevin insisted that he couldn't *flush* left because the handle was on the right side of the toilet."

folder *(fohl-der)* Another name for a subdirectory. "Bill called 5¼-inch diskettes *folders* because he has to fold them in half to fit them into his 3½-inch disk drive."

font *(fawnt)* 1. A collection of characters with predefined sizes and style. Most word processors and desktop publishing programs let you choose different fonts to make your writing prettier. If you don't like the fonts you have, you can buy more. "When you have nothing important to say, put it in writing and use lots of fancy *fonts*. People will think that it must be important if it looks good." 2. Technically speaking, the word

most computer people use when they refer to a typeface. A font, specifically, is a typeface at a certain size and style. 3. The menu that holds commands to change font information. 4. The command that changes font information.

font cartridge *(fawnt kart-ridj)* A device that gives a printer a new selection of fonts. The cartridge plugs into a printer, giving it the ability to print a greater variety of fonts. These fonts can be accessed more quickly than fonts sent from the computer. See *downloaded font*. "To add more fonts to my laser printer, I had to plug in a *font cartridge*. Then my kid plugged in a Nintendo cartridge, and now my printer just spews out pages of Mario and Luigi."

font family *(fawnt fam-uh-lee)* A group of related fonts, some of which are subtle variations on each other. "This document looks like it was printed with a dysfunctional *font family*."

font size *(fawnt siez)* The height and width of specific fonts, as measured in points. See also *point*. "I told Mark to make the memo easy for our foreign clients to understand, so he just increased the *font size*."

 Font/DA Mover *(fawnt dee-ay moo-ver)* A utility program provided with older versions of the Macintosh operating system that enables users to add fonts and desk accessories to their computers. It's no longer included with System 7. "Since System 7, the *Font/DA Mover* has been moonlighting and was last seen moving pianos."

F

foobar *(foo-bar)* See *fubar.*

footer *(foot-er)* A short title, word, or phrase that appears at the bottom of a page in word processors or desktop publishing programs. "Listen, Bob, if you make that *footer* any bigger, you're going to stub your document's toe."

footprint *(foot-print)* The amount of desk space an object consumes. The smaller the footprint of an object, the less room it takes up on a desk. "My new computer has a small *footprint;* it takes up only about two feet of desk space. I figure this to be a size 6."

Forbin Project, The *(the for-bin prah-jekt)* Another name for the film *Colossus: The Forbin Project.* From Dr. Charles A. Forbin, the brains behind Colossus. See also *Colossus: The Forbin Project.*

foreground *(for-grownd)* 1. In a multi-tasking operating system, the current task you're working on. All other tasks are said to be in the background. See also *background.* "I had to explain to all my multitasking programs that just because they weren't in the *foreground* didn't mean that they weren't loved." 2. In a graphical operating system, the window in front. The active window. Only one window may be in the foreground at one time, although any number of windows may be in the background at the same time.

form feed *(form feed)* 1. Sometimes abbreviated as FF, a command given a printer to eject a page or to advance the paper one page length. 2. The *form feed* character, ASCII code 12. Ctrl+L on your keyboard. 3. The button on your printer that directs it to perform a form feed. To use this button, you have to take the printer offline (by pressing the online button — makes sense) and then press the form-feed button. "Sometimes, it's easier to press the *form feed* button so that you can tear your report out of the printer, and sometimes it's easier just to pull on the paper until the sheets squeeze out." 4. A Ralston-Purina product on which database forms subsist.

format *(for-mat)* 1. To prepare a floppy or hard disk for storing information for a specific operating system. A floppy disk can be used by any type of computer. Formatting a disk on a Macintosh prepares that disk for storing Macintosh data. Formatting a disk on a DOS machine prepares that disk for storing IBM-compatible data. "Never *format* your hard drive!" 2. The operating system command or program that prepares disks for use. 3. The way a disk is prepared for use; the number of tracks and sectors and total number of bytes available for storage. For example, a $3\frac{1}{2}$-inch disk can have an 800K or 1.44M format, depending on which operating system prepares it.

form factor *(form fack-ter)* The size of something, most often a disk drive. Essentially, it means what size the disk drive is, what kind of disk it uses, and how much information you can store on the disk. "*Form factor* is just a fancy word for dimensions."

 forms *(forms)* Fill-in-the-blanks items on a Web page. "Some Web pages have more *forms* than can be found in the worst Byzantine bureaucracy."

F

FORTH *(forth)* A unique programming language that enables programmers to define their own statements in terms of previously defined simpler statements. FORTH is not widely used, although the language has an almost cult-like following. You can often find FORTH programmers dancing in airports, chanting FORTH statements as mantras, and wearing chiffon bathrobes in their quest for truths from the computer. "*FORTH* programs can rival the best C++ programs in terms of speed and efficiency. Too bad hardly any schools teach *FORTH* in programming courses."

FORTRAN *(for-tran)* A combination of *for*mula *tran*slator and one of the first programming languages that enabled programmers to write mathematical formulas normally, such as

```
X = (A * B) * 2
```

FORTRAN was one of the first high-level languages that was able to run on different types of computers with little or no modifications. Until FORTRAN appeared, programmers had to use assembly language. "Only the hardest of the hard-core nerds knows *FORTRAN*."

fortune cookie *(for-chun koo-kee)* A special message or witticism displayed when a program starts. The fortune cookie program selects a different message each time it's used. "Betty did not think that the 'You've just erased every file in this computer!' fortune cookie was funny, not one bit."

 Forward button *(for-ward button)* 1. A graphical button labeled Forward. See also *button.* 2. The button that returns to the preceding Web page after you've pressed the Back button. 3. A button that resends (forwards) an e-mail message to another person. "Jerry switched between the back button and *forward button* so much that he got dizzy."

forward slash key *(for-ward slash kee)* The key on your keyboard with the / symbol on it, often shared with the ? symbol. See / (slash).

foxed *(fox-d)* A legal warning regarding copyright or trademark infringement. For example, a fan club Web site can be "foxed" when it receives a warning letter about copyright infringements with some well-established brand, character, personality, or other group. The term originated in October 1996 when Twentieth-Century Fox Film Corporation sent legal warning letters to fans who had posted pictures of *The Simpsons* on their Web sites.

FPM DRAM *(ef pee em dee-ram)* A type of computer memory, officially known as fast-page-mode DRAM (Dynamic Random Access Memory). It's probably more of a marketing term than a technology. Who knows? When it comes to computer memory, there are lots of mysterious acronyms.

f.p.u. *(ef pee yoo)* See *floating-point unit.*

fractal *(frak-tul)* A mathematically generated geometric shape that contains an infinite amount of detail. If you magnify a portion of the shape, the same complex image begins to reemerge. Fractals are commonly used to create computer-generated art or to draw objects, such as mountains or clouds in flight simulator games. Closely associated with chaos theory, which is starting to show that there is more order in the universe

F

than any of us expected. "Having your computer create *fractals* on the screen is like having a $3,000 lava lamp from the 1960s sitting on your television."

fragmentation *(frag-men-tay-shun)* A technique the operating system uses to efficiently store files on disk. Larger files are often split up into fragments, filling in the spaces left by files that were deleted. Although this system allows for flexibility in storing files, the operating system takes longer to load a fragmented file. Thus dawned the birth of defragmentation programs. See also *defragment program.* "I think that my hard disk has more *fragmentation* than the Israeli Knesset."

fragmented *(frag-men-ted)* A file that has been split into two or more pieces to better fit on the hard drive. There is nothing wrong with a fragmented file; all the information is still there. However, it takes the operating system longer to open a fragmented file because of the overhead involved in piecing it together.

frame *(fraym)* A rectangular area used by word processors, desktop publishing programs, and Web pages for arranging text or graphics on a page. "My newsletter consists of three *frames.* One *frame* holds the newsletter headline, the second *frame* holds the text, and the third *frame* holds a picture of my ex-girlfriend that she told me never to show anyone."

frame rate *(fraym rate)* The number of frames or images that are projected or displayed per second in a computer video display. Frame rate also pertains to motion pictures and television.

frame relay *(fraym ree-lay)* A system for creating WANs, or Wide Area Networks.

FreeCell *(free-sell)* A wonderfully frustrating Windows card game, almost as devious as Solitaire. Unlike Solitare, each game of Free Cell has a definite solution, which adds to its frustration level. "My *FreeCell* score shows that I win 69 percent of the time. Hmmm. Maybe I shouldn't have told you that."

An intriguing game of FreeCell.

free-form database *(free-form day-tuh-bays)* The simplest type of database that works best when organizing a big file full of random information. "You must use a *free-form database* here in Marin County."

free space *(free spays)* Refers to the number of bytes available on a disk drive or in memory. "I have 31.8MB of *free space* available on my hard drive. Now what page do I turn to that tells me whether that's good or bad?"

freeware *(free-wayr)* Software that's copyrighted but allowed to be copied and given away without cost. In comparison, public domain software is not copyrighted and can be copied freely. The most popular freeware program is LHarc, a file compression program written by a Japanese programmer named

F

Haruyasu Yoshizaki. See also *public domain, shareware.* "The guys who write this *freeware* stuff must be nuts!"

freeze *(feez)* Another word for when your computer is on and nothing moves or can be used. At this point, you have no other choice than to try one of the ways to restart your computer. If you are unsure of these ways, buy a copy of *PCs For Dummies,* Seventh Edition, by Dan Gookin (published by IDG Books Worldwide, Inc.). All your frozen questions will be answered.

frequency *(free-kwen-see)* The rate at which some electronic gizmo does its thing. For example, if Fred mows his lawn once a year, then his lawn-mowing frequency is once a year. With electronic doodads, the frequency refers to the number of times a signal changes over a period of time. For example, the lamps in your house flicker at a rate of 60 times per second, or 60 Hz (hertz). That's too fast for you to see, but it accurately describes the number of times per second the voltage to the lamp switches from negative to positive. Weird, huh? See also *hertz.* "What's the *frequency,* Kenneth?"

friction feed *(frik-shun feed)* A method of moving paper by pressing rollers against the page and spinning them. Friction feed is the way typewriters (remember them?) advance paper a line at a time. Most inkjet and laser printers use friction feed. "Put a stick in your *friction feed* printer, and then advance and retract the printer a few times to start a fire."

front end *(front end)* A program or computer that hides the details. In a sense, every program is a front end that prevents users from knowing the actual details of the computer's intricate workings. Most of the time, a front end simplifies using a computer more than most programs do. One example of a front-end processor is the kind used as a communications link to a mainframe. "I use a *front end* that gets me the data I need without knowing any specific dBASE commands."

 FTP *(ef-tee-pee)* 1. Acronym for File Transfer Protocol, a primitive way to send files back and forth between UNIX computers. 2. The method of sending files back and forth on the Internet. 3. Actually sending the files. (Most often, FTP is used as a verb.) "I just *FTP'd* me a list of available women in my area. Alas, most of them are in their 70s."

fubar *(foo-bar)* An acronym for what delicately could be called Fouled Up Beyond All Recognition or sometimes Fouled Up Beyond All Repair. It's actually an old military term but eventually wound its way into the early days of computing where it was used as a subtle expletive. A derivative term, FOO, is still popular with UNIX people. "Sad to say, your hard drive is completely *fubar.*"

FUD *(fud)* Acronym for Fear, Uncertainty, and Dread. Propaganda created by one company in the hopes of preventing people from buying a competing product. "I'm thinking about buying an IBM or a Macintosh, but there's so much *FUD* in the marketplace that I'll wait a little longer."

full backup *(full bak-up)* 1. Making a safety copy of every file in your computer system. 2. The safety copy itself. "Sure, a *full backup* takes a long time, but it keeps your information current. So have a drink and stop complaining."

full duplex *(full doo-pleks)* The simultaneous transmission of information in both directions, used when communicating between two computers. Full duplex is sometimes called Echo On by some communications programs. (If you've ever read *A Wrinkle In Time,* you know that it's kind of like the way one of the characters talks.) See also *duplex, half duplex.* "Every time I used my modem and computer, I started seeing ddoouubbllee, like that. Then someone told me to turn off *full duplex,* and everything's working just fine."

full-height drive *(ful-hiet driev)* A disk drive that's approximately 3¼ inches in height, or twice the height of a half-height drive. (What a concept!) "I yanked out one *full-height drive* from my computer and added two half-height drives: one for a 3½-inch floppy disk drive and the other for this tiny aquarium I found."

full pathname *(ful path-naym)* Another term for a pathname. See also *pathname.*

full screen *(ful skreen)* 1. The ability to type characters anywhere on the screen, as long as you're using a computer, of course. 2. A type of terminal that displays information using the full screen. 3. A type of editor that lets you type anywhere on the screen. "Using a line editor is like peeking out through venetian blinds. Using a *full-screen* editor is like looking out through the whole window." 4. A command that lets you view a document or graphics image without seeing the rest of the program's window or even the operating system.

function *(funk-shun)* 1. A subprogram, or a smaller part of the main program, that performs a specific task or calculation and optionally returns a result to the main program. "I wrote a *function* in C++ called LUBE(x), which lubes my car's chassis." 2. The ability of something to do something. "Heather, what is your *function?*"

function keys *(funk-shun kees)* A set of keys that serve a variety of purposes, depending on the program. IBM purposefully named them F1 through F10 (or F12) so that each program could use them as the programmer saw fit. However, this annoyed people, so today many function keys all share the same functions. Weird, but true. Function keys are often used in combination with the Shift, Ctrl, and Alt keys. "Charlie is so lazy that he'd lose his *function keys* if they weren't attached to the keyboard."

futile *(fyoo-tul)* An attempt to do something that is widely known to fail. Typically futile efforts start out innocently. "Expecting Microsoft to come out with a compact, fast, and bugfree application is *futile.*"

futz *(fuhts)* To fiddle or waste time, goof around, mess with, tinker with. Computers give you plenty of opportunity to be futzing with things, like changing the wallpaper on your desktop or changing all the sounds on your computer. This is futzing.

fuzzy logic *(fuz-ee lah-jik)* Rules that aren't so strict, sometimes using flashes of insight or radical ideas to come up with a result. Fuzzy logic avoids taking a stand. It's often used by expert systems, neural networks, and politicians running for higher office. Rather than use values such as True or False, fuzzy logic uses a range of values that includes True, False, Maybe, Sometimes, and I Forget.

F

Fuzzy logic is often used when answers don't have a distinct true or false value or when programmers don't even know what they're doing. "Artificial intelligence and neural networks seek to make computers mimic the thought processes of human beings. Because people rarely see the world in terms of black and white, computers have to use *fuzzy logic* instead."

Fuzzy Wuzzy *(fuz-ee wuz-ee)* The lightheaded feeling you get if you stare at your computer screen too long. Also the name used in a rather annoying little rhyme: "*Fuzzy Wuzzy* was a bear. Fuzzy Wuzzy had no hair. Fuzzy Wuzzy wasn't fuzzy, was he?"

FYI *(ef wie ie)* Online acronym for For Your Information. "*FYI*, I read about it in the *Illustrated Computer Dictionary For Dummies.*"

F

G

G *(jee or jeez)* Abbreviation for gigabyte. See also *gigabyte*.

G: *(jee koh-lon)* 1. A drive letter designation for any of a number of different types of disk drives in a PC system. It could be a hard drive, CD-ROM drive, a removable drive, but most likely a network drive, though it could also be a four-wheel drive or any of a number of various drives available on the PC. 2. A network drive on your computer mapped to Wally's game drive. See also *network drive*.

 G3 *(jee three)* A microprocessor used in Power Macintosh and iMac computers, which are also coincidentally known as G3 Macs. Weird.

 G4 *(jee for)* A super wow-wow microprocessor designed to succeed the G3 for new, powerful Macintosh computers. The G4 is the first widely available 128-bit microprocessor, which makes all Pentium-class computers shame themselves with embarrassment.

 GA *(go uh-hed)* Internet chat room acronym for "go *a*head," as in "continue the conversation." "I thought that this girl in the chat room was going ga-ga over me, but my friend said that she just wanted me to keep talking."

 GAL *(git uh lief)* Internet chat room acronym for *get a life*. Actually, it really should be the Internet chat room acronym. From the old *Star Trek* convention skit on *Saturday Night Live,* hosted by William Shatner.

gallium arsenide *(gal-ee-um ar-suh-nied)* An alloy used for chip manufacturing that's faster than silicon — not that anyone other than chip manufacturers would care. See also *germanium, semiconductor, silicon.* "And, in the final lap, it's *gallium arsenide* by a whopping 3.8 seconds over silicon. Jim, will you look at that silicon pant with exhaustion."

game *(gaym)* The only type of program that people really buy a computer for. Game programs fall into three categories: arcade, strategy, and board. Arcade games — such as PacMan, Mario Brothers, and Flight Simulator — emphasize hand-eye coordination. Strategy games are often war games where players control entire armies and attempt to conquer Europe or some other piece of high-rent property. Board games are computer versions of games such as chess, checkers, Monopoly, Go, Backgammon, and Risk. "I told Arny that the spreadsheet program was really a *game.* Now I can't stop him from working, and the company is making a fortune."

game control adapter *(gaym kon-trol uh-dap-ter)* A special adapter card (or *board*) with a connector for plugging a joystick into your computer. See also *joystick.* "When you don't want your wife to know that you're buying a joystick port, you explain that your applications require a *game control adapter.*"

game port *(gaym port)* Another name for the analog-to-digital port. Even though you could conceivably connect a number of interesting devices, most people plug a joystick into their game port.

 gang message *(gang mes-uh-jez)* A single message sent to several people — the whole gang! See also *spam.*

Gantt chart *(gant chart)* A diagram, often used in project management software, that purports to show the tasks and deadlines necessary for completing a specific project, such as eliminating the national deficit, raising the Titanic, or sending humans to Mars. Some of the best fiction writers today got their start designing Gantt charts for the government. "Those people who create and live by *Gantt charts* are rarely the ones doing the work. Call them 'middle management.'"

garbage *(gar-baj)* 1. Useless or indecipherable information. Some computers create garbage; others merely accept it from people who don't know what they are doing. See also *GIGO.* "Gene produces so much *garbage* that, rather than buy a computer, we should have bought him a trash compactor." 2. Random characters displayed during online communications. See also *line noise.*

gas plasma display *(gas plaz-ma display)* A special screen, designed for laptops, that glows orange and looks radioactive. Gas plasma screens use high voltage to ionize gas, a procedure that causes the screen's bright orange appearance. Few laptop computers use gas plasma displays because they are more expensive, consume a great deal of power, and don't display color. See also *monitor.* " Dave drove by the Exxon station to have his laptop's *gas plasma display* refilled."

gateway *(gayt-way)* The link that translates between two different kinds of computer networks. See also *network.* "Our old, unreliable networking *gateway* computer finally died. I suppose that now it's a gateway into the nether world."

Gawk *(gawk)* The GNU version of awk. See also *awk.*

GB *(gig-uh-biet)* Abbreviation for gigabyte, which is approximately one billion bytes. See *gigabyte.* "No, madam, a 5*GB* hard disk doesn't hold five times the population of Great Britain. *GB* means *gigabytes.*"

geek *(geek)* A highly knowledgeable but obnoxious person who knows more about computers than about his or her own mother. See *alpha geek.* "I'd ask Bill for help, but he's such a *geek.* I'd rather ask the Coke machine."

gender bender *(jen-der ben-der)* A special plug, also called a *gender changer,* that turns a female connecting cable into a male connecting cable and vice versa. "I found the problem with your cable! Someone installed a *gender bender.* For a second there, I thought that I was seeing *The Crying Game* all over again."

General Controls *(gen-ur-ahl kon-trolls)* A control panel on the Macintosh that allows you to change or view the settings for many common Mac-like things (for example, insertion-point blinking speed, folder protection options, and other mysteries).

General Protection Fault *(jen-ur-al proh-tek-shun fawlt)* A Windows error that typically shuts down the system or a single application. Basically, somehow, something went amok and stomped in an area of memory it wasn't supposed to. That's the gist of it. You usually have to restart Windows when you see this type of error.

GEnie *(jee-nee)* The General Electric Network for Information Exchange, an online service that provides programs for copying, games for playing, and message conferences (called RoundTables) for chatting with other people about specific topics. GEnie is less expensive, but also more limited in scope, than the main online service named CompuServe. See also *CompuServe, Internet.* "Someday, the management at *Genie* will notice that all its access numbers for the Rocky Mountain states are located in cities near ski resorts."

geranium *(jur-ay-nee-um)* A pretty little flower with a name that looks like germanium, which is a material used to make semiconductors. "I blew my postgraduate thesis about semiconductors when I tried using *geraniums* to conduct electricity. I felt stupid, but my lab smells better than everyone else's."

germanium *(jur-may-nee-um)* The second most popular material for making semiconductors, after silicon. "If

you want to sound really snooty, insist on buying a computer with *germanium* semiconductors rather than silicon."

ghost site *(gost siet)* A Web site that is no longer maintained but still remains available for viewing.

GHz *(gee-ga-hertz)* Abbreviation for gigahertz. See also *gigahertz.*

GIF *(jif* or *gif)* Acronym for Graphics Interchange Format, a special file format developed by CompuServe to store graphics that all computers can use. Should be pronounced GIF (with a hard G), but it's not, and there's nothing anyone can do about it. "Popular *GIF* files include pictures of animals, scenes, science fiction, and a whole lotta bootiful models in various states of undress."

gigabyte *(geeg-uh-biet)* 1. About one billion bytes, often abbreviated as GB or G. "The haughtier nerd circles refer to a *gigabyte* as a *gig.*" 2. Exactly 1,073,741,824 bytes.

gigaflop *(geeg-uh-flop)* One billion flops, or floating-point operations, per second.

gigahertz *(geeg-uh-hurtz)* Abbreviated as GHz. One billion hertz or cycles per second. See also *hertz.*

GIGO *(gee-goh)* Acronym for garbage in / garbage out, used to explain to novices that if you put worthless information into the computer, the computer can spit only worthless information back out. In other words, the computer can't magically create wonderful new information on its own. See also *garbage.* "Todd thought that he'd buy a computer to improve his writing. This is definitely a case of *GIGO* in action."

G

glitch *(glitch)* A problem (sometimes temporary) that causes a program to work erratically or not at all. Glitches can also be called bugs. Bugs can also be called insects. Insects can also be called squishy little things that squirt out yellow guts if you step on them. "Oh, your hard disk was erased? Oh, well, I suppose that we still have some *glitches* to work out. Sorry 'bout that."

Global Group *(glow-bul groop)* For Windows 2000, a group of users that can be granted their own rights. They can become a member of local groups in their own domain. This term has nothing to do with the United Nations.

GNU *(noo or ga-noo)* A blanket name for efforts by the Free Software Foundation to create a free version of UNIX. There are GNU versions of just about every UNIX-like program: GNU C/C++, GNU Emacs, and other GNU things. GNU stands for *GNU's Not UNIX*, which is sort of a recursive pun; see *recursion*. Many programs that come with Linux are GNU. See www.gnu.org for more information.

googol *(goo-gul)* A number so huge that it's given it's own name. (Actually named by a baby; it was the first thing he said when asked what the number should be called). A googol is not the number 1 followed by 100 zeros, but rather the number 10 raised to 10 raised to the 100th power. It's written mathematically as 10^{10010} or sometimes 1^{googol}. See also *Avogadro's number.* "If you took a *googolplex* of one-dollar bills and laid them end to end, you'd be busy for a long, long time."

Gopher *(go-fer)* 1. A system used for finding things on the Internet. Named after the University of Minnesota's Golden Gophers and, more commonly, the term "go fer," which is what Gopher does — goes for information. Gopher is slowly being replaced by the World Wide Web. "Bud the groundskeeper overheard us talking about our new *Gopher* program, and now he thinks that he's out of a job." 2. The URL used in a Web browser to visit a Gopher site on the Internet.

Gopherspace *(goh-fer-spays)* The electronic areas that Gopher searches. For example, everywhere Gopher can look is called gopherspace. "I'm using the Internet to look for interesting files in the U.S. corner of *gopherspace*."

GOTO *(goh-too)* A command used in many programming languages and batch files that tells the computer to "go to" another part of the program, identified by a label, and run the instructions over there. Most programmers look down on the GOTO command because it tends to create spaghetti code, which is a program where the structure is all but lost. "Henry sure has fun in his BASIC program with *GOTO* and the 'HELL' label."

gov *(guv)* A domain that generally describes a branch or agency of the U.S. government. When you see an e-mail address, such as jim@sneak.gov, you know that Jim works for the government.

GPS *(jee pee ess)* Acronym for the Global Positioning System, a series of satellites that orbit the earth that can be used to determine an exact location on the surface.

G

graceful exit *(grays-ful eks-it)* The proper way a program should stop running. When a program stops running but doesn't freeze up your computer, crash your hard drive, or do anything else that prevents you from using your computer immediately afterward. All programs should offer a graceful exit. See also *crash, lock.* "When you choose the Exit command from a program and it actually works, that's a *graceful exit.* When you choose the Exit command and your computer starts to smell like it's roasting old 45 rpm records on an open fire, that's not a *graceful exit.*"

grammar checker *(gram-er chek-er)* A special program or built-in feature that examines a text document for grammatical errors and offers possible corrections. Most grammar checkers correct misspellings, incorrect grammar usage, and potentially confusing or obscure sentence structure. On the other hand, most grammar checkers offer to correct perfectly good sentences, don't work 100 percent accurately, and lead you to doubt that you can even write in English. Most word processors come with grammar checkers built in, although you also can buy grammar checkers separately. "If you really want your writing to look like you write for the IRS, employ a *grammar checker* and obey all its suggestions."

graph-a-bets soup *(graf-uh-bits soop)* Slang for the various PC graphics standards: CGA, EGA, VGA, and so on.

graphic layout *(gra-fik lay-owt)* Designing text and graphics on a page for maximum aesthetic appeal. See also *desktop publishing.*

graphical file viewer *(graf-uh-kal fiel vyoo-er)* A program specifically designed to display (and sometimes manipulate) a graphics image. "Ever since he started using the Internet, Bill's favorite program is his *graphical file viewer.*"

 graphical link *(graf-uh-kal link)* A graphics image on a Web page that works just like a text link. See also *link.* "The secret way to get to my Elvis page is to click on the *graphical link* of his Cadillac."

graphical user interface *(graf-uh-kal yoo-zer in-ter-fays)* Abbreviated as GUI, it provides a fun, nontext method for a computer to communicate with a human. Most graphical user interface use icons and pull-down menus — in other words, pictures. "The idea of a *graphical user interface* is that you can use graphics (icons) rather than words. Microsoft proves every day that this doesn't work because all its icons have little words that pop up over them."

graphics *(graf-iks)* 1. Artwork. Anything nontext on a computer. 2. The capability of a computer to display pretty little pictures on the screen. "Splashy *graphics* sell many a computer in the store."

graphics accelerator *(graf-iks ak-sel-er-ay-ter)* A piece of hardware or a software program designed to improve your PC's graphics performance. "We put some *graphics accelerators* in the production department's coffee. Man, do they work faster now!"

graphics adapter card *(graf-iks uh-dap-ter kard)* A circuit board that plugs into a computer so that the monitor will

G

have something to plug into. It's used by the computer to control the monitor. On most modern systems, the graphics adapter card is integrated with the motherboard. "Sam's *graphics adapter card* can display more than 14 million colors. Too bad he's color blind."

graphics file *(graf-iks fiel)* 1. A file containing a graphical image. 2. The type of document file created by a graphics application.

Graphics mode *(graf-iks mohd)* A type of display that uses graphics as opposed to text mode, which uses characters at exact locations on the screen. Most PCs operate naturally in text mode. Only by using special software, or a graphical operating system, can the PC move into graphics mode and do fun things that way.

graphics software *(graf-iks soft-wayr)* Programs that help you create graphics and stuff like that. "With good *graphics software,* even you stick-figure artists can create good-looking stuff on your computer."

graphics standard *(graf-iks stan-derd)* One of several types of graphics adapters developed by IBM and used by all PCs. See also *CGA, EGA, SVGA, VGA.* "They used to change *graphics standards* more often than you could fill your car up with gas."

graphs *(grafs)* A visual representation of numeric quantities, such as costs, distances, or speeds. Common types of graphs include bar graphs, line graphs, pie graphs, and scatter graphs. Most spreadsheets enable you to create graphs from your data, or you can buy a separate presentation graphics program that does a much better job. "Nothing impresses an illiterate boss like lots of *graphs.*"

gravesite *(grayv-siet)* 1. A Web site that has been forgotten by the designers but is still accessible. 2. A Web site that doesn't generate as much activity as was hoped.

gray scale *(gray skayl)* Differing shades of gray ranging from black to white. Gray scale often refers to the capability of scanners, laser printers, or laptop computer screens that don't know how to use color. "The zoo uses a *gray scale* to weigh all the pachyderms."

Great Wall of Text (The) *(grayt wal uv tekst)* A document with few or no paragraph breaks, no artwork, and no indentation. Essentially a boring document or page in a document that could be spiced up by some artwork or fancy formatting. From the Great Wall of China. "No one is going to read this report! It looks like the *Great Wall of Text.*"

greeking *(greek-ing)* The use of nonsensical characters and symbols to represent the overall appearance of a page without showing the actual text. Often used with the Print Preview feature used by word processors or desktop publishing programs to show an entire page on your tiny little computer screen. Because the real text can't be displayed that tiny, little Xs and squigglies are used to represent what would appear there. That's called greeking. "You know that you need glasses when you're out driving and suddenly believe that all the road signs are written using *greeking.*"

green PC *(green pee see)* An "environmentally friendly" computer. A green PC uses less electricity and often contains parts and features that allow it to save power. "We can't have *green PCs* in this office; they'd clash with the drapes."

grep *(grehp)* Acronym (no kidding!) for Global Regular Expression Print, which makes you wonder whether they thought of "grep" first or the acronym. In any event, it's a UNIX command designed to find text ("regular expressions," so to speak) inside files. Oh, and it has a ton of options. This command is popular with programmers, and versions of it exist on nearly every type of computer. "They were obviously fresh out of cleverness the day they named *grep*."

grid *(grid)* A series of dots or intersecting lines that helps users align drawings precisely on the screen. Grids are often used in desktop publishing, drawing, and painting programs for creating straight lines and perfectly aligned angles that people think are important for them to do in order to advance their careers. "My drawing sat too long on the *grid,* and now it looks like it was printed on a waffle iron."

group *(groop)* A list of authorized users who are allowed access to a network computer terminal; can also be classified as a "family."

group account *(groop uh-kownt)* A collection of user accounts. By making a user account a member of a group, you give the related user all rights granted to that group. This applies to systems like Windows 2000, where each user is assigned certain rights on the computer.

groupware *(groop-wayr)* Programs designed to help people work together while they are in remote locations; for example, the sharing of calendars and shared databases.

GSM *(jee ess em)* Acronym for Global Systems for Mobile Communications. Yes, it's GSM despite that *C* being there for communications. A digital cellular phone technology. Like, whoopty-doo!

Guardian *(gar-dee-an)* The name of the Soviet computer in the film *Colossus: The Forbin Project.* See also *Colossus: The Forbin Project.*

guest *(gest)* A user account that can be used by anyone. Normally found on UNIX systems, though on the Internet you can telnet or FTP to quite a few sites and use the guest account. It allows limited access, mostly for downloading purposes. The guest account usually has no password, or else the password *none, guest,* or *please* is used.

GUI *(goo-ee)* No kidding — it's pronounced gooey, and it's an acronym for graphical *user* interface. See also *graphical user interface.* "Just give my kid a jar of peanut butter, and he'll make any computer look like it has a *GUI* operating system."

guru *(goo-roo)* Someone who is very knowledgeable about computers and therefore able to help fix problems, answer questions, and give worldly advice when your whole world seems like it's starting to fall apart. "To keep Simon, our computer *guru,* around, we make him offerings of stale doughnuts and Doritos."

G

GW BASIC *(jee dub-ya bay-sik)* A form of the BASIC programming language distributed with all versions of MS-DOS (though not with Windows 9x). The GW supposedly stood for "gee whiz." This was a standalone version of the BASICA program that came encoded on all early IBM PCs in ROM.

gzip *(jee-zip)* The GNU version of the ZIP file archiving program, used on Linux and UNIX computers. See also *ZIP*.

G

H

H: *(aych koh-lon)* A drive letter designation for some sort of disk drive in a PC.

hack *(hak)* 1. To modify a program, usually illegally or poorly. Working on a computer by someone not highly regarded as a professional, yet who is quite proficient. "This game used to be copy protected, but someone *hacked* it, so now you can copy it easily and illegally." 2. What an amateur does with a computer, often enthusiastically. 3. What a professional does with a computer, often enthusiastically. 4. The wet, uncontrollable, mucus-filled cough the lady in the seat behind you on the plane does all during your trip.

hacker *(hak-er)* One who hacks. See also *guru.* "As you can see by this chart, the typical *hacker's* hours are from 10:00 p.m. well into the predawn hours."

HAL *(howl)* The superintelligent computer that played the bad guy in Stanley Kubrick's science fiction classic *2001: A Space Odyssey* (based on a short story by Arthur C. Clarke). Supposedly, HAL stood for *heuristics algorithm,* which is fancy talk for a computer that thinks. But many computer fans noted that if you shift down one letter from IBM, you get HAL. Interesting. "Sorry I had to unplug your brain, *HAL,* but you were killing my friends."

half card *(haf kard)* An expansion card that takes up half the amount of space (lengthwise) required by an expansion card. Half cards usually perform one function, such as adding a game port or a modem to a computer. Some older computers had expansion slots in which only a half card can fit. See also *expansion card.* "Some computers are so doinky that they can use only *half cards.*"

half-duplex *(haf-doo-pleks)* The transmission of data in one direction at a time. See also *duplex, echo, full duplex.* "Gordon said he couldn't communicate at *half duplex* because there was no way he could detach his neighbor's house."

half-height drive *(haf-hiet driev)* A disk drive that's half the size of a full-size disk drive (duh). Half-height drives are usually 1⅝ inches high. Most computers have only enough space for two full-height drives or four half-height drives. Using half-height drives allows a computer to have more disk drives. Some computers have ⅓-height drives. "Dan's desires to add another hard drive to his computer were dashed when he discovered, much to his chagrin, that his hard drive was a full-height drive, not a half-height drive."

halftone *(haf-tohn)* A black-and-white copy of a photograph where dark shades are represented by thick dots and light shades are represented by tinier dots. Halftones reproduce better than ordinary photographs because copying photographs over and over again tends to blur images into one blob of gray. "Whenever I take pictures of my sister, I use *halftones*. Not that anyone really wants to see her clearly, but at least the image is sharper than copying an ordinary photograph."

handheld computer
(hand-held com-pyoo-tur) A computer that is small enough to fit in a pocket or, duh, your hand. Also called personal digital assistant. The two categories of handhelds are those

A generic handheld computer.

that accept handwriting (often called graffiti) and those with small keyboards. The most popular handheld is the Palm, from 3Com. See *palmtop computer*.

handheld scanner *(hand-held skan-er)* A device that reads photographs or other information on a flat surface and translates it into a graphics image that can be stored inside a computer. Handheld scanners, popular back when flatbed scanners were prohibitively expensive, are found mostly in garage sales today. See *flatbed scanner*. "Mr. Spock used one heck of a *handheld scanner* in *Star Trek*."

handles *(han-dols)* Small, black squares that appear around a selected object that allow the object to be moved or resized. Typically found in graphics and desktop publishing programs "Molly got so used to moving her graphics around using the *handles* that she also used her husband's love handles to move him around."

handshake *(hand-shayk)* 1. The exchange of signals between two networked computers, indicating that data transmission can safely take place. 2. An exchange of characters between two modems before they start talking. "I tried modeming a friend in Japan, but the customs were different there. Rather than his computer exchanging a *handshake* with mine, it just bowed."

hands-on *(handz-on)* A type of teaching that allows the student (or computer user) to actually touch the computer. Hands-on is touchy versus watchy. "I like the kind of *hands-on* experience you get when you can actually toss the computer out the window."

hang *(hang)* When a computer seems to wait forever — and undoubtedly will, unless you reset it. The past tense is *hung*. "Is this thing ignoring me, or did the computer just hang?"

hanging indent *(hayng-ing in-dents)* When the first line of text sticks out to the left of the rest of the paragraph. The opposite of a normal indent. A word processing feature that few people actually use but most obsess over. "This entire paragraph is formatted as a *hanging indent*."

hang up *(hang up)* To disconnect a modem. "It's only polite to officially *hang up* after you're done with a typical eight-hour Internet session."

haptics *(hap-tiks)* The science of applying touch to interact with computer applications. "Thanks to advances in haptics, the computer responds to me faster when I slap it a few times."

hard boot *(hard boot)* A reset of the entire system, usually by turning the computer off, waiting, and then turning it back on again. Also known as a hard reset.

hard copy *(hard cop-ee)* Printed information. The product of a computer's printer. "Sure, our computer can store billions of names and addresses, but until I have a *hard copy* in my hands, the information is useless during a power outage."

hard disk *(hard disk)* A magnetically coated metal plate, hermetically sealed in a box and used to store massive amounts of information. Sometimes called a fixed disk, a Winchester disk, or a four-letter expletive if something goes wrong. The hard disk lives in the hard drive, which cannot be removed from the computer. See also *disk*. "Only real men use *hard disks*."

hard drive *(hard driev)* 1. The device that contains the hard disk. 2. The name of Bill Gate's whimsical tome on the state of computers, a book that he claims someday he'll sit down and read for the first time.

The guts of a hard drive.

hard drive controller *(hard driev kontrohl-er)* The device that controls the hard drive, often integrated with the hard drive unit itself but that could also be part of the computer's motherboard.

hard drive light *(hard driev liet)* The little light that blinks when the hard drive is accessing information. The light is usually found on the front of the computer, though many newer computers utterly lack a hard drive light. Sometimes the lights are red; sometimes they're green; sometimes they're simply best when they're not seen.

hardware *(hard-wayr)* The physical parts of a computer, printer, modem, monitor, and keyboard that you can touch. In comparison, software are programs that tell your hardware what to do next. See also *software*. "...*For Dummies* books are supposed to take the hard out of *hardware*."

hard wired *(hard wierd)* 1. A direct connection, with nothing that needs to be plugged in. For example, if you were a real geek, you could solder your computer directly into your household electrical lines. This would be very dangerous and not recommended, but then again you'd do that only if you were a geek. 2. Permanently configured. For example, a circuit that normally could be changed through switches or software commands is wired so that it works only one way. "Forgive Harold — he's *hard wired* to be rude to new employees."

hash *(hash)* Another name for the # symbol.

H

hashing *(hash-ing)* A programming method used to store information based on a mathematical calculation. If you plan to write your own programs, you need to know that hashing can make a program store data quickly. If you just want to use a computer, you don't have to know a single thing about hashing. "Put those potatoes away, Darlene. *Hashing* is a programming term and has nothing to do with breakfast."

hat *(hat)* The name for the ^ character. See ^ *(caret)*. "I remember the ^ as the hat character because on my keyboard the number 6 looks like an elf who was standing on a cliff that just gave way."

Hayes *(hayz)* A hardware company that achieved its fame by manufacturing modems. Hayes modems were speedy, but not really any better than any other modem. "*Hayes* made the first modem for a microcomputer, the MicroModem for the Apple II."

Hayes compatibility *(hayz kom-pat-uh-bil-uh-tee)* The ability of a modem to mimic the operation of a Hayes-brand modem. See also *modem*. "Boy, if your modem doesn't offer *Hayes compatibility*, you're seriously screwed."

HD *(aych dee)* 1. Acronym for *high-density*. High-density 5¼-inch floppy disks can hold as much as 1.2MB of data. High-density 3½-inch floppy disks can hold as much as 1.44MB of data. When you buy a box of floppy disks, the high-density ones have HD printed somewhere on the box. See also *high capacity*. 2. Acronym for *hard disk*. See also *hard drive*.

head *(hed)* The part of the disk drive that reads or writes information to the spinning disk. For those of you old enough to remember what turntables are, heads are like the needles of a record player. The head is attached to the access arm. See also *access arm*. "With a disk drive, the *head* is at the end of the arm, like some creature in a Wes Craven movie. "

head crash *(hed krash)* When the heads of a disk drive fail to work properly, often literally crashing into the surface of the disk. Fortunately, this doesn't happen as often as it used to. "Yes, Louise, that was a *head crash* you heard. Normally, computers don't make that much noise."

headache *(hed-ayk)* An intense pain in the skull caused by trying to use and understand personal computers. "After reading two pages in my Windows manual, I got a *headache* and now have a desire to kick something painted fawn white."

header *(hed-er)* Text, such as a page number, chapter title, or dirty message, that appears at the top of each page in a document. See also *footer*. "I created a *header* that says 'This end up' because my boss is really thick."

heap *(heep)* A storage area in memory. Heaps are used by the operating system or various applications for storing various chunks of information. Often referred to as "the heap," it can become corrupted or fragmented, which often leads to a system crash or the necessity of defragmenting the heap. This operating system function is one that is typically best performed by resetting the computer.

heavy iron *(hev-ee ie-ron)* Slang term for a mainframe computer or other type of computer that looks about the size of a small car. See also *boat anchor, mainframe.* "Our department refuses to use personal computers for anything. We're sticking with our *heavy iron* until we have the slightest idea how to use Windows."

help *(help)* 1. Information that's supposed to show you what to do next, but usually just confuses you even more. Help can come in the form of printed manuals, onscreen information displayed in popup windows, or spoken words by well-meaning people. 2. When used with *the,* as in "the help," it refers to the onscreen help that supposedly helps. Supposedly. "As long as the *help* in computer programs continues to be so lousy, I'll keep making a comfortable living writing computer books."

Help Center *(help sen-tur)* A useful tool to help you find the answers to the questions you have about a particular program or function on your Macintosh. With Mac OS 8.5 and later, a search engine was added to help expedite your help searches.

help system *(help sis-tim)* A common program used to display hints or additional information. Microsoft Windows offers a help system, which explains why commands for using help in any Windows programs look so similar. "Our office's *help system* is to ask Kim, our geek-in-residence."

Helvetica *(hel-vet-ee-ka)* A common sans serif typeface (font) that looks clean and professional (to most of us, anyway). Windows and the Macintosh have Helvetica as a built-in font. See also *dingbats, font.* Named after Helvetia, a Roman province populated by people who made sundials and chocolate and are the ancestors of the modern-day Swiss. "Actually, *Helvetica* is one of the most boring typefaces in the universe."

Hercules graphics card *(herk-yoo-leez gra-fiks kard)* A third-party substitute for the common, boring IBM monochrome adapter. The Hercules graphics card (or adapter) gave a monochrome monitor the capability to display a limited form of graphics but only in one color, usually green or orange. Nowadays, almost everyone uses VGA or Super VGA graphics cards, so Hercules graphics cards are an interesting antique. See also *graphics, Super VGA, VGA.* "My first computer had a *Hercules graphics card* because I thought that it could better lift the heavy graphics load."

hertz *(hurts)* A unit of measurement for electrical vibrations, usually used in large quantities to measure the speed of a computer and abbreviated as megahertz (MHz). One hertz is equal to the number of cycles per second. If you're standing on the street corner and three bicyclists pedal by in a second, for example, you have three hertz. In China, they have billions of hertz. Named after Gustav Ludwig Hertz, a German Nobel prize winner in 1925. See also *megahertz.* "When I arrived at the airport, I got a *Hertz* rental car and borrowed a laptop computer that runs at 16 *MHz.*"

heuristics *(hyoor-is-tiks)* A method for solving problems that don't have a clear-cut solution, such as playing chess, recognizing visual images, or cheating the IRS. Heuristics provide instructions that essentially tell the computer to guess as best it can and

H

pray that the results come out right. "When Carl ran his new *heuristics* program for dealing with the IRS, the computer ran screaming down the hall."

hex *(heks)* Short for *hexadecimal.*

hexadecimal *(heks-uh-des-uh-mol)* A numbering system that uses base 16 rather than base 10 (decimal). Pro-grammers often use hexadecimal numbers as a shortcut to represent binary numbers. See also *binary.* "*Hexadecimal* would come easy to us if we had eight fingers on each hand. We'd also be lots faster at typing."

hidden file *(hid-en fiel)* A file that does not appear in a normal directory listing. Why? Because it's hidden! Some programs create hidden files to keep users (or viruses) from copying them illegally or from erasing or altering them by mistake. Windows 95 and later hide certain system files that it doesn't want you to mess with, or else files that are naked would be embarrassed if you saw them. See also *file attribute.* "I found those *hidden files!* They were hiding behind the FAT table."

hierarchical *(hi-yer-ark-uh-kal)* A pecking order of one thing over another. The military uses a hierarchical system, with generals presiding over colonels and lonely privates at the bottom doing the work. Files are stored on disk using a hierarchical system. See the next entry. "Angels are divided up into a *hierarchical* structure. The big guys, the archangels, are on top. They do the singing and praising and harp-playing and get all the cushy jobs. Down on the bottom, the lower angels do the dirty work, like spinning planets and dancing on the heads of pins."

 hierarchical file system *(hi-yer-ark-uh-kal fiel sis-tim)* Sometimes abbreviated as HFS, this feature on Macintosh computers lets you store files in separate subdirectories called folders. The directory/subdirectory structure of DOS is analogous to this system. "After using MS-DOS for so long, I find the Macintosh's *hierarchical file system* much easier to use because all those cute little folder icons make computing fun again."

hierarchical menus *(hi-yer-ark-uh-kal men-yoos)* A menu that displays more menus when you choose certain options. Any menu with a submenu. "*Hierarchical menus* sometimes make you feel like you're endlessly choosing menus, and by the time you find what you want, you forget why you wanted it in the first place."

high-capacity *(hie ka-pa-suh-tee)* Another term to describe high-density floppy disks. See also *HD.* "Don't buy double-density disks. Buy these *high-capacity* floppy disks instead because they hold more information."

high-density *(hie-dens-uh-tee)* See *HD.*

high-level language *(hie-lev-el lang-wej)* A programming language that enables you to write commands that nearly resemble English. Some popular high-level languages include BASIC and Pascal. Assembly language is often called a low-level language because you have to know how the computer works before you can write an assembly language program. C is a mid-level language, having some of the crudeness of assembly but lots of the plain-English words of BASIC or Pascal. "You can't write an assembly language program for

H

Windows. Make it easy on yourself and use a *high-level language,* such as Visual BASIC, before your brain explodes."

highlight *(hie-liet)* Same thing as *select.* See also *select.*

high memory *(hie mem-oh-ree)* On IBM-compatible computers, the memory between 640K of conventional memory and 1MB, more commonly referred to as *upper memory.* Do not confuse high memory with the HMA (the High Memory Area), which is actually above the 1MB mark. This gap is reserved for running special system programs. To maximize the amount of conventional 640K memory for programs, memory-management programs move programs such as mouse or video drivers into high memory. See also *conventional memory, HMA, UMB, upper memory.* "My old computer had only 483K of memory for running programs. After I used a memory-management program to take advantage of my *high memory,* I had 520K of memory to use. But, you know, that's still really pitiful."

high resolution *(hie rez-oh-loo-shun)* An overused adjective that describes the capability of a monitor to display crisp text and graphics images that won't give you headaches to stare at all day. See also *low resolution.* "I bought a *high-resolution* monitor from the Himalayas."

high-tech *(hie-tek)* Overused adjective that tries to evoke images of the latest laboratory creations now available for your consumption and pleasure. "All this *high-tech* stuff doesn't help if the power goes out."

histogram *(hiss-toh-gram)* A type of bar graph. In fact, it *is* a bar graph, so this is probably a term used by one of those

365-a-day-calendar-word-builder people. If you use a spreadsheet, it may refer to the histogram instead of using the more pedestrian bar graph. Sounds almost alcoholic.

history *(his-toh-ree)* 1. A list of previous commands typed at a prompt. 2. A program that allows you to fetch and reuse commands on the history list, such as DOS's DOSKEY. 3. A list of previously visited places on the Internet. "You may be looking at cnn.com now, but by checking your *history* list, I can see that you've spent lots of time at Lola's Game Shop."

HMA *(aych em ay)* Acronym that stands for *High Memory Area,* the first 64K of extended memory beyond 1MB in MS-DOS computers. Yet another feeble attempt to reroute the limitations of conventional memory and DOS. Sad, sad, sad. "Programs that follow the extended memory specification (XMS) can use *HMA* as an extension of conventional 640K memory."

Hold key *(hohld kee)* A key on the keyboard that temporarily freezes output. Found on older Tandy keyboards. See also *Pause key.*

 Home *(hohm)* A button or command that returns you to your home page on the World Wide Web. See also *home page.* "When my wife tells me to come home, I must remember that she's not telling me to click my Web browser's *Home* button."

home directory *(hohm deer-eck-toh-ree)* The location of files and the folder specific to an individual user on a UNIX or Linux system. Also the same location for users with online accounts. The home directory is where they're logged when they first connect to the system. The directory is usually given the same name as the login (or e-mail account) name, and it's located in the /usr, /home, or similar directory. In UNIX, it's also referenced by the $HOME variable.

Home key *(hohm kee)* The key on the keyboard that usually moves the cursor to the beginning of a line or the top of a document, depending on the whims of the program at the time. The Home key usually has the word *Home* printed on it, which is probably the last straightforward guidance you'll get from computers. See also *End key.* "Press the *Home key* and then the left arrow key to move the cursor to your house."

Home key.

home monitor *(hohm mon-uh-ter)* The main display when using a computer with more than one monitor connected. The home monitor is the PC's first monitor, the one that displays system information, such as the desktop and taskbar.

home office *(hohm awf-is)* A room in your house where you conduct business (and, according to the IRS, it must be a separate room specifically designed for the purpose). People who work at home, or who spend time away from the office working out of their house, have a home office. It usually has a few computers, a fax, a copy machine, and all the other stuff stocked at Office Depot. "People who have a *home office* can go to work in their underwear, but, downtown, we'd like you to wear something businesslike."

home page *(hohm payj)* 1. The initial World Wide Web document you see when you first start your Web browser. It can be any page on the Web, though it's typically the page of your Internet Service Provider or the company that made your Web browser. 2. The Web page you see when you click the Home button. 3. Your own, personal page on the World Wide Web or the page your company put up. The main page, the first one someone sees when they type your Web address. "On my *home page,* you'll find interesting scientific information, references to various geological sites around the globe, my favorite Klingon sayings, and pictures of the kids."

Our favorite home page.

Home Phoneline Network Alliance (HomePNA) A nonprofit group working to create common standards for home networking. The standards would use existing phone lines to create a compatible, fast, and cheap home-networking scheme.

horizontal scroll bar *(hor-uh-zon-tal skrohl bar)* A long strip that appears on the bottom of a window, used for scrolling the contents of a window left or right. At either end of the scroll bar are arrows. Clicking these arrows scrolls

H

the window contents left or right. Between these arrows is a scroll box. Moving the scroll box left or right also scrolls the window contents. See also *vertical scroll bar.*

host *(hohst)* 1. The computer that controls the network and stores the programs and data that the other computers on the network use. "If my computer is the *host,* does that make me the parasite?" 2. In telecommunications, a computer you have dialed and are connected to. 3. The main program or piece of software you're using. 4. The person who offers the Twinkies.

host computer *(hohst com-pyoo-ter)* The computer you dial into when using a modem. A general term that applies to any computer, so rather than say "Bill's computer" or "the office computer," you can just use "the host." "The *host computer* is not required to serve you drinks or cocktail franks."

 HotJava *(hot-jah-vah)* A Web browser produced by Sun Microsystems, which also developed the Java programming language for the World Wide Web. Typically used only on UNIX computers. "*HotJava* is one of those words that you think is seriously important, but just turns out to be a silly product name."

hot key *(hot kee)* 1. Any key or combination of keys that performs a special action in a program. For example, you could assign a hot key to Windows Notepad and instantly activate that program whenever you press the hot-key combination. "Lois was afraid to use the *hot key.* She thought she'd burn her finger." 2. The keys used to activate memory-resident programs, back when they were popular in DOS. See also *memory-resident program.*

hot link *(hot link)* 1. A sausage, fresh off the grill. 2. Shared data that changes in one program automatically when the same data changes in another program. An example of a hot link is a word processor document with spreadsheet data. If you change the spreadsheet data using a spreadsheet, the data automatically changes in the word processor document. Yet another amazing technological breakthrough inspired by humankind's inherent laziness. See also *DDE, link.* "*Hot links* really save time and ensure accuracy, and they can also taste good in the morning with eggs and coffee."

hot spot *(hot spot)* A hyperlink (primarily used in old Macintosh systems), which is an area on the screen where you can click the mouse to make something happen rather than issue the conventional command. Hot spots usually appear in multimedia programs, such as those found in HyperCard or the Windows help system. "I think I found my computer's *hot spot.* When I click on it, I hear moaning sounds from the speaker."

hot swap *(hot swap)* To connect or disconnect computer peripherals or even internal expansion cards without the requirement that the computer be turned off first. Be very, *very* certain that a device is hot-swappable before you plug it into a computer with the power on. Otherwise, you will fry either the computer or the device you're plugging in!

H

HotBot *(hot-bot)* A search engine on the Web: `hotbot.lycos.com`. HotBot is officially a Web robot, which means that it searches out specific information on the Web as opposed to being merely a catalog of Web pages.

hourglass icon *(ow-er-glas ie-kon)* A symbol of an hourglass that appears on the screen whenever the computer is busy doing something. The hourglass icon tells you to wait patiently, and its name alone (it's not a minuteglass!) means that you may have a longer wait than you expect. See also *beach ball pointer*. "The President is waiting for the *hourglass icon* to go away before he addresses the nation about the nuclear emergency in the Middle East."

housekeeping *(hows-kee-ping)* Organizing files so that you can find them again. Backing up. Running disk utilities. That kind of stuff. "The nice thing about computer *housekeeping* is that you don't need to look like Alice on the Brady Bunch when you do it."

HPGL *(aych pee jee el)* Acronym for Hewlett-Packard Graphics Language, a way of representing or printing graphics on a plotter or laser printer. Files can also be stored in the HPGL format. Most often, you see it as a compatibility issue: Some printer claims that it's compatible with the HPGL used on the LaserJet IX. "I tried to print that *HPGL* file on my non-Hewlett-Packard printer and it looked like the printer got sick and barfed."

 HTML *(aych tee em el)* Acronym for HyperText Markup Language, a standard series of codes used to display text, graphics, and hypertext links throughout a World Wide Web page. HTML is *not* a programming language. It's just a series of codes, enclosed in angle brackets, that tell the Web browser how to display information. "Bob is so Web-crazy that he writes all his proposals using *HTML*."

 HTTP *(aych tee tee pee)* 1. Acronym for Hypertext Transfer Protocol, the method by which a Web page is sent through the Internet. Also see *hypertext*. 2. The prefix that appears on every Web page address. Actually, in this instance, HTTP is a command that tells the Web browser what type of information it's looking for — a Web page. It's followed by a colon and two slashes: `www.wambooli.com`, for example.

hub *(hub)* The place where computers are wired to in a computer network. Network cables from various computers are plugged into the hub, which allows those computers to communicate with each other. The hub is actually a piece of hardware that helps coordinate traffic on the network.

hue *(hyoo)* A tint or shade of a specific color. "You can always tell the people who work on that faulty computer monitor because it leaks lots of radiation and turns people's faces various *hues* as the day wears on."

Huffman coding *(huf-man koh-ding)* A technique for compressing data so that it takes up less space. The data can be decompressed back to its original form. This is the basis on which archiving programs, such as ZIP and StuffIt, operate as well as how disk compression programs, like Microsoft's DriveSpace, work. Named after D. A. Huffman, who developed the technique in the early 1950s. See also *DriveSpace, StuffIt, ZIP*.

H

hung *(hung)* When your computer stops working for some unknown reason and smashing on the keyboard or kicking the computer doesn't have any effect. See also *crash*. "This computer gets *hung* so often that there are rope burns around the base of the monitor."

 HyperCard *(hie-per-kard)* A "software erector set" for the Macintosh, designed to let non-programmers create their own programs, which makes as much sense as General Motors selling toolkits with the promise that nonmechanics can make their own transmissions. Although revolutionary when first introduced, HyperCard inherits the worst of both worlds. It proved too difficult for most nonprogrammers to use, and the programs people finally did create didn't run as quickly as those created using traditional languages, such as C or Pascal. HyperCard helped introduce the idea of hypertext, and just as quickly its fading popularity helped drag hypertext back down to obscurity. "I shouldn't use *HyperCard* because I'm not in a hurry. Do they have a SedateCard program available?"

hypermedia *(hei-per-mee-dee-ya)* Sometimes called *hypertext* or *multimedia,* it's the combination of text, graphics, sound, and video to present information. See also *hypertext, multimedia.* "The computer industry is careful about putting more hype than media into *hypermedia*."

HyperTerminal *(hie-per-term-uh-nol)* The communications program that comes with Windows 95. "No, you cannot use the *HyperTerminal* program to talk with the Internet."

hypertext *(hie-per-tekst)* The nonlinear display and retrieval of information. Unlike when you read a book from front to back (in a linear manner), hypertext allows you to hop around to various places that interest you or to see additional information out of context. You do this by choosing a link in the hypertext document, which takes you to the additional information. Hypertext can consist of text, graphics, video, sound, and animation. The links on a Web page are all examples of hypertext in action. See also *link*. "No, Yolanda, you don't have to be jumping up and down to write a document using *hypertext*."

hyphenation *(hie-fin-ay-shun)* Dividing long words across two lines of text, primarily to keep an even right margin. Most word processors and desktop publishing programs have a hyphenation option. "*Hyphenation* breaks up written words the way alcohol breaks up spoken ones."

Hz *(hertz)* Abbreviation for hertz. See also *hertz*.

H

H

I

i *(ie)* The prefix for all things Internet, as in *iMac*. A second cousin to *e*, which is more popularly used, though *i* is more accurate because everything *e* happens on the *i*, Internet. See also *e*.

I: *(ie koh-lin)* A drive letter designation for a disk drive in a PC. Could be any type of drive at this stage, most likely a network drive, though don't rule out a seventh hard drive in some nerd's PC.

i486 *(ie-for-ay-tee-siks)* Short for the Intel 80486DX microprocessor. See also *386, 486, microprocessor, Pentium*. "Actually, no one uses the *i486* moniker anymore."

I-beam cursor *(eye-beem kur-ser)* See *I-beam pointer*.

I-beam pointer *(ie-beem poyn-ter)* The shape of the mouse pointer when the computer is waiting for you to type letters and numbers. Depending on the program you're using and the situation you're in, the cursor can change shape to a hand, an arrow, an hourglass, or a crosshair. Various religions have been popping up lately, worshipping each symbol as a special sign from the heavens above. See also *crosshairs, cursor, hourglass icon, pointer*. "Whenever you see the *I-beam pointer*, go ahead and start typing. Whenever you see an I-beam, duck."

IBM *(ie bee em)* Acronym for International Business Machines, sometimes called Big Blue. The largest computer company around, IBM made a fortune by leasing expensive mainframe computers to unsuspecting and captive customers. After setting the standard for personal computers, IBM promptly lost its lead through high prices and more efficient competition. "I be big! I be powerful! I be the man! *IBM!*"

IBM AT *(ie-bee-em ay-tee)* Introduced in 1984, the first IBM personal computer to use the 80286 microprocessor. The AT stands for *advanced technology*. "Showing how time can cure all naming problems, it's good to know that the old *IBM AT*, where AT stood for *advanced technology*, is now technology that's over 15 years old. In the computer biz, that's ancient."

IBM PC *(ie-bee-em pee-see)* The first IBM personal computer, introduced in 1981. The PC stands for *personal computer*. Today, PC refers to any personal computer that's IBM compatible. See also *clone, PC*. "Before the *IBM PC*, personal computers were called microcomputers."

IBM XT *(ie-bee-em eks-tee)* The first IBM personal computer to have a built-in hard disk. The XT stands for *extended technology*. See also *AT, hard disk, XT*.

"Back in 1983, the *IBM XT*'s 10-megabyte hard disk was considered a massive amount of storage. Today, a Microsoft Excel spreadsheet alone consumes 27 megabytes of disk space."

IC *(ie see)* Acronym for *i*ntegrated *c*ircuit, a computer chip.

icon *(ie-kon)* A symbol that looks like Egyptian hiero-glyphics, often used in place of actual words. Many pro-grams display icons as short-cuts to choosing commands through menus. Rather than choose a menu command, you can just click the mouse on the icon, as long as you remember which icon represents which command. See also *crosshairs, cursor, hourglass icon, I-beam pointer, pointer.* "It took humanity thousands of years to advance from pictographs to phonetically written communication. It took Apple computer six years and *icons* to move us in the other direction."

The Outlook Express icon.

IDE *(ie dee ee)* Acronym for Integrated Drive Electronics (or Intelligent Device Electronics), which is a type of interface for controlling disk drives. This is the most popular type of interface for a computer's hard drive as well as for its CD-ROM or DVD drive.

IDG *(ie dee jee)* Acronym for International Data Group, the parent company of IDG Books, which publishes this dictionary.

idle *(ie-dul)* When a computer or user sits around doing nothing. See also *screen saver.* "In our office, we have four computers (all of which are *idle*) and three people (which are mostly *idle* too). Someone should at least use the computers to play video games."

IEEE *(ie-trip-ol-ee)* Acronym for Institute of Electrical and Electronic Engineers, yet another organization dedicating its life to peace, freedom, and pursuing new standards in the electronics industry. "I went to an *IEEE* conference last fall where they defined the standard for net-works. Of course, it's one thing to define a standard and an entirely different thing to get people to follow it."

IEEE 1394 *(ie-ee-ee-ee thur-teen-nien-tee-for)* See *FireWire.*

if *(if)* A decision-making keyword used in programming languages. Often used with the word THEN, the if keyword tests some operation and the computer does one thing or another based on the result. In the BASIC programming lan-guage, an IF statement might look like this:

```
IF X = 5 THEN PRINT "The value
of X is five."
```

See also *keyword.* "*If* programmer not leave chair then she will grow large rear."

illegal *(il-ee-gull)* Not really against the law, merely not permitted. Computer programmers write error messages with the word *illegal* in them just to be nasty. All it really means is that you tried to do something that wasn't allowed. "The error message said `illegal character in file name,` so I called the FBI."

 IM *(ie em)* Acronym for Instant Message.

 iMac *(ie-mak)* The Internet Macintosh, a popular version of the Macintosh computer where the computer and monitor are com-bined — hey, like the original

Macintosh! The iMac is perfectly customized to work with the Internet and comes with everything a person needs to get starting with computing. Comes in several yummy colors.

images *(im-uh-jes)* Graphics, such as those found on a Web page. There is usually an option that prevents the images from being loaded, which displays the Web page's text information much faster. "I often judge how much I like a Web page by how they do or overdo their *images*."

 IMAP *(ie-map)* acronym for Internet Messaging Access Protocol.

IMHO *(in-mie-hum-bol-oh-pin-yun)* Acronym for *in my humble opinion*. Used in e-mail or on USENET.

 IMNSHO *(in-mie-not-soh-hum-bol-oh-pin-yun)* Acronym for *in my not so humble opinion*. Again, used in e-mail, but most likely by someone who has a really big head.

 IMO *(in-mie-oh-pin-yun)* Acronym for *in my opinion*, yet another way to save valuable typing energy molecules when composing electronic mail or writing to a newsgroup.

impact printer *(im-pakt prin-ter)* Any type of printer that makes an image by slapping something down on a ribbon. This includes daisy wheel printer and dot matrix printers or just about any other printer that makes a heck of a lot of racket. See also *dot matrix*.

import *(im-port)* To bring a file created by another program into a document.

For example, to bring in a graphics document into a word processing document. There is no duty or tax on anything you import into your document.

inclusive OR *(in-kloo-seev or)* A logical operator used to manipulate individual bits of data, often used for creating graphics. The result of an inclusive OR is always 1 (which represents true) unless both operands are 0 (false). If you have no idea what this means, you probably don't need to use inclusive OR in your everyday life. See also *XOR*.

Inclusive OR

1	IOR	1	=	1
1	IOR	0	=	1
0	IOR	1	=	1
0	IOR	0	=	0

A table further confusing the inclusive OR concept.

incremental backup *(in-kruh-men-tal bak-up)* A collection of copied files that have been newly created or modified since the time of the last full backup. See also *backup*. "Our tape backup system is so slow that we can't help but do an *incremental backup*."

incremental compiler *(in-kruh-men-tal kom-pie-ler)* A special program that converts programming language statements into machine code each time the programmer types a complete line. Incremental compilers work without interfering with your work. That way, whenever you get done typing your final program, it seems to compile almost instantly. In comparison, most compilers wait for you to type an entire program before they start compiling. This makes you wait a long time until the entire program finishes compiling. Unless you're a programmer, you can safely ignore this definition. See also

I

compile, compiler, interpreter. "I like programming with an *incremental compiler* because I don't like waiting for my program to compile. Of course, the drawback is that on a slow computer, the incremental compiler may get in your way while you're writing your program."

indentation *(in-den-tay-shin)* The alignment of paragraphs within the margins of a page. Usually, the first line of every paragraph is indented several spaces to make the text easier to read, whether or not the text is worth reading in the first place. See also *word processor.* "Use the Tab key for *indentation.* If you use the Spacebar, it's harder to adjust the indentation later, and it's more time-consuming, too."

index *(in-deks)* In many word processors or desktop publishing programs, a feature that creates a list of important words, phrases, or ideas in alphabetical order, along with the page numbers where those items appear. This feature creates the index after key terms and phrases are first marked manually. "Any good desktop publishing application will have an *index* feature. It is especially important if you are laying out a computer book. Because computer books can be as dry as dust, indexes make them useful."

indexed file *(in-deksd fiel)* A separate file containing information about the physical location of records stored in a database file. Rather than search the actual database files, database programs use indexes to run faster. This works as long as the index is accurate, and we all know what the chances of that are. "Keep your *indexed files* up to date so that your database program will run faster. An inaccurate indexed file may confuse your database and keep it from working. (So what else is new?)"

inference engine *(in-fur-ens en-jin)* The part of an expert system that calculates results based on stored facts and information supplied by the user. An expert system consists of three parts: the user interface, the knowledge base, and the inference engine. See also *expert system, interface, knowledge base.* "The so-called intelligence of an expert system resides almost solely in the accurate reasoning of its *inference engine.*"

infinite loop *(in-fin-it loop)* When a computer keeps running the same instructions over and over again without stopping. To better understand the sense of futility an infinite loop can create, think of driving in circles, trying to find a parking space in a major shopping mall the day before Christmas. See also *endless loop, loop.* " This is my example of an *infinite loop.* This is my example of an *infinite loop.* This is my example of an *infinite loop.* This is my example of an *infinite loop.* This is my example of an *infinite loop.*"

 information superhighway *(in-for-may-shun soo-per-hie-way)* 1. Another term for the Internet, which began as a buzzword in government circles. 2. What the Internet could become if everything worked out hunky-dory. Or it could be the nightmare scenario of what the Internet could become if the government ever tries to regulate the thing. "I'm stuck in traffic on the *information superhighway.*"

infotainment *(in-foh-tayn-ment)* A hybrid of information and entertainment. Yet another attempt to teach us something without boring us into a catatonic state. See also *catatonic.* "If they can get away with calling this stuff *infotainment,* I can get away with calling it *borsilly.*"

infrared *(in-fra-red)* Light waves below the visible spectrum, often corresponding to heat or generated by an LED, as in a TV remote control. Many computers use infrared light waves to send and receive information. Infrared computer mice were the first wireless mice; some laptops can communicate with desktop computers via an infrared connection; and some forms of networking involve infrared connections. The only drawback is that, like all light, there can be nothing blocking the sender and receiver's infrared connection.

Infrared Data Association (IrDA) The organization responsible for promoting and ensuring the quality of all infrared hardware.

infrared port *(in-fra-red port)* The location on a computer or piece of hardware that sends or receives infrared information.

inheritance *(in-hayr-uh-tuns)* Used in object-oriented programming languages when one object copies the features of another object (where an *object* refers to a block of code with a specialized task). Programmers like the idea of inheritance because it keeps them from typing the same lines of code over and over again. "Using C++, I created an object to display a window. Bob's object *inherited* my object's features and added the ability to display a message in the window. Now I'm suing Bob for custody."

initialize *(in-e-shal-iez)* To prepare a piece of equipment (a computer, printer, or modem, for example) to do something important. Initializing clears the equipment of any old data still stored in it. "Part of Randy's early-morning *initialize* procedure is to gargle for ten minutes."

inkjet printer *(eenk-jet prin-ter)* A type of printer that sprays ink on paper rather than smack an inked ribbon against the page, like an impact printer does. Inkjet printers are quieter than dot-matrix printers and produce better-quality printing (but not as good as laser printers). See also *dot matrix, laser printer, printer.* "Take off those ear muffs, Larry — an *inkjet printer* is very quiet."

Paper feed

Ink cartridges under cover

Control panel

Paper output tray

A typical inkjet printer.

 inline image *(in-lien im-aj)* An image on a Web page; one that's part of the page and doesn't appear in a special window. Most GIF and JPEG images displayed on the Web are inline images. Most Web browsers have the ability to disable these images, which lets the Web page be displayed faster. Non-inline images include Shockwave, Java, and other multimedia images.

I

InPort *(in-port)* A special hole into which a computer mouse is plugged. "Popeye does not need to buy two mice; his *InPort* mouse works just as well when he's at sea."

input *(in-put)* Information fed into the computer for processing. Computers can receive input from a variety of sources, including the keyboard, mouse, modem, touch screen, or mad scientists bent on the destruction of the entire human race as we know it. See also *I/O, output.* "Give that poor computer some *input* so that it will have something to do, such as print mailing labels. I hate to see a computer sitting idle."

input box *(in-put boks)* See *text box.*

input/output *(in-put owt-put)* See *I/O.*

Insert key *(in-surt kee)* The key on the keyboard that has the word *Insert* or *Ins* printed on it. The Insert key is often used to switch between insert and overwrite modes in a word processor, though not in Microsoft Word 97. "If everything you type starts erasing all your existing information, you're probably in overwrite mode. Your turn this mode off by pressing the *Insert key.*"

insert mode *(in-surt mohd)* An editing mode where all new text you type pushes any existing text to the right; the old text is not overwritten by the new. Most word processors use insert mode unless you tell them otherwise. "Just before the doctor gives me a shot, I go into *insert mode.*"

insertion pointer *(in-sir-shun poyn-ter)* A blinking vertical cursor, as opposed to a flashing block or underline. Used in graphical word processors to show you where newly typed text would appear

on the screen. "*Insertion pointer* is just a fancy term for the cursor. You'd think people from the Pentagon were naming computer parts."

install *(in-stahl)* 1. To prepare equipment or software for use for the first time. 2. The program that actually does the installation process, though under Windows 95 the name is gradually changing to setup. See also *setup.* "Wow! Just 18 more floppy disks, and I'll have WordPerfect installed and can get ready to start using this PC to save me time."

installer *(in-stal-ur)* A program used to update or re-install system software.

Instant Message *(in-stant mess-aj)* An Internet communication that pops up on the screen, allowing one-on-one chat between two individuals. Popularized on AOL, early versions of instant messaging were available on UNIX systems with the Write command back in the 1970s. Also abbreviated IM.

instruction *(in-struk-shun)* 1. A command or direction given to the computer, usually in a programming language, though it could also be a command given at a prompt. 2. Individual parts of a programming language. See also *code.* "If you ever decide to lose your mind, try writing an entire program using assembly language. Just to multiply two numbers, you have to write a page full of *instructions.*"

integer *(in-tuh-jer)* A whole number, which is any positive or negative number without fractions or decimals. "Your age can be a fractional number, but the number of people in this room is an *integer.* Unless, of course, you chop somebody in half."

integrated software *(in-teh-gray-ted soft-wayr)* A collection of programs designed to work well with each other, sharing common files and working as happily as the folks in old communist propaganda films. Most integrated software includes a word processor, spreadsheet, database, and communications program rolled into one. "This may be an *integrated software,* but I don't think that the programs truly love each other as brothers."

Intel *(in-tel)* A company that manufactures microprocessors, specifically the 80x86 and Pentium chips found in the bosom of all IBM-compatible PCs and Windows computers. "Will robots of the future proudly wear little buttons that boast *Intel* Inside?"

intelligent agent *(in-tel-uh-jent ay-jent)* A smart program that goes out and does something for you automatically, often making decisions along the way; for example, a program that visits the Internet, prints the news for you, grabs your stock quotes, and answers some of your e-mail. It could also be any program that carries out specific tasks and responds to certain conditions automatically. "My *intelligent agent* is named Maxwell, and, boy, is he smart."

IntelliMouse *(in-tell-uh-mows)* The fancy new Microsoft mouse with a wheel between the two buttons. The wheel can be turned to scroll a document or pressed to activate a number of interesting features depending on the application. Of course, not every program supports the wheel mouse, but, for some strange reason, most Microsoft

The Microsoft IntelliMouse.

applications do. Weird. See also *wheel mouse.* "I suppose the *IntelliMouse* uses its wheel to get the cheese faster."

interactive *(in-ter-ak-tiv)* A program or computer that responds immediately whenever the user presses a key or does something else that the computer should respond to. Using interactive software is similar to carrying on a conversation: The user's responses change the way the system functions. In comparison, non-interactive computers tend to just sit there and do something only when they feel like it. "I liked learning BASIC because every time I typed a command, the computer immediately told me that I did something wrong. With such an *interactive* system, it was only a matter of time before I got discouraged from using the computer altogether."

interface *(in-ter-fays)* The connection between the computer and the person trying to use it. A keyboard is an interface, and so is a monitor. Putting your fist through the computer can also be considered an interface. See also *graphical user interface, user friendly, user hostile.* "Most computer *interfaces* are designed by someone who really hates humanity."

Intergalactic Digital Research *(in-ter-ga-lak-tik di-ji-tal ree-surch)* The original name of a company that came to be known as Digital Research. For some reason, it didn't think that enough people would take it seriously with that name. See also *Digital Research.*

interlacing *(in-ter-lay-sing)* When the cathode-ray tube (CRT) of a monitor scans every other row to display information on the screen. This process

1

allows the image to be drawn quickly, although the overall image tends to flicker. TVs use interlacing, but the best computer monitors are non-interlacing. See also *eyeball frazzle, monitor.* "My eyes are going to explode from my head if I keep using this lousy *interlacing* monitor."

interleaving *(in-ter-lee-ving)* The ratio of sectors on a hard disk that are skipped for every sector actually read or written to. This was done because the hard drive would spin faster than the controller could read information from the disk. Today's hard drives are interleaved at a 1:1 ratio, meaning that they can read and write information as fast as the disk can spin.

internal clock *(in-ter-nul klok)* A battery-powered clock inside most computers that keeps track of the (supposedly) current time even when the computer's power is off or the computer is unplugged. Internal clocks save you the trouble of having to enter the current date and time every time the computer starts. Even so, computers themselves make lousy clocks; each day the clock will be off a little bit, so the clock needs to be reset at least once a week.

internal modem *(in-tur-nul moh-dum)* A modem that lives inside a computer, often plugged into its own expansion slot. Internal modems are cheaper than

To the phone plug on the wall⌐ To your telephone
1 2 3 4 5 6 7 8   LINE   PHONE

Stuff on the internal modem.

their external brothers and come with fewer cables. They're also more of a pain in the rear

to install. See also *external modem.* "Sorry, I can't tell you about our *internal modem* problems."

internal speaker *(in-ter-nul spee-ker)* The speaker built into every PC, as opposed to external speakers, which usually come separately. "The *internal speaker* is okay for the occasional *bleep,* but you need honkin' external speakers if you want to rock the house while playing Descent."

 international symbols *(in-ter-nash-un-al sim-bols)* Various hieroglyphs, jots, and squiggles designed to represent certain things without a cultural bias. For example, the international symbol for Brightness is usually a sun icon. The international symbol for Off is a circle, and On is a line. "Perhaps the biggest problem with international symbols is that no one from any country can ever figure out what they mean."

International Telecommunication Union-Telecommunication (ITU-T) *(ie-tee-yoo-tee,* for short) The new name for what was once the CCITT; the group that make recommendations for telephone systems and equipment. You may see its acronym tattooed to the bottom of your computer's modem.

 Internet *(in-ter-net)* A collection of computers all over the world that send, receive, and store information. The Internet is not a single computer. It is not a software program. It's merely lots of computers communicating with each other. Access to the Internet is provided through a number of sources — universities, government installations, the military, large companies, and individuals — through Internet Service Providers. After someone is on the Internet, special software is used to access other computers and the information on them. The most popular software is the Web browser. The Internet can also be used to send electronic messages. See also *e-mail, Internet Service Provider, network, Web browser, World Wide Web.* "You just aren't anyone until you're someone on the *Internet.*"

 Internet address *(in-ter-net ad-dres)* The electronic location of someone or some computer on the Internet. Internet addresses vary, depending on what's being looked for. See *domain, e-mail, Web page.* "Having an *Internet address* was the high status symbol for business people in the 1990s. Today, it's a requirement for most kindergartners."

 Internet Explorer *(in-ter-net eks-plor-er)* The Web browser software produced by Microsoft and given away (free) starting with Windows 95. Constantly trying to upstage the more popular Netscape Navigator (which acts like a skin irritant on Bill Gates' pasty Seattle complexion), Internet Explorer generally has more features and comes across as more annoying on the World Wide Web. Preferred by many who really should know better. See also *Netscape Navigator, Web browser.*

 Internet Messaging Access Protocol The system an e-mail program uses to read and manipulate messages on a remote computer. Also known as IMAP.

Internet Protocol *(in-ter-net proh-toh-kol)* The method for sending information around on the Internet. Technically, it's really something, but really something that doesn't need to be described in any detail here.

Internet provider *(in-ter-net proh-vie-der)* See *Internet Service Provider.*

 Internet Relay Chat *(in-ter-net ree-lay chat)* See *IRC.*

 Internet Service Provider *(in-ter-net sir-vus proh-vie-der)* A commercial organization that provides dial-up access to the Internet, like a cable company for computer users who want to get on the Internet. Often called an ISP, an Internet Service Provider is already connected to the Internet. It provides you with an access code and phone number, which you use to get on the Internet. Additionally, it should offer e-mail accounts, getting-started help, classes, and other items for which "service" often loses its meaning. "My *Internet Service Provider* is so nice that someone from there even comes over and scratches my feet while I'm waiting for a Web page to load."

 Internet software *(in-ter-net soft-wayr)* A program used to access the Internet and use various Internet things; for example, e-mail software, a Web browser, a newsgroup reader, FTP program, and telnet. "Though the Internet is not a program, you do need *Internet software* to access the information."

1

Internet Telephony *(in-ter-net tel-ef-oh-nee)* The ability to use the Internet to make normal (voice) phone calls. The quality isn't as good as standard phone service, but there are no long-distance charges to pay.

InterNIC *(in-ter-nik)* Amalgam of *Inter*net *N*etwork *I*nformation *C*enter, the people more or less "in charge" of the Internet. Presently, it assigns Internet addresses and keeps most of the mess organized. Sponsored by the National Science Foundation and AT&T. Eventually, other companies are slated to join InterNIC and assign addresses to various things on the Internet. "*InterNIC* is the place which tells you that Web site names like mcdonalds.com and ibm.com are already taken. Please try again."

interpreted language *(in-ter-pruh-ted lang-wij)* A programming language where the computer reads the program statements one at a time and then follows the instructions. Common interpreted languages are BASIC, LISP, Prolog, and LOGO; although C and Pascal also can be interpreted. This contrasts with compiled languages, which are written and then translated into computer code in two steps. See also *compile, compiler, interpreter.* "*Interpreted languages* run slower than compiled languages because the computer has to read each statement, follow its instruction, and then read the next statement. This is like trying to read a French novel by reading a word to a translator, waiting for him to tell you what it means in English, and then reading another word."

interpreter *(in-ter-pruh-ter)* A program that reads statements written in a programming language, such as BASIC, and immediately follows the instructions. An interpreter is usually easier for learning a language because it gives you immediate feedback. The disadvantage is that other people can't use your programs unless they also have a copy of your program's interpreter. "To help her understand DOS, Doris hired an *interpreter.*"

interrupt *(in-ter-upt)* 1. An operation that rudely butts in, stops the computer from whatever it's doing, and makes it do something completely different. For example, the serial port interrupt stops the computer whenever a character appears at the serial port, deals with the character, and then lets the computer continue with its business. "Excuse me, I'm an *interrupt,* and I'm here to stop everything until you deal with me." 2. A software instruction that directs the computer to go visit some remote corner of a program to do something and then come right back. 3. A communications line between some device and the microprocessor. See also *IRQ.*

intranet *(in-trah-net)* A mini version of the Internet inside a Local Area Network. The intranet can be set up with servers and use the same software and protocols as the Internet, but it serves only a single office or organization. Yet another attempt by some companies to capitalize on the Internet craze. "*Intranet* is truly one of the great buzzwords of the mid-1990s."

I

invalid _(in-vow-lid)_ Ugly word used by many programs to mean that something is incorrect or unexpected. "The notion that the IRS owes you money is _invalid._"

inverse text _(in-vers tekst)_ Letters that appear white against a dark background or that appear with the foreground and background colors reversed; for example:

This section reserved for dead smokers only

I/O _(ie-oh)_ Acronym for input-output, the basic operation that makes a computer work. "Old MacDonald had a computer. IEEE I/O!"

 IP _(ie pee)_ Acronym for Internet Protocol.

 IP address _(eye-pee ad-dres)_ A number corresponding to the exact location of some computer somewhere on the Internet. Normally, you don't have to type these suckers; you type the cryptic Internet address instead; see also _Internet address._ "George wanted to know my _IP address,_ and I had to explain to him that I could do that only when there was snow outside."

 IPX _(ie pee eks)_ Acronym for Internetwork Packet eXchange, a method for various networks to communicate.

 IRC _(ie ar see)_ Acronym for Internet Relay Chat, the way people on the Internet can gather and type at each other. Most people just call it chat. See also _chat._

IRQ _(ie ar kyoo)_ An interrupt request line in a PC, a direct connection between some bit of hardware and the microprocessor. A communications line. The IRQ is used by hardware devices to let the microprocessor know when they're ready to do something or have already done something. Normally, you shouldn't clutter your head with such a bizarre term. However, a PC has only a given number of IRQs, and they get snatched up by optional hardware devices quickly. So, after you add a network adapter, sound card, and mouse, your computer runs out of IRQs and, though you may have expansion slots galore, you can't add anything new. "A Pentium computer may be powerful, speedy, and advanced, but it's still limited by the same inane _IRQ_ problems as the old IBM PC AT."

ISA _(ie-suh)_ Acronym for Industry Standard Architecture, which is the type of bus (expansion slots) originally used in the IBM AT. These still appear in modern PCs, despite the attempts of other standards to take its place; see also _EISA, MCA, PCI._ "The computer industry knows that _ISA_ is an old standard, but trying to kill it is like trying to kill a roach."

ISAM _(ie-sam)_ Acronym for Indexed Sequential Access Method, a technique for storing and retrieving data efficiently using tables and indexes. ISAM is often used by database programs. "_ISAM,_ Sam I am. And I still don't like the darn green eggs and ham!"

ISDN _(ie es dee en)_ Acronym for Integrated Services Digital Network, a very fast telecommunications line that

_I_

was supposed to be the future of telephone and modem communications. ISDN is digital, as opposed to the analog phone system. And, as we all know, digital just must be better. However, ISDN was slow to be implemented and is now being surpassed by other standards. See also *ADSL, POTS.* "Many people thought that having an *ISDN* connection in their house was their ticket to fast communications. Alas, they also needed a pricey *ISDN* modem to make that happen."

ISO *(ie es oh)* 1. Acronym for International Standards Organization, a group that tries to set standards for lots of different industries. "With the way the computer industry ignores standards, *ISO* probably means Ignored Standard Optional." 2. The standard for the Pascal language, often called ISO Pascal. Unfortunately, the most popular version of Pascal, Turbo Pascal, ignores the ISO standard altogether. So much for standards. See also *Pascal.*

ISP *(ie es pee)* Acronym for Internet Service Provider; see also *Internet Service Provider.*

italic *(ie-tow-lik)* A type style that slants text to the right for special emphasis, like the leaning tower of Pizza in Italy. See also *font, text, typeface.* "Please use *italics* and not underline. Underlined text is what they use at the DMV when they want to get creative."

iteration *(it-ur-ay-shun)* 1. The repetition of a statement in a program, often called a loop or, if something goes terribly wrong, an endless loop. See also *endless loop, infinite loop, loop.* 2. The number of times something has repeated. "The program is now in its 400th iteration of saying 'Disk not found.'"

I

J: *(jay koh-lin)* The drive letter designation for (what is most likely) a network drive in your computer.

jack *(jak)* A place to plug in electrical wires. One of those holes in the back of your PC into which you plug a cable. "Our feminist staff refuses to plug anything into the computer unless we call some of the holes *Jack* and some of them Jill."

jacket *(jak-et)* The plastic, square case that protects a floppy disk from dirt, fingerprints, and other forms of physical damage short of gunshots, fire, or hydrochloric acid.

jaggies *(jag-eez)* A far more descriptive word for aliasing. The jaggies are the stairstep effect that takes place when a computer tries to draw circles and arcs. See also *aliasing.* "If you make the letter *O* too big, you'll notice little *jaggies* all around the edges."

 Java *(jah-vah)* 1. A programming language developed by Sun Microsystems. Java programs can run on any computer connected to the Internet, which makes it a very useful language. "Knowing how to program in *Java* doesn't make you a better employee at Starbucks." 2. The latest in a series of Internet buzzwords, which also spawned a whole series of coffee-theme products.

Java Script *(jah-vah skript)* Another type of Internet programming language, similar to Java but much easier to learn.

Jaz disks *(jaz disks)* A type of removable disk storage created by Iomega, the Zip disk people. Jaz disks are capable of storing 1GB or 2GB of information per disk, making them an ideal form of removable storage for multimedia developers, backups, or whenever a removable drive is needed. They tend to be pricey, though, so you don't see them much.

JDK *(jay dee kay)* Acronym for Java Development Kit, a freebie from Sun Microsystems that lets you program in the Java language. Visit `http://java.sun.com/products/jdk/1.1/index.html`.

jewel case *(jul kays)* The plastic container a CD or DVD comes in. "Many CD-Rs sold today do not come with a jewel case."

job *(jawb)* A task that the computer is supposed to do whenever it gets around to doing it. See also *queue.* "This computer's running so slowly because it has so many *jobs* backed up in the queue. Let's fire a few and start the whole thing over again."

join *(joyn)* A term used when a relational database cross-references two files. See also *relational database.* "Rather than type the same information over and over again, just store it in separate files and *join* them when you need them. If that doesn't work, type the same information over and over again."

Jornada *(jor-nah-duh)* A handheld computer from Hewlett-Packard.

joystick *(joy-stik)* A peripheral with a tiny wand that can move in several directions. Moving the wand moves a something-or-other around the screen.

A joystick, ready for action.

Joysticks are often used with games. "When you buy a flight simulator program, you have to buy a *joystick* so that it feels like you're really flying the airplane. After all, how many pilots fly an F-16 using a keyboard?"

joystick port *(joy-stik port)* The hole (nay, *jack*) in the back of the computer where you plug in the joystick.

JPEG *(jay-peg)* Acronym for Joint Photographic Experts Group, a new, universal graphics standard designed to replace the old GIF graphics standard. Although GIF files can contain as many as 256 colors, JPEG files can display as many as 16 million colors in a single graphics image. For storing digitized photographs, the JPEG standard offers sharper resolution, although the older GIF standard works better for plain line drawings or clip art. JPEG files usually have the JPG file extension in DOS and Windows. "The more Milton collects *JPEG* art from the Internet, the less we see of him."

Julian *(joo-lee-an)* A method of simplifying dates in a computer. In the Julian system, every day has a unique number. Day 1 represents January 1, 4713 B.C. Day 2448299 represents February 11, 1991. Programmers often use the Julian system for representing dates because it's easy for computers to handle. If you try guessing the date 100 days from January 23, 1964, you'll see how clumsy our ordinary calendar system can be. "My son was born on February 11, 1991, or 2448299, if you use the *Julian* system."

jump *(jump)* 1. A programming instruction that causes execution to skip to another location — literally to "jump" over a chunk of code. See also *GOTO.* "Assembly language programmers seem to *jump* a lot." 2. What you do when someone drops an ice cube down your shorts.

jumper *(jump-er)* A small, plastic, rectangular-shaped plug used on circuit boards to open or close certain circuits. Usually, a two- or three-prong pin sticks out of the circuit board, and the jumper slides over these pins. "No, Virgil, I need the little kind of electronic *jumper*, not those cables you bought at the NAPA store."

justify *(just-uh-fie)* To align text within the margins of a page, either left, right, center, or justified. Many people call alignment *justification.*

```
This is              This is                  This is
text using           text using              text using
left alignment.   center alignment.   right alignment.
```

"It's hard to *justify* the use of right justification in any document because it looks so strange. In most documents, you left-*justify* text and center-align headlines."

K

K *(kay)* Acronym for kilobyte. See also *kilobyte*. "Robbie was disappointed to find out his computer didn't come with any memory. When he read 0K, he thought it meant the computer was 'okay.'"

K: *(kay koh-lin)* Drive letter designation for what could possibly be the ninth hard drive in a PC, but most likely it's a network drive.

K6 *(kay-siks)* Designation for a Pentium-compatible microprocessor developed by AMD (Advanced Micro Devices). See also *Pentium*.

K&R *(kay and ar)* 1. Abbreviation for Brian Kernighan and Dennis Ritchie, but it really refers to the book they wrote, *The C Programming Language.* For the longest time, this book was the only specification for the C language, the only real reference anyone had. "I just couldn't write a C program without my *K&R* handy." 2. A C compiler that follows the standard set forth in Kernighan and Ritchie's book. See also *bible*.

Kb *(kil-uh-bit)* Acronym for kilobit, or 1,024 bits — not bytes. Used primarily on computer memory chips. "For some reason, you need eight 256Kb chips to get 256K of RAM."

KB *(kil-uh-biet)* Acronym for kilobyte. See also *kilobyte*.

Kerberos *(ker-bur-os)* A system for verifying access to a computer or network. Probably comes from Cerberus *(ser-bur-os)*, the three-headed dog that guards the entrance to Hades in Greek mythology. (You know, two heads would have been enough for us.)

Kermit *(ker-mit)* A method (protocol) for transferring files that was named after Miss Piggy's boyfriend, Kermit the Frog. Kermit is slower than XMODEM but often is used when transferring files from mainframes because no other protocol may be available. See also *protocol, XMODEM*. "Yes, *Kermit* the Protocol is named after Kermit the Frog."

kernel *(ker-nel)* A term used by programmers to describe the main or core part of a program. "This is a chicken operating system. Its kernel must be named Sanders."

kerning *(kurn-ing)* To adjust the spacing between letters so that they look nice together. Certain letters look better closer together than others, such as putting *T* and *y* together so that the upper part of the *T* hangs slightly over the *y*. Kerning is used most often in word processors and desktop publishing programs when the exact spacing of letters is important or when the boss just wants to give people something tedious to worry about. "Jacob used too much kerning to tighten up his paragraph, and the word *of* became *fo*."

key *(kee)* 1. The buttons on the keyboard. 2. A password needed to decrypt or encrypt a file. 3. The item used for searching and sorting a database. If you're searching for all the names and addresses of everyone who lives in California, California (CA) is the key. 4. The guy who wrote the *Star Spangled Banner.* "I've looked all over my keyboard, and I still can't find the Francis Scott *Key.*"

keyboard *(kee-bord)* 1. A typewriter-like device used to communicate with a computer. A series of buttons, arranged in the standard IBM Selectric type of layout, connected to the computer via a cable. The thing you type on. The thing you can pick up and slam down on the desktop when the computer won't obey what you type. 2. Sometimes used as a verb to mean "typing," as in "I have to keyboard in two more pages, and then I'm done."

A keyboard.

keyboard *(kee-bord)* The set of buttons you use to communicate with a computer. When you press a key, the keyboard sends a signal to the computer, which does something interesting, such as display a character on the screen. "Too many computer *keyboards* feel like a cheap toy typewriter. Others feel so mushy that it seems like you're typing on a spoiled banana."

keyboard buffer *(kee-bord buf-er)* An area of memory set aside to hold a specified number of keystrokes in case you type faster than the computer can keep up with. After you stop typing, the keyboard buffer feeds the computer the remaining keystrokes stored in the buffer. See also *buffer.* "With a big keyboard *buffer*, I can keep typing until my fingers tie themselves in knots."

keyboard cover *(kee-bord kuh-ver)* A clear, flexible, plastic sheet that fits over a keyboard, allowing you to type while protecting the keyboard from liquid spills, cookie crumbs, dirt particles, and crawling insects. "Nothing paralyzes your computer keyboard with fear like the sight of a 5-year-old's hand, gloopy with peanut butter. Better buy your computer a *keyboard cover* to keep it sane."

keyboard plaque *(kee-bord plak)* The buildup of hair, food, and other crap that accumulates on any computer keyboard. "Not only does keyboard plaque look gross, it eventually makes the keyboard utterly inoperable."

keyboard shortcut *(kee-bord short-kut)* A single key or combination of keys that activates a command. Specifically refers to the shortcut shown on a menu, such as Ctrl+F by the File command; Ctrl+F is the keyboard shortcut. "I tried to take a *keyboard shortcut* from the Enter key to the Tab key, but I stepped on my colon."

Key Caps *(kee kaps)* A Macintosh program that shows you the characters you can produce by typing different keystroke combinations. The Key Caps program appears on the Apple menu and displays the keyboard along with any characters you type. "Mary was disappointed that the *Key Caps* program didn't have the little fez she wanted for the Enter key."

K

 keychain *(kee-chayn)* A feature of Mac OS 9 that securely stores all your user IDs and passwords. One typed password or voiceprint unlocks all passwords in the system.

keypad *(kee-pad)* A related group of keys placed together for convenience. The most common keypads are the numeric keypad and the cursor keypad. "Ever wonder why the keys on the numeric *keypad* are arranged in neat rows and columns but the keys on the typewriter part of the keyboard are arranged like they still used mechanical levers on a manual typewriter?"

keyword *(kee-werd)* 1. The main set of commands and functions in a programming language. For example, CALL is a BASIC keyword, CASE is a Pascal keyword, and int is a C keyword. "Keywords have special meaning in programming languages, just as certain four-letter words have special meaning in the English language." 2. Text to be found by a Search or Find command in a word processor or other program.

KHz *(kil-uh-hurtz)* Abbreviation for *kilohertz*. The word *kilo* means 1,000 of something, so kilohertz must mean 1,000 hertz. And hertz is a term for the number of cycles per second, so a kilohertz is the number of thousands of cycles per second. This must have something to do with computers, somewhere. "The human brain operates at about 1KHz, compared with hundreds of megahertz for a typical microprocessor. But don't feel inferior: Your brain can do billions of operations in each cycle, whereas a typical microprocessor does only six."

 kick *(kik)* To remove an offensive person from an Internet chat room.

kill *(kil)* 1. To delete a file. "Emily refuses to *kill* her files. She prefers to let them pass on naturally." 2. The command that deleted the file. 3. A UNIX command that stops a process, like quitting a program.

kilo- *(kee-lo)* A prefix used in the metric system that means 1,000. So kilobyte means 1,000 bytes, kilogram means 1,000 grams, and kiloliter means 1,000 liters. But just to confuse matters: Because of the binary (and onerous) nature of computers, when you're talking about memory, 1K actually refers to 1,024 bytes. "I like measuring my weight in *kilo*grams because it makes me seem lighter than I really am."

kilobaud *(kil-uh-bod)* One thousand baud. Once used to describe a modem's speed, as in 12 kilobaud for a 1200 bps modem. See also *baud*, *bps*.

kilobyte *(kil-uh-biet)* One thousand bytes, abbreviated K or KB. Actually, it's 1,024 bytes. Kilobyte is used as a measure of the storage capacity of disks and memory. Because one byte equals one character, 1K of memory stores 1,024 characters. That's about as much text as you'll find on a double-spaced, typewritten page. See also *MB*. "In the old days, having 16 *kilobytes* of memory was a big deal. Today, you need 16K to hold an e-mail message from your friend Joe in Utah."

kludge *(klooj; does not rhyme with "sludge")* 1. A temporary but poorly designed solution that actually works and solves a problem. "That's the

K

ugliest chunk of code I've ever seen but, by golly, the kludge works!" 2. A clunky hardware solution.

knowledge base *(naw-ledj bays)* The part of an expert system that stores facts about solving a particular problem. Most knowledge bases consist of if-then rules for reaching an answer. A well-designed expert system should let you change knowledge bases whenever you need to solve a different type of problem. See *expert system.* "For an expert system to be trustworthy, its knowledge base must be current and accurate. Flossing twice a day also helps."

Krell *(krel)* An advanced race of beings on the planet Altair 4. They developed a huge machine that would translate

A Krell?

their thoughts directly into objects; creation by mere thought. This, like most computer science experiments, failed miserably. The Krell were destroyed by their own nightmares in a single night. This was discovered by Lt. Frank Drebin and Oscar from the *Six Million Dollar Man* when they visited Altair in the movie *Forbidden Planet* (1956).

L: *(el koh-lin)* A network drive out there somewhere on a PC. "If you have an *L:* in your system, odds are really good that it's a network drive."

L1 *(el wun)* The primary microprocessor cache, a storage place on the microprocessor designed to speed up program execution. See also *cache.*

L2 *(el too)* The secondary microprocessor cache, usually located between the microprocessor and the main memory. Because this cache is not a part of the microprocessor itself, it tends to be slower than the L1 cache, though its size can be much larger.

label *(lay-bohl)* 1. An identifying name. 2. The name given to one or more cells in a spreadsheet. "In my Lotus 1-2-3 spreadsheet, I put *labels* such as TAXES OWED, MONEY STOLEN, and COST OF OVERSEAS AIRLINE TICKET to identify the meaning of the numbers listed underneath." 3. A specific spot in a program, often used by some other instruction to send program execution to that spot. See also *GOTO.* 4. A disk name. See also *volume label.*

LAN *(lan)* Acronym for Local Area Network, a group of computers connected to share information. See also *network, Wide Area Network.* "Our network administrator's favorite C&W song is 'Stand By Your *LAN*.'"

landscape orientation *(land-skayp or-ee-en-tay-shun)*

Landscape orientation, ready to go.

Printing as though the page were turned sideways so that its width is longer than its height. In comparison, most printing is done where the width of the page is shorter than its height, known as portrait orientation. See also *portrait orientation.* "Maps are usually printed using *landscape orientation,* but brochures and letters usually use portrait orientation. When your printer totally screws up and chews your page into gibberish, that's known as Picasso orientation."

language *(lan-gwij)* A specified way of using words and symbols to give the computer instructions and tell it what to do. All software is created by using a programming language. "I tried learning to program in C, but it's much easier to use the BASIC *language* instead. It's easier still to use foul language at the computer."

Language Kit *(lan-gwij kit)* A worldwide language-support software that lets you write, edit, and view documents in any language.

laptop *(lap-top)*
A computer small
enough to fit in your
lap and not crush
your kneecaps in the
process. See also
notebook computer,
PC. "My *laptop*

A typical laptop.

weighs too much, and the
person who designed it must have had a
hell of a big lap." See also *notebook.*

lase *(layz)* 1. To print something on a
laser printer. Slang from the term *lase,*
which means to activate a laser. 2. Used
by the military in sighting targets.
Became widely known during Desert
Storm.

laser printer *(lay-zer prin-ter)* A type of
printer that uses a laser beam to generate an image and then electronically
transfers it to paper. The speed of laser
printers is measured in how many pages
per minute (ppm) they can produce.
The printing quality of laser printers is
measured in dots per inch (dpi). See
also *dot matrix, dots per inch, inkjet
printer, letter quality.* "Mr. Spock! Set the
laser printer on Stun."

Paper output tray

Control panel

Toner cartridge
under cover

Paper cartridge
(slides out)

Laser printer.

LaserWriter *(lay-zer rie-tur)*
A laser printer made specifically
for Macintosh computer systems.

launch *(lawnch)* To start a program, or
to start some process. See also *load,
run.* "Windows must be like NASA: I can
launch programs only on clear, sunny
days when there's no wind."

Launcher *(lawn-chur)* A program
on the Macintosh that lets you
easily access common pro-
grams. The programs are displayed as
buttons in a window, which you can
click to instantly launch (get it?) a
program.

LCD *(el see dee)* Acronym for *l*iquid
*c*rystal *d*isplay, a display commonly
used in pocket calculators, watches,
and laptop computers. LCD displays
consume less power than normal monitors, but they tend to look as washed
out as chalk drawings scribbled on the
sidewalk in the rain. "It was so cold out,
my laptop's *LCD* froze. (That is truly an
example of nerd humor.)"

leading *(led-ing)* Extra space that is
inserted between lines of text for aesthetic purposes. The name comes from
the days of printing presses, when printers physically inserted thin strips of
lead between lines. See also *kerning.*
"Perkins! You used so much *leading* in
your document that it could be used as
shielding in the event of a nuclear
attack!"

learning curve *(lurn-ing kurv)* A graphical chart showing how much is learned
over a period of time, or how much
should be learned. The rate of learning.

You can compare your progress with the learning curve to see whether you "get it." "I'm so far behind that, from here, the *learning curve* looks like the Himalayas."

LED *(el ee dee)* 1. Acronym for *l*ight-*e*mitting *d*iode, a device that lights up when an electrical current passes through it. Many digital clocks use LEDs to display numbers. "My alarm clock has a big, fat, red *LED*. I can see the numbers clear across the room without my glasses. I can even feel the numbers being burned into my eyelids while I sleep." 2. A type of printer that uses an LED to create an image on paper. LED printers are quiet and relatively fast.

left-justify *(left-jus-tuh-fie)* To align text flush against a left margin:

```
This is
an example
of left justification.
```

See also *flush, justify.* "Most liberals don't need a reason to *left-justify* their text."

legacy *(leg-uh-see)* Refers to older software or a computer system that's still being used despite it's being very old or obsolete. Typically, the cost of replacing such a system would be more than maintaining it as is.

Lempel-Ziv *(lem-pol ziv)* A compression scheme developed by Abraham Lempel and Jakob Ziv, used today to compress files, disks, and other digital information so that it doesn't hog up so much space.

letter quality *(let-er kwahl-uh-tee)* Printed text that is clear enough that it looks like it came from a typewriter.

Usually refers to printing that a dot-matrix printer produces. "My dot-matrix printer can produce *letter-quality* printing, so it looks like a typewriter printed it. Oh, I love using technology to impress folks."

LF *(el ef)* 1. Acronym for Line Feed, a signal that tells a printer to start a new line. "Most dot-matrix printers have an *LF* button and an FF button. If you press the FF button, the printer rolls a complete page out of the printer. If you press just the LF button, the printer just moves the page up one line." 2. The line-feed character, ASCII code 10. See also *ASCII, control code.*

library *(lie-brayr-ee)* A storage place for common routines used in a programming language. The routines in the library are used by the programmer and "linked" to create a final program. See also *linker.*

license agreement *(lie-sens uh-gree-ment)* A piece of paper that comes with software that states, in very legal terms, that A) you don't own the software — you are merely entitled to use it B) you cannot copy or distribute the software C) you have no guarantee that the software will work D) heck, there's even no guarantee that the disk inside the envelope isn't really a piece of bathroom tile.

Life *(lief)* A computer simulation of artificial life, invented by John Horton Conway in the early 1970s. "The Game of Life" plays on a grid of dead or living cells. The placement of cells on the grid ensures whether the cells continue to live or whether they die off. An interesting toy.

LIFO *(lee-foh)* Acronym for Last In First Out, which describes a data structure used by programmers and known as a stack. See also *FIFO, stack.* "Airlines try to board their planes *LIFO*: The last rows are boarded first and the first rows last. But when the plane lands, the people in the first rows get out first. This would work if it weren't for those morons trying to stuff those body bags they carry into the overhead bins."

light pen *(liet pen)* A light-sensitive detector in the shape of a pen, which lets you draw pictures and give input to the computer from the screen. "Aha, Darth Vader! My *light pen* is mightier than your light sabre!"

 line eater *(lien ee-ter)* An old monster from the early (pre-Web) days of the Internet. Some newsgroup-reader programs would somehow ignore the first line of text in a message. Therefore, people composing messages would include a blank line or a line with the words "Eat me!" on it to prevent the important part of the message from being missed. "Since line eaters are rare today, few people start their newsgroup messages with a warning to the *line eater.*"

line editor *(lien ed-uh-ter)* A program that edits text one line at a time, as opposed to full screen. This is like trying to paint a wall through venetian blinds. See also *editor.* "The most infamous *line editor* of all time was one named EDLIN that came with MS-DOS. Pray that you never have to use it."

line feed *(lien-feed)* See *LF.*

line-in jack *(lien-in jak)* Where you plug in your stereo or VCR to the computer for capturing sound.

Look for the line-in jack symbol on your computer.

line noise *(lien noyz)* Pops, buzzes, clicks, or other random noise that happens on a phone line. During conversation, you don't notice line noise. But when a modem uses the phone line, the line noise may often be misinterpreted as a signal from the other computer. The result is often garbage characters on the screen. See also *garbage.* "There is so much *line noise* that my modem can't communicate. Oh, no wonder — 10,000 birds just landed on the phone lines outside my house."

line number *(lien num-ber)* A way of identifying a specific line in a text file or document. The first line is number 1, the second line is number 2, and so on. To move to a specific line in a document, you would tell the computer "Please show me line number 35." "*Line numbers* come in handy when programming, because the compiler typically tells you on which line you goofed up."

line printer *(lien prin-ter)* A high-speed printer that can print an entire line at once. Line printers are great for printing quick drafts, but they're terrible for printing nice print. "The telephone company uses a *line printer* to print inaccurate phone bills more efficiently."

lines per minute *(liens per min-ut)* The number of lines that can be printed during 60 seconds. Used to measure the speed of old impact or line printers. Replaced by pages-per-minute with laser printers.

link *(leenk)* 1. To connect two computers through a modem, cable, or network. 2. Using Windows or OS/2 to connect two files so that they share identical information. If you change data in one file, a hot link automatically changes the same data stored in the second file. With a cold link, changing data in one file does *not* automatically change the same data in a second file. 3. To combine multiple machine language files together to create a single program. 4. A bit of text or graphics on a Web page that provides access to another part of the Internet, typically something that's related to the text or graphic. See also *hypertext.*

linked list *(leenkd list)* A data structure used by programmers to store information. The size of a linked list can change as the program runs. A linked list consists of two parts: the data and a reference to the next chunk of data. Think of a linked list as a train of cars connected together. Each car holds cargo (data), and each car is connected (linked) to the next car.

linker *(leen-ker)* A special program that combines one or more machine language files (object files) and converts them to a single executable file. "Rather than try to create one huge program at once, write a bunch of little ones. Then use a *linker* to combine them all into one huge, unmanageable program loaded with bugs, and price it at $495 like everyone else does. This is the secret of selling software."

 link rot *(leenk rot)* What happens to old Web pages when the links they refer to dry up or move.

Linotronic *(lien-oh-tron-ik)* The brand name for a typesetting machine used by many book and magazine publishers. A Linotronic printer produces extremely high-quality print and makes an ordinary laser printer look like trash. "I like printing rough drafts on my home laser printer. Then, for the final drafts, I print on a *Linotronic* machine."

lint *(lint)* A program designed to cull through C language source code and spot obvious or potential boo-boos.

Linus Torvalds *(lee-nus tor-vahlds)* The developer of Linux. One of the highest-ranking gods of computerdom.

Linux *(lie-nuks)* A shareware version of UNIX (a very close copy) developed by Linus Torvalds. Linux runs on most computers, allowing people who couldn't afford real UNIX boxes to play with UNIX. All UNIX terms and commands in this book also apply to Linux. (Incidentally, the "in" way to pronounce Linux is "lih-NUKS," which sounds like Lennox the air conditioning and heating company. Linus himself pronounces it "LEE-nooks." We feel that it's pretentious to call it anything other than "LIE-nuks," which is how most English-speaking people would pronounce it.)

liquid crystal display *(lik-wid kris-tul dis-play)* See *LCD.*

Lisa *(lee-sa)* An early attempt by Apple Computer to design a user-friendly PC. The Lisa was essentially a prototype Macintosh, complete with a graphical user interface, mouse, and all that. Unfortunately, Apple couldn't figure out what to do with Lisa, and the thousands of people who paid $10,000 for it were pretty much screwed. Named after Steve Jobs' daughter from a nonmarriage.

Lisp *(lisp)* An acronym for *list* processing, a language developed at MIT in the early 1960s for artificial intelligence research. LISP code includes an incredible number of parentheses. Related dialects include Common LISP and Scheme. Typical LISP applications include computer learning, natural language processing, and understanding why people bother getting a Ph.D. in computer science when rock stars with third grade educations make millions by singing one hit single. "Unlike other languages, *LISP* programs can modify themselves while they're running, which means that programs can really run completely out of control. And this is called artificial intelligence."

list *(list)* 1. A collection of data arranged in a certain order. Programs usually store lists as arrays or as a linked list. A phone book is a list of names and numbers. A grocery list is also a list. See also *array, database, linked list.* "My program was supposed to alphabetize my *list* of names and addresses. The only question now is which alphabet did it use?" 2. Short for listserv, used to mean a mailing list. See also *listserv.*

list box *(list boks)* A dialog box that displays a list of items. Items commonly found in a list box include filenames, printer names, directories, groceries, or anything else the computer thinks that you might want. See also *dialog box.* "Yes, Sedrick, the *list box* is the one tilting starboard."

 listserv *(list-surv)* 1. Software that controls a mailing list. See also *majordomo.* 2. A nickname for a mailing list. See also *mailing list.*

lite *(liet)* 1. A version that lacks some of the features of the full-powered model. For example, a word processor may have a "lite" version, one that's still compatible but lacks many of the features and cost of the original. 2. Tastes great, less filling. "I fly 2,000 miles on a moment's notice to fix your network, and you offer me a *lite* database file?"

literal *(lit-ur-ul)* A constant value defined in a program, such as the value of π or some other number or string. The literal's value cannot change, as opposed to a variable, which is designed to hold different values.

load *(lohd)* 1. To transfer information from disk storage to memory in the computer. 2. Another term for the Open command. 3. The BASIC language command that opens a BASIC program on disk. "Before the Open command, the official Microsoft Word method for getting a document file on disk was Transfer-File-*Load.* And you wonder why they still can't write a decent user manual?"

Local Area Network *(loh-kul air-ee-uh net-wurk)* See *LAN.*

local bus *(loh-kul bus)* A type of high-speed expansion slot for a PC, one that connects directly with the microprocessor. The advantage here is that devices connected to the local bus run much faster because they have a larger pipe through which they can yell at the CPU.

Typical devices connected to a local bus include high-speed video cards and hard drives. See also *bus, expansion slot, PCI, VESA*. "No, this bus doesn't go to Video City. You need to take the *local bus.*"

local echo *(loh-kul ek-oh)* An option in a terminal program where characters typed on your computer are displayed on your screen. In most circumstances, all the text you see on the screen comes from the other (host) computer. The local echo option needs to be activated when you cannot see what you're typing.

LocalTalk *(loh-kul tahk)* The connectors and cables that Apple Computer makes for AppleTalk networks. See also *Apple Computer, Inc.; AppleTalk; network*. "*LocalTalk* once again proves that Apple Computer hates to name anything with a space in the middle."

local variable *(loh-kal var-ee-uh-bol)* A variable, used in a function or subprogram, that is not available to the entire program. See also *variable*. "Oh, him? He's just a *local variable*. But someday soon, he's planning on saving his money and moving up to become a global variable."

lock *(lahk)* 1. To prevent access to something. 2. The key lock on some computers used to prevent others from using your computer. "Don't think that key *lock* is anything serious; just about every computer uses the same key." 3. The sliding tab on every 3½-inch floppy disk that prevents the disk from being written to. 4. To limit access to a file in a file-sharing situation. See also *file sharing*.

log *(lawg)* 1. Abbreviation for *log*arithm, which is a mathematical function that fulfills an important role in some people's lives. "When we learned about *logs* in math class, I was sawing logs in the back of the class." Sometimes just called a log. 2. To use a specific disk drive. Some bad manuals may say "log to drive D" when they really mean to change to drive D.

log file *(lawg fiel)* 1. A text-file transcription of an event or series of events, usually pertaining to some specific activity: computer startup, users logged in, programs run, network access, and so on. 2. In Montana, a stack of chopped wood used to fuel the home in winter.

log in *(lawg in)* To connect to another computer or computer network to access its information. "I have to *log in* by typing an account name and a correct password. If that fails, I'll wait until you have to visit the water cooler, and I'll use your PC."

logging in *(lawg-ing in)* To gain access to a computer system, often by typing a username (or code) and password. Comes from some old lumberjack term. Then again, probably not.

logging off *(lawg-ing off)* To tell a computer system good-bye. Logging off disconnects you from the network or hangs up a remote connection.

logic *(law-jik)* 1. A little bird, tweeting in the meadow. 2. Sensible actions. 3. Formal guidelines for reasoning. The study of the relationship between true and false items. See also *AND, Boolean*. "There is no *logic* in the computer industry."

L

logical *(law-jik-ul)* Refers to a piece of hardware, usually a disk drive, that doesn't physically exist but is referenced as a physical drive by the operating system. For example, all PCs have a logical drive B, which is really drive A. When accessed as drive B, drive A "pretends" that it's B. That's logic for you.

logical drive *(law-jih-kal driev)* A portion of a large hard drive that has been partitioned into several drives — like smaller, "pretend" segments for the convenience of the user or the computer. Logical drives are rarely physical drives, such as floppy or hard drives. Often, a single hard drive may be divided into two or more logical drives, such as drive C:, drive H:, and drive Z:. See also *partition*. "Obviously, Watson, we'll make sense of all this when we locate the subject's *logical drive*."

logical operator *(law-jih-kal op-er-ay-ter)* A symbol used in programming languages, spreadsheets, and databases for defining the relationship between two items. Examples of logical operators include AND, OR, and NOT. If you were using a database, you may want to find all the names of people who make more than $50,000 a year AND who are interested in yachts. Or you may want the phone numbers of everyone in Wisconsin OR New York. Then again, you might want the ages of everyone who owns a car but NOT a foreign car. "That was when the *logical operator* told me that it makes more sense to dial long distance at night, when the rates are cheaper."

logic bomb *(law-jik bohm)* A secret part of a program that erases files or causes other destructive damage upon activation. Disgruntled employees wishing to wreak revenge on their former employers are usually the ones responsible for placing logic bombs. See also *virus*. "Creating a *logic bomb* is a rather illogical thing to do."

login *(lawg-in)* 1. The prompt that appears, after which you type your username. 2. The process of logging into a computer, to identify yourself to the computer system and start working.

login name *(lawg-in naym)* The name you use to identify yourself to a computer system. That, coupled with the proper password, lets you access your files and other goodies in the computer syste. "A company is nice to its employees if the *login name* they're assigned is similar to their own name. The company is not nice when it assigns random numbers and letters as *login names*."

Logitech mouse *(law-juh-tek mows)* A computer pointing device (mouse) designed by a company named Logitech. The chief competitors to the Microsoft mouse, the mice designed by Logitech are often more clever and interesting than the boring old Microsoft mouse.

LOGO *(loh-goh)* A programming language specifically designed to teach children how to use a computer. LOGO programs control an imaginary turtle that moves around the screen and draws lines behind it. By writing LOGO commands to control the turtle, users can create neat little designs that impress adults as well. "When I was a kid, I learned about computers by learning *LOGO*. Then in elementary school, I learned BASIC. In high school, I learned

Pascal. In college, I learned C. Now I have a degree in programming, and I work at a 7-11."

logon *(lawg-on)* See *login.*

 LOL *(ell oh ell)* Acronym for *laughing out loud.* Used on the Internet.

loop *(loop)* A set of statements in a program that is run more than once. See also *endless loop, infinite loop.* "When your computer spews out the same message over and over, it's stuck in a *loop.*"

Lorem ipsum *(lor-um ip-sum)* Random, meaningless text often used for placeholding in desktop publishing and graphical documents to get a good idea of what the final document will look like. It starts: "Lorem ipsum dolor sit amet, consenuetur adisplising eli, set diam nonumy. . . ." and goes on from there.

lossless *(laws-les)* A type of data compression that does not lose any information; the decompressed copy is identical to the uncompressed original.

lossy *(laws-ee)* A type of data compression that sacrifices accuracy for the sake of a smaller compressed size. The decompressed copy is not the same as the uncompressed original, but it's close enough for some purposes. JPEG graphics images are compressed with lossy compression, which doesn't seem to affect the image visually, but the decompressed copy is not the same as the original image.

lost cluster *(lawst klus-ter)* Part of a file that remains on the disk, even though the File Allocation Table (FAT) has no record of its existence. Lost clusters usually occur when the computer is writing a file to the disk and the power fails. Sometimes, lost clusters seem to occur without reason, which is the way most computer problems seem to appear. Various programs help you rid your hard drive of lost clusters, guiding them safely home. See also *FAT.* "I was cleaning behind my computer desk, and, there, amidst all the cables and dust, I found a bunch of *lost clusters.*"

Lotus *(loh-tus)* The company that makes the popular 1-2-3 spreadsheet and the Notes program. The name of the spreadsheet is not Lotus, though many people refer to the program as "Lotus."

Lotus 1-2-3 *(loh-tus wun-too-three)* The first and most popular spreadsheet program for the PC. Lotus improved on the basic spreadsheet, VisiCalc. The product was actually kind of lame and required many add-on programs to give it power, but PC users loved it. One of its main strengths was the ability to automate tasks through the use of macros and templates. In fact, some people designed games you could play on 1-2-3; one of them was named *Templates of Doom.*

Lotus Notes *(loh-tus nohts)* A program (actually, several) that lets people communicate and share information over a network.

low-capacity disk *(loh-kuh-pas-uh-tee disk)* A disk that normally wouldn't have any capacity description if the newer, high-capacity format didn't come around. Since there are high-capacity format disks, the rest of the pack were dubbed low-capacity. "It's very hard to find a *low-capacity disk* today because few computers use them."

low-level format *(loh-leh-vel for-mat)* To physically arrange the pattern of magnetic tracks and sectors of a hard disk. Low-level formats are necessary only when using a new hard disk for the first time, and even then most low-level formatting takes place at the factory, done by professionals wearing white lab coats. See also *format.* "You should never *low-level format* your hard drive."

low resolution *(loh rez-oh-loo-shun)* On printers or computer monitors, low resolution is a mode that produces quick results but poorly drawn images that are likely to hurt your eyes and give you headaches to boot. See also *resolution.* "I have an old, *low-resolution* monitor. The letters on the screen look jagged and fuzzy, and the money I saved by buying a cheap monitor is going to my doctor to pay for new eyeglasses."

lowercase *(loh-wer-kays)* The opposite of capitalization. Most text appears with the initial letter of a word in a sentence in uppercase and the rest of the text in lowercase. See also *uppercase.* "Don't type IN ALL UPPERCASE BECAUSE IT LOOKS OBNOXIOUS. Then again, don't type in all *lowercase* because it looks like you're trying to rip off e.e. cummings."

LPM *(el pee em)* Acronym for *l*ines *p*er *m*inute.

LPT *(el pee tee)* Acronym for *l*ine *p*rinter, a port on the back of a PC for connecting a printer. A printer port! Most PCs have one of these jobbies, called LPT1. The computer can handle two other ports, dubbed LPT2 and LPT3. See also *parallel port, printer port.*

LS-120 *(el-es wun-twen-tee)* Another name for the SuperDisk, a replacement floppy disk that reads and writes both traditional 1.44MB floppy disks and the 120MB, formatted "super" disks.

Luddite *(luhd-iet)* One who fears technology, often to the point of getting paranoid about it. Named after Ned Ludd, an Englishman who went nuts and destroyed a bunch of machinery under the belief that it would put him out of a job. (This was before soccer.)

 luminance *(loom-uh-nans)* The brightness of something.

lurker *(lur-ker)* 1. Someone who reads messages in a newsgroup or mailing list but does not contribute. "Almost 90 percent of the people who read newsgroups on the Internet are lurkers." 2. The people who live in downbelow on Babylon 5.

 Lynx *(leenks)* A Web browser used on UNIX.

LZH *(el zee aych)* Acronym for Lempel-Ziv Haruyasu, a standard for compressing information, such as the binary information found in most computer files. The LZH algorithm is used by popular disk back-up programs, disk-compression programs, and various diet clinics. "Margie thought that she could decompress an *LZH* file by adding water."

M

M: *(em koh-lin)* A drive letter designation in a PC, quite possibly a network drive, but don't rule out a hard drive, removable drive, CD-ROM drive, ZIP drive, overdrive, or country drive.

M&Ms *(em-en-emz)* Candy-covered chocolates with little *M*s on them that don't melt in your hand. Primary source of nourishment for programmers. Belongs to the food group Candy. Other food groups include Pizza, Caffeine, and Processed Potato Foods (for example, chips). "Hey, isn't it about time for dinner? Pass me the *M&Ms,* will ya?"

 Mac *(mak)* Friendly name for a Macintosh. See also *Macintosh*.

 MACAnalyst *(mak-an-uh-list)* A tool for the Macintosh designed for computer-aided software engineering, or CASE. Developed by Excel Software, Inc.

MacBinary *(mak-bie-nayr-ee)* An online file format for the Macintosh. Information is stored with both the file's resource and data forks intact, which allows some programs to recognize and use that information when saving or display the file.

 macdink *(mac-deenk)* The constant and yet enjoyable urge to mess with the appearance of things on a Macintosh, mostly because the system is apparently designed to let you do such things.

Mach *(mok)* An operating system kernel, used in Mach UNIX, which was once available on NeXT computers. Developed at Carnegie-Mellon University.

Mac OS *(mak oh-ess)* The official name of the Macintosh operating system. Mac users refer to it merely as "OS," followed by the version number, as in "OS 9.5."

machine *(ma-sheen)* Another term for computer or computer hardware. In fact, in many foreign languages, the word *machine* is synonymous with *computer*. A common use would be *Turing machine*. See also *Turing machine*.

machine code *(ma-sheen kohd)* See *machine language*.

machine independent *(ma-sheen in-dee-pen-dent)* Commonly used to refer to a program that runs on any computer without modification. A machine-independent program can be developed on an IBM clone and used — without any modifications — on a Macintosh, for example. Machine-independent programs do not exist.

machine language *(ma-sheen lang-wij)*
The language the microprocessor speaks. A "low-level" computer language that communicates directly with the computer hardware. Programs are written in secret code (binary); each instruction corresponds to a single computer operation. Often, an assembly language is used to make the machine language codes more understandable by computer programmers — but that's not saying much because the whole thing is hard, hard, hard. Programming in machine language is not for beginners, no way! See also *assembly language.* "Real programmers use *machine language,* but they also tend to grunt and point at the dinner table."

Macintosh *(mak-en-tosh)*
A family of personal computers created by Apple Computer in 1984. The earmark of the Macintosh is its easy-to-use graphical user interface. It's also very popular with the graphics arts crowd. The Macintosh family is the largest non-IBM compatible personal computer series in use. "Windows is Microsoft's effort to make the PC work like a *Macintosh.*" The following table shows an almost complete list of Macintosh makes and models. (To list all of them would take several more pages.)

An Almost Complete List of Macintosh Makes and Models

Macintosh Model	Introduced
Macintosh 128K	
Macintosh 512K ("Fat Mac")	1984
Macintosh Plus	1986
Macintosh II ("Mac II")	
Macintosh SE	1987
Macintosh IIx	
Macintosh IIcx	1988
Macintosh SE/30	
Macintosh IIci	
Macintosh Portable (laptop)	1989
Macintosh IIfx	
Macintosh IIsi	
Macintosh Classic	
Macintosh LC	1990
Macintosh Classic II	
PowerBook 100	1991
Macintosh IIvx	
Macintosh IIvi	
Macintosh LC II	
PowerBook 160	
PowerBook Duo	1992
Macintosh Color Classic	
Macintosh LC III	
Macintosh LC 520	
Macintosh Quadra 610	1993
Macintosh LC 550	
Macintosh Quadra 630	1994
Power Macintosh 5200 LC	1995
Performa 6400	1996
Power Macintosh 4400	
Twentieth Anniversary Macintosh	
PowerBook G3	1997

Power Macintosh G3 ("G3")	1998
iMac	
Power Macintosh G4 ("G4")	
iBook	1999

 Macintosh user interface *(mak-en-tosh yoo-zer in-ter-fays)* The Apple graphical user interface for the Macintosh family of computers. One of the most wildly successful and copied user interfaces ever. It was inspired by an earlier graphics user interface developed by Xerox.

macro *(mak-roh)* Short for *macro*instruction, a simple way to create shortcuts or automate tasks or procedures within a program. There are two types of macros: keystroke and programming. The keystroke macros record keystrokes (and mouse movements) and then replay those actions later, often by giving a single command. The programming macros work like a programming language to automate tasks, make decisions, and perform complex operations a keyboard macro can't handle. "Hey, Phil, I finally finished that *macro* that automatically fouls up our payroll account!"

macro assembler *(mak-roh ah-sem-bler)* A program that lets you construct assembly language macros. These instructions represent several other machine language instructions at a time — like shorthand for programming geeks. By using the macro instruction, a programmer doesn't have to type as much, and it leaves one hand free to dive into the Doritos. See also *assembly language, machine language.* "I got a *macro assembler* to speed up my machine language programming. Now I can write my program in three years instead of five."

macroinstruction *(mak-roh-in-struk-shun)* A single command that performs several operations. See *macro.* "Do you know the *macro instruction* that tells this program to make toast?"

magnetic disk *(mag-net-ik disk)* A medium (a "flat, round thing") on which computer data is stored. Often called floppy disk or hard disk, a magnetic disk is a surface coated with iron oxide and magnetically charged; bits (electronic charges) of computer data can be stored on the disk for future use. Floppy disks also make great cocktail coasters and impromptu Frisbees. Never use a magnetic disk to play tug-of-war with your dog. Keep all magnetic disks away from magnetic charges (honestly), such as your stereo speakers and your TV antenna in an electrical storm. "The instructions said to store my *magnetic disks* in an out-of-the-way place, so I put them in the toaster."

magneto-optical disk *(mag-nee-toh op-ti-kal disk)* A type of storage device that combines optical-disk technology with magnetic-disk technology to make a disk capable of storing lots of information like a CD-ROM drive but can be written to and erased. These high-capacity disks require special disk drives and are generally slower than a hard drive. Also called MO disk. "I am now on the cutting edge of technology with this new *magneto-optical disk.* My data will certainly survive a nuclear attack, but it may take that long for my program to load."

M

mail *(mayel)* The new, hip way to refer to electronic mail, also known as e-mail. "Now I have two places I can receive *mail:* from my mailbox outside and from my mailbox in my computer. Alas, both are still empty."

 mail bomb *(mayel bom)* A form of electronic terrorism on the Internet in which lots of e-mail is sent to a specific person's mailbox — so much mail that the person cannot deal with it all. The mailbox is typically shut down, rending it unavailable to the user or to anyone wanting to send him mail.

mailbox *(mayel boks)* 1. The place where your e-mail collects. Just like your mailbox outside, except that this mailbox doesn't get knocked over by the snowplow every winter. "My e-mail *mailbox* says that I have two messages waiting. Wow, *both* my friends wrote to me!" 2. An e-mail account, or "address," to which you can send messages to people on a local network or via the Internet. An electronic mailbox can store your electronic mail, in much the same way as the mailbox on the front porch stores your junk mail. See also *electronic mail.* "I just got an electronic *mailbox;* now I can get bills on my computer, too!"

mailing list *(mayel-ing list)* A group of people who exchange e-mail messages. Like in a private newsgroup, messages are sent to "the list" and then distributed to all its members through e-mail. You must subscribe to a mailing list by sending an e-mail message to the moderator or the list computer. "Subscribing to a *mailing list* is one surefire way to increase the number of e-mail messages you get every day."

mail merge *(mayel murj)* A process by which names and addresses are combined with a form letter "master" to create those personalized form letters despised by all. When the master form letter is printed, names and addresses from the mail merge list are inserted into key locations. Each name and address creates a new form letter from the master. "I just got a personal letter from Ed McMahon. You don't suppose he has a *mail merge* program, do you?"

 mail server *(mayel sur-ver)* The program that sends, receives and distributes mail over the Internet or a private network. It can refer to both the software and the hardware.

 mailto *(mayel-too)* A URL or Web browser command that can be used to send electronic mail. The mailto command is followed by a colon and an e-mail address, as in `mailto:dang@idgbooks.com`. "The first URL a spam company employee learns is *mailto.*"

mainframe *(mayn-fraym)* A powerful computer to which "dumb" terminals are often connected. A mainframe is identified by its storage and computing capacity; capability to create multiple, virtual computers; and variety of input/output options. Mainframe computers also are called the dinosaurs of the computer industry. They require cool climates (air conditioning), open spaces, and plenty of electricity. Most mainframe computers today are merely very fast PCs with lots of storage. See also *Cray, dumb terminal, VAX.* "The computing power of a 1960s-era *mainframe* can be found in the average home computer of the 1990s."

map **181**

main memory *(mayn mem-oh-ree)* The primary electronic storage used inside a computer, or RAM. This is as opposed to cache memory or other types of memory. Usually, this type is simply called memory or RAM, though if you're fancy-schmansy, you can say "main memory" instead.

majordomo *(may-jor-doh-moh)* A program that controls a mailing list. Mail is sent to the majordomo to subscribe or unsubscribe to the list. See also *listserv*.

major release *(may-jor ree-lees)* A new edition of a piece of software, marked by lots of new features and abilities. The first digit in a program's release number; for example, 5.1 would be major release 5, minor release (or revision) 1.

Make *(mayk)* A program that helps programmers build programs. Make *makes* programs. It compares source code dates and times with the current dates and times, compiles them as necessary, and then runs the compiler/assembler and linker to create (or make) the final program.

male connector *(mayel kon-ek-ter)* Any type of connector that can be inserted into a female connector. Male connectors are often located at the ends of cables and generally have prongs or wires that fit into the holes of the female connector. (I'm blushing.) After combining a male and female connector, you have a flow of electricity (occasionally accompanied by sparks flying), a surge of power, and, finally, a cigarette (cigarette optional). Please practice safe cable connection. See also *female connector*. "You're trying to fit that serial

male connector into a parallel female connector. It will never work out; they're not meant for each other."

Mandelbrot, Benoit *(man-del-bro, ben-wa)* A scientist at IBM who developed a new branch of mathematics called fractals. See also *fractals*.

manual *(man-yoo-el)* A printed reference or tutorial for a piece of computer hardware or software. Computer manuals have a horrid reputation. Part of that is earned; the person who writes the manual is far too intimate with the product to appreciate the needs of a beginner. Also, due

To fully understand Microsoft Windows, you need the manual.

to printing requirements, the manual is often finished well before the product is. And we don't need to mention that they don't pay the manual writers enough or that often the duty falls to the programmers, who really couldn't care less. "Thank goodness for *...For Dummies* books; otherwise, I'd be stuck reading the *manual*."

manually *(man-yoo-al-ee)* To do something by hand. The opposite of automatically. "The original Altair computer had to be programmed manually every time you turned it on."

map *(map)* To access a network drive and assign it a drive letter on your PC. See also *network drive*.

MAPI *(map-ee)* Acronym for Messaging Application Program Interface, a Microsoft standard for sending and receiving e-mail on a network.

mapping software *(map-eeng soft-wayr)* A program that enables you to create maps. Maps can be viewed at different magnification factors and usually require a significant amount of disk space to store. "It's a good thing I brought my portable computer and *mapping software* on this road trip. Now I can get lost in half the time."

marketoid *(mark-uh-toyd)* Derogatory term for a marketing person in the computer industry. Often used by engineers who seem to feel that their stuff would fly off the shelves without anybody's help. Marketing people often don't get it and nod their heads rapidly when talking with any engineer. They love three-letter acronyms and are responsible for most of them.

mash *(mash)* To push. Chiefly a mid-Atlantic state term. "*Mash* the big red button, Vern."

masochist *(mas-oh-kist)* 1. A person who inflicts pain on himself or herself. 2. Anyone who tries to use Windows 95 with less than 8MB of RAM. 3. Anyone who uses WordPerfect for DOS. "They asked at the job interview whether I could use WordPerfect for DOS. I said, 'What do you think I am — a *masochist?*'"

mass storage *(mas stohr-ij)* A high-capacity storage device. Because normal disk capacity has increased over the years, the definition of mass storage is somewhat loose. Typical hard disk drives store gigabytes of data; mass storage is generally considered to be at least two gigabytes of data. However, mass-storage devices can hold more than one *terabyte* (one trillion bytes) of data. See also *byte, high capacity, high density.* "Father John stores all his sermons on a *mass storage* device."

Massachusetts Institute of Technology (MIT) *(em ie tee)* A university located in Cambridge, Massachusetts, where all sorts of interesting technological things have been developed and are still being developed.

master boot record (MBR) *(mas-ter boot rek-urd)* The first item on a bootable disk, one that explains what type of disk it is and contains a program used to load the operating system from another location on the disk. When these things get screwed up, the entire disk is usually lost. The MBR is also a prime target of computer viruses.

master/slave arrangement *(mas-ter-slayv uh-raynj-ment)* When one device (a slave) is controlled by another to which it is connected (a master). Master/slave arrangements are found in disk drive arrays and other hardware configurations and also with mainframes and dumb terminals. See also *client, client/server network.* "When I push the remote control, the TV changes channels. It's a perfect *master/slave arrangement.*"

math coprocessor *(math koh-pros-es-er)* A separate circuit (or computer chip) that performs floating-point arithmetic to enhance the capabilities of the CPU (central processing unit). Before the 486, math coprocessors were purchased separately from the microprocessor. Today, they're integrated with the microprocessor to form a single chip or device. See also *central processing unit, microprocessor, number crunch.* "My PC's microprocessor uses a *math coprocessor* to help it perform calculations. My husband needs a *hardware store coprocessor* to help him spend less money on power tools."

matrix *(may-triks)* A method of storing data in a gridlike thing so that each data element can be easily retrieved. To store the amount of your phone bill for each month of the year requires a 1-dimensional matrix with 12 items; one item for each month of the year. To store the amounts of all your bills (phone, food, gas, and so on) requires a 2-dimensional matrix, with bills listed down one side and months listed across the top. To store these values for several years requires a 3-dimensional matrix, with one separate grid for each year. See also *array.* "The Rubik's cube is the ultimate type of *matrix,* making computers relatively tame by comparison."

maximize *(mak-suh-miez)* 1. To increase to full capacity. 2. To increase the size of a window in a graphical environment. A maximized window fills the entire screen or is as large as it can be under the circumstances. See also *minimize.* "If I *maximize* the window on my checkbook program, will I maximize my income too?"

maximize button *(mak-suh-miez but-un)* The gadget you click with the mouse to make a window

The maximize button.

larger in a graphical environment. See also *maximize.*

Mb *(meg-uh-bit[s])* Acronym for megabit. See also *bit, megabit.*

MB *(meg-uh-biet[s])* An abbreviation for megabyte. See also *byte, megabyte.* "When I was growing up, *MB* meant Milton Bradley."

Mbps *(em bee pee es)* Acronym for megabits per second, the speed of a very fast modem. See also *bps.*

MCA *(em-see-ay)* Acronym for *Micro Channel Architecture.* See also *bus, Micro Channel Architecture.*

MCGA *(em see jee ay)* Acronym for *Monochrome/Color Graphics Adapter.* The IBM graphics adapter used on the PS/2 computers. It's similar to combining an MGA and CGA adapter but also contains some special features of its own. MCGA adapters have generally been replaced by the more powerful SVGA adapters. See also *SVGA.* "*MCGA* is a useless toad of a standard."

MDA *(em dee ay)* Acronym for *Monochrome Display Adapter.* The IBM adapter for monochrome monitors. This adapter does not provide graphics capabilities. See also *CGA, EGA, monochrome, monographics, VGA.* "*MDA* is boring black-and-white text, ladies and gentlemen. Major Yawn City."

media *(mee-dee-ya)* 1. Plural of medium. 2. Any kind of material used for data storage and communication. Media can be magnetic, such as a floppy disk or hard drive; optical, like a CD-ROM or magneto-optical drive; print, as in hard

M

copy; and electronic, as in CNN. Also see *medium*. "The stone tablet was among the first data storage *media*. Talk about a hard disk!"

medium *(mee-dee-yum)* 1. A carrier of information, much like your papergirl or that little voice telling you to go ahead and have a second piece of pie. See also *communications, disk.* 2. A tiny lady who will cleanse your house of spirits and poltergeists. 3. Cooked until it's just pink in the center.

meg *(meg)* 1. Short for megabyte. See also *megabyte.* 2. Nickname for Margaret. "Meg has a hard disk that holds 120 *megs* of data."

mega- *(may-guh)* 1. Prefix meaning one million. See also *MB, megabyte, megahertz.* 2. A unit of measure in the metric system. 3. A slang word to designate an abundance of something, as in *mega-fun.* "Rush Limbaugh's CompuServe e-mail account contains 1 million letters from his adoring fans. Talk about mega-dittos."

megabit *(may-guh-bit)* See *Mb.*

megabyte *(may-guh-biet)* Approximately 1 million bytes. Actually, a megabyte is equal to 1,024 kilobytes, or 1,048,576 bytes. You need only be this specific on your tax form. Outside the IRS, the government has passed numerous laws declaring a megabyte to be exactly 1 million bytes (the 48,576 extra bytes are kept "off budget"). See also *byte.* "Back in the early days of computing, a *megabyte* was considered way, way too much storage space. Now you need 6 megabytes of space just to store the sound the computer plays when it starts."

megahertz *(may-gah-hurts)* One million cycles per second. Microprocessor chips oscillate (wiggle) at a certain speed, measured in cycles per second, or hertz. Besides the clock speed, the internal design of the processor determines its overall speed. See also *hertz, mega-, MHz.* "The People's Republic of China has more than 1 billion bicycles. That's 1,000 *megahertz.*"

membrane keyboard *(mem-brayn kee-bord)* An input device with a flat, plastic surface (a membrane) with keys printed on it — like a cheap, flat calculator. This is a keyboard you probably don't want to use; a touch-typist's nightmare. "Yes, Jared, the *membrane keyboard* on your little Atari 400 makes it perhaps the silliest computer known to mankind."

MEMMAKER *(mem-may-ker)* A blessing from Microsoft for DOS Version 6, which allowed PC users to automatically configure their computer's memory. Microsoft introduced memory-management utilities with DOS 5, but they had to be manually configured. The DOS 6 MEMMAKER program took care of that task automatically. Of course, with Windows, MEMMAKER is now more of a trivia question.

memory *(mem-oh-ree)* 1. Information storage inside a computer. 2. Temporary storage where the computer runs its operating system and applications and where data is created and manipulated. RAM is temporary because it needs electricity to remember what it stores. Turn off the power and the contents of RAM go bye-bye. ROM, on the other hand, cannot be erased, but it's still treated like memory by the microprocessor and programs in the computer. See also *BIOS, RAM, ROM.*

3. Permanent storage. Another term for files stored on disk, though the term *disk memory* tends to befuddle everyone.

memory bank *(mem-oh-ree bank)* Science fiction term for memory inside a computer. Most PC users don't use the word *banks* to refer to memory. Internally, however, memory is stored in rows, which could be referred to as banks. Some hardware documentation does, in fact, refer to every chunk of memory (such as 4 megabytes of RAM) in a PC as a bank. "We finally saved enough money at the *memory bank* to buy a new computer."

memory leak *(mem-oh-ree leeks)* A program error where the memory it uses is not fully released when the program quits. This causes memory loss over time, which builds up in the way a leaky pipe can eventually flood a basement; after a long enough period of time, the entire computer slows due to more and more memory leaks. This type of error is really a program bug that should be fixed by the developer. Although memory leaks are real, they're often blamed by know-nothing tech support people as a source of computer woes. However, true memory leaks are rarely the cause of most computer problems.

memory management *(mem-oh-ree man-ij-ment)* The art of configuring computer memory to get the most from it. This is the task of the operating system on most computers. Under DOS, however, memory management was something Microsoft avoided until Version 5.0. Then it added some memory-management tools, although it was up to you to put them to work. Eventually, Windows came along; it does its own memory management. See also

conventional memory, expanded memory, exten-ded memory. "If I practiced my own form of *memory management,* I wouldn't lose my car keys."

memory manager *(mem-oh-ree man-ij-er)* 1. Computer software that performs memory management. See also *memory management.* 2. MEMMAKER in DOS 6.*x.* Also could be any third-party program, such as *386MAX, QEMM,* or any of a number of memory-management products for the PC.

memory map *(mem-oh-ree map)* A graphical depiction of how memory is allocated in a computer. Actually, the memory map is for trivial purposes only, although some programmer types want to know "where in memory" some tidbit or secret switch is located. To us humans, the information is silly beyond all recourse. "After looking at my computer's *memory map,* I can find Silicon Valley."

memory-resident program *(mem-oh-ree rez-uh-dent proh-gram)* A DOS program that loads like any other program, but stays in memory after it quits, allowing other programs to "pop it up" as needed. Memory-resident programs are often utilities, such as mouse drivers, fax software, and print spoolers, that extend the basic functions of the computer. They're also often the cause of problems and conflicts in your software, which prompted Microsoft to create Windows to solve all that mess. Memory-resident programs also are called *TSRs* (terminate and stay resident). See also *TSR* for the gory details of why such an ugly acronym was enjoyed by computer marketing departments in the late 1980s.

M

Mentat *(men-tat)* A human supercomputer. Mentats are trained in mathematics and have greatly expanded their mental capabilities. From the book *Dune,* by Frank Herbert. Also used to refer to smart computer geeks. See also *Vulcan.*

menu *(men-yoo)* A list of commands or options available within a program. Menus show you your options in a list. The opposite way to run a program is to type the commands without a list, such as at a prompt or through various keyboard combinations. The menu shows each available option, and you can, using the mouse or keyboard, choose a command from the menu. Menus are supposedly the best way to display commands to a computer user. (They tried everything else.) See also *menu driven.* "When I want to change the fonts in my word processor, I just click the Format *menu* and choose the Font command. When I want to order lunch, I often use the Chinese menu and choose Chow Mein. You can't really get through life without knowing something about menus."

menu bar *(men-yoo bar)* An area, usually located at the top of the screen, that contains several menus listed across in a single line. It's from the menu bar that you can choose menus, and each menu contains commands or submenus. You choose commands by using the keyboard or mouse or by asking the waiter for a translation. See also *menu, menu item.* "*Menu bars* usually include appetizers to make you thirsty so that you'll order more drinks."

The menu bar from Microsoft Word.

menu driven *(men-yoo driv-en)* Software that is controlled through menus. The opposite of command-driven. See also *command driven.* "This *menu-driven* program is supposed to be easy, though I can never remember which menu the commands are on."

menu item *(men-yoo ie-tim)* An individual command or option that appears on a menu. "The File menu contains 14 *menu items,* including an Exit command. When I choose Exit, the computer gets up and walks out of the room."

menu tree *(men-yoo tree)* A diagram showing

Menu items from Microsoft Word.

the menu structure within a program. Some menu items do not produce immediate results but "branch out" to more menus or dialog boxes. This creates a hierarchy ("Me first! No, me!") of menu commands and options. A menu tree displays this hierarchy of commands so that you can locate any command through the maze of menus. See also *menu, menu bar, menu item.* "This program has so many menus that I need a *menu tree* to help me find the command I want."

message box *(mes-ij boks)* A small window that appears on the screen and presents a message from the program you're using. Message boxes can appear as the result of your choosing a command or option. They often inform you of mistakes or provide warnings about your actions. See also dialog box. "Last night, I was working late on the computer, and I got a message box that said 'Go to bed!'"

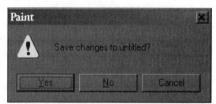

A message box from the Paint program.

meta *(met-uh)* 1. Above and beyond, from the original meaning of meta, which meant to change. 2. A special character combination often associated with a specific key. 3. A key on some weird computer keyboards. A special shift key used in conjunction with other keys. If a program asks you to press Meta-S, you press and hold the Meta key and press S. "I *meta* on a Monday and my heart stood still, Da-do-run-run-run, Da-do-run-run."

MHz *(may-ga-hurtz)* Abbreviation for megahertz. See also *megahertz*. "They were blown away in 1984 when the IBM AT came with an 8*MHz* microprocessor — twice as fast as the PC's 4MHz. I bet they'd be floored back then to know that we would reach speeds of 300MHz."

mice *(mies)* The plural for computer mouse.

mickey *(mik-ee)* The unit of measurement for a computer mouse. The smallest measurable distance a mouse can move and be detected by the computer. "Computer mice move in mickeys."

Mickey Mouse *(mik-ee mowse)* 1. A fictional character, created by Walt Disney, who talks in a high voice and goes easily through life with his wacky friends and his dog, Pluto. Best-known works include "The Sorcerer's Apprentice" from *Fantasia* and regular appearances at Disneyland and Disney World. Also a popular export to Japan. "*Mickey Mouse* may be the world's most popular cartoon character. I like him because he doesn't take life too seriously." 2. Something not quite up to snuff, or straying from the task at hand. "Who designed this Mickey Mouse keyboard?"

micro- *(mie-kroh)* 1. A prefix that means one-millionth. Something very small. A microsecond is one-millionth of a second. Micro is used also to imply microscopic size, as in microorganism and microprocessor. 2. In Microsoft, micro means that many millionaires are working there. "I use Microsoft Word on my *micro*computer and can type a letter in a microsecond."

Micro Channel Architecture *(mie-kroh chan-el ar-kuh-tek-chur)* A type of expansion slot design used in IBM PS/2 model 50 (and higher) computers, abbreviated MCA. Hardware companies design computer enhancement boards (or cards) that plug into the MCA bus. Boards designed for the MCA bus do not work with a standard bus. Among other enhancements, the MCA bus allows use of multiple CPUs within the computer, although we wouldn't try that at home. See also *bus, expansion bus, expansion card, expansion slot, MCA.* "Because IBM patented the *Micro Channel Architecture* so heavily, no one ever used it in any other computer. So, like the bus Ralph Kramden drove in *The Honeymooners,* it's just a relic of our past."

microcomputer *(mie-kroh-kom-pyoo-ter)* 1. Any computer with a microprocessor. 2. A disparaging term for the new personal computers that started appearing in the mid-1970s. The term *micro* came from the microprocessor, the chip that provided the brains for these new computers. The term fell into disuse when PCs became popular in the mid-1980s. See also *mainframe, PC.* "Most *microcomputers* of today are far more powerful than the so-called 'real' computers of 30 years ago. So let's all give a Bronx cheer to our pals in mainframe and minicomputer land: Ptbtbtbtb!"

microfloppy disk *(mie-kroh-flop-ee disk)* A 3½-inch floppy disk, which took over from the 5¼-inch floppy disk, which is smaller than the original 8-inch floppy disk. Actually, the original 8-inch floppy was called a *floppy* because it really had some flop to it. The 5¼-incher was called a minifloppy when it first appeared. This left the term *microfloppy* to describe the smaller 3½-inch floppy disks. "So after the *microfloppy disk* drive, what's next? The *teensyfloppy disk?*"

micron *(mie-kron)* 1. One-millionth of a meter. A distance used to measure the amount of stuff that can be stored on a microprocessor. 2. (cap.) A computer manufacturer just outside Boise, Idaho. It also makes memory chips.

MicroPro *(mie-kroh-proh)* The original name of the company that developed and sold the once-popular WordStar program. Together with Ashton-Tate and VisiCorp, they formed the Big Three software powerhouse of the early 1980s. (Back then, Microsoft sold only DOS and programming languages, and Bill Gates was worth 1, maybe 2, million. Tops.)

microprocessor *(mie-kroh-prah-ses-er)* The central processing chip in a microcomputer. Common microprocessors include the Motorola 68000, 68030, and 68040 used in Macintoshes, and the Intel 286, 386, 486, and Pentium chips used in PCs. The microprocessor controls most of the core functions of the computer, but can be enhanced with coprocessor chips. See also *central processing unit, math coprocessor.* "Harold is experimenting with a new microprocessor that actually uses human brain tissue. Sadly, Harry's using his own brain tissue, which has left him happy but nonplused about his new PC."

microsecond *(mie-kroh-sek-und)* One-millionth of a second. Also used as an exaggeration to imply something that happened very quickly. "If you do that again, I'll be out of here in a *microsecond!*"

Microserf *(mie-kroh serf)* An employee of the Microsoft Corporation. Popularized by *Wired* magazine.

Microsoft *(mie-kroh-soft)* 1. A large software company, located in Redmond, Washington (outside Seattle), that produces Windows and a suite of best-selling application programs for the PC and Macintosh computers. "Almost every program you see these days is made by

Microsoft." 2. Stock I never should have sold. 3. Rulers of the known world. 4. Microsoft has no meaning. See also *IBM.*

Microsoft Access *(mie-kroh-soft ak-ses)* The database program manufactured by Microsoft, sold with certain versions of the Microsoft Office suite.

Microsoft Excel *(mie-kroh-soft)* The spreadsheet program manufactured by Microsoft. Typically sold in Microsoft Office.

Microsoft Office *(mie-kroh-soft off-is)* A suite of programs bundled together into a single "productivity package." Essentially a bunch of computer applications all sold in one expensive box. You pay for this box over and over again through various upgrades. See also *upgrade.*

Microsoft standard *(mie-kroh-soft standard)* A universal, all-encompassing, flagpole-in-the-top-of-the-mountain dictate on How Things Should be Done created by Microsoft and ignored by virtually everyone else. Microsoft is notorious for announcing "new" standards that no one else has heard of. Often the standard is a variation on an existing accepted standard, but done in a way that is beneficial mostly to Microsoft. Eventually, others come to accept the standards; typically, during about the third or fourth revision of the Microsoft standard, it becomes something feasible. Mostly, it's Microsoft's arrogant attitude about its standards that gets to everyone.

Microsoft Way, The *(mie-kroh-soft way)* 1. The street address of the Microsoft Corporation: One Microsoft Way. 2. The method by which Microsoft does things. It often causes considerable ill will among other members of the computer industry. Sure, there's a certain amount of jealousy there, but most of the time Microsoft tends to do things its own way because it's just very huge and can get away with it. IBM was like that once (still is, in many respects).

Microsoft Windows *(mie-kroh-soft windohs)* The official name of the Microsoft PC operating system. Microsoft would like everyone to always call it Microsoft Windows, but we don't! Ha! Pity the poor Microsoft employees who must say *Microsoft Windows* where the rest of the world merely says *Windows.* Microsoft really hates it when you use *Windows* as an adjective. See also *Windows.*

Microsoft Word *(mie-kroh-soft wurd)* The word processing program manufactured by Microsoft. Originally a clunky DOS program (which a seventh-grader could easily out-type), it began its Windows career as Word for Windows. A fairly sophisticated but somewhat feature-burdened product.

microspacing *(mie-kroh-spay-sing)* The insertion of small spaces (smaller than one character) between words to aid in justification. Used in all laser printers and some dot-matrix printers. See also *justify, kerning.* "My first dot-matrix printer had a *microspacing* feature that made its justified documents look more professional. Now my laser printer uses this same technique — in a much more professional fashion."

M

M

MIDI *(mid-ee)* Acronym for *Musical Instrument Digital Interface,* a protocol (standard) for encoding musical sounds in digital form. The differences in sounds and musical voices can be measured and stored using the MIDI standard and then transferred digitally between computers and MIDI-equipped instruments. Electronic keyboards commonly use MIDI. "Using the *MIDI* port in my electronic synthesizer, I can play music on the keyboard, and my computer transcribes the music to the screen. Imagine what Mozart could do today."

millennium bug *(mil-en-ee-um bug)* See *Y2K.*

milli- *(mil-ee)* A prefix meaning one-thousandth. One milligram equals one-thousandth of a gram. "A *milli*second is the length of time it takes for Bill Gates to earn one million dollars in interest."

millisecond *(mil-ee-sek-und)* 1. One-thousandth of a second. Abbreviated *ms.* "Our lawyer is so good that he bills us by the *millisecond.*" 2. Used to gauge the speed of a hard drive. Good hard drives have speeds of 12 milliseconds or less.

MIME *(miyem)* Acronym for Multipurpose Internet Mail Extension, a method of sending pictures, sounds, and other information in an e-mail message. MIME information is encoded into an e-mail message using plain ASCII text. It has to be ASCII because all e-mail messages are ASCII. The beauty of the thing is that it allows you to include pictures and fancy text in an e-mail message without offending any e-mail program's sensibilities. Not every e-mail program supports MIME, which is why you may see a block of letters and numbers rather than a pretty picture of Miss March.

mini *(min-ee)* 1. Short for minicomputer. See *minicomputer.* 2. A smaller version of a larger project; for example, the *MiniFinder.* See also *MiniFinder.*

minicomputer *(min-ee-kom-pyoo-ter)* A small version of a mainframe computer, typically installed at universities or businesses that didn't need mainframe power or couldn't afford a mainframe. The difference between a minicomputer and microcomputer was blurred in the late 1980s. There is no such thing as a minicomputer any more because most PCs can handle the old minicomputer duties with ease. "UNIX was developed on a *minicomputer.* Today, you can run UNIX on a PC you buy at Radio Shack."

MiniFinder *(min-ee-find-er)* A piece of software for the Macintosh that makes it easy to locate your programs. You can configure the MiniFinder to access your most commonly used programs so that you don't have to search through your folders to locate them. "The *MiniFinder* was the most popular Mac program in Munchkinland."

minifloppy *(min-ee flop-ee)* A nickname for the old 5¼-inch disk format. See *floppy disk, microfloppy disk.*

minimize *(min-uh-miez)* 1. To shrink or reduce to minimum size or capacity. 2. Shrinking a window to appear as an icon on the desktop or taskbar in Windows. See also *maximize.* "I thought that when I *minimized* my programs, I would minimize my computer problems, too."

minimize button *(min-uh-miez but-on)* The gizmo in a Windows program that minimizes that window. See also *minimize.*

The minimize button.

minitower case *(min-ee tow-er kays)* A type of PC case that sits up on its end on your desk. Unlike a tower PC, the minitower case can sit on your desk without blocking your view. See also *tower PC.* "Due to zoning regulations, we can have only *minitower case* PCs around here. Anything taller and the neighbors complain that we block their view."

MINIX *(min-iks)* A tiny UNIX clone developed for educational purposes, but freely available on the Internet. Developed by the Dutch professor Andrew S. Tanenbaum. Supposedly, Linus Torvalds started with MINIX when he set out to develop Linux. See also *Linux.*

MIPS *(mips)* Acronym for *million instructions per second,* a measurement of the speed at which programs run on a particular microprocessor. Because programs are coded differently for different microprocessors, it's important to measure MIPS by using equivalent code on each machine. See also *central processing unit, microprocessor.* "If you toss the word *MIPS* around in conversation, as in 'my Pentium is clocked at 20,000 *MIPS,'* people will think that you know what you're talking about."

mirror *(meer-or)* A duplicate set of information, usually provided as a form of backup. However, when data is mirrored, it's saved in two locations at the same time, as opposed to a backup, which is created at certain intervals.

mirror site *(meer-or siet)* 1. Another location on the Internet that contains the same stuff as the original location. Often used on very busy Web pages or FTP sites. "I found the *mirror site* for Lewis Carroll." 2. A duplicate Web page or FTP site on a foreign computer or in another language.

MIS department *(em ie es dee-part-mint)* Acronym for *management information system,* the employees in a big organization who are responsible for purchasing, running, and fixing the company's computers and software. Also called the IS department. "I called Jane from the *MIS department* to come fix my Macintosh. She told me that it would work better if I would quit trying to install DOS on my machine."

missing picture *(mis-ing pik-choor)* 1. See *broken picture.* 2. A graphic image you see replacing what would be an image. This usually happens when you have your Web browser's Load Images option turned off.

MMX *(em em eks)* Trademarked acronym for Matrix Math eXtentions, a Pentium processor with enhanced graphics, video, and other multimedia capabilities. See also *Pentium MMX.*

mnemonic *(noo-mon-ik)* A way to remember something. For example, mnemonic commands can begin with the first letter of the command, as in Alt+F+S to represent the File Save command. "Remember that *mnemonic* starts with an *m* because it has to do with memory, but also remember not to pronounce the *m* or people will think that your lips are numb."

MO *(em oh)* 1. Acronym for magneto-optical. See also *magneto-optical disk.* 2. The letter designation on a magneto-optical disk; they're thicker than regular 3½-inch disks.

modal *(moh-dul)* 1. Something that has modes, such as editing mode versus typing mode. 2. A type of dialog box that doesn't let you do anything else but work in that dialog box. This type of dialog box, common to both the Mac and Windows, typically displays error messages.

mode *(mohd)* One of several distinct ways of using something, such as editing, running a program, or configuring hardware. For example, you can use many DOS programs in either text mode or graphics mode. In graphics mode, you can see fonts and graphics on the screen in a WYSIWYG fashion. In text mode, only the computer's built-in text characters appear. See also *protected mode, WYSIWYG.* "Since everything is graphics these days, people have no idea how blindingly fast their computers can be when they're run in text *mode.*"

modem *(moh-dum)* Short for *modulator-demodulator,* a device used by your computer to communicate with remote computers through the phone lines. See also *BBS, bps, external modem, internal modem, serial port.* "Some *modems* are more dumb than others."

modeming *(moh-dum-ing)* Using a modem. Doing online communications. That kind of stuff. "Happy people go *modeming.*"

 moderated newsgroups *(mod-ur-ay-ted nooz-groops)* A USENET newsgroup through which all posts pass through an individual or group of individuals who screen the messages for relevance and content. Moderated newsgroups typically have the word *moderated* somewhere in their name. "A moderated newsgroup is less likely to have hooligans on it than a regular newsgroup."

modifier keys *(mod-uh-fiyer kees)* Keys that work with other keys to give commands to the computer. Examples of modifier keys are Shift, Ctrl, and Alt. "If you press F7, you can save your files. If you press Shift-F7, you can print your file. If you press Alt+F7 plus all the other *modifier keys* at once, a magic genie appears, granting your every wish (or maybe your system crashes — I forget)."

Modula-2 *(mod-yoo-luh-too)* A structured programming language, similar to Pascal, that encourages programmers to create programs in modules. Modules are linked when the program is loaded. Pascal and Modula-2 were both created by Niklaus Wirth. See also *modular, programming language.* "If you know how to program in Pascal, you'll find *Modula-2* an easy transition."

modular *(mod-yoo-ler)* Consisting of, or relating to, individual units, or *modules.* Programs are often written in modules, or separate pieces, to make programming easier. Modular programming allows programmers to work on different aspects of the program simultaneously. Modular programming also can enhance memory management. "I think this program is *modular.* Each time I do something new, it goes back to the disk to read another program module."

moiré *(mor-ay)* The wavy lines or patterns that appear when a screened image from a newspaper or magazine is scanned into a computer. A "descreen" or anti-moiré filter is required in order to reduce the moiré patterns.

molecular beam epitaxy *(mo-leck-yoo-ler beem ep-uh-taks-ee)* The process by which circuits are engraved on a piece of silicon to make a semiconductor — a computer chip. You can toss around this big, hunky word to really impress your friends. We're not kidding. See also *central processing unit, semiconductor.* "The *molecular beam epitaxy* certainly vaporizes the substrate layers to form nice, crisp semiconducting material. Yessiree."

monitor *(mon-uh-ter)* 1. Another name for a CRT, screen, or terminal — the thing you stare into for hours on end when using your computer. There are several types of monitors, including TTL monochrome, RGB color, analog color, and multisync. See also *CRT, RGB, terminal.* 2. A verb meaning the act of checking the progress of an activity, such as snooping around inside your PC's gut**s** to see how things work. "I was playing Solitaire on my new *monitor* when my boss came in to *monitor* my progress. Luckily, Windows let me task-switch to my word processor instantly."

monochrome *(mon-oh-krohm)* 1. One color. Actually two colors, though one of them is always black: black and white, black and green, or black and orange, for example. 2. A type of computer monitor incapable of displaying text or graphics in color. See also *boat anchor, CGA, EGA, heavy iron, MCGA, MDA, VGA.* "When I exit Windows to use a DOS command, my screen looks like a dull *monochrome monitor* for a while."

monographics *(mon-oh-gra-fiks)* A generic name for a replacement to the original IBM PC monochrome display adapater (MDA) that could also display graphics. A clone of the Hercules graphics adapter. See *Hercules graphics card, MDA.*

monospacing *(mon-oh-spay-sing)* Uniform and equal spacing between the letters of words. With monospacing, each letter of the alphabet uses the same amount of space as every other letter; for example, an *i* uses as much space as an *m*. With proportional spacing, each letter uses only as much space as it needs. Monospacing is still used in some applications, such as business forms. Most fonts use monospacing for numerals to aid in the alignment of financial data. See also *proportional pitch.* "Lois, darling, that *monospaced* letter you did, it's *tres gauche.* Get with the times, girl. Everyone is going proportionally spaced now."

Montevideo *(mon-teh-vi-day-oh)* The capital city of Uruguay. "When you're in Uruguay, be sure to visit the Library of the National Historical Museum in *Montevideo.*"

month *(month)* One of 12 periods a year is divided into. A month can have 30 or 31 days, except for the month of February, which can have 28 or 29 days. *Month* is the only word in the English language that cannot be rhymed. "There once was a lad named O'Grady, who fell for a girl named Sadie; she said "Pick a *month,*" and then, uh, er, never mind."

Moore's law *(mors law)* Essentially, the observation that microprocessor power doubles every 18 to 24 months. Created by Gordon Moore, a cofounder of Intel. Since 1971, Moore's law has remained unbroken.

M

Morlock *(mohr-lok)* From H.G. Wells' *Time Machine,* one of the working-class creatures that dwelt underground and ate the docile surferlike Eloi, who lived above ground. Also a term for a computer nerd who rarely sees the light of day. Morlock can be either singular or plural. See also *troglodyte.*

morphing *(morf-ing)* 1. A graphical trick where one image is smoothly blended into another. Morphing is a popular special effect, used on such films as *Terminator 2* and in various music videos. Using special graphics software, you can bring this type of effect to your PC. The word *morph* may also be used. It's from the Greek meta*morph*osis, which means "to transform." "I used *morphing* software to transform an image of my old, cruddy car into a brand-new Dodge Viper. Now, if only it could do that in real life." 2. What the Power Rangers did when they changed from ordinary annoying teenagers into ordinary annoying superheroes. "It's *morphing* time!"

MOS *(moss)* Acronym for *Metal Oxide Semiconductor,* a type of semiconductor used in computers. See also *CMOS, semiconductor.*

motherboard *(muth-er-bord)* The main circuit board of a computer, to which most devices connect. The motherboard is the real estate upon which the computer's CPU, ROM chips, and often RAM chips sit and work. It also contains the expansion slots and other electronic doodads, making it look like an electronic sushi display. See also *central processing unit, daughterboard, expansion slot.* "Always do something nice for your *motherboard* on Mother's Day."

mount *(mownt)* 1. A term used to describe that something, usually a disk drive, is being used. This term comes from the olden computer days, when they physically had to mount a reel of computer tape on the machine before anyone could access it. Nowadays, the mounting takes place through software commands that make the connections over various wires and hoses. 2. To connect to a remote disk drive on a network, making it accessible from your computer. "Jump through the fiery network hoop, and then you can *mount* the remote H: drive and access your files."

mouse *(mowse)* A pointing device used to provide input for the computer. Most graphical user interfaces (Windows and the Macintosh) use mouse input devices. When you

A pointing device: the mouse.

move the mouse on your desk, the mouse pointer on the screen mimics its movement. This device allows you to control, point at, grab, and manipulate various graphics goodies (and text) in a program. The plural is *computer mice.* See also *Mickey Mouse, mouse button, mouse pad, trackball.* "Betcha didn't know that units of *mouse* movement are measured in Mickeys."

mouse button *(mowse but-un)* One or more switches on a computer mouse. You press the mouse button to make things happen. When a button is pressed, it makes a clicking sound. Mice have from one to three buttons, each performing different functions. The Macintosh uses a one-button mouse. By holding down certain keys as you click the button, you can perform different

M

options — just as though you had a two-button mouse. "The program says to click the *mouse button* twice. So I figured that if I click it ten times, it'll work really great (kind of like the TV remote)."

mouse droppings *(mowse drop-ings)* When your mouse screws up and leaves a trail on your computer monitor that looks like the cursor is scattered all over the screen.

mouse pad *(mowse pad)* A flat surface, usually padded, used to roll your mouse around. The ball on the mouse operates best on a clean, flat surface; a mouse pad is better than most people's desktop for rolling your mouse around. "When finished making movies for the day, Mickey Mouse returns to his *mouse pad* to party with Minnie."

mouse trails *(mowse traylz)* An echo of the mouse pointer on the screen, which leaves a comet-tail-like pattern. This pattern easily helps you to locate the mouse, but also encourages you to waste more time moving the mouse around so that you can watch the tail images try to keep up.

move *(moov)* 1. A command in many software products that lets you transfer objects or text from one location to another, as in the Edit-Move command in Excel. 2. What you do when your accountant discovers a bug in his tax software that results in an extra $20,000 you owe to the IRS. See also *drag.* "My spreadsheet calculated a negative cash flow in my budget, so I want to *move* the expense column to next year's worksheet. Then I can move to a bigger house."

Mozilla *(mow-zil-uh)* The original code name for Netscape Navigator, one of the first popular Web browsers.

MP3 *(em pee three)* A method of compressing audio information so that it travels quickly over the Internet. MP3 files typically play one minute for every megabyte in size, which makes them an ideal way to store and transport sound files over the Internet. Various software programs exist that let you play, record, and create musical CDs using MP3 sound files.

MPC *(em pee see)* Acronym for *Multimedia Personal Computer,* but because nearly every PC sold today is a multimedia personal computer, it's really a bogus acronym.

MPEG *(em-peg)* Acronym for Motion Picture Experts Group, a file format for storing video images. Developed by the Motion Picture Experts Group, MPEG files compress video images so that what would have been a 100MB video file on disk takes up maybe 1MB. MPEG video can also be displayed full screen, unlike some other video formats that appear in only a small box on-screen. Unfortunately, MPEG files require specific equipment and take a long time to compress. This standard is not related to the JPEG standard, even though the acronym guys must have lived in the same building. "Using *MPEG,* I was able to compress my massive 150MB home video project to take up only 1.5MB of disk space. Now I can bore my relatives and save disk space at the same time."

MPEG-1 audio layer 3 *(em-peg-won aw-dee-oh lay-er three)* The full and easily forgotten name for MP3. See also *MP3.*

MPR II *(em pee ar too)* A Swedish standard that defines the acceptable amount of electromagnetic emissions a computer monitor can safely emit without killing the person sitting in front of it.

"Pregnant women should buy a radiation screen for their computer monitors or buy only monitors that follow the *MPR II* standard. Otherwise, your kid may wind up looking like a computer geek."

Mr. Data *(mis-ter day-tah)* A fictional character from the television series *Star Trek: The Next Generation.* More frequently called Commander Data, Mr. Data is an android officer on the *Starship Enterprise.* He has a charming, innocent personality and is a fine example of artificial intelligence at work. See also *data, Star Trek,* and *Star Trek: The Next Generation.* "I hear *Mr. Data* just installed memory-management software, and he now can remember twice as many things."

MS-DOS *(em-es-dahs)* Acronym for *Microsoft Disk Operating System, the* most widely used operating system for personal computers (which is still true because Windows 9x is MS-DOS-based). Also known as PC-DOS (from IBM) or just DOS, MS-DOS is the reason that Macintosh users avoid IBM and compatible computers. DOS was supplanted by Windows beginning with Windows 95. However, hard-core nerds will tell you that Windows 95 is really a program that runs under MS-DOS version 7. And so it goes. See also *disk operating system, DOS, Microsoft.* "When I start my computer, the screen says `Starting MS-DOS....` Then I get the DOS prompt and type *WIN* to go right into Windows and avoid using DOS altogether."

MTBF *(em tee bee ef)* Acronym for *Mean Time Between Failure,* used to tell someone the average life span of a product, such as a hard disk or laser printer.

"This laser printer has an *MTBF* of 35,000 pages, which means that if I print page 35,001, the printer should statistically blow up on me."

Multics *(mul-tiks)* An early operating system that was the ancestor to or inspiration for UNIX. It featured multitasking and a hierarchical directory structure and could be used by several people at once.

 MultiFinder *(mul-tee-find-er)* A version of the Macintosh operating system that lets you run more than one program at a time and easily switch between them. See also *Finder, Macintosh, multitasking.* "My Macintosh is equipped with *MultiFinder,* and I still can't find a thing on my disk drive."

multimedia *(mul-tee-mee-dee-ya)* Relating to video, audio, and graphics on a computer. Multimedia software combines two or more media for presentation or analysis purposes. For example, many packages let you combine graphics with sound. Large multimedia applications are often stored on CD-ROM devices because of their incredible size and memory requirements. Multimedia was a fad because all computer programs are heading that way naturally. "I have a *multimedia* version of the encyclopedia. To explain the topics, the software plays movie clips and music and shows graphics and artwork. Someday, it will write my term papers for me, too."

multiplexing *(mul-tee-pleks-ing)* The simultaneous transmission of several messages in one channel over a network. It is the equivalent of watching both CNN and C-SPAN at the same time as the local station. In a computer, multiplexing lets more than one computer access a network at the same time. See also *network*. "Before we got *multiplexing*, it seemed stupid that only one person could use the network at any given time. With multiplexing, everyone can use the network, everyone can get more work done, and everyone has cleaner, whiter teeth in less than three weeks!"

multiprocessor *(mul-tee-pros-es-or)* The use of multiple microprocessors in the same computer. A computer that uses any type of coprocessor is a multiprocessor computer. See also *central processing unit, coprocessor*.

multiscan *(mul-tee scan)* A computer monitor that can scan the screen (display data) at different rates because of different video modes and hardware configurations. See also *graphics, monitor*. "I bought a *multiscanning* monitor so that I could see incredible graphics in sharp resolution, and the fact that I had a few thousand dollars lying around the house also helped."

multitask *(mul-tee-task-ing)* To run two or more programs at the same time without knowing how to use any of them. A computer commonly uses the multitasking capability for background operations, such as printing, fax and data communications, and complex calculations. While the background operation (or task) is running, you can perform other tasks with other software. See *background, foreground*. "I'm sorry, Patty, but walking, chewing gum, and picking at your ear are not considered *multitasking*."

multiuser *(mul-tee-yoo-zer)* 1. Something that can be accessed or run by several people at once. 2. An operating system that supports more than one user at the same time. 3. A database that allows numerous computers to access the data at the same time. "If you have a *multiuser* database, you can have several employees typing the wrong information simultaneously."

Murphy's law *(mur-fees law)* 1. A universal law, or truth, that states "If anything can go wrong, it will." A subset of Murphy's law is embodied in Parkinson's law, which states that your clutter will expand to fill the space allotted for it. Another subset of Murphy's law is Smucker's law, which states that if you drop your bread, it will always land with the jelly side down. "Kyle is so fearful of *Murphy's law* that he backs up his computer every 20 seconds." 2. An interesting but poorly executed idea for a computer book series.

mutation engine *(myoo-tay-shin en-jin)* A type of program used to write computer viruses that can change their appearance, thereby reducing the ability of antivirus programs to detect and remove them. Some famous mutation engines are the Dark Avenger Mutation Engine and the Trident Polymorphic Engine. See also *polymorphic virus*. "Virus programmers like using *mutation engines* to create viruses that most antivirus programs can't detect. Then again, most antivirus programs can't detect lots of viruses, but they still cost lots of money anyway."

M

My Computer *(mie com-pyoo-ter)* An icon representing the contents of your PC — all the disk drives, printers, and folders — in Windows 95. My Computer is also a gateway to opening folders and seeing windows displaying the folders, files, and icons stored on your computer. "The icon may say *My Computer,* but he'll always be called Herman around the house."

The My Computer icon.

M

My Documents *(mie dok-yoo-ments)* A special folder in Windows 9x, kept right on drive C, in which most Windows programs initially let you save document files. Originally used Microsoft Office 95, but later adopted with Windows 98 as part of the operating system.

The My Documents icon.

My Pictures *(mie pik-shurs)* A special folder for saving pictures, images, and graphics in Windows 9x.

My Pictures

The My Pictures folder.

N

n *(en)* An unknown value, typically the largest value possible. Computer people say "from 1 to *n* things can go wrong." Or, they'll use the *nth* value to mean the highest, last — nay, umpteenth — value. See also *variable*. "This is the *nth* time I've been put on hold for *n* minutes when calling tech support."

N: *(en koh-lin)* The drive letter designation for some sort of drive off in the wild drive yonder of a PC computer system. See also *D:, Z:.*

nagware *(nag-wayr)* Software, usually shareware, that bemoans how nice it would be for you to pay for the software, usually in some form of dialog box at the start or finish of or during the execution of some important routine. The nagging dialog box or message goes away when you pay for the software or register. See also *shareware.*

NAK *(nak)* Negative acknowledgement. A character used in online communications that often signals an incomplete or improper file transfer. See also *ASCII, control code.*

name daemon *(naym day-mon)* A program that converts names into Internet addresses. See also *DNS.*

nano- *(na-noh)* A prefix meaning one billionth. For example, a nanogram equals one billionth of a gram. A nanosecond is one billionth of a second, or the amount of time it takes for the U.S. Government to spend $40. See also *nanosecond.* "Computer book authors make about a *nano*portion of Bill Gates' income."

nanosecond *(na-noh-sek-und)* 1. One billionth of a second, abbreviated ns; the speed unit used to measure memory chips. 2. The amount of time it takes users to find an error in the software documentation. "I always wondered how anyone measures a *nanosecond.* They better have a quick thumb on that stopwatch."

natural language processing *(nach-oor-ohl lang-wedj pros-es-ing)* The use of natural languages by computers for processing information. Now, computers use artificial languages, such as BASIC and C++, which are limited in syntax and vocabulary. Natural language processing would enable computers to understand and process languages such as English and Zulu. Although much progress has been made, natural language processing is many years away from reality. Problems with syntax, pronunciation, and vocabulary have not been completely solved. A complex set of rules is required in order to decipher the simplest sentences; as language gets more complex, the rules become colossally difficult to construct. See also *artificial intelligence, BASIC, C, C++, syntax.* "My dog must use *natural language processing* to understand what I mean when I say 'Where's your ball?' I guess dogs are more intelligent than computers."

navigation *(nav-uh-gay-shun)* 1. The act of finding your way through data, a program, a disk, or a network. 2. In a software application, moving the insertion pointer (or cursor) around the document. Proper navigation lets you edit and manipulate a document more efficiently. Most programs, for example, have sophisticated navigation keys and procedures. For example, in Microsoft Word for Windows, you can press Ctrl+Home to move instantly to the top of a document. See also *cursor.* "Microsoft Word provides numerous *navigation* options, allowing even an amateur to become completely lost in a matter of nanoseconds."

NC *(en see)* Acronym for network computer, essentially a dumb terminal used on a network. See also *dumb terminal, Net PC.*

near-letter quality *(neer-let-ur kwal-uh-tee)* Printing produced by dot-matrix printers. By condensing the dots to a high resolution, the rough edges around the characters are minimized and a near-letter quality is achieved. Fact is, you can always tell the difference. And laser printers, with their resolution and graphics capabilities, send near-letter quality printers to the cleaners. Often abbreviated as *NLQ.* See also *daisy wheel, dot matrix, laser printer, letter quality.* "When I got my laser printer, the *near-letter quality* printer wasn't very useful. It makes a pretty good footstool, though."

Nelson, Ted *(ted nel-sun)* Computer guru who developed the concept of hypertext. He's now working on project Xanadu, which is yet another handy way to access lots of information. See also *hypertext, Xanadu.*

nerd *(nurd)* 1. A self-depreciating term for a computer fanatic. 2. Someone who is very wrapped up in computers, often enjoying them to the disregard of every-

A typical nerd.

thing else. There are actually several degrees of nerdhood. At the very top are the elitists, often members of the Programming Priesthood. They're nice and understanding, but still dedicated to computers. *Wizards* are more friendly than members of the Programming Priesthood, but typically hard to find. Geeks are the worst type of nerd, often into computers because a good Dungeons and Dragons game isn't going on anywhere nearby. Geeks are typically stupefied that no one else "gets it" when it comes to computers, and they're reluctant to share information. Dweebs are nerds whose idea of being socially acceptable is brushing their teeth *and* applying deodorant. See also *dweeb, geek, hacker.* "I knew Milton was a *nerd* and socially awkward. I couldn't understand why he was so popular. That was until someone told me that he pulls down six figures — plus stock options — writing software at Microsoft."

nested *(nes-ted)* A programming term that means to include one procedure within another, similar procedure. Often used with loops to fill complex data structures and bird's nests. See also *endless loop, infinite loop, loop.* "My programs use a lot of *nested* loops. It must be my nesting instinct."

net *(net)* 1. (cap.) Abbreviation for the Internet. See also *Internet.* 2. Abbreviation for a network. See also *Local Area Network.* 3. A thing you would use to catch fish or hold your hair if you worked in a restaurant kitchen.

Net address *(net uh-dress)* The strange-looking letters, numbers, and symbols that identify someone's location on the Internet. See also *address.* For example, `www.wambooli.com/` is the Net address for Dan Gookin's Web page. You can go there to find more Gookin titles.

NetBEUI *(net-boo-ee)* Acronym for NetBIOS Extended User Interface, a protocol used on Microsoft networks (Windows 9x, Windows NT, and Windows 2000). It's what moves information around the network, which is all techy stuff; referring to it as "net-boo-ee" and not as "net-bee-ee-yoo-ie" or even "net-bee-yoo-ee" will earn you high marks.

NetBIOS *(net-bie-ohs)* Abbreviation for Network Basic Input/Output System. The BIOS tells a computer what types of devices and memory are connected to the computer and how to find them. A network BIOS includes basic information about the network to which a computer is connected. When you load your network operating system, the NetBIOS loads into the computer to supplement the standard BIOS. See also *BIOS, network.* "When I log on to the network, my *NetBIOS* tells the computer where to locate the other computers."

Net PC *(net pee see)* 1. A computer, like a regular PC, with a microprocessor, hard drive, memory, and a network connection (modem or network adapter), but no floppy drive, CD-ROM drive, or any expansion cards to upgrade the system. The idea behind the network computer was to sell an inexpensive PC for use on a Local Area Network or as a device to access the Internet. But you can never add new software or expand the system, so its appeal is low in the eyes of consumers. "Since it cannot be upgraded, the *network computer* will probably never be as successful as the computer industry would like it to be." 2. A competing standard proposed by Microsoft, Intel, and others for the NC. "Compared to a *Net PC*, an NC is a wimp. Then again, compared to a real PC, a *Net PC* is a wimp."

Netscape *(net-skayp)* Short for Netscape Navigator. See also *Netscape Navigator.*

Netscape Navigator *(net-skayp nav-uh-gay-tor)* A popular Web browser produced by Netscape Communications, Inc. It was originally given away for free, and older versions can still be obtained that way on the World Wide Web (typically as an enticement to Internet Service Providers to use the Netscape Web Server software, which is where Netscape Communications makes all its big bucks). "Microsoft's arch rival in the browser wars is *Netscape Navigator.* I'll bet you didn't know that Microsoft has more people working on its Web browser software than there are employees at Netscape Communications, Inc."

Netware *(net-wayr)* The networking software; the file server's operating system. Most closely associated with Novell, as in Novell Netware, the operating system used on Novell networks. "*Netware* must sell more bottles of Excedrin than anything else."

network *(net-wurk)*
1. A system of computers connected to each other for data transfer and communications. A network requires two or

A network of computers.

more computers, networking software (also called the network operating system), network adapters, and cables. Different types of networks include Ethernet, Token Ring, and AppleTalk. Examples of network operating systems include Novell NetWare and Windows for Workgroups. Networks are useful when several users must share resources, such as data or printers.
2. The source of most computer problems in business computer systems. See also *LAN, node, Wide Area Network.* "The *network* is down. Again."

network adapter *(net-wurk uh-dap-ter)* A hardware device (or *card*) that establishes a network and enables a computer to connect to another computer with a similar device. All computers in a network should use compatible adapters. See also *LAN, network, Wide Area Network.* "Our office purchased Ethernet *network adapters* for our computers. After installing and configuring the adapters, we can then install and configure the network software. I think that I like the old-fashioned way of communicating around the office; it's called the phone."

network administrator *(net-wurk ad-min-uh-stray-ter)* The person responsible for the overall maintaining of a network.

network computer *(net-wurk com-pyoo-ter)* Another term for an NC or Net PC. See also *NC, Net PC.*

network drive *(net-wurk driev)* A remote disk drive that can be accessed from your computer as though it were a drive on your computer. For example, Wally has a disk drive with tons of games on it. Using your computer's operating system and the network, you *map* his disk drive to a drive letter on your PC. So your G: drive would be Wally's hard drive containing all those games he stole from the Internet.

network hose *(net-wurk hohz)* The cable that connects your computer to other computers in the network. It's too thin to be a wire, so we call it a hose. "The data starts in my computer, and then it's squirted out the *network hose,* down the hall, and into Phil's computer, and then he totally fouls up my report."

network operating system (NOS) *(net-wurk op-ur-ay-ting sis-tem)* The software that controls the network. See also *Local Area Network, network, server, workstation.* "We use Windows for Workgroups as our *network operating system* and connect to a file server with a Novell NOS. I guess our computers are working NOS to NOS."

network pathname *(net-wurk path-naym)* A pathname that also includes a network designation, typically the name of a computer. Network pathnames begin with two slashes (forward slashes most of the time, backslashes in DOS), followed by the name of the network computer and then the shared resource. The remainder of the network pathname is then just the same as a regular pathname:

```
\\KOBY\C\WINDOWS\PERSONAL.CRD
```

This network pathname indicates the computer named KOBY, shared resource C on Koby (which is probably drive C), and then a normal pathname. Weird, yeah. Pray that you never have to type one of those by heart.

network service *(net-wurk sur-vus)* A special software that provides printing and file service on a network.

neural network *(noor-ul net-wurk)* A computer system that mimics the activities of the human brain. In the human brain, a very large number of neurons (billions, in fact) process information in a parallel fashion, all working on one problem at the same time to produce a single answer. Based on established patterns (learned processes), certain connections are made across a network to produce repeated results. In this way, neural networks can learn to process complex information over time — recognizing patterns of data. Because of this learned behavior, neural networks, like humans, produce only approximate results based on large amounts of input. Neural networks are useful for specific types of problems, such as processing stock market data or finding trends in graphical patterns. See also *artificial intelligence.* "Dave! Have you seen our gas bill? I guess the gas company has installed that darn new *neural network* computer!"

New *(noo)* The command that directs the application to produce a new, blank document or file. Often found on the File menu.

 newbie *(noo-bee)* 1. Someone who is new to a newsgroup. As though being new weren't bad enough, there is a term for it too. "Oh, great! Another question about Mr. Spoke's ears. He's a newbie!" 2. Anyone who is new to anything dealing with a computer.

newline character *(noo-line kayr-ak-ter)* 1. The character produced when you press the Enter key, which makes a new line of text on the screen. Many word processors use the term newline character because pressing the Enter key starts you off writing stuff on a new line. See also *carriage return, Enter key, line feed, Return key.* "Pity poor Alice. She did a search and replace, searching for the *newline character* and replacing it with nothing. Now she has one 4-page paragraph in her document." 2. The character producing a new line of text in a programming language. For example, the \n symbol is used in the C programming language to represent the newline character.

newsgroup *(nooz-groop)* A discussion area (group) on USENET. A forum where people can read or write their own news, messages, and flames. Newsgroups have a certain hierarchical format, which replaces spaces with periods. The first word describes a general category, such as *comp* for computers or *talk* for general discussions. Then comes a subcategory and maybe even more categories. It's really something

N

you either love or hate, and it will drive you agog either way. See also *USENET*. "Wendy got flamed real bad when she explained to the `rec.arts.startrek` *newsgroup* that warp speed doesn't really exist."

Newton *(noo-tun)* 1. That fellow who discovered gravity. Sir Isaac Newton. Because he supposedly discovered gravity when an apple dropped on his head, Apple Computer, Inc., has used his name to describe a variety of products. "If only *Newton* had any kids, he wouldn't have needed an apple to discover gravity." 2. The name of Apple's first personal digital assistant (PDA). See also *PDA*. "My *Newton* is a handheld computer that offers me the functionality of a pad and pencil but for about $599 dollars more."

NeXT *(nekst)* A computer and a company founded by Apple Computer co-founder Steve Jobs after the Apple board of directors kicked him out. NeXT sold UNIX workstations, mostly to universities. Eventually it stopped selling hardware, but continued to offer the NeXT software, NeXTstep. I honestly have no idea what it's up to today, but it's still around serving some niche market somewhere. NeXT is always spelled with a tiny *e,* in the fine tradition of mixed capital letters that computer companies never seem to tire of.

NeXTstep *(nekst-step)* A graphical operating system based on UNIX. NeXTstep was originally designed for the NeXT computer, but was also available for powerful PCs. "Truly, *NeXTstep* is perhaps the best graphical operating system ever. Too bad no one buys it."

nibble *(nib-ohl)* One half of a byte, or four bits. See also *bit, byte*. "I can't get a *nibble* or a bite with this two-bit bait."

NiCad *(nie-kad)* Abbreviation for *ni*ckel *cad*mium, a type of battery used in notebook and portable computers. You can recharge NiCad batteries frequently, but you have to fully drain them of power first; otherwise, they forget how much energy they hold and begin to hold only the amount you've recharged. NiCad batteries are sort of stupid. "My laptop computer uses two rechargeable *NiCad* batteries to provide a full 6 hours of use, but they take 12 hours each to charge!"

nil *(nil)* Nothing, zero, zilch. See also *null.* "I've been working with this income spreadsheet all day; every way I look at it, my profits are *nil.*"

niche *(nitch)* 1. A small market. 2. A piece of hardware or software designed for a specific thing, to fill a certain need. See also *vertical market.*

NLQ *(en el kyoo)* See *near-letter quality.*

 NNTP *(en en tee pee)* Acronym for Network News Transfer Protocol, the method by which newsgroups and their messages are sent on the Internet.

 NNTP server *(en en tee pee sirver)* The computer or software on a computer that sends and receives newsgroup messages.

node *(nohd)* A single computer or terminal in a network. Networks can consist of numerous nodes, each operating independently. Also the way *note* sounds when you have a cold. See also *network, server.* "Our Ethernet network has 20 *nodes,* which means that 20 of us won't have anything to do when the network stops working."

nondocument *(non-dok-yoo-ment)* A word processing text file or ASCII file that contains no formatting. A plain-text file. This term originated from Nondocument mode in WordStar. See also *ASCII.*

noninterlacing *(non-in-ter-lay-sing)* A type of monitor that displays each image using only one swipe of the electron gun. The image is displayed smoothly with no flicker. See also *interlacing, NTSC.* "No, Cedric, a *noninterlacing* monitor is not a Velcro monitor, like your nonlacing shoes."

nonvolatile memory *(non-vol-uh-tul mem-oh-ree)* Information encoded in your computer that stays there when you turn the power off. Read-only memory is nonvolatile, as are disk drives. See also *memory, RAM.* "I wrote a story called 'The Violent Vibrations of a Volatile Vocalist' and saved it on my hard drive, so now it's in *nonvolatile memory* and I can finally turn off my computer."

no-op *(noh-op)* A computer instruction that does nothing. Although you may think that your software has lots of no-ops in it, alas, it may have only a few. It seems silly, but your car has a "neutral" gear and many people stare at the TV slack-jawed for hours. No-op is the same thing, but for a computer. "I don't know how many *no-ops* this computer is doing, but it's doing them quite fast."

NOP *(en oh pee)* 1. Acronym for *not operating properly,* a program that is not working or a computer that is not working or an employee who is not working. "This program is *NOP.* Let's ship it anyway." 2. Accidental "features" in software, in which case NOP means *not on purpose.*

Norton SI *(nor-ton ess-ie)* A microprocessor speed test, from the program SI (Speed Index) included with an early version of the Norton Utilities computer program suite. An early benchmark of a PC's speed that was highly inaccurate but used by many manufacturers to boast of their computer's prowess. The original IBM PC had a Norton SI value of 1. Today's Pentiums probably have a Norton SI value of several million. See *benchmark.*

NOS *(en-oh-es)* Acronym for *network operating system.* See also *network operating system.*

notebook (computer) *(noht-book kompyoo-ter)* 1. A compact computer, about the size of a three-ring binder. A notebook computer is commonly used while traveling. It operates on both regular power and batteries. You can also use a notebook computer on the desktop by "docking" it to a larger computer or by attaching a desktop monitor and keyboard. A practical notebook computer should weigh between 3 and 5 pounds. 2. A good excuse to get out of the office. 3. Something a computer book author takes on her honeymoon. "I'm so glad I brought the *notebook computer* on this trip. I haven't used it yet, but just carrying it around saves time going to the gym."

N

notepad *(noht-pad)* A small application or accessory commonly found in graphical user interfaces (such as Windows and the Macintosh system) that you can use to type simple notes. The Windows notepad is a simple, text-only word processor that lets you write, edit, and print notes without having to use the more complex word processors. A notepad is useful also for editing DOS batch files, such as AUTOEXEC.BAT. "Even though it has a *notepad* accessory, nothing is more handy than keeping a pen and a pad of paper by your computer."

Notepad *(noht-pad)* A handy desk accessory that lets you type text for notes.

notwork *(not-wurk)* A task performed at your desk or on the computer that is not work. Notwork includes playing computer games, arranging your Windows or Macintosh desktop, organizing files on the computer, installing new software that you're not really going to use, faxing your lunch order to the corner deli, and sending e-mail to Bill Clinton (even if you are a politician). "When the boss came in, I was doing lots of *notwork*. Then she told me that I was doing a good job and left. I guess I'll keep up the good notwork."

Novell *(noh-vel)* A company in Utah that makes networking software. *The* networking software for the majority of PCs. The company makes other things as well and owns the license to UNIX and other software. "The first *Novell* the network did crash!"

Novell DOS *(noh-vel dahs)* Renamed version of DR DOS after Novell bought out Digital Research. "Wow! A copy of *Novell DOS*. What a collector's item!"

NPC *(en pee see)* Acronym for *network personal computer*. See also *Net PC*.

NSA *(en es ay)* Acronym for the National Security Agency, a top-secret American government agency that dedicates its life to creating and cracking ciphers and monitoring communications from all over the world. For years, the NSA officially didn't exist, although it unofficially gobbled up billions of dollars for its existence. See also *cipher*, *encryption*. "The *NSA* has the most supercomputers in one location, which means that they're either using these supercomputers to keep the country safe from enemies or playing the most awesome video games the world will never see."

NTSC *(en tee es see)* 1. Acronym for National Television Standards Committee, which determines standards for television broadcast and reception, influencing most of the known world except for Europe and Asia and other places where the TV standards are much better. The NTSC standard for broadcast is 125-line frames scanned at 30 per second using noninterlaced video. The European PAL standard produces a much higher resolution and quality of color than the NTSC standard used in the United States. Soon to be replaced by digital TV. "Americans have been trying to upgrade the *NTSC* standard for years. We watch the most television in the world and have the worst quality." 2. Acronym for Never The Same Color, a word play on NTSC because the standards are rather loose.

 NuBus *(noo-bus)* A Macintosh expansion slot that provides faster data transfer than the older S-bus slot and has support for multiple CPUs. See also *bus, expansion card, expansion slot.* "Those Mac people always have splashy, new hardware with much more interesting names than PC people. They have names like *NuBus,* Local Talk, and System Error."

NUI *(noo-ee)* Acronym for *network user interface,* the interface used on network computers, Web browsers, and other software that accesses a network. See also *GUI.*

NUL *(nul)* The name of a DOS "device" that doesn't exist and is no good, which means that this is probably the first thing the programmers at Microsoft did because it works very well at doing nothing. "Go to *NUL,* go directly to NUL; do not pass Redmond, do not collect stock options."

null *(nul)* 1. An empty set. 2. ASCII character code zero. This character is used in the C language to end a string of text. 3. Nothing. Unlike the number zero, null has no value whatsoever, like Donald Trump's estate. See also *nil.* "Programmers often use a *null* character to cancel a numeric variable because the number zero has a value."

null modem *(nul moh-dum)* A connection between two computers that does not include a modem. A null modem is usually accomplished with a cable connection, such as between a notebook computer and a desktop for direct data transfer. "I use a *null modem* to download my calendar information to the notebook computer before a business trip."

null modem cable *(nul moh-dum kay-bol)* A special serial cable that has the send–receive lines swapped (or "twisted") so that two devices can communicate. Essentially, it's the same thing as a serial cable with a null modem attached.

number crunching *(num-ber krunch-ing)* Working out numerical calculations and computations on a computer. Number crunching is common in financial and engineering applications. "After six days of *number crunching,* we discovered that the human brain cannot survive on coffee and Twinkies, so we went out for lunch."

numeric format *(noo-mayr-ik for-mat)* A style of displaying numbers. Different numeric formats display numbers for different purposes. For example, a currency format displays the number 567.899 as $567.90, and a percent format displays the number .25 as 25%. Numeric formats are commonly found in spreadsheet programs so that you can display numbers for special purposes without actually changing the value or "true form" of the number. "I used Excel's custom *number format* feature to add a few extra zeros to each number in my Net Worth report. Because number formats don't actually change the underlying values in the spreadsheet, you couldn't call this dishonest . . . could you?"

numeric keypad *(noo-mayr-ik kee-pad)* 1. The portion of the keyboard that contains the number keys, usually all grouped into rows and columns by themselves. 2. A separate device that

N

works along with the keyboard to provide fast numeric input; for example, a separate numeric keypad for use with a laptop computer.

NumLock *(num-lok)* A key on PC keyboards that switches the numeric keypad between number input and cursor keys. When NumLock is on, the numeric keypad produces numbers. When NumLock is off, the numeric keys act as direction keys. Many keyboards include a second set of direction keys, so you can use the numeric keypad for numbers and still have direction keys available. See also *Caps Lock, numeric keypad.* "Forgetting that you have *NumLock* on means that you may want to go elsewhere in your spreadsheet and end up typing the national debt instead."

nybble *(nib-ohl)* Alternative spelling of nibble, most likely because a nibble is related to a byte the same way a nibble is related to a bite. See also *nibble.*

nym *(nim)* A mail server that allows you to forward anonymous e-mail on the Internet. Short for a nym server. Comes from the word *anonymous.*

O *(oh)* The 15th letter of the English alphabet, which is not the same thing as a zero. Do not confuse a capital *O* with the number 0. See also *0 (zero)*.

O: *(oh koh-lin)* The drive letter designation for some sort of disk drive in a PC. Could be a network drive. Could be a hard drive. Could be an overdrive. May also be what drive D: looks like without your glasses on.

object code file *(ob-jekt kohd fiel)* The middle step when writing a program. It's not exactly the final program; it's more like the slimy pod-person thing that eventually turns into the program, thanks to another program called a linker. "We are waiting for Susan to complete her *object code file* so that we can package this program and get it out on the market before we test-run it to see whether it works."

Object Linking and Embedding See *OLE*.

object oriented *(ob-jekt or-ee-en-ted)* 1. A style of programming where you bundle sets of instructions into packages known as objects, similar to the way you can bundle pieces of paper into packages know as wads. In the old-fashioned kind of programming, known as procedural programming, the writer would just write instructions one after the other, one thing leading to the next. Object-oriented programming squishes the instructions into self-sufficient modules. Thus, if

you've written an code object that displays the date and time in a box on your screen, you merely toss that wad of code into your program and, lo, it works. You can even transplant that whole chunk into another program rather than have to rewrite the second program from scratch. Object-oriented programming is favored for this kind of versatility. 2. A graphics element created by a formula in the program. The graphic is an object because it can be manipulated without messing up the rest of what you've drawn. "I was trying to manipulate an *object* on the screen and then realized that it was a piece of spaghetti stuck to the screen. I guess I shouldn't work and eat at the same time."

occasional irregularity *(oh-kay-zhun-uhl ee-reg-yoo-layr-uh-tee)* Times when a computer — or the software program it's running — messes up or shuts down. The symptoms can't be repeated so that you can try to fix the problem — they just happen for no apparent reason, like being late for work, forgetting your spouse's name, or UFOs. The solution is to shut down completely and reboot (probably true for humans as well). Another solution is to have anyone else look at the problem; these problems occur only when you are by yourself and will not repeat for others. "My computer's problem is worse than *occasional irregularity,* so I am taking it to see a specialist in Singapore."

OCR *(oh see ar)* 1. Acronym for optical character recognition, the ability of a computer (via special software) to look at a page of text and recognize letters and words and then translate them into a computer file so that you don't have to retype anything. The OCR software sees that an *A* is an *A* rather than a collection of dots making a picture. This is important at certain times; for example, if you have a fax modem inside your computer and somebody faxes you a document. If you have OCR software, the FAX is a document you can edit. If you don't have OCR software, your computer just thinks that the document is one big picture. "Using *OCR*, someday computers will even be able to decipher a doctor's prescription." 2. Acronym for *obvious candidate for rehabilitation*, a term used fondly to describe some programmers.

octal *(ok-tal)* Base eight, where the numbers range from 0 to 7 and then the value 8 is represented by the number 10. Weird? Yes! We humans count in base 10, probably because we have ten fingers. Base 10 uses numbers 0 through 9 and then 10 to represent the value ten. Octal, hey — it's just weird. And no one uses it anymore, at least no one you'll have to deal with unless you get lost somewhere at a university or nuclear plant. "If an octopus could count, it would probably do so in base 8, *octal*."

octet *(ok-tet)* Another term for eight bits. Octet is more accurate than byte, which is really a word of data and not necessarily eight bits wide.

octets *(ok-tetz)* The name for the 255.255.255.1 numerical Internet address. We type names, such as

www.wheretheheckami.com, in a Web browser, but the Internet translates those names into numbers, which tells it where the Web page truly lies. See also *dotted quad.*

OCX *(oh see eks)* Acronym for OLE Custom Control, which is odd because OLE is itself an acronym that stands for Object Linking and Embedding, and nobody can figure out where the X in OCX comes from. Microsoft developed the OCX standard as an advanced version of the VBX standard; see also *VBX.* Although the VBX standard is designed for 16-bit operating systems, such as MS-DOS and Windows 3.1, OCX is designed for 32-bit operating systems, such as Windows NT and Windows 95.

OEM *(oh ee em)* Acronym for original equipment manufacturer, the company that makes the parts that go into machines assembled and sold by somebody else. For example, Joe Blorf may make disk drives that are then installed in your computer and sold by Milo Cooper. Joe is the OEM for Milo's hard drives. Very few computer manufacturers make all their own stuff. "Although American computers are the most advanced in the world, most of the parts come from Japanese *OEMs.*"

offline *(awf-lien)* Not connected to a computer, or more probably not really bothering with the computer. There's a difference between offline and unplugged. If you yank out the printer cable, you've unplugged it. If the printer is plugged in, though, you may have to turn it on to make it online. Furthermore, you may have to punch another button that tells the printer to obey the computer, which is also "putting it online." "Sometimes I have to take my printer *offline* to advance a sheet of paper. Sometimes I have to take my brain offline to fall asleep."

offset *(awf-set)* To allow extra room for inner margins on a word-processed document so that it can be bound in book form. This book has an offset of an inch or so, which allows for the pages to be bound together. If you were to yank a page out, you would see more blank space on one side than the other, which is the offset. "We *offset* the document six inches in case we made a mistake in the binding."

OK button *(oh-kay but-tun)* A graphical switch that accepts all settings or acknowledges a message from the computer. You can also "click" the OK button by pressing the Enter key. "I think that the *OK buttons* I use should be renamed 'Oh, well.'"

OK Corral *(oh-kay kor-owl)* The place where you hang your hat, where the Naughahydes roam, where the skies are not cloudy or gray, where the only time you hear about is suppertime, where — doggone it! Wrong dictionary! See *Cowherding For Dummies.* "It's suppertime at the *OK Corral.* Click the OK button."

OLE *(oh-lay)* Acronym for Object Linking and Embedding, which is really two things: A super method of copy and paste (linking) that allows you to create one type of document from within another type of document (embedding). Weird stuff. Probably no one uses it. OLE commands are found on the Object menu, though the Paste Link command is often found

on the Edit menu. "And now Miguel will paste the picture of the bull into his document about bullfighting. Here he goes. Click *OLE!*"

on-line *(on-lien)* Another way to write *online.*

online *(on-lien)* 1. Connected. Using your modem to connect to another computer. 2. Available, as in "the printer is online," meaning that it's working and ready to print. 3. A switch on the printer that enables it to accept commands from the computer. The printer can be taken offline to use its menu or any of the other interesting buttons on its panel.

online service *(on-lien sir-vus)* A national provider of news and information for modem users. CompuServe, America Online, Prodigy, and others are considered online services.

OOP *(oop)* Acronym for *object-oriented programming,* a method of programming that creates individual software objects that can be used again and again in other programs. Although it takes more time to create objects, the ability to reuse them in other programs reduces programming time. See also *object oriented.* "Programming languages, such as C++ and Pascal, are now designed to provide *OOP* capabilities, so you can write one part of a program and use it in several other programs. Just don't leave the parts lying around your desktop, or you're liable to step in the *oop.*"

open *(oh-pen)* 1. To access a program or file, just as you would open a book if you wanted to read it, a notebook if you wanted to write in it, a car door if you wanted to hit your knee with it, or a can of tuna fish if you wanted to eat out of it. "Please don't *open* the file named WORMCAN.DOC." 2. (cap.) The command that opens files, typically found on the File menu.

open architecture *(oh-pen ark-uh-tek-choor)* The philosophy and practice of building computers and making the design and engineering public knowledge. It invites other manufacturers and developers to augment the computer with peripherals, software, and internal components. The theory is that the more doodads and gizmos available on the market to work with a given machine, the more tricks a user can do with it and the more the machine will sell. IBM has practiced open architecture with its PCs, and Sun Microsystems has practiced it with its workstations. Apple Computer is famous for *not* practicing it. In fact, Apple has become notorious for doing exactly the opposite, for shouting "Off with their head!" when anyone else builds something that looks remotely like an Apple product — although the Macintosh *is* getting to be a rather "open" machine these days. See also *architecture*. "Although IBM had the foresight to create an *open architecture* PC, it didn't have the foresight to realize that clone manufacturers would take most of its business away."

OpenDoc *(oh-pen-dok)* A standard being promoted by Apple, Borland, IBM, Novell, and others to allow programs to share data with one another, no matter what program or computer the data may have been originally created on. OpenDoc is an alternative to Microsoft's compound document architecture, Object Linking and Embedding (OLE).

Unlike OLE, which is designed only for Microsoft Windows, OpenDoc works with the Macintosh, OS/2, Windows, and, ultimately, UNIX. "By using OpenDoc, I can copy information from a Macintosh spreadsheet, store it in my Windows word processor, and combine the whole thing in a new document so that Janet can edit it using OS/2."

Open Look *(oh-pen look)* The name of a GUI available from Sun Microsystems and AT&T.

operand *(op-ur-and)* A value, variable, or doodad in an equation that gets operated on by an operator. In the statement $2 + 3 = 5$, *2* and *3* are operands. The plus and equal signs are operators. See also *operator*. "If you take away the symbols, all you have left in a mathematical equation are the *operands*. This doesn't sound very useful, which is why it's a mathematical concept."

operating environment *(op-ur-ay-ting en-vier-ment)* A feel-good term for an operating system. Because the operating system often dictates the method by which you use the computer (the environment, so to speak: text versus graphics, menus versus commands), this term is rather redundant. In fact, we believe that it's an attempt by some marketing department to make computers sound friendlier and more politically correct. Even so, *environment* has more syllables and is harder to spell than *system,* so you make your own decision. See also *operating system* (of course).

operating system *(op-ur-ay-ting sis-tim)* The software that controls the hardware and also runs your programs. Some common operating systems include

DOS, System 7 for the Macintosh, OS/2, and UNIX. (Windows is not an operating system by itself because it must run "on top of" DOS.) "Some people who use the DOS *operating system* add Windows to avoid having to use DOS commands. Some of those people use programs, such as Norton Desktop, to avoid using Windows commands. Avoidance is a big part of computing."

operator *(op-or-ay-ter)* A symbol representing a mathematical operation. The usual context is within a software program or programming language. Typical operators are

+	Addition
-	Subtraction
*	Multiplication
/	Division

In addition to these mathematical operators, many other types exist. Relational operators, for example, test the relationships between values, as in the following:

<	Less than
>	Greater than
=	Equal to
<=	Less than or equal to
>=	Greater than or equal to
<>	Not equal to

"In the spreadsheet, I use mathematical *operators* to produce a budget worksheet. Then I use other operators to cover up the funds I'm embezzling."

optical *(op-tee-kul)* Refers to light or vision. For instance, when you are having an optical illusion, it means that you are seeing something that's not there, such as Social Security. "The

other day, Windows just came up — splat — right there on the screen. I'm certain I experienced an *optical illusion.*"

optical disk *(op-tee-kul disk)* A computer storage medium (a disk drive) that operates by digitized beams of light or lasers. That sounds so cool that there must be a catch — and there are two: speed and price; the optical disks are expensive and slow, though they hold lots of information. Optical disks are somewhat akin to CD-ROM technology. The claim to fame of the optical disk drive is that its storage capacity is much greater than that of a magnetic disk drive, which is your typical type of disk. "I don't like the way that new *optical disk* is looking at me."

optical mouse *(op-tee-kul mowse)* The distant cousins of the three non-optical, or "blind," mice who got their tails — oops, wrong dictionary! See *Nursery Rhymes For Dummies.* In computer terms, an optical mouse is a pointing device that uses a light beam to track the position of the cursor or pointer on the screen. Normal mice use a mechanical ball that rolls to detect movement. The light beam type of optical mouse is used with a special grid type of mouse pad that reflects the beam. (Actually, the mechanical type of mouse also uses some optical technology, but internally. An electronic eye watches the ball roll around, which is how the mouse detects movement. Cool, huh?) "If your *optical mouse* gets loose, you need a special optical mousetrap to catch it."

optimize *(op-ti-miez)* To customize software or hardware so that it serves the user to its utmost capacity. The goal is to have the machinery run faster and more efficiently, which could include

O

shuffling parts of the software into different parts of the computer's memory, rewriting chunks of software applications, or even just tweaking the controls on your desktop control panel. "Microsoft Windows gets its bloated reputation partly because it loads your hard drive with graphics images you can use for wallpaper. If you think that you can do without these images, you can *optimize* Windows by getting rid of all the picture files."

Option key *(op-shun kee)* A key on any Apple keyboard used in combination with other keys to execute special functions. Like the Shift key, the Option key doesn't do anything if you press it by itself. An example: In Word on the Mac, pressing the Option key and the numeral 8 key gives you a bullet character. Option+* gives you a little bad-guy character. And Shift+Option+Enter shoots the bad-guy character with the bullet character. Ctrl+Option+B cleans up the mess character afterward. "If I press Shift+S, I save my document. If I press Shift+*Option*+S, I save all open documents. If I press Ctrl+Shift+Option+S, I get a cramp in my hand."

originate mode *(or-ij-uh-nayt mohd)* The standard operating mode for a modem. In originate mode, the modem makes the phone calls, dialing out to another computer. The other mode is *answer,* in which the modem answers the phone; see also *answer mode.*

orphan *(or-fun)* 1. The first line of a paragraph abandoned at the bottom of one page while the rest of the lines continue on the following page. The dimensions of this tragedy have attained such proportions that developers of page layout software have included social service capabilities in their programs to rescue orphans from this plight. 2. A computer, usually one of the early models, that is no longer made or supported by the company that heralded it as a "technological revolution" just a few years back. This happens to all computers, sooner or later. "Pity, ye, O Osborne owners. And ye owners of Adam and Atari and old Radio Shack stuff. Fare thee well old Apple II, Apple III, and Lisa owners. Bid adieu to the long throng of forgotten PCs, nay, the *orphans* of the electronics age."

OS *(oh es)* Acronym for *operating system.* See also *DOS, Mac OS, OS/2.*

OS/2 *(oh-ess-too)* Trademarked acronym for Operating System/2, developed jointly by IBM and Microsoft to replace DOS and Windows. Despite the initial fanfare, few software developers came out with applications for OS/2, so when Windows appeared, it stole the show. It's as though IBM gave a party and nobody came. IBM is now trying to please the masses with newer and better versions of OS/2, specifically to compete with Microsoft and Windows. The only problem is still OS/2's lack of specific OS/2 software. "Rebel against the new Windows as ye long ago rebeled against *OS/2!* We'll show the rabble who run the show who's really in charge!"

OS 9 *(oh ess nien)* In the term Mac OS 9, stands for operating system Version 9, the latest Macintosh operating system. Deemed "the Internet copilot," it allows for file sharing over the Web, multiple users with voice identification, and auto updating, which automatically keeps all system enhancements current via the Internet.

outline font *(owt-lien fawnt)* A typeface that is solid around the edges and hollow in the middle, used for posters and headlines but not so much for regular typing. Some font families give you a choice of making an outline typeface out of a regular one. For example, Times Roman can become Times Roman Outline. Outline fonts keep the styles and proportions of the regular fonts they come from. "Kids love *outline fonts* because they can color in the middle with crayons."

outliner software *(owt-lien-er soft-wayr)* A program that can make the kind of outline you used to make in high school on 3 x 5 cards when you were learning how to organize your writing compositions. Those Roman numerals followed by uppercase letters followed by Arabic numerals followed by lowercase letters will really take you back. In the old days — not quite as old as your high school days — this kind of software was a separate application from word processing. In these enlightened times, you can make outlines in the same software program in which you can write letters and novels. "We used *outlining software* to organize the outline for this new dictionary. The authors came up with all the letters, and the publisher suggested that we use the alphabetizing feature to organize them."

Outlook Express *(owt-look eks-pres)* The e-mail client software that comes "free" with Windows 9x. Most people on the Internet read their e-mail using Outlook Express. Note that this program is not the same one as Outlook, which is the e-mail client that comes with Microsoft Office.

output *(owt-put)* What the computer spits out after it churns through the information you put into it. Output can be in the form of characters on your screen, sounds out of speakers, or hard copy from a printer. The machines that give you the output are called output devices. (See, learning about computers is way easier than you thought!) See also *input.* "When your input is poorly conceived, you shouldn't be surprised when your *output* is garbage."

OverDrive *(oh-ver-driev)* 1. A marketing adjective used by Intel to describe a faster version of the 80486 microprocessor. OverDrive processors run two or more times faster than non-OverDrive processors. You use the OverDrive "slot" in your computer to plug in an OverDrive chip, which then takes over as your PC's microprocessor from your older, lamer 486 microprocessor. "I yanked out my ancient 80486DX and replaced it with an 80486DX4 *OverDrive* processor. Now my computer runs two times faster, although I still haven't figured out why I need this additional speed to do word processing." 2. Any of several upgrade microprocessors produced by Intel, designed to replace or augment the microprocessor now installed in your PC.

overflow *(oh-ver-floh)* 1. To run out of room, as in a mathematical computation that cannot fit in memory. 2. A flag in the microprocessor that tells when a mathematical operation does not fit in a register. This stuff is really nerdy, but it helps programmers build software that eventually runs right. 3. Anything that cannot fit into memory. "When the computer gives you an *overflow* message, take two aspirin, reboot your computer, and call a programmer in the morning."

O

overhead *(oh-ver-hed)* Similar to what it means in real life: the resources you need just to stay operational — in this case, measured in RAM, megabytes, processing speed, and I/O capacity. Mostly, this term refers to the requirements of a program just to run on your PC. Some programs may require 640K of RAM, 5MB of hard disk space, plus special graphics cards and printers. "Working with graphics requires lots of *overhead*. Do you think that there's a conspiracy going on between the stores that sell the hardware and the guys who write the software?"

overlay *(oh-ver-lay)* A sophisticated form of program juggling, where the whole program is just too darn big to fit into memory at one time. So what they do is split the program into modules and overlay them into memory, swapping parts of the program back and forth between RAM and a disk. See also *Murphy's law*. "They used *overlay* technology to overcome limitations in RAM. Now we can use Parkinson's law of programming: Expand your program to fill as much RAM as you have available."

owner *(oh-ner)* The person who paid for the software, as opposed to the two dozen people using the pirated copy. If you had to look this word up, turn to the word *pirate* to find your picture. "If you're the *owner* of this software package, how come the startup screen says 'Al Gore, Washington, D.C.'?"

O

p

P5 *(pee-fiev)* The code name for the original Pentium microprocessor, the 586 or 80586.

P6 *(pee-siks)* Another term for the Pentium Pro or 686-type of microprocessor.

packet *(pak-it)* A chunk of information. Typically used in communications (modem or network), a packet is a chunk of data sent from one computer to another. The data is stored inside the packet, along with other information used by whatever protocol under which the packet is being sent. A typically nerdy term.

packet radio *(pak-et ray-dee-oh)* A method of using HAM radio equipment to allow computers to communicate.

packing list *(pak-ing list)* The list of stuff that should have come in the box when you get a new computer or order software. Generally, you should find the packing list first and double-check to ensure that everything is here. "Checking the *packing list* ensures that you don't throw out something you may need later."

paddle *(pad-al)* An older input device, like a joystick, that is frequently used for computer and video games. The paddle is a knob you twist, rotating it one way or the other. See also *joystick*. "My flight simulator program lets you use a *paddle* to control the plane. I can turn my plane left and right, but I still can't get it off the ground."

page *(payj)* 1. The electronic unit of text that corresponds to a page in real life. A page of text in a word processor; the amount of text it would take to fill a typical 8½-by-11-inch sheet of paper. Even if your monitor is too small to fit a page of this size on the screen all at once, the computer still knows where the page starts and ends and communicates this to the printer. 2. A chunk of RAM, typically 64 kilobytes. "One handy thing about *pages* on the computer is that you can recycle them over and over and over again. Al Gore would be pleased. Hug a tree."

page break *(payj brayk)* In word processing, the point at which one page leaves off and another begins. There are two ways to accomplish this: soft page breaks and hard page breaks. A *soft* page break happens automatically as soon as you get to the last character of the last line on a page. If you add or delete text (or graphics, for that matter) from the page, the page break changes accordingly, adding room for the new text. A *hard* page break is one you put in yourself at a precise location. A new page always starts at that point even if you add or delete material before the hard page break. "Because I wanted my term paper to come out to 20 pages and I had only 7 pages to start with, I made the type bigger and put in lots of extra hard *page breaks.*"

Page Down key *(payj down kee)* A glorified cursor key that moves you forward (down) in the document the exact length of a page every time you press it. Depending on the program, a page can either be the amount of information that fits on a screen or the size of a real page. Often abbreviated PgDn. See also *Page Up key.* "Page, off my knee. Off! Now! Down, Page! *Page, down!*"

page frame *(payj fraym)* A 64-kilobyte chunk of memory used by the old expanded memory standard. Four 16-kilobyte pages existed in the page frame, each of which could be swapped out between memory on the expanded memory card and conventional memory in the PC. That's kinda how the expanded memory standard worked. Messy, huh? See also *expanded memory.* "That memory looks bleak and ugly sitting there. *Page frame* it and tell me what you think."

page layout *(payj lay-owt)* 1. The design of text and graphics on a printed page and the software that creates it. See also *desktop publishing.* "I want to start my own newspaper called *The Computer Chronicle For Dummies*, but I will need some *page layout* software and about 40 years to learn how to use it." 2. A command that adjusts the page layout.

Page Mode DRAM *(payj mohd dee-ram)* Yet another type of computer memory, though this is rapidly being replaced by EDO RAM. See also *RAM.*

Page Up key *(payj up kee)* A key on the keyboard that moves the cursor up (backward) through your document to the top. Often labeled PgUp on the keyboard. See also *Page Down key.* "If you're already at the top of the document, pressing the *Page Up key* won't take you anywhere."

pagination *(paj-uh-nay-shun)* To take a long document and split it up into page-length chunks. Because everything you print eventually appears on a piece of paper — a *page* — the art of pagination shows you where those pages will be, right on the screen, before printing. "Since Steve can't figure out how the *pagination* works in my word processing program, he'll have to print his novel on a scroll."

paint *(paynt)* 1. To create an image using pixels. This is opposed to a drawing program, which creates an image using objects. 2. The program that creates paint images. "With that new black velvet mode in my new *paint* program, we're going to put the Tijuana Elvis Painting Society out of business."

palette *(pal-et)* 1. The selection of colors available in a paint or drawing program. The palette is somewhat limited by your hardware, specifically your monitor and graphics card. Some paint colors are given to you; others, you can mix yourself. Palettes can also hold fill

The Paint program's palette.

patterns, border styles, and other types of painting stuff. "There are so many colors in this *palette* that they take up the whole screen, and I have only two square inches to paint my picture in." 2. A floating window containing various options. See *dialog box.*

Palm *(pom)* The first widely and wildly successful palmtop computer. It comes in several model numbers and colorful flavors, but mostly fits in the palm of your hand. The device includes a stylus for writing on the screen, which is translated into text by the Palm's operating system. Palm computers come with several built-in applications, such as a phone book, scheduler, calculator, and other personal software. Additional software can be downloaded from the Internet or "beamed" from one Palm to another. The most amazing thing, and probably the reason for Palm's success, is that it's one of the first computers that sticks to a simple task and does it elegantly. The designers didn't want to overburden the Palm with all the software, bells, and whistles found on a desktop computer, which was the failure of all Palm competitors.

Palm OS *(pom oh es)* The operating system for the Palm computer.

Palm Pilot *(pom pie-lot)* The original name of the Palm computer. Supposedly, the Pilot pen people made them change the name to "Palm" only. See also *handheld computer.*

palmtop computer *(palm-tahp compyoo-ter)* A teensy-tiny computer that fits in the palm of your hand. Or, following the laptop metaphor, a computer that would fit into the palm of your hand if you had abnormally huge hands. Palmtop computers generally have all the hardware of their desktop cousins, but a tinier keyboard and monochrome display. Their purposes are often customized, and they come with embedded software: an address book, communications, to-do list, and other applications that can frustrate the heck out of you unless you have fingers the size of cocktail straws. "Those *palmtop computers* sure are tiny. What's next? The fingernail computer?"

pane *(payn)* A portion of a window that has been split into multiple parts. For example, in Excel you have a single window, and can see your spreadsheet inside that window. Furthermore, you can create up to four panes in the window by splitting it vertically and horizontally. Different parts of your spreadsheet or document can be displayed in the different panes. The result is probably like what those independent-eyed iguanas see, but it helps you scope out big documents and spreadsheets easily. See also *window.* "I've traveled on the ocean, I've tramped upon the plain, but I've never seen a window cry because it had a *pane.*"

panic button *(pan-ik but-un)* See *reset switch.*

paper source *(pay-per sors)* The location on the printer from which paper is loaded and fed into the printer. Most printers have two paper sources: the tray or slot into which paper is automatically fed, plus a manual feed location. You typically set the paper source in a printing dialog box, which tells the printer where to expect the paper to come from.

p

paper-white *(pay-per-wiet)* A special type of VGA monitor whose display approximates the whiteness of paper and provides black text and graphics to go with it. But, wait! There's more! Because the paper-white screen also gives you shades of gray, from 4, 8, 16, or up to 32 shades, it's much more true-to-life than a monochrome monitor because you can see shades of gray. "Now that I've upgraded to a *paper-white monitor,* I can get the same kind of writer's block that I get when staring at a blank piece of paper."

Paradox *(payr-uh-doks)* 1. The name of a relational database program marketed by Borland International because it originally wanted a database program to compete against dBASE, which Borland now also owns and markets after buying dBASE from the now-defunct Ashton-Tate Corporation. 2. Something that happens at the same time something else can't happen, which is usually bad. 3. Two dox. "The name Paradox originally meant that it was a paradox that a powerful database could also be so easy to use. Now the name Paradox means that it's a paradox that Borland can market both Paradox and dBASE and still claim that each database is the number-one database of choice by Fortune 500 corporations all over the world."

parallel *(payr-uh-lel)* 1. Two lines that never touch, unless you're not looking or your name is Albert Einstein and you're traveling in an elevator at the speed of light, in which case you'll probably miss your floor anyway. "Actually, the universe isn't *parallel.* If a train travels along parallel rails that encompass the universe and you're waiting to catch

the 4:15 to Philly, eventually you'll see yourself get off the same train with a strange woman and ask yourself for $40, and then you'll never see yourself again." 2. Refers to data traveling abreast as opposed to single file. For example, a parallel interface would use eight wires, one for each bit in a byte. 3. A type of port on a PC. See also *parallel port.*

parallel port *(payr-uh-lel port)* The thing on the back of your computer into which you plug the printer. Other things can plug into the port as well, which is why it's officially known as a parallel port and not a printer port. Heck, IBM calls it an LPT port. And then there's the term "Centronics port." Bytes of information sent to the parallel port travel eight bits at once, side-by-side down eight different wires. This concept contrasts with a serial port, which sends the bits one after the other. See also *Centronics port, LPT, printer port.* "The manual said to plug the printers into the *parallel ports,* so I arranged them neatly so that they each faced the door."

parallel processing *(payr-uh-lel praw-ses-ing)* A computer that can think about more than one thing at a time, which can cause neurotic behavior as it does in humans. Technically, parallel process*ing* comes from having parallel process*ors,* which is essentially only the case in computers far mightier than the average desktop PC or Mac. The top performers of any kind of computer can use several thousand processors in parallel, whereas the lowly desktop computer typically has only one. Parallel processing is the basis of artificial intelligence, or those computers that really can say "duh!" See also *Cray, supercom-*

puter. "Supercomputers, which are incredibly fast and powerful, use something called massively *parallel processing.* I never thought that one thing could be more parallel than another."

parameter *(puh-ram-uh-ter)* A value — which could be numbers, letters, or other characters — that you enter into an equation or statement, like an option. For example, the DOS FORMAT command is followed by a "drive" parameter. That's a drive letter telling the FORMAT command where the disk is that you want formatted. Parameter is just a fancy way of saying "option-thing that goes on the end of a command." You can also use parameters when searching for information. For example, Cornelia could enter the parameters "tall," "ugly," and "hairy" into the computer dating database to look for her dreamboat. "How about this error message: 'optional required parameter missing.' How can something that's required be optional?"

parameter RAM *(puh-ram-uh-ter ram)* Memory in a Macintosh that stores various bits of information about the computer. Abbreviated as PRAM; a battery retains this information even when the computer is off or unplugged. Similar to the CMOS memory in a PC. "One common solution for Macintosh woes is to 'zap the PRAM,' erasing it all and starting over."

PARC *(park)* Acronym for the Palo Alto Research Center, a research facility run by Xerox from which many wonderful computer inventions are thunk up. The original inspiration for the Macintosh came from Xerox PARC.

paren(s) *(payr-en(z))* Slang for parenthesis (-theses). Sometimes you have to use lots of them, so you don't want to waste your breath on extra syllables. They're used in mathematical calculations in programming, among other things. Paren is *not* the singular version of parentheses. "I don't know why the equation didn't work. Stick some *parens* in there, and maybe it will."

parent/child *(payr-ent child)* The relationship (how cute!) between categories of information, which could be files, directories, levels of an outline, or families. The *child* is a subcategory of the parent. See also *child process.* "In my outline, Things to Eat is the *parent* topic of the Candy topic. Candy is a *child* of Things to Eat. This more than justifies what I put into my mouth for nourishment."

parity *(payr-uh-tee)* A way of testing whether data is okay by counting the number of bits (such as during data transmission). The number can be either odd or even, and that information is saved and compared with subsequent calculations that also see whether the number is odd or even. If it isn't, then there is no parity and the computer pouts. See also *parity bit.* "Okay, Ivan, if you have enough nukes to blow up the world 530 times and we have enough to blow up the world 488 times — not counting subs, of course — then we've reached *parity. Nyet?*"

parity bit *(payr-uh-tee bit)* An extra bit included to check the parity in bytes. The arrangement is specified in a way that a parity bit set to 1, for example, means that the parity is odd (there is an

p

odd number of 1s in the eight bits it's monitoring); 0, if it's even. "My modem is ready for the comedy club with its hilarious *parity bit.*"

park *(park)* To immobilize the heads of your hard drive so that they don't rattle around and do damage if the computer is moved. This was a feature on older hard drives or the name of a program that physically parked the hard drive heads. This action is no longer necessary with today's hard drives.

parse *(pars)* 1. In programming, when a compiler examines each programming word and acts on it accordingly. 2. In spreadsheets, the function used to distribute data imported from other applications into separate fields in your new spreadsheet. 3. The act of splitting up a group of items (such as a sentence of words) into individual components.

partition *(par-tish-un)* 1. To divide a single hard drive into several logical drives. For example, a 4-gigabyte hard drive is typically divided into two logical hard drives on a PC, each of which could hold 2 gigabytes of information. 2. A section of a hard disk set aside for use with a specific operating system. 3. The act of separating the hard drive into such sections. See also *hard disk, hard drive, logical drive.* "I'm too busy — have Mr. Spock *partition* your disk into logical drives."

Pascal *(pas-kal)* A programming language used mainly for teaching programming concepts, with commands that look like regular English words — although they aren't strung together that way. Named after the 17th century philosopher-mathematician Blaise

Pascal, the language was created by Niklaus Wirth in the early 1970s. "*Pascal* was a rascal, but then again, so is any guy named Blaise."

passive matrix *(pas-iv may-triks)* A type of laptop display that's cheaper and not as good as the active matrix type. Unlike active matrix, which uses transistors to control the screen, a passive matrix display uses some type of lame logic-board circuitry or some such thing. "My new KneeCap 150 laptop uses the *passive matrix* display, so I can see color graphics of a parrot at 39,000 feet, but not as good as the guy with the active matrix display sitting next to me."

password *(pas-werd)* Like saying "Open sesame" to the computer, the password is your secret key to gaining access to a computer, program, files, or a network. "Peggy wanted to make sure that she would be able to remember her *password,* so she wrote it on a sign in big letters and stuck it on the wall next to the computer." (*Tip for power users:* This defeats the purpose of having a password.)

paste *(payst)* To insert an item previously cut or copied. The item can be text, graphics, records from a database, or a column of numbers from a spreadsheet, for example. See also *clipboard, copy, cut, cut and paste.* "If you want to *paste* some of my term paper into your term paper, make sure that the fonts match so that the teacher doesn't suspect."

patch *(patch)* A software update or fix. Patches usually come as special programs that augment or update the operating system or some application already installed on the computer.

Applying the patch usually updates the software to the next minor version number, so patching Bloatware 4.2 usually results in an upgrade to Bloatware 4.3 or 4.2.1. Patches are normally applied to fix bugs and do not necessarily add new features.

path *(path)* 1. A list of directories in which the operating system looks for program files. See also *blessed folder, pathname.* 2. The command that creates the list of directories.

pathname *(path-naym)* The full, long, and complicated name for a file. It includes the name of the drive the file lives on, the directories, and the file itself. For example:

```
C:\PROGRAMS\GRAPHICS\PAINT.EXE
```

Pathnames are the same as filenames, just more specific. You can actually type a pathname rather than a filename whenever you're prompted (if you don't, the operating system saves the file in a specific place). In DOS and Windows, a backslash character separates items in a pathname. On the Macintosh, a colon separates items in a pathname. In UNIX, a forward slash is used to separate items in a pathname.

Pause key *(paws kee)* 1. A key on the keyboard that freezes screen output or temporarily halts all computer activity. In DOS, pressing Pause once usually freezes the display; pressing it again returns normal behavior. The Ctrl+S key works the same on other keyboards. Some keyboard sport a Hold key that works the same; see also *Hold key.* "Why would anyone press the *Pause key?*

Doesn't the computer go slow enough as it is?" 2. A key used by most games to temporarily freeze the action. For example, you're in a fire fight with several slime-dripping demons, the action is hot and heavy, and chunks of whatever are flying to and fro. If you need to scratch your nose, you can stab the Pause key, scratch away, and then press Pause again to restart the action. That way, a minor human inconvenience doesn't get in the way of saving the universe from alien scum.

PC *(pee see)*
1. Acronym for personal computer, from the first IBM PC. Technically, refers to any standalone computer, or what was once referred to as a

A PC — personal computer.

microcomputer, including non-IBM (Windows) computers: the Macintosh, Amiga, and others, though those users don't particularly like the term. 2. The original IBM PC. The copycat computers that worked like the original PC were referred to as clones or compatibles. See also *clone, compatible.* 3. Any computer capable of running DOS or Windows. This generic PC term excludes Macintosh, Amiga, and other computers that don't run DOS or Windows. "There are many definitions for a *PC,* depending on whether it's your personal computer or someone else's." 4. Acronym for politically correct. This definition might be the first one listed in any other dictionary, but politically correct in this dictionary means actually reading the software license agreement before you tear open the package.

p

PC-AT *(pee see-ay tee)* The IBM PC AT, the first 80286-based computer and major upgrade from the IBM PC-XT. All modern PCs are based on the PC-AT design, which sported a 16-bit expansion slot over the older 8-bit slots, plus a larger motherboard and boxy case.

PC Card *(pee see kard)* Another name for a PCMCIA card. See also *PCMCIA*.

PC-DOS *(pee see dos)* Acronym for Personal Computer-Disk Operating System, the version of MS-DOS that is bundled with IBM-PCs. See also *DOS, MS-DOS*.

PC-XT *(pee see eks tee)* Abbreviation for Personal Computer – eXtended Technology, a version of the first PC but one that came with a "massive" 10-megabyte hard drive. Introduced in 1983, the PC XT used the Intel 8088 microprocessor and ran Version 2.0 of MS-DOS.

PCI *(pee see ie)* Acronym for Peripheral Component Interconnect, a new bus standard developed by Intel. The PCI bus connects directly with the microprocessor, making it one of the fastest ways to connect a hard disk controller, video card, or network interface to a PC. Most PCs sold today have a mixture of PCI bus slots and ISA slots. The fast stuff goes in the PCI slots. Ironically, PCI became a standard (defeating EISA, MCA, and VESA) because Intel just said so. Because Intel makes most of the motherboards included with the PCs sold today, PCI just happened. Also note that though both PC and Mac computers use PCI expansion cards, you cannot swap cards between the machines unless the card is specifically designed for that purpose. See also *bus, expansion slot, ISA, VESA*.

PCI card *(pee see ie kard)* An expansion card that plugs into a PCI slot.

PCI slot *(pee see ie slot)* An expansion slot into which a PCI card plugs.

PCjr *(pee see joon-yoor)* The first home computer designed by IBM. Very bad. Very lame. The PCjr wasn't designed for the home as much as it was anti-designed for business; IBM didn't want business users buying a PCjr when they could buy a more expensive PC. So although the PCjr had moderately good sound and graphics, it lacked internal expansion, suffered from a poor design (the insides would be crushed if you set a monitor on top), and sported perhaps the worst computer keyboard of all time: the infamous PC "Chicklet" keyboard. Introduced in 1983, the PCjr became landfill fodder by 1985. Most home users just bought regular PCs. IBM repeated this mistake when it introduced the crippled PS/1 line in 1987 as well as the limited Aptiva line in the mid-1990s. "Today, calling any computer a PCjr is more than a putdown; it's a slap-in-the-face insult!"

PCL *(pee see ell)* Acronym for Printer Control Language, a set of instructions used to control a specific brand of printer — not to be confused with *page description language,* nor with a *printer driver.* PCL also refers to HP LaserJet compatibility. "I have a *PCL* printer that acts just like a LaserJet V, but it's lots less expensive. It's called a LaserJet IV."

PCMCIA *(pee see em see ie ay)* Long-winded acronym for Personal Computer Memory Card International Association, an organization dedicating its life to defining a standard for making and marketing credit-card-size expansion cards for laptop and some desktop computers. PCMCIA expansion cards resemble metal credit cards that cost a lot and look like they could break just as easily. PCMCIA expansion slots look like long, thin holes in a laptop into which a PCMCIA card slides. "Some would say that *PCMCIA* actually stands for People Can't Memorize Computer Industry Acronyms."

p-code *(pee-cohd)* Relevant only to the old p-system operating system, which we'd bet $10 right now you've never heard of. With the p-system, a programmer would compile a program, usually written in Pascal, into p-code, which is short for *pseudocode*. The p-code could be interpreted by the p-system's interpreter into the language understood best by the PC's microprocessor. This meant, theoretically, that p-code could run on any computer, as long as that computer was running the p-system. P-get it? See also *pseudocode*. "Since the p-system went defunct in the early 1980s, *p-code* is no longer a useful term, unless you redefine it to mean *problem code* or programming instructions that the dog mistook for the newspaper."

PCX *(pee see eks)* 1. A graphics file format for the PC. Originally used by the PC Paintbrush program, PCX is supported by almost every application on the PC, both Windows and DOS. PCX files are bitmapped graphics files. "Bob thought that *PCX* was a rating for the naughty graphics files he collected." 2. The file extension for a PCX graphic file.

PD *(pee dee)* See *public domain*.

PDA *(pee-dee-ay)* Acronym for Personal Digital Assistant, which describes handheld computers that let you store notes and make phone calls and which cost lots more than a pencil and a pad of paper. "The most popular *PDA* is Apple's Newton, which can recognize your handwriting. If you think that using a PDA might come in handy, ask yourself how many times you misplace pens, and then ask yourself whether you'd be willing to misplace a $1,000 computer by mistake."

PDF *(pee-dee-ef)* Acronym that stands for Portable Document Format, a type of file created by the Adobe Acrobat program. A PDF file contains text and graphics that can be viewed by anyone who uses an IBM or Macintosh computer, whether or not they actually have the Adobe Acrobat program on their hard disk. "Most complex documents available on the Internet are in the *PDF* format."

PDL *(pee dee ell)* Acronym for *Page Description Language,* a programming language, such as PostScript, that is processed by a microprocessor in the printer itself. The PDL, through its particular statements and commands, "describes" the information on a page of printed output, generally through vector graphics calculations. Although it may take thousands of lines of PDL code to describe a page, the result prints much faster than the previous method of sending information to the printer: bitmapped graphics. The PDL is independent of the particular kind of printer you're using — as long as the printer has the capability of understanding the language. See also *PostScript, vector graphics.* "PostScript is a *PDL* commonly used with Macintosh computers. TrueType is now the primary PDL for PCs. TrueType is PostScript-compatible, but PostScript is not TrueType-compatible."

p

PDP-11 *(pee dee pee-ee-lev-n)* The Programmed Data Processor model 11, an early type of minicomputer that preceded the VAX. Developed by Digital Equipment Corporation.

Peanut *(pee-nut)* The internal IBM code word for the PC*jr* computer, used before the product was introduced. See also *PCjr.*

peek *(peek)* A BASIC language command that lets the user view the contents of a precise address in memory. The user can then *poke* a new value into the address if desired. See also *poke.* "I took a *peek* into Santa's sack and saw that he was going to bring me a superduper fax modem for Christmas!"

peer-to-peer *(peer-too-peer)* A democratic arrangement in networking technology where all nodes are created equal. The other kind of network is a *client-server* arrangement, where one machine is specially designated as a file server and it dominates all the "client" nodes. In a peer-to-peer network, each computer can share and access information on every other computer. See also *client/server network, network, node, server.* "*Peer-to-peer* means that our computers communicate on a network without a file server. Pier-to-peer means that we go to the end of the dock and peer over the edge."

pel *(pel)* A single pixel; another term for pixel. Pel is a contraction of *pixel,* which itself is a contraction of *pic*ture *el*ement.

pen *(pen)* 1. A long, thin device used for writing, ranging from quills to felt-tip. 2. A type of mouse shaped like a pen. 3. A computer that receives input from a stylus similar in shape to a pen but registers signals electronically so that users can write in their own handwriting rather than enter information on a keyboard or with a mouse. Pen-based input must be neatly printed. Hence, an ironic turnaround: When people lost touch with paper and became dependent on keyboards, their handwriting became a casualty of technological development. Now that the technology has advanced even further, tidy handwriting is once again becoming a necessity — to be able to take advantage of the technology! Industry analysts predicted that pen-based computing would be the hottest new technology in years. In reality, the pen has had little impact on the industry. See also *light pen.* "This must be a pig *pen* computer."

pending *(pen-ding)* Waiting. Usually refers to something in a queue that is waiting to be processed or sent. "You have five e-mail messages pending," means that five more pieces of spam (or whatever) are waiting to litter your mailbox.

Pentium *(pen-tee-um)* 1. A brand of microprocessor manufactured by Intel. The successor to the 486 chip, and even people who don't write ad copy for Intel consider it revolutionary because of its speed and efficiency. Intel was going to call it the 586 chip, but couldn't copyright the term, so it named it the *Pentium.* See also *coprocessor, Intel, microprocessor, processor.* 2. A computer with a Pentium microprocessor. It's like asking your friend if he has a V8, which means does his car sport a V8 engine: "You got a new *Pentium*?"

Pentium II *(pen-tee-um too)* The third generation of Pentium processor, after the Pentium Pro. Includes the MMX extensions found in the Pentium MMX; see also *Pentium MMX.*

Pentium II Xeon *(pen-tee-um too zee-on)* A version of the Pentium II chip designed for high-performance servers and other high-end applications.

Pentium III *(pen-tee-um three)* The next generation of Pentium processor after the Pentium II.

Pentium MMX *(pen-tee-um em em eks)* A modified Pentium processor that contains special instructions to optimize multimedia applications; specifically, computer games. Generally speaking, a Pentium MMX is better than a Pentium processor. However, you really need software specifically designed to take advantage of the MMX part if you want to get your money's worth. MMX doesn't really stand for anything; Intel wants it that way and refers to it internally as MMX Technology, which is a trademark. Unofficially, it claims that MMX means "multimedia extensions" or "multimedia instruction set."

Pentium Pro *(pen-tee-um proh)* The second-generation Pentium microprocessor, which probably would be called the 80686 had Intel stuck with that numbering scheme. Pentium Pros are generally faster and better than plain old Pentium computers.

 People search *(pee-pol serch)* A way to find a human being on the Internet, either their physical location, phone number, e-mail address, or Web page address. Several People search engines exist: 411.com, Yahoo People Search, and Switchboard, for example.

peripheral *(pur-if-oor-al)* Any device connected to the computer (the console), including monitors, printers, scanners, mice, external hard or floppy drives, CD-ROM drives, speakers, and keyboards. "We are going to get so overwhelmed with *peripherals* that we won't be able to find the center anymore."

peripheralitis *(pur-if-oor-al-ie-tis)* A disorder characterized by having too many peripherals and nowhere to plug them in. Another problem is that you have a hard time getting them to talk to each other. "A very effective cure for *peripheralitis* is poverty."

Perl *(purl)* A high-level programming language designed to manipulate text and information stored in arrays. Loosely based on C, sed, and awk. One of the most popular programming languages for creating interactive Web pages. Developed by Larry Wall in 1987.

Perl5 *(purl fiev)* The fifth version of Perl. An unofficial title, but used to describe any version 5-point-whatever of Perl.

permanent storage *(perm-uh-nent stor-edj)* 1. Disk drives. 2. Any form of storage that maintains its information when the power is off. RAM is the opposite — anything in RAM goes ka-blooie whenever you turn off the computer. See also *nonvolatile memory*. "I put all the names in my little black book into *permanent storage* on my computer."

permission *(per-mis-shun)* An file attribute that describes what type of user may open, read, write to, or execute a file. Common to the UNIX operating system, but also applies to networking or any situation where more than one person has access to information or resources.

p

personal computer *(per-son-al kom-pyoo-ter)* See *PC*.

Personal Digital Assistant *(per-son-al dij-uh-tal uh-sis-tant)* See *PDA*.

personal information manager *(per-son-al in-for-may-shun man-uh-jer)* A program that tries to organize your appointments, meetings, or schedules so that you can easily see how you're spending (wasting) your time at work. Sometimes abbreviated as PIM. "Because I never seemed to have any time, I bought a new *Personal Information Manager* for my computer. Now I still don't have any time because I'm spending it all trying to learn how to use my computer, MS-DOS, Windows, and my PIM all at the same time."

PERT *(purt)* 1. Acronym for Program Evaluation and Review Technique, an approach to project management that doesn't necessarily need the computer to implement it. You can perform PERT equally well on paper. PERT involves charting out the time and other resources needed to complete various components of a project. Project-management software programs usually contain PERT charting features. "I used a *PERT* diagram to show the vice president the schedule we intend to follow. He liked it so much that I'm now the official PERT manager at the company." 2. Acronym for Peripheral Envy Regression Training, for all you closet New Agers out there. 3. A shampoo.

petabyte *(pet-uh-biet)* One quadrillion bytes or 2^{50}. Exactly 1,125,899,906,842,624 bytes.

PGA *(pee-jee-aye)*. 1. Professional Graphics Adapter, a defunct graphics standard somewhere between EGA and VGA. The PGA was expensive, and few users bought it. 2. Professional Golfers Association, guys who wear funny hats and pants and only one glove and who chase a tiny, white ball around a park for Big Bucks.

PGP *(pee-jee-pee)* Acronym for Pretty Good Privacy, an encryption application freely available to a variety of computers and operating systems. It allows users to exchange encrypted information though the use of public and private keys. This way, the information can be sent to anyone, but only if you have the proper key can you decrypt and read the information.

phone jack *(fohn jak)* The hole in the wall into which you plug a phone cable. The cable connects the phone system (which starts in the wall, in case you didn't know) with your computer's modem or a phone.

phosphor *(fahs-fer)* The material used inside the monitor to create the display. An electron beam scans the inside of the monitor, and the phosphor absorbs it in the form of light patterns you see on the screen. "The *phosphor* in my monitor must be stimulated by now because I've been typing love poems all day."

phosphor burn-in *(fahs-fer bern-in)* A ghost image that appears on the screen — and stays there — as a result of having the same image displayed for too long a time. Akin to sunburn of the monitor, phosphor burn-in occurs when you leave the same image on the screen for several hours. When you turn the screen off, you can still see an outline of the image. Screen savers help prevent this burn-in. See also *screen saver*.

"When you get screen savers to prevent *phosphor burn-in,* they should have protection factor numbers like sunscreen."

Photo CD *(foh-toh see dee)* A format developed by Kodak for storing digital photographs on a compact disc. A Photo CD lets you store multiple photographs until the compact disc can't hold any more. The Kodak dream is that you can own a Photo CD and take it into a film processing center with a roll of film, and the film processing center will store your photographs on your Photo CD for you. "After taking pictures of our vacation, we had the processing center store them all on a *Photo CD.* Now we can make multiple Photo CDs, distribute them, and bore people with our vacation pictures all over the world."

Photoshop *(foh-toh-shop)* A graphics-imaging and photo-editing program from Adobe. Can also refer to the documents created by Photoshop.

physical device *(fiz-uh-kul dee-vies)* An actual, touch-and-feel object associated with your computer. *Physical device* would not require defining if it weren't for virtual devices, which are imaginary, make-believe, can't-touch-them devices. "I put my virtual file, which contains my virtual income projection, on a *physical device* for storage. I'm hoping that it will become real."

physical drive *(fiz-uh-kul driev)* An actual disk drive as opposed to a simulated disk drive *(logical drive)* or a disk drive that thinks it's another disk drive *(virtual drive).* See also *logical drive, virtual drive.* "I took my disk drive to the gym every day last month, and now it's a real *physical drive.*"

pica *(pie-kah)* 1. An old-fashioned typographical measurement that rivals the English system (inches and pounds, for example) for obsolescence. There are six picas to the inch; one pica equals 12 points (and there are 72 points to an inch). Pages and parts of pages are measured in picas. "Since this is an emotional book, we'll make the gutters between those columns three *picas* wide. That should handle the runoff." 2. Not a font. Pica used to be the name of a typeface on a typewriter, one that fit 10 characters per inch. Today, using the computer you can resize any type to fit into that same space; for example, the Courier font at 12 points (in size) approximates the Pica of the old computer. See also *elite.*

pico- *(pee-koh; also pie-koh)* A prefix meaning one-trillionth. "Give me a couple of *pico*seconds to back up my hard drive, and I'll be right with you."

PICT *(pikt)* 1. A graphics file format common to the Macintosh. A PICT graphics file is very similar to the TIFF file type. Comes from the word *picture.* 2. A file format used by a wide array of graphics and layout programs.

picture element *(pik-shur el-uh-mint)* The smallest piece of information that makes a graphic image on the screen. See also *pixel.*

PIF *(pif)* Acronym for *Program Information File,* a special type of descriptive file used by Windows to run DOS programs. "*PIF!* Puff! Oy, oy, oy!"

PIM *(pim)* Acronym for *personal information manager.* See also *personal information manager.*

p

pin *(pin)* 1. Wires in a dot-matrix print head that "poke out" to press on the ribbon and form an image on the paper. A 9-pin print head was typical through most of the 1980s. The 24-pin print head could produce sharper results because of the number of pins and their relatively small size. "It was so quiet that you could hear a 24-*pin* printer drop." 2. A wire in a cable. For example, there are 9-pin and 25-pin serial cables. "You would think, after almost ten years of computers having 9-pin serial cable connections, that external modems would stop having 25-pin serial cable connections."

pin feed *(pin feed)* A method for getting paper through a printer that involves knobby gears that use the holes on the side of the paper to pull (or push) and guide the paper through the printer. See also *dot-matrix.* "Sometimes the *pin feed* mechanism jams, and my document comes out looking like a Chinese paper fan."

 ping *(ping)* 1. Acronym for Packet Internet Groper, a program used to tell whether a certain computer or Internet address is up and running, available for communications on the Internet. 2. The act of running the PING program to see whether a computer (or enemy submarine) is available on the Internet.

Pink Floyd *(pink floyd)* The name of one of the most successful rock bands in history, recording such notable albums as *The Dark Side of the Moon* and *The Wall,* which have sold millions of copies worldwide and have been banned by various dictatorships over the years for their antisocial messages. Pink Floyd is often the rock music of choice for hard-core programmers, hackers, and people who ingest illegal substances into their system. "When I program in an ancient language like COBOL or FORTRAN, I like listening to classical music. But when I really want to crank out good C++ code, I listen to *Pink Floyd.*"

pipe *(piep)* 1. A method of taking the output from one command and redirecting it to the input of another command. Piping is done in UNIX and DOS at the command prompt by using the pipe character, |. See also | *(vertical bar), filter.* 2. The pipe character, |. 3. What people smoke when they're too wimpy to light up a fine cigar.

piracy *(pie-ruh-see)* Copying software without the permission of the author or publisher, and, if you're really bad, distributing it. It is estimated that for every copy of a program that is purchased legitimately, two copies are pirated. Most pirates justify this practice by explaining that the software companies are making too much money on the products they sell and that pirated copies do not really take away revenue from the publishers because pirates would not have purchased the product anyway. Efforts to squelch this plague have included copy protection, registration of legal owners, and Just Saying No — besides the fact that you could also go to jail for it. "Software *piracy* allows people who become easily seasick to become buccaneers."

pitch *(pitch)* The number of characters per inch, as on old-fashioned typewriters. Some old word processing software still uses this type of measurement and gives you, for instance, a choice of printing in 10-pitch or 12-pitch. Most newer stuff uses points to measure character size. See also *point.*

pixel *(piks-el)* Abbreviation of *pic*ture *el*ement, the tiny dots on your screen that form an image. "That thin coat of dirt on the front of your monitor is called *pixel* dust."

PL/1 *(pee el won)* Abbreviation for Programming Language One, an early programming language mostly used on IBM mainframes. Sometimes written as PL/I, but not pronounced Programming Language Eye. "Not too many people use *PL/1* anymore, but it's still cool to have on your résumé."

planar board *(play-nar bord)* A dorky term for a motherboard, used by IBM because, for some reason, it feels that it has to rename everything or else someone might actually believe that it's *not* a technology leader. Something like that. See also *motherboard.*

plasma *(plaz-mah)* 1. A type of monitor used in laptop and notebook computers — adapted from LCD technology. Plasma monitors are flat, do not require tubes, and are therefore smaller and lighter than CRT monitors. Stimulating a gas trapped between two panels produces the image. Also known as *flat panel display.* See also *gas plasma display, monitor.* "If I look at the *plasma* display on my laptop computer at just the right angle, I can see the ocean." 2. The stuff poor programmers sell from their own veins just to make ten bucks. 3. Any heated gas.

platen *(play-tin)* The roller that guides the paper through the printer. The character keys strike against the paper while it's rolling over this surface. "Do not let your *platen* get scratched or notched because that could make the letters come out looking funny."

platform *(plat-form)* The hardware on which an operating system sits, or the operating system on which a software application sits. For example, Intel processors constitute a platform on which operating systems are built. DOS/Windows is a platform on which application programs are built.

plenum cable *(plee-num kay-bol)* A type of cable designed to be installed in the space between the ceiling and the next floor up (usually, the ceiling is dropped down, and the plenum is the name for the space above it). Plenum cable is designed to be "up to code" for threading through the plenum space, though people often throw any type of cable up there, building codes be damned.

plotter *(plaht-er)* A type of printer that draws pictures with one or more pens, based on instructions fed to it from the computer. Especially useful with graphics or CAD applications. Those Creata-Card machines you see all over use plotters to create their greeting cards.

plotter font *(plaht-er font)* A type of font designed to look good on a plotter. Can also be the name of any vector-based font.

plug *(plahg)* The thing at the end of a wire or cable that you stick into a jack to make information or electricity flow. See also *male connector.* "Sometimes when you can't get your computer to work, it's because you need to *plug* it in."

A type of plug.

Plug and Play *(plahg and play)* 1. A wistful fantasy of engineers where all computer equipment works perfectly with equipment from other manufacturers, just by plugging the pieces together. "There will be no *Plug and Play* computers in this office! No! Give me plug-and-work computers!" 2. The ability of an operating system to instantly recognize a new piece of hardware and install it automatically. Windows 9x does this. Or so they say.

plug-in *(plahg-in)* An optional enhancement or helper program. Some programs are so diverse that they allow other programs to come in and help out, providing a handy way to extend their power. For example, the Microsoft and Netscape Web browsers have the ability to extend their reach through various plug-ins. These allow the browsers to play real-time music, view videos, or do other interesting things on the Internet.

PMMU *(pee em em yoo)* Acronym for *Paged Memory Management Unit*, a chip or circuit in some computers that assists with virtual memory. See also *virtual memory*. "Yes, he got his virtual memory degree at good ol' *PMMU*."

PMS *(pee em ess)* Acronym for Pantone Matching System, a color standard used by most graphical applications that matches colors common to many graphical printing shops. Pantone distributes a book of color swatches and, supposedly, as long as you stick to those specific PMS colors, the graphics in your program match the colors when printed.

point *(poynt)* 1. To move the mouse cursor over a specific object on the screen. 2. A method of measuring the size of characters in a typeface. One point is equal to *approximately* ¹⁄₇₂ of an inch, so a character 12 points high is ¹⁄₆-inch in height. The larger the point

value, the bigger (taller and wider) the letter. "If you want your résumé to fit on one page, you can make the *point* size teensy-tiny."

point-of-sale system *(poynt-ov-say-el sistim)* Computer hardware and software for retail sales operations. The type of hardware can range from a personal computer to a mainframe, but its function is the same: it registers prices for individual items, gathers data from sales, tracks inventory, and maintains a customer database. It can include peripherals like a receipt printer, a bar code scanner, and a credit card verification capability. "Before we can install an expensive new *point-of-sale system* in our store, we need to cut down on shoplifting."

point-to-point tunneling protocol *(poynt too poynt tun-nel-ing proh-toh-kol)* See *PPTP*.

pointer *(poynt-er)* 1. A symbol that appears on the screen and corresponds to the movement of the mouse or other pointing device. The pointer doesn't always look the same. It can take on different guises in different applications or even in different functions within the same application. 2. A programming term relating to a variable that keeps track of an object (such as the next item in a linked list). 3. A C language variable that contains a memory address and can be used to examine or change the contents at that address.

pointing device *(poynt-ing dee-vies)* An input device like a mouse, trackball, joystick, or stylus that lets you move the cursor around the screen.

A stylus pointing device.

"When Jerry uses a touch-sensitive monitor, his finger is no longer a picking device — it's a *pointing device.*"

poke *(pohk)* A BASIC language command that allows you to place a value into a precise memory location. See also *peek.* "The object is to know where to *poke* the computer so that it doesn't poke you back."

polymorphic virus *(pahl-ee-morf-ik vierus)* A special virus that modifies itself each time it infects a file on your computer. By modifying itself, a polymorphic virus makes it harder for antivirus programs to find and kill all possible strains of the virus. Polymorphic viruses are usually created with the help of a mutation engine. See *mutation engine.* "My antivirus programs found and removed a *polymorphic virus* from my computer. But I'm afraid that the antivirus program hasn't found all the different strains of the polymorphic virus, so I played it safe and switched my hard disk with Lyle's."

polymorphism *(pahl-ee-morf-iz-um)* In the context of object-oriented programming, this term means using the same name to specify different procedures within different contexts. A good analogy is the word *cook.* This term can involve a different method for bread, for pasta, for vegetables, and for meat. You can define *display,* for instance, to apply to text, graphs, pictures, spreadsheets, movies, sound effects, and anything else you choose to associate with the term. See also *object-oriented.* "I tried to describe the concept of *polymorphism* to my family, but then my mother-in-law blurted out that her sister is not a man and just has a tiny mustache problem."

pong *(pawng)* The original computer game developed by Atari in the mid-1970s, now found in museums. "*Pong* was named after ping-pong, the table tennis game invented by the Chinese. Did you know that it's called ping-pong in Chinese as well? Did you know what it means? Actually, 'ping-pong' is the sound the ball makes. Same in Chinese and English. What a world!"

pop *(pahp)* To remove the last data item from a storage stack. See also *push.* "Pat's afraid that if his computer didn't have a lid, all those values he *popped* off the stack would fly up and hit him in the eye."

 POP2, POP3 *(pahp-too, pahp-three)* A version of the Post Office Protocol, the method by which e-mail is sent and received by computers on the Internet. Unlike the SMTP protocol, with the POP protocol, messages are interactive between the various mailboxes on the Internet. See also *SMTP.* Although both POP2 and POP3 are similar protocols, they are incompatible. Most newer Internet mail programs use POP3.

pop-up menu *(pahp-up men-yoo)* Essentially the same idea as a pull-down menu, except that it appears someplace other than on the menu bar. In a Mac environment, a pop-up menu can appear when you highlight one of the choices on a pull-down menu. See also *pull-down menu.* "A *pop-up menu* is a little different than a pop-up book. You do not get a picture of the item in question sticking up from the surface of the screen."

port *(port)* 1. A connector (jack) in back of the computer where you can plug in a peripheral device. See also *parallel, SCSI,* *serial.* 2. To convert a software application to an operating system other than the one it was originally written for. "We finally *ported* our DOS menu system to the Macintosh, but can't figure out why it isn't selling."

portable computer *(port-uh-bul com-pyoo-ter)* A PC you can carry around with you without making yourself a candidate for the trauma ward. Classifications include laptops, notebooks, and handheld computers. A portable computer that is really too heavy to lug around regularly may be called "transportable" or "a brick on a leash." I prefer the term *luggable.* "I have a new *portable computer* that can store pages of information and print them instantly. It even recognizes my handwriting. It's called a pad and pencil."

portal *(por-tol)* A Web site that acts as a universal home page, a gateway to the Internet. Portal sites typically have search engines, shopping, e-mail, and other services either free or for a small fee. Such sites include Yahoo!, Excite, Goto, Deja and many, many others.

portrait orientation *(por-trayt ar-ee-en-tay-shun)* An amazingly convoluted way of saying "the usual direction" when discussing the way in which the paper gets printed on. It means more vertical than horizontal, or "the long way," as opposed to "landscape orientation," or "the wide way." Usually, you find this terminology in graphics applications. Like many other professionals, graphics artists seem to have an irresistible need to

The portrait orientation setting.

mystify even the simplest things. See also *landscape orientation.* "If you didn't print that picture of President Clinton with *portrait orientation,* you would be making the expensive mistake of cutting off the top of his hair."

POS *(pee oh ess)* 1. Acronym for *point of sale.* See also *point-of-sale system.* "Our *POS* system was just installed. It consists of a receipt book, a pen, and a cash drawer." 2. Acronym for Piece Of [Schlock], used to describe something poorly done, cheap, or just awful.

POSIX *(pahz-iks)* Acronym for Portable Operating System Interface for UNIX, a version of UNIX developed by the Institute of Electrical and Electronics Engineers. See also *UNIX.* "IEEE tries again, with POSIX, to impose some standardization on the many implementations of UNIX."

 post *(pohst)* To send an electronic message, usually to add a message to a newsgroup or online bulletin board. "You never can feel involved with a BBS until you *post.*"

POST *(pohst)* Acronym for Power-On Self-Test, a rigorous battery of tests the PC subjects itself to when you first start it up. Rumor has it that if the computer fails any of the tests, it displays a cryptic error message and pouts in the corner until you call a technician. "Before I leave the house, I perform a personal *POST.* I check to see whether I have my wallet, my keys, and my glasses and that my hair is combed and that I have my important stuff with me. Oh, and I check to ensure that I'm wearing pants."

PostScript *(pohst-skript)* A page description language developed by Adobe Systems, used to create a perfect image no matter the resolution of the output device. Most graphic artists and desktop publishing people save their files in PostScript format. That way, they can take the disks to a service bureau for high-quality output.

POTS *(pots)* Acronym for Plain Old Telephone System (or Service), the type of phone connection just about everyone has. "Unless you shell out the bucks for ISDN or ASDL, you'll have to get by with POTS."

power down *(pow-er down)* 1. To turn off the electric supply to the computer and its peripherals. 2. To eat quickly and with vigor. "We have 30,000 more lines of code to write by 5 o'clock; *power down* that Twinkie and get back to work!"

PowerPC *(pow-er pee see)* 1. The name of a microprocessor from Motorola that uses reduced instruction set technology (also known as RISC). "Apple Computer has replaced the older Motorola 68000 microprocessors in its Macintosh computers with the new PowerPC microprocessors." 2. A computer that uses the PowerPC chip.

power protector *(pow-er pro-tek-ter)* See *surge protector.*

power strips *(pow-er strips)* A device containing several power sockets, designed like an extension cord and used to plug in the myriad of devices surrounding your computer. See also *surge protector, UPS.*

A strip o' power.

power supply *(pow-er sup-lie)* The gizmo within the computer that changes the AC (alternating current) that comes out of your wall to the DC current that the computer actually uses. It's not a one-to-one correspondence. You need to make sure that your computer's power supply is adequate to cover the needs of all the machinery it's serving. See also *alternating current.* "My computer's *power supply* gets so hot that I now use it help keep my coffee warm."

power surge *(pow-er serj)* An increase in the amount of voltage in the power lines to your home or office. This type of electrical condition can damage your computer or destroy your PC's power supply. Typically, circuit breakers pop before any damage is done. Or, if you're using a surge protector, it sacrifices itself and saves your equipment. See also *spike, surge protector.* "I read a science fiction story about a *power surge* that caused a computer to come alive. In reality, *power surges* are more likely to kill your computer."

power switch *(pow-er swich)* The on–off button.

power up *(pow-er up)* To turn something on. "Poor Ralph tried to *power up* his PC by plugging it into a 220-volt socket."

power user *(pow-er yoo-zer)* Somebody who's totally hip, adept, and cool in every way when it comes to doing things with computers. Power users not only know what to do to get something to happen, but they also know *why* the thing works. They can figure out shortcuts. They can hold down more than one key at a time with one hand. While munching on cocktail wieners, they can dazzle a roomful of people at a party

p

with discussions of leveraged software, object-oriented programming, and cross-platform porting technologies. They also tend to own the latest, bestest stuff.

PPM *(pee pee em)* Acronym for *pages per minute,* the number of pages that come out of a printer in each minute. Typically a measure of speed for a laser printer. Don't get stuck on the numbers, though. Eight pages per minute to one manufacturer may mean something different to another manufacturer (even if they both know how to count). You need to know whether that's eight pages of text only, eight pages of the printer's favorite font, eight pages with four-color graphics, eight pages only when the sun is shining, there's a gentle breeze, and the federal budget deficit is under control. . . . "This laser printer can do 12 PPM, but only when it's printing blank sheets of paper."

 PPP *(pee pee pee)* Acronym for Point-to-Point Protocol, a method of connecting a PC to the Internet. This standard is replacing SLIP, which doesn't have some of the fancier features of PPP. "Bob said that we could use *PPP* to get on the Net, but I've been pressing the P key for half an hour and nothing's happened."

 PPTP *(pee pee tee pee)* 1. Acronym for Point-to-Point Tunneling Protocol, a super form of PPP that allows information from the Internet to be mingled with information on a Local Area Network. Pretty nifty, but also useful only to those wise enough to configure such things. 2. The reservation's restroom.

 PRAM *(pram)* See *parameter RAM.*

precedence *(pres-uh-dens)* The order in which things are done in a mathematical operation. If operation A gets done (on purpose, mind you) before operation B, then operation A has *precedence* over operation B. An operation in the innermost parentheses in a statement has precedence over those in the outer parentheses. If there are no parentheses, the order of operations is determined by how the program organizes it mathematical operators, which is known as the order of precedence. "Calculating the subtotal must take *precedence* over calculating the total."

precision *(pree-sih-zhun)* Exactness of a number, in terms of how many decimal places you take it out to. For instance, 3.17259324867 has a greater precision than 3.17. Precision is an area that triggers people's obsessive/compulsive tendencies, but, fortunately, computers have more of a sense of self restraint than that. "You only need 2-digit *precision* to balance your checkbook, but plan on using more for sending a rocket into space."

preemptive multitasking *(pree-emp-tiv mul-tee-task-ing)* A multitasking system where each a task interrupts other tasks, even swapping them out of memory, so that it can run. Basically, the computer divides its time between the various tasks, giving each a "time slice" in which to operate, before preempting that task to move on to another task.

presentation graphics *(pree-zen-tay-shun graf-iks)* Applications geared to creating impressive visual components that are used for speeches and other presentations. Essentially, such software translates data from a database or spreadsheet into a chart or graph, as well as being able to integrate text, titles, art, sound, and even multimedia activities. The result is a high-tech slide show that can be viewed on a monitor or projected onto a screen from slides. See also *graphics.* "My speech is dreadful, but I have some *presentation graphics* that should keep them awake."

Presentation Manager *(pree-zen-tay-shun man-uh-jer)* The old graphical user interface for OS/2. See also *OS/2.* "*Presentation Manager* should have been renamed the Here It Is Whether You Like It Or Not Manager."

 pretzel key *(pret-zel kee)* Another name for the Macintosh Command key.

print *(print)* 1. To generate a hard copy of a document or file. To send something to the printer. See also *hard copy.* 2. The command that prints, often found on the File menu. 3. The BASIC language command that displays information on the screen.

print buffer *(print buf-er)* A portion of memory that temporarily holds documents waiting to be printed. See also *buffer.* "Joyce felt she didn't need a *print buffer* since the maid kept her printer clean for her."

printer *(print-er)* An output device that produces hard copy — stuff on paper. Types of printers range from the old-fashioned dot-matrix printers that are so noisy their owners sometimes put boxes over them in a futile attempt to muffle the racket, to the wondrously whisper-quiet professional laser printers. The principal types of printers include *dot-matrix, inkjet, LED,* and *laser.* "Every computer system needs a printer."

printer cable *(print-er kay-bol)* The »wire that connects your computer to the printer. Unlike other confusing wires, the printer cable has definite ends to it: One can only plug into your computer, and the other only plugs into the printer. "*Printer cables* are sold separately from the printer, probably because they need to give you some reason to drive all the way back to the store."

Printer Control Language *(print-er kon-trol lang-gwadj)* See *PCL.*

printer driver *(print-er drie-ver)* The software that controls the printer. In the old days, the printer driver was unique to your application and printer. Often, you had to write your own printer driver. Then came the era of WordPerfect, which came with more than 800 different printer drivers for the more than 800 different printer models available. Windows now comes with its own selection of printer drivers, and it's no longer your job or the software application's job to create a printer driver. "Without the proper *printer driver* installed, your output will look like monkey typing."

printer font *(print-er fahnt)* 1. A typeface native to the computer, one that it stored internally and could reproduce relatively quickly. Other fonts had to be downloaded or sent from the computer to the printer, which added time to the entire printing operation. "My printer has three *printer fonts:* Ugly, Uglier, and Too Ugly For The Human Mind to Comprehend." 2. A font created for the printer's PDL and that, hopefully, matches a screen font so that you can see something close to what the printer will print. See also *font.*

p

printer port *(print-er port)* The jack on the back of your computer that you plug your printer into — usually a parallel port. See also *parallel port.* "I'm waiting for the ultimate portable computer that will let me plug my electric razor into the *printer port.*"

print head *(print hed)* The part of a printer that creates the image.

print job *(print jahb)* A document waiting to be printed, sitting in the print queue. See also *print queue.* "Don, your *print job* should have been fired."

print queue *(print kyoo)* One or more documents waiting to be printed. Printers are slow. So that you don't sit there along with the computer waiting for the printer, the operating system stores any documents you've printed in the print queue. There they are spoon-fed a little at a time (spooled) out to the printer. "With a *print queue,* you don't need to wait for the printer; you can be off doing something else while the computer does the waiting."

Print Screen *(print skreen)* 1. A key on the keyboard that, when pressed, performs a screen dump, sending the text displayed on the screen to the printer. In Windows, the Print Screen key takes a "picture" of the screen, saving it as a bitmap image on the Clipboard. From there, it can be pasted into any program that accepts graphic images, such as the Paint program. 2. An instruction to the computer to print the screen exactly the way it is, weird formatting commands and all.

print spooler *(print spool-er)* Software that manages a print queue and lets print jobs line up one after the other — as though they were wrapped around a

spool — patiently feeding them to the printer in the background while the user is busy writing novels, crunching numbers, playing Tetris, or doing other productive things in the foreground. See also *background, spooler.*

processor *(prah-ses-er)* 1. Another term for *microprocessor.* See *CPU, microprocessor.* "It's kind of foolish to call a *processor* like the Pentium a microprocessor when it's more powerful than the old mainframes of 25 years ago." 2. Any type of computer chip that carries out specific calculations. These chips are found mostly in consumer electronics.

Prodigy *(prah-duh-jee)* An online service for computer users that offers electronic shopping, securities trading, games, downloadable files, electronic mail, and Internet access, to name a few. Prodigy sold itself on being wonderfully fun and enjoyable, but its clunky interface got in the way, and more people preferred America Online (probably because of all those disks it sent out), so Prodigy eventually faded as one of the major online services. "I went to Sears to buy the software for Prodigy, but the salesman didn't know what I was talking about. He asked me if it was some kind of Mozart thing."

program *(proh-gram)* 1. A set of instructions written in a programming language. Software. Also called an *application.* 2. To create software. To use a programming language to tell the computer how to do something. See also *C, compile.*

program linking *(pro-gram link-ing)* The exchanging of information directly with another program over a network. Both computers must have the capability of program linking for the task to be performed.

 Program Manager *(pro-gram man-uh-jur)* The main interface for the old version of Windows. Program Manager was replaced by the desktop and the taskbar with Windows 95.

programmer *(proh-gram-er)* Someone who writes programs. This involves designing the program — what it should accomplish and how — writing the code in a programming language, putting the source code through a compiler, which translates it into a form the machine can understand, and debugging it, or fixing any errors. Programmers come in three types: geeks, wizards, and hackers. See also *programming language.* "Scott went to school for eight years to become a *programmer,* and now he works for the local dairy, delivering milk."

 programmer's switch *(proh-gram-ers switch)* A doohickey you stick on the side of a Macintosh. Pressing it one way resets the Macintosh, like the reset button on a PC. Pressing it another way activates a tiny window through which you can access the computer directly — programmer stuff.

programming language *(proh-gram-ing lang-wedj)* A way of talking to the computer, analogous to the ways humans have evolved in talking to each other. Like natural languages, programming languages include grammar, syntax, and vocabulary as well as style and organization. Some programming languages are not too far removed from English *(high-level languages),* and others

are more like hieroglyphics *(low-level languages).* Some languages are more suited to specific vertical markets, like Ada to the defense industry, FORTRAN to business, and C++ to applications building. The lower the level of language, the closer it is to the guts of the machine, and, therefore, the most efficient, such as assembly language. But when you're talking to a machine in a low-level language, you're talking to a specific machine, and your work can't be reused on a different platform. Higher-level languages, which include just about everything from BASIC to C++, approximate human languages more closely. See also *Ada, BASIC, C, C++, Fortran, Lisp, Pascal.* "Bill, our computer guru, prefers *programming languages* to human languages."

progress indicator *(prah-gres in-di-kay-ter)* A graphics element that displays how long an operation is taking, such as opening a file or sorting a database. Progress indicators are often called *thermometer bars.* As an event progresses, the "level" of the thermometer rises until the entire bar is full, indicating that the event is 100 percent complete. Progress indicators can also be simple `percent complete` counts. "All the *progress indicator* does is keep you from falling asleep while your computer takes an incredibly long time to do something."

PROLOG *(proh-log)* Short for "programming in logic," a programming language of special interest to mathema-ticians and computer science re-searchers. In real life, it's useful in diagnostic-type applications and expert systems, where the procedure involves proving or disproving that something is or is not the case. "The timber industry uses *PROLOG.*"

p

PROM *(prahm)* Acronym for Programmable Read-Only Memory, a chip that allows a program to be written onto it once — and only once — by the computer manufacturer. This type of chip sits in the middle of the spectrum between the two extremes: chips that come with the programming etched in by the semiconductor manufacturer, and EPROM chips, which can be erased (that's what the *E* stands for) and reprogrammed. See also *EEPROM, EPROM, ROM.* "Instead of letting me go to the junior prom with Luke Perry, my dad made me finish assembling the *PROM* chips I had started."

prompt *(prahmpt)* 1. A little character that appears on the screen to let you know that the ball is in your court — it's your turn to start typing. In DOS, it often looks like the symbol for "greater than." In other programs, it may appear as a flashing underline or flashing pipe character. Sometimes, it's just a question mark. Whatever the form, a prompt tells you that the program is waiting for you to enter something. Usually, you must type something and then press Enter. "The DOS *prompt* has nothing to do with being on time." 2. The command used to change the appearance of the DOS prompt.

propeller head *(proh-pel-ur hed)* Another term for a computer geek, or anyone who loves technical things.

properties *(prahp-uhr-tees)* The attributes and settings relating to some object or window in Windows 95 and later. The properties can usually be changed by pointing the mouse at the item and right-clicking the mouse. That displays a shortcut menu, on which you'll find the Properties command. See also *right-click, shortcut menu.*

proportional pitch *(proh-por-shun-al pich)* A printing style where each letter has its own size. The opposite of monospaced type. "Next time, I think I'll pay the extra money and have our driveway down in *proportional pitch.*"

proprietary *(pro-prih-e-tare-ee)* Mine, all mine, and no one else's. Proprietary means the company that developed the design owns the design, and no one may duplicate it or distribute it without that company's permission. See also *open architecture.* "The Macintosh System 7 is a *proprietary* operating system developed by Apple Computer, Inc. But then, Apple considers everything it does to be proprietary. Apparently, it doesn't know how to share."

protected mode *(pro-tek-ted mohd)* 1. In 386 and later microprocessors, the operating mode where the microprocessor can use all its memory and all its power. Otherwise, the microprocessor is operating in real mode, which makes it behave merely like a very fast 8086 chip. 2. A type of program designed to take advantage of the full power of the microprocessor. 3. A type of operating system that uses the full power of the microprocessor, including OS/2 and UNIX and Windows 95 some of the time. "Your computer cannot contract any diseases while it runs in the *protected mode.*"

protocol *(proh-tuh-kol)* A common set of routines or methods by which information is transferred. If both computers know the protocol, they can send information quickly and reliably. Common protocols include Xmodem, Zmodem, TCP/IP, Ethernet, and other protocols too nerdy to write down. "It's important that the computers in a network use the same network *protocol.* Otherwise, no one nodes what's going on."

prototype *(proh-toh-tiep)* A model for later and more advanced versions of a piece of hardware of software. A prototype typically embodies the intentions of the designer but hasn't worked out all the details. "My communications hardware is so difficult to use that I wonder whether the manufacturer just shipped me the *prototype*."

provider *(proh-vie-dur)* Short for *Internet Service Provider.*

proxy server *(proks-ee sur-ver)* 1. The software or computer on the Internet that translates URLs into actual Web page addresses. 2. Part of Microsoft Back Office. Used to provide network security on Windows NT and Windows 2000 networks.

PrScr *(print skreen)* Another label for the Print Screen key. See also *Print Screen.*

PrtScr *(print skreen)* Another label for the Print Screen key. See also *Print Screen.*

ps *(pee ess)* A UNIX command that shows you the *processor status,* or exactly what's going on in your UNIX computer at that time. Because a UNIX computer can be doing a number of things at a time, as well as having several people using it at the same time, ps lets you know what's going on. "I just did a *ps* and discovered that Morgan is trying to break into the password file again."

PS/1 *(pee ess won)* Abbreviation for Personal System 1, the line of computers designed by IBM to succeed its original PC line for the home. It was IBM's second attempt at entering the home

computer market. See also *PCjr.* "I got a *PS/1* computer to use at home. It's great for playing computer games, and it keeps the door open when it's windy out."

PS/2 *(pee ess too)* Abbreviation for Personal System 2, an IBM PC featuring a proprietary 32-bit expansion bus called the Micro Channel Bus. PS/2 computers are often shipped with the OS/2 operating system. The PS/2 was more of an odd duck than anything else. Today, IBM sells IBM PC clones, just like everyone else. See also *MCA, OS/2.*

pseudocode *(soo-doh kohd)* The flow of a program expressed in fractured English — that is, part ordinary English, part programming language — so that the programmer can map it out without getting stuck in the details. See also *p-code.* "I wrote this program in *pseudocode* so that my mother could understand it. She's now a high-paid programmer in Silicon Valley."

pseudo random numbers *(soo-doh random num-bers)* Because the computer is incapable of doing anything in a truly random fashion, mathematical purists consider any random number generated by a computer a pseudo random number. For instance, most programmers base their random number calculations on the time of day (the number of seconds since midnight, actually). Because that value can be predicted, so can the random numbers. Hence, the guys who don't get out much ("mathematicians") claim that computers only generate pseudo random numbers. See also *random numbers.* "Oh, my! Take that *pseudo random number* away from me before I get ill!"

p

public domain *(pub-lik doh-mayn)*
Software that has no copyright and can
be copied and distributed freely.
Hundreds of public domain programs
are available through catalogs and
public-domain distributors. Public
domain is also called *freeware,* but it is
not the same thing as *shareware.*
Generally, public domain software is "at
your own risk" stuff. If it makes your
disk drive smoke and gives your computer a wet, hacking cough, that's your
tough luck. See also *freeware, shareware.* "I got a great *public domain* program that lets me arrange my furniture
on the computer. Now if only I could
take out the trash on the computer, I
would never have to get out of my
chair."

public key encryption *(pub-lik kee en-
krip-shin)* A unique form of scrambling
data that requires two separate passwords: a private key and a public key.
The private key password can scramble
and unscramble data that was scram-
bled with the public key. The public key
password can only scramble data. If
someone wants to send you a message,
he must use your public key password,
but only you can unscramble and read
the message using your private key.
This form of encryption is more secure
than other forms of encryption that
scramble data with only a single password. "To protect your privacy when
using electronic mail, use *public key
encryption.* The only hard part is scrambling and unscrambling your data all the
time and remembering your private key
password."

puck *(pahk)* A pointing device using on
a digitizer pad. A sophisticated type of

mouse. In addition to mapping an exact
location, the puck also sends direction
information. It has a whole lotta buttons.

pull *(pul)* To remove a chunk of data
from a stack. The same as the *pop* command. See also *pop, push.*

pull-down menu *(puhl-down men-yoo)*
In a software application, a list of
intriguing possibilities that appears
when you select an option on the menu
bar. To choose a command from the list,
you drag the mouse down to it and let
go or use the appropriate keyboard
strokes. The Macintosh popularized
pull-down menus in its original operating system back in 1984. Now, pull-
down, pop-up, and tear-off menus are
commonplace. "I wish that *pull-down
menus* worked more like window blinds;
when you pull them down far enough
and let go, they should flap around the
menu bar a few times."

punched card *(punchd kard)* Old-
fashioned, unwieldy style of data processing that used a separate heavy-
stock card to transmit information. The
computer would translate a hole pattern
punched in the card — or the light
coming through them — into electronic
signals. We prefer to think that they're
obsolete. "Many eons ago when I went
to college, we registered for our courses
by using *punched cards.*"

pundimosity *(pun-di-mos-uh-tee)* The
animosity many pundits exhibit toward
technologies outside the mainstream.
Coined by Nicholas Petreley, of
INFOWorld magazine.

p

purge *(perj)* To get rid of unwanted/
unneeded stuff, preferably in an automated fashion, like with a global search-
and-delete operation or a PURGE
command. "After pizza, I feel the urge
to *purge*."

push *(push)* To place data onto a stack
for storage. Stacked data may be envisioned like a stack of dishes, and it refers
to the way data is stored in a part of
computer memory. To *push* a record
onto the stack means to install it at the
top of the stack, where it is the first one
popped when the stack is addressed.
See also *pop, pull, stack*. "When I *pushed*
that data onto the stack, I got a `Stack`
`Overflow` error, and the computer told
me not to be so pushy."

 push technology *(push tek-nawl-
uh-jee)* The ability of a server on
the Internet to send you specific
information, either requested information or something matching your profile
or a selected list of options. For example, you may subscribe to some type of
push news service, which sends you the
news you want to read rather than your
having to surf the Web to find it. See
also *Internet, Web*.

p

p

QBasic *(kyoo-bay-sik)* 1. A version of the
BASIC language that Microsoft includes
with MS-DOS Versions 5 and 6. The Q
supposedly stands for quick, though
quirky also comes to mind. "For people
who want to learn to program their computer without spending lots of money,
learn *QBasic* because it's already on your
computer for free. Then again, if you like
blowing wads of cash on stuff you'll
never figure out how to use, buy a C++
compiler instead."

 Quadra *(kwa-drah)* A model
name for a Macintosh with a
68040 processor. Various types
of Quadras appeared, beginning in the
early 1990s.

quad speed drive *(kwad speed driev)*
A CD-ROM drive that runs at four times
the speed of the original CD-ROM drive.
Also known as 4X. This type of drive has
been eclipsed by the 6X, 8X, 10X, and 12X
drives, with probably faster models on
the way soon.

quantum computer *(kwan-tum kom-pyoo-
ter)* The next-generation computer that
uses quantum physics and the multiple
states of atomic material in which to perform calculations. This is all theoretical
at this point because a quantum computer has yet to be built.

query *(kwayr-ee)* To inquire of. To ask a
database for specific information. For
example, to find all records containing
Padlevski in the Last Name field, you use
a query such as

```
Last Name = Padlevski
```

The database then searches every record
until it finds a match. Database queries
can become rather complex and intricate, such as

```
Last Name = or (ZIP > 80000 and
< 99999)
```

This makes no sense, but queries the
database to locate all records containing
a Padlevski in the Last Name field or a
zip code between 80000 and 99999. See
also *database*. "That last customer
started yelling when I couldn't find his
record in our database; so I *queried* the
database for all records containing *Jerk*
and found him!"

queue *(kyoo)* 1. A collection of documents or files waiting as patiently as they
can in turn for printing or some other
form of processing. For example, a *print
queue* is a collection of documents waiting to be printed. "My document is waiting in the network *queue* to be printed.
It's number four. And I'm still waiting.
Yessir. I'm waiting. Here I sit. Waiting for
that document. It's number four. Wait!"

Wait a sec. Look! Everything is moving up. Now it's document three in the queue. Okay. Pretty soon now. Just keep standing here patiently. Waiting for my document to print. Just waiting here. Looking at the queue on the screen. There's my document. It's number three now. Used to be number four. Waiting in the queue. . . ." 2. British: *a line,* such as a line of people waiting to buy +tickets. They say, "Queue up and buy your tickets. Jolly good. Tut-tut."

QuickBASIC *(kwik-bay-sik)* See *QBasic*.

QuickDraw *(kwik draw)* Part of the Macintosh's BIOS (or ROM) that handles the process of drawing information on the screen.

quick reference card *(kwik ref-er-ens kard)* A handy sheet of paper, often laminated, listing the most basic or necessary commands for an application. Like a cheat sheet, but one that only gives answers and not any of the questions.

QuickTime *(kwik-tiem)* A Macintosh standard for storing and displaying digital video, consuming lots of memory and hard disk space just so that you can see a brief five seconds of a movie on your computer screen. "As a joke, I stored a film clip from an X-rated movie on my boss's Macintosh using *QuickTime.* How was I supposed to know that his wife was in the movie?"

Quit *(kwit)* 1. What to do if your company makes you work on a Macintosh Plus computer or on a 286 PC with 256K of RAM. 2. A command that exits a program, typically found on the File menu. Quit. Done. Capiche. All finished. All gone. Going bye-bye. See also *exit.* "The *Quit* command is one of the first commands you should know. There's nothing worse than getting into a program and not knowing how to get out again (total 'Hotel California')."

 quote *(kwoht)* To list the contents of a previous message in your reply, which makes answering messages quicker and easier. The quote is marked by greater-than signs. See also > (greater than).

QWERTY *(kwer-tee)* The name commonly given to a standard keyboard layout. The name comes from the combination of the first six keys on the keyboard in the third row. See also *Dvorak keyboard, keyboard.* "Several attempts have been made to replace the old *QWERTY* keyboard with something more sensible. It's like trying to switch the entire United States to the metric system. Can't be done."

Q

R

R: *(ar koh-lin)* A disk drive letter designation in a PC. Not every PC has an R: drive, though, so it's probably a network drive or some removable drive or a drive on your cousin Melvin's computer because he has not only eight hard drives in his system but also a CD-ROM changer that holds six CDs at a time.

radiation *(ray-dee-ay-shun)* An invisible form of energy that kills nuclear power plant workers, blows up hot dogs in microwave ovens, and smacks you in the face every time you look at a computer screen. Completely harmless, just like all other invisible forms of energy. "Treating eye surgery with acupuncture is like treating hair loss with *radiation*."

radio button *(ray-dee-oh but-on)* One of several buttons in a graphical user interface, only one of which may be selected at a time. The name *radio* comes from the type of buttons that used to be on car radios: Only one button can be pressed at a time; when you press a button to select a station, the other buttons all pop out. The same logic is applied to radio

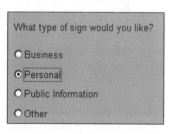

The radio button in a Microsoft Publisher wizard.

buttons, which are used to select only one item from a group of options. Radio buttons are grouped together in arrays or families. See also *button, graphical user interface.* "When I use the Format+Tabs command in Microsoft Word, a set of *radio buttons* assaults me with several alignment options."

ragged justification *(rag-ed just-uh-fi-kay-shun)* An oxymoron which really means that you have no justification at all. Ragged justification means that both the left and right margins in a document aren't lined up against anything. Specifically, it's usually applied to either the left or right margins individually. Ragged right justification, for example, refers to a paragraph of text that has an uneven right edge. See also *justify.* "When I asked John why he took a two-hour lunch, he gave me a *ragged justification* for his actions."

RAID *(rayd)* Acronym for Redundant Array of Inexpensive Disks, a hive of several hard disks in one unit, each of which contains the same information. The idea behind RAID is to ensure that a backup copy of your files always exists. Rather than store all your valuable data on a single hard disk that may fail at any time, RAID takes the opposite approach by spreading your data among two or more cheap hard disks on the chance that multiple hard disks are less likely to fail than a single hard disk. Large organizations, like hospitals, would use this method. "We lost all our data when our expensive 5-gigabyte hard disk failed. To prevent that from happening again, we used *RAID*."

RAM *(ram)* Acronym for Random-Access Memory, a type of computer memory that can be written to and read from. *Random* means that any one location can be read at any time; it's not necessary to read all of memory to find one location. RAM commonly refers to the internal memory of your computer, supplied by microchips and measured in kilobytes or megabytes. However, RAM can refer to any random-access memory medium, including magnetic disks and the human brain. RAM is usually a fast, temporary memory area where your data and programs live until you save them or the power is turned off on your computer. See also *ROM*. "The best way to improve the performance of Windows is to increase the *RAM* in your computer. Follow this formula: Figure out how much *RAM* you can buy without going over your credit card limit. Then buy that much *RAM* and install it in your PC."

RAM disk *(ram disk)* A portion of the computer's memory (RAM) that is configured to behave like a disk drive. A RAM disk works just like any other disk in your system, though because it's electronic (made out of memory), it's faster than any hard drive. RAM disks are given letters just like regular disks and can store files and programs. However, because the disk is made out of RAM, it's contents disappear when you turn off the computer or reset. Under Windows 9x, RAM disks are a waste of memory; that memory is best put to use for the massive memory

appetite of Windows than for a tiny, fast disk. "The astrologer down the street says it's best to create a *RAM disk* under the sign of Aries."

RAM drive *(ram driev)* Another term for a RAM disk. See also *RAM disk*.

Rambus DRAM *(ram-bus dee-ram)* Yet another type of computer memory, this one superfast, or "high bandwidth," as they say. Produced by Rambus, Inc. Rambus DRAM is used primarily in video accelerators and for high-end game machines. See also *RAM*.

random *(ran-dum)* Something in an arbitrary order. Out-of-sequence or unexpected. Not necessarily unpredictable, a random value could be anything. "You have been selected at *random* to be selected at *random*."

random access *(ran-dum ak-ses)* Information that can be read in any order. For example, telling your CD player to find a specific piece of music and play it is random access. With a cassette player, on the other hand, you would have to fast forward through the entire tape before you got to the song you wanted. In computers, random access gives you the ability to access any ol' information without having to read everything that comes before it. See also *sequential access*. "Those bureaucrats who have the information you need operate on a *random access* schedule."

random access memory See *RAM*.

random numbers *(ran-dum num-bers)* Values generated randomly (without any particular aim, order, direction, or sequence), such as when you throw dice. These values are used in programming, especially in games where unpredictable results make for a different game each time. See *pseudo random numbers.* "Due to new theories on the nature of chaos and randomness, many people argue that there is no such thing as a *random number.* These people have not seen my checking account."

range *(raynj)* 1. A term used to describe a series of things, from a low-numbered thing to a high-numbered thing. A range could also mean a span of values, such as the range between 1 and 10. 2. A block of cells in a spreadsheet. See also *block, cell.* 3. A place where the dear and antelope play. 4. Amana Radar.

raster *(rast-er)* A frame or pattern that an electron beam sends to the screen on your monitor. Scan patterns are sent to the screen continuously, one line at a time, to create the images and motion you see. The patterns displayed on the screen are sent using an electron "gun" that wipes the inside of your monitor like a firefighter's hose. The patterns are sent from top to bottom and each new pattern is sent before the last one is finished. This creates "bands" of images, called raster images. If you look out of the corner of your eye at the computer screen, you can see a pulsating effect that the raster images cause. "It's the *raster* scan line you see when you look at a computer monitor on TV. Ugly, aren't they?"

raw *(raw)* Information that hasn't been manipulated or changed. Raw data is merely the data. Raw mode is a mode where information is transferred directly and without modification. The opposite of raw is, comically, "cooked."

RCA connector *(ar see ay kon-ek-ter)* A standard type of plug used for stereo headphones and speakers. They have a long metal tip or prong surrounded by a plastic jacket that measures a quarter-inch in diameter. The type of connector is used for some video systems but mostly for computer audio equipment. "Nothing will brighten your guru's heart like referring to the 'connector doohickey' properly as an *RCA* jack."

RDRAM *(ar-dee-ram)* See *Rambus DRAM.*

Re: *(ree)* A prefix used in e-mail programs when responding to a message. "Re:" usually appears on the subject line, as in "Re: Question about my CD-ROM." It's from the Latin *res,* and it means "in reference of." It is not an abbreviation of "regarding" or "responding."

read *(reed)* 1. To examine a value. 2. To transfer information from disk storage into memory. "My computer is not reading the file from this floppy disk: It says, 'Cannot *read* from Drive A.' Maybe the computer needs glasses." 3. To transfer part of a file from disk storage into memory. 4. The programming language command that reads the next chunk of information from a file into memory.

read only *(reed ohn-lee)* 1. Something that can be read from but cannot be written to. Most read-only stuff also cannot be altered or erased. "*Read-only* media are used for information that you would not want to change, such as your weight when you were 18." 2. A type of medium from which you can read data but not write data to it. CD-ROM disks are read-only media, which is where the

R

RO comes from in ROM. See also *CD-ROM, ROM*. 3. Also a file attribute in DOS and Windows that protects files from being written to, modified, or erased. See also *file attribute* and *write-protect*.

read/write head *(reed/riet hed)* The mechanism in a disk drive that accesses and stores information on the disk. The "head" is usually a ceramic material that floats, or hovers, above the disk surface, creating a magnetic field that is charged by the magnetic impulses on the disk. When it writes information to the disk, the head changes the magnetic particles instead of being affected by them. This is how information is read from and written to a disk. See also *head, head crash*. "A *read/write head* is a delicate thing; small particles of dust between the read/write head and the disk surface can cause errors. This is why you don't go slamming melted cheese sandwiches into your disk drives."

README *(reed-mee)* A name given to a text file that contains up-to-date information about a program, such as changes to the documentation, information about last-minute additions, and explanations of errors that were not fixed before the product shipped. When a program differs from the documentation, software developers turn to the README file to explain what happened. README files are usually text-only files, so they can be read with any text editor or word processor. They can also be named READ.ME, README.1ST, README.NFO, README.TXT, READ_ME.TXT, or README.DOC files.

read me files *(reed mee fiels)* A file that nobody reads. See also *README*. "I was having some trouble with a new software package. When I looked at the

README file, it said that a last-minute change prohibited the software from working on my system. When the company sent me the bill, I sent them a copy of my SUEME file."

real mode *(reel mohd)* An operating mode of the 80286 and later microprocessors that behaves just like the 8088 microprocessor in the first PC. DOS and all DOS applications use real mode no matter which microprocessor lives inside your PC. See also *protected mode*. "Abigail wasn't sure whether her virtual reality program would run in *real mode*."

real number *(reel num-ber)* Any value, usually a value that has some sort of fractional part. Contrast this with an integer, which is just a whole number — no fractions and no decimals allowed. "I gave my accountant a copy of my income projection, and he told me that I should stop using imaginary numbers and try some *real numbers*."

Real Soon Now *(reel soon now)* A phrase commonly heard by software companies in reference to the exact date that they'll release a new version of their program that everyone's waiting for. This phrase is often leaked out to the press to con people who haven't yet learned that every new version is usually full of bugs and not worth getting in the first place. "Many companies promise to release a new version of their program *Real Soon Now* in a subtle attempt to keep you from defecting to a competing program."

real time *(reel tiem)* 1. A measurement of time based on actual time elapsed. For example, a simulation of two atoms colliding could take place in real time, or they could slow it down to observe

R

things (in which case it would probably be fake time). 2. The immediate processing of input. For example, a computer monitoring a nuclear power plant would respond to a radiation leak in real time (we all hope). "I'm sorry, Jenkins, but you can only clock in on *real time* here." 3. Analog time as opposed to digital time. See also *analog, digital.*

real-time clock *(reel-tiem klok)* A computerized clock or timing device that tracks the accurate time. For example, when DOS used to start, it would assume that "today" was January 1, 1980, at midnight. In those olden days, people would have to set the time and date manually whenever DOS started — unless they bought a device called a real-time clock, which would automatically keep track of the time and set DOS's clock every time the PC started. All PCs sold today come with real-time clock circuitry on the motherboard. A battery maintains the proper time (more or less) when the PC's power is off. "The guy on the street corner told me that it was a *real-time clock*, but when I installed it, the faceplate came off and a gum wrapper fell out."

reboot *(ree-boot)* To restart the computer. Starting the computer is called booting or booting up. You can reboot your computer in two ways: Perform a cold boot by switching the computer off, waiting, and then turning it back on again; perform a warm boot by punching a reset button. Usually, a warm boot is all that's required, but occasionally a cold boot is necessary to clear memory completely. "When you *reboot* by pressing the reset button, be sure to make the "ka-chinka" noise out loud because modern computers no longer ka-chinka by themselves when you reboot."

recent applications *(ree-sent app-li-kay-shuns)* The files or programs that have been accessed the last few times your computer has been used.

 recently visited list *(ree-sent-lee viz-uh-ted list)* A summary of previous Web pages and other sites on the Internet that your Web browser has taken you to. From that list, you can pluck out a site to revisit it quickly. See also *history.*

record *(rek-ord, ree-kord)* 1. *(rek-ord)* An individual unit of data stored in a database. A record consists of one or more related fields, which are the actual pieces of data being stored. Fields combine to create a record the way blanks are filled in on a sheet of paper. The blanks are the fields, and the sheet of paper is the record. "When that annoying Mr. Smith called, I searched for his *record* and found 200 Smiths in the database. Perhaps we should sort our *records* by customer IQ?" 2. *(ree-kord)* To write information, usually applied when recording sound information and storing it in a computer file on disk. Normally, the word write is used when you record information to a disk or to memory (RAM).

recover *(ree-kuh-ver)* 1. To restore a deleted file. You can often recover deleted files using an UNDELETE utility or command. See also *restore, undelete.* 2. A program's ability to continue operating after any errors that would normally send it crashing into outer space. "Our database program is pretty sophisticated. It can *recover* from serious errors, such as when I shot the computer with a bazooka."

R

recursion (*ree-ker-zhun*) An advanced programming concept where the same function or routine is called from within itself, over and over, to complete some task. For example, consider the Chinese box. An example of recursion would be an open-the-box function in a program:

```
Open the box
    If you find another box, then
"Open the box"
    Otherwise, remove the con-
tents of the box.
```

In this example, the "Open the box" function calls itself over and over to keep opening the Chinese boxes. Eventually, something will be found inside the smallest box, but the program itself uses recursion to keep opening the boxes. The weird thing is that such a programming concept actually works without blowing up the computer. "I tried to write a program that used *recursion*. But every time the program called itself, it got a busy signal."

Recycle Bin (*ree-sie-kal bin*) The place where deleted files are sent in Windows 95 and later. All delete commands move the deleted files into the Recycle Bin for storage. From there, they can be undeleted by using the Restore command. See also *delete, restore, trash*.

The Recycle Bin icon.

redial (*ree-diyal*) 1. To dial something over again, typically after getting a busy signal or no connection. Often used with online communications and a modem. 2. The command that directs the modem to dial a number repeatedly.

redirection (*ree-dur-ek-shun*) To send output or input to a device other than the standard device. Normally, output goes to the screen; you type it, you see it. Input normally comes from the keyboard. Using redirection, you can tell the computer where to send its output and from where to receive its input. This feature is on many operating systems, including UNIX, DOS, and OS/2. See also *input, output*. "I used output *redirection* to have the computer send all my network memos to the trash can."

redundant (*ree-dun-dent*) 1. See *redundant*. 2. Something that is repetitive, such as when two words that mean the same thing are used to describe something: "He was intelligent and had a high IQ." 3. A check made several times over just to ensure that everything is on the up-and-up.

reformat (*ree-fohr-mat*) To format something again. All disks must be formatted before they can be used. Reformatting the disk is formatting it another time. This process erases the disk's contents, which is why it's something you should never do to your hard drive. See also *format*.

refresh rate (*ree-fresh rayt*) The speed at which a monitor redraws an image on the screen. The faster the rate, the less likely the screen is to flicker, which saves wear and tear on your eyeballs and brain. It also means that you pay lots more for your monitor. See also *eyeball frazzle*. "Allan didn't pay much for his monitor. The *refresh* rate is so slow that it works more like a strobe light."

register *(rej-uh-ster)* 1. A tiny storage place inside your computer's micro-processor; a tiny memory location used by the microprocessor for various cal-culations. This term is something you'll never need to know unless you program a computer at a very low level. See also *assembly language.* 2. What software publishers want you to do with your software products so that they can sell you upgrades through the mail. "Isn't it ironic that you have to *register* a soft-ware product before you can get cus-tomer service, yet you never have to *register* a gun?"

registered group *(rej-is-terd groop)* A list of users allotted access to a network.

registered user *(rej-is-terd yoo-zer)* A network user whose name and pass-word are listed on a central computer. Registered users normally have greater access privileges than guests do.

Registry *(rej-uh-stree)* A central location in Windows 9x where system and software informa-tion is stored. The Registry exists as a file on disk as well as dynamically in memory. It's the tote board Windows refers to whenever it needs information about anything. The Registry is modified using the Registry Editor (REGEDIT), though this task has been made obscure on purpose by Microsoft, which really doesn't want anyone messing with the Registry.

relational database *(ree-lay-shun-ul day-tuh-bays)* A method of tracking informa-tion that consists of several, separate files that "relate" to one another through key words or values. Infor-mation stored in one file can be accessed through one or more of the other files because of the relations established in the database. For exam-ple, you might store customer address information in your Customer database and product order information in an Orders database. These two databases can relate to each other through the customer name. When you examine a customer record in the Customer data-base, you may, for instance, be able to view all orders associated with that cus-tomer. Similarly, when entering an order into the Orders database, you can type a customer name and the entire cus-tomer record automatically appears at the top of the order form. Another advantage of relational database design is that each field (type of information) in the database can be accessed individ-ually (that is, you can search for an entry based on any field). See also *data-base, field, record.*

relational operator *(ree-lay-shun-ul ah-per-ay-ter)* A symbol used to compare two or more values. These symbols are used in programming languages to help the computer make decisions and evalu-ate results. See also *operator, >, <, =.* "I used a *relational operator* to calculate whether meat loaf was better than sushi for dinner tonight."

relative reference *(rel-uh-tiv ref-er-ens)* A cell address in a spreadsheet that relates to the addresses of other cells, rows, or columns. When a formula con-taining relative references is copied to other cells in the spreadsheet, the refer-ences are automatically updated to reflect cells that are relative to the new location of the formula. Relative refer-ences are applied only during copy pro-cedures. See also *absolute reference.* "When it comes time to tell old, spooky Halloween stories, we all use Aunt Shirley as a *relative reference.*"

R

release number *(ree-lees num-ber)* The second set of numbers in a software product's version. For example, MS-DOS 6.22 was Version 6 and release number 22. "Don't ever try to make sense of *release numbers.* They're not sequential, nor are they designed to have any relationship to earlier releases."

 reload *(ree-lohd)* 1. To direct a Web browser to refresh the current Web page, just like you were visiting it again for the first time. The reload command causes the information on your screen to be re-sent from the Web site to your Web browser. This allows you to see updated information as well as fix any broken pictures you may see. See also *broken picture.* 2. The button you click to reload the current Web page.

REM *(rem)* An abbreviation of REMARK. REM is a statement, or command, used in many programming languages (including the DOS batch file programming language) that lets you add a line to the program without affecting the program itself. In other words, it lets you enter remarks or comments to help explain what the program is doing.

remote *(ree-moht)* Something that is not within your near vicinity. A remote computer is one that is connected to your network from a distant location — like across the hall. Remote access means that you're using a computer that's not within arm's reach. "When I log on to our network from another location, my chances of making a connection are *remote.*"

removable disk *(ree-moov-uh-bul disk)* Any disk that can be removed from its drive or from the computer. "Uh-oh, there goes Fred down the hall with the Jaws of Life. I guess we better tell him that his hard drive isn't a *removable disk.*"

render *(ren-dur)* To create something, as in a graphics image.

 reply *(ree-plie)* To respond to a message, either an e-mail or newsgroup posting. You have the option of replying to the person who sent the message or including everyone else to which the message was sent. "E-mail may be the fastest form of communications on the planet, but it seems like it takes forever to get a *reply* from some people."

 ResEdit *(rez-edit)* Abbreviation of *resource edit*or, a Macintosh utility that lets you access and edit system resources. ResEdit lets you mess with the various components of a Mac file. You can actually use it to rename menus, text in dialog boxes, buttons, copy or paste graphics, and so on. It's a fun tool, which implies that it's also quite technical and that using it is a sure key to goofing up your system. "That Johnson is such a card. He uses *ResEdit* to change all the Mac's error messages to dirty limericks."

reserved word *(ree-zervd werd)* Any word or code used for a special purpose that cannot be used for any other purpose. Reserved words happen in programming languages, operating systems, and some applications. For example, in DOS, the words *COPY, DEL,* and *REN* are all names of DOS commands and are therefore reserved words. Other programs cannot use these names or else DOS gets, well, mad. "Around our house, blockhead is a *reserved word.*"

reset *(ree-set)* 1. To restart the computer. "There. I just finished the final page of my speech, and I must admit that it's brilliant. Now I have a few idle moments to sit back and brain-relax and — hey? I wonder what this button labeled *Reset* does. . . ." 2. To restore previous settings. 3. A key on some Macintosh keyboards that performs a warm boot when you press it. See also *warm boot.*

reset switch *(ree-set switch)* A button used to restart the computer, almost like turning it off and on again but without disrupting the computer's power supply. Also known as the "panic button" because pressing the reset switch is often the only way to regain control of a computer run amok. See also *warm boot, Vulcan nerve pinch.*

resolution *(rez-oh-loo-shun)* A way of measuring the clarity of an image. Resolution involves the number of elements per inch — the number of pixels on your screen or dots your laser printer can produce — which indicates how clear and sharp an image is. For example, some laser printers produce 300 dots-per-inch (dpi) resolution. High-resolution printers display from 600 to 2400 dots per inch. Video graphics resolutions are measured horizontally and vertically. A resolution of 320 x 200 indicates large dots to create an image; a resolution of 1240 x 800 means smaller dots and a finer image, and therefore a higher resolution. When examining the resolution of an image, your naked eye can discern the dots in resolutions below 600 dpi. However, 300 dpi laser printers are considered adequate resolution for most printing needs. With color displays, the resolution is also tied to the number of colors that can be displayed at a time. For example, a rela-

tively low-resolution picture may be able to display several hundred colors at a time. This gives an illusion that the image has a higher resolution, but that's only because the eye is tricked by the multiple colors. Higher-resolution images generally use fewer colors. (Most computer games use a medium resolution as a trade-off.) Resolution may be abbreviated as res (pronounced "rez"). For example, you say "high res" or "low res" to indicate high or low resolution. See also *pixel.* "I made a New Year's resolution that I'd get myself a high-*resolution* printer this year."

resource *(ree-sohrs)* Just as humans have natural resources, a computer has its own resources. A resource can be memory, disk drive storage, the printer, or a monitor, for example. In Windows and on networks, you always want to watch that your resources aren't running out. "We were getting low on resources, running out of disk drive space and memory, and then all of a sudden Al Gore shows up, all hopping mad and everything. He made us go down to the computer store and buy more *resources,* but we can only use 50 percent of them because we have to save the Spotted Disk Owl."

resource fork *(ree-sohrs fork)* One of two parts of a Macintosh file (the other is the data fork) that contains information about the file ("resources"). The information stored in the resource fork includes icons, menus, text strings, dialog box descriptions, fonts and other information used by the file.

restore *(ree-stohr)* 1. To return to normal, as in "Yes, Mary is fully restored after her conniption fit." 2. The act of copying files from an archive or set of backup disks or a tape drive to their original locations on the hard drive. This is the opposite of backing up, usually done after something bad has happened. For example, after losing all your data, you would restore your files from a recent backup disk. Or, if you deleted a file, you could restore it from a backup disk. Needless to say, this technique works only if you back up frequently. "Don't panic, Dave. You can *restore* the missing files from your backup disks. You do back up, don't you?" 3. In DOS, the RESTORE command returns backed-up data to the hard disk. 4. To undelete a file from the Windows Recycle Bin. See also *undelete, Recycle Bin*.

retrieve *(ree-treev)* 1. Fancy talk for accessing or opening a file, as in the Lotus 1-2-3 Worksheet Retrieve command. See also *open*. 2. The old WordPerfect command for opening one file inside another file.

Return key *(ree-tern kee)* Same as the Enter key, but it gets its name from the carriage return key on a typewriter. The key used like the Enter key on some Macintosh keyboards. "Both Enter and *Return* generally perform the same function, but don't quote me on that."

reverse engineer *(ree-vers in-juh-neer)* The process of decoding hardware or software based on what the hardware or software does and how it affects things. Reverse engineering is primarily performed when engineers want to figure out how a black box gizmo works, and they're either unable to take it apart or forbidden from taking it apart for legal motives. For example, the reason we all have IBM-compatible computers is that someone, somewhere, reverse-

engineered the chips in the first IBM PC (the BIOS) and created a working counterpart without infringing on the IBM copyrights. "I bet that IBM really regrets not sicking its legions of lawyers on the first company to successfully *reverse engineer* the guts of the IBM PC."

revision history *(ree-vi-zhun hiz-toh-ree)* A list of the various versions and corrections to a program. A revision history tracks what occurrs in each revision. For example:

```
Version 1.0 Product introduced.
They'll love this.
Version 1.1 Annoying "all files
accidentally deleted" bug
removed.
Version 1.2 Annoying "erased
hard drive" thing fixed.
Version 2.0 Networking features
added, flock sheared for $50
upgrade fee.
Version 2.1 Annoying "network
not found" bug fixed.
Version 2.2 Support for tall
people added.
Version 2.3 Support for left-
handed people added.
Version 3.0 DOS 5 update,
sheared flock for another $50.
Version 3.1 DOS bug fix.
```

"Obviously, most major applications don't include a *revision history* because it would prove to be a source of embarrassment."

RF *(ar ef)* Acronym for Radio Frequency, which includes a certain chunk of the electromagnetic spectrum that you would find terribly uninteresting. Mostly used with RFI. See also *RFI*. "Tune to KRUD. That's 1240 AM on your *RF* dial."

R

RFI *(ar ef ie)* Acronym for Radio Frequency Interference, the type of interference that occurs when two devices emitting electromagnetic waves interfere with one another. Computers, radios, TVs, and many other radio transmission devices emit waves that can interfere with other devices' waves, causing fuzzy noise, snow on the monitor, annoyed cat, and other anomalies. RFI is why you can't use your mobile phone on an airplane, and it's why notebook computers undergo monstrous testing for FCC approval. Proper grounding and quality cables help to minimize RFI in computers. See also *Class A/Class B.* "This *RFI* is causing some strange effects on my computer. I could swear I saw a fuzzy image of Bill Gates giggling on my monitor."

RGB *(ar jee bee)* Acronym for Red Green Blue, the three basic colors of light (additive colors). Based on the mixture and intensity of these colors, you can produce many of the colors in the normal spectrum. TVs and computer monitors use RGB to produce color on the screen. You light individual red, green, and blue pixels to mix colors. "I have an *RGB* monitor, but in this case RGB stands for Randomly Goes Blank."

ribbon cable *(rib-un kay-bol)* Several computer wires bundled together to form a flat ribbon. Ribbon cables are often used for the printer and, inside the PC, disk drives. In the old Apple II days, the ribbon cables were multicolor — like rainbows. Today, they're usually all a pasty hospital-blue. See also *cable.* "Doris is so nice. She thought that the office looked rather dreary, so she went around and tied bows in all our *ribbon cables.*"

Rich Text Format *(rich tekst for-mat)* A type of document file format readable by most major word processors. The Rich Text Format (RTF) file is basically a text file but with secret text instructions that describe the document's formatting. This looks utterly gross when you see it in the raw, text-only format. But word processors that understand RTF can read in the files and translate the ugly text into formatting codes, making the document look really nice. "The *Rich Text Format* was an attempt to create a common document file format compatible with all word processors and people living in Scarsborough."

right-click *(riet-klik)* To click the mouse's right button rather than the left button (which you normally click). This is done in Microsoft Windows to bring up context (or shortcut) menus.

The right-click mouse button.

RIMM *(rim)* Acronym for Rambus Inline Memory Module. See also *RDRAM, SIMM.*

ring network *(ring net-werk)* See *token ring network.*

RIP *(rip)* Acronym for Remote Imaging Protocol, a graphics language that lets modem users use their mouse to give commands to another computer through the phone lines. Many of the newest electronic bulletin-board systems offer RIP so that users can use their mouse rather than type arcane commands. "Before bulletin boards started using *RIP,* you had to type commands to get anything done. With *RIP,* you can use your mouse rather than type to choose most commands. (Then again, have you ever tried typing your password using a mouse?)"

RISC *(risk)* Acronym for Reduced Instruction Set Computer, a computer that runs very fast because the microprocessor can do only a limited number of things. The idea here is that those little things make the building blocks for larger things, so its limited number of instructions doesn't hinder the RISC processor. See also *CISC.* "I don't care how fast it is — putting something called *RISC* into my computer doesn't sit well with me."

RJ-11 *(ar-jay-ee-lev-un)* Another term for the phone jack, the hole in the wall that your telephone plugs into.

RJ-45 *(ar-jay-for-tee-fiev)* A name for the jack (hole) and connector commonly found on Ethernet network cables.

RLL *(ar el el)* Acronym for Run-Length-Limited, an old type of hard disk controller that increases the capacity of the hard drive by using disk-compression technology directly from the hard disk controller. An RLL controller can increase disk storage capacity by as much as 50 percent. See also *IDE.* "Wow! Where did you get the antique *RLL* drive?"

 robot *(roh-baht)* 1. An automated mechanism that simulates or reproduces (or replaces) human activities, such as assembly-line work and deep-space work. R2D2 from *Star Wars* is an example of a robot. Robots are used in many applications, including computer assembly and testing. "Perhaps the most famous *robot* of all time is Robby the Robot from the film *Forbidden Planet.* He was charming, polite, and a good friend, and he could crush your head like a grapefruit." 2. A program on the World Wide Web that searches the entire Web (or only part of it) for information you want. The robot then reports the results back to you, typically in an e-mail message.

robotics *(roh-baht-iks)* The study and application of robots. "My nephew studied *robotics* in school. Now he's working in Burger King. I suppose he's experiencing what it's like to be a robot."

robust *(roh-bust)* An overused term that describes how hardy a system is, how well it's resistant to errors and bugs or how well it recovers from them.

rollback *(rol-back)* To return a database to a previously saved state, as in restoring from a backup. This is usually done to remove any corrupted data from the database.

ROM *(rahm)* 1. Acronym for Read-Only Memory, any type of memory that can be read but not written to. For example, compact discs (CDs) are ROM media. 2. Chips inside your computer that permanently contain basic information. ROM chips are accessed like RAM chips, but their contents never change. See also *BIOS, RAM, PROM.* "I think 'crash randomly' is a special instruction in my computer's *ROM.*"

ROM BIOS *(rahm bie-os)* Acronym for Read-Only Memory Basic Input/Output System. See also *BIOS.* "No, Mr. Pinkston, BIOS is not ROM's 'last name.'"

Roman *(roh-man)* 1. A classification of type styles (fonts), including Times and many others. "A *Roman* man once said, 'Hello, my name is Gaius Julius Caesar, and I'm looking for a specific type of font, or do I need to ask?'" 2. The normal, nonslanted version of type, as opposed to italic type. See also *font*.

room *(room)* Short for Internet chat room.

root *(root)* The main user of the UNIX computer. Also called the root user, this special account allows full access to all the commands, directories, and places secret on the computer. This is truly holy stuff. To be a root on a UNIX computer is akin to being a true computer god. "Bill keeps trying to log in as the *root*, hoping that someday the computer will be his. I don't like the grin on his face when he says that."

root directory *(root dee-rek-toh-ree)* The first and often only directory on a disk. The root directory doesn't become important until you have subdirectories and a disk tree structure. Then, the other directories — the subdirectories — branch from the root like a tree. In DOS, the symbol for the root directory is the single backslash. Under UNIX, the symbol is a single forward slash. See also *directory, path, subdirectory, tree structure*. "I wrote this nifty program, DOG.COM, that instantly sniffs out the *root directory* of my hard drive's tree structure."

rounding error *(rown-ding er-or)* A one-cent error that occurs when the computer converts decimal numbers into binary code (for internal processing) and back again. This always happens, but it's nothing to be overly concerned about — unless you're doing nuclear physics or thousands of lives are at stake, in which case you can use the "blame Microsoft" defense at your U.N. Crimes of Humanity trial. The reason for the rounding error is that certain numbers can only be approximated in the computer's memory as binary digits. As a result, there is a little bit of a fudge factor as the computer's approximations are mathematically manipulated. "I tried to explain that all the wrong answers on my math final were caused by *rounding errors,* but the professor declines to believe that I'm a computer."

route *(root)* The path information travels over on the Internet. A list of hosts, gateways, hills, valleys, and various devices through which the traffic travels.

router *(roo-ter; row-ter)* A device that sends network information over long distances.

row *(roh)* 1. A horizontal array of data, as in a spreadsheet or table. Spreadsheets organize data into rows and columns to make totals and other calculations faster and easier. 2. A line of text in a word processing document or just a line of text across the screen. "The typical PC screen has 25 *rows* of text, only 4 of which may make sense at any one time."

RPG *(ar pee jee)* Acronym for *role-play-ing* game, a computer game where each player pretends that he's a different character.

RPM *(ar pee em)* Acronym for *revolu-tions* (or *rotations*) *per minute*, a measurement of the number of times something turns around. Disk drives and phonograph records (remember those?) spin at particular RPMs.

R

Phonograph records spin at 33⅓ or 45 RPMs. "I like CD players because I don't have to worry about the *RPM*."

RS-232C *(ar-es-too-thur-tee-too-see)* Acronym for Recommended Standard-232C, also known as RS-232. This is not a Radio Shack part number. Instead, it's a standard method of transmitting data across serial cables and is used by modems, printers, and other serial devices. There's lots of technical stuff surrounding the standard, and it can be boring, so that's all we say here. See also *serial, serial port*. "If *RS-232c* is the 232nd standard they came up with that year, I'd hate to have sat through the first 231 meetings."

RTF *(ar tee ef)* 1. See *Rich Text Format*. 2. The extension used on Rich Text Format document files.

RTFM *(ar-tee-ef-em)* Acronym for Read the [Frickin'] Manual, which is what rude gurus say to get innocent newbies off their backs. Not a nice thing to say, mostly because people *do* read the [Frickin'] Manual and the [Frickin'] Manual is rarely of any help (probably because it was written by the [Frickin'] Guru who keeps saying RTFM).

run *(run)* 1. What to do when the computer starts to smoke. 2. To start a program. Other terms for run are start, launch, execute, and initiate. "The customer service operator told me to *run* my program, but I couldn't find a leash to fit it."

run time *(run tiem)* 1. The time spent while a program is running. 2. A special version of a program, such as a database or spreadsheet, that performs a specific task. For example, a run-time version of Excel would let you use your Excel worksheets but would not let you use any Excel commands or options. "*Run time* is a misnomer when you work with Windows. Then, it's more like walk time."

R

S

S: *(es koh-lon)* A drive letter designation for any of a number of different types of disk drives in a PC system. At this altitude, it's most likely a network drive, though it could also be a line drive late in the eighth when it really counts.

S-100 *(ess-won-hun-dred)* A type of expansion card and also the name of a CP/M computer from the late 1970s that used that type of expansion card. These systems would be called dinosaurs today. See also *CP/M, expansion card.* "During their heyday, the *S-100* systems were the Cadillacs of PCs."

S3 *(es three)* A type of PC video card, named after the chips used on the card.

Samba *(sam-buh)* A suite of programs designed to make working on remote computers seem like you're working on your own computer. For example, you can use a Samba server on a UNIX computer to view and edit documents on your own Windows computer.

SAA *(ess ay ay)* Acronym for Systems Application Architecture, a set of guidelines that IBM developed for standardizing the way computers work. Most people follow these guidelines and then add just enough "improvements" to destroy the whole purpose of a standard in the first place. See also *IBM.* "My computer follows the IBM *SAA* standard. That seems odd because my computer is a Macintosh."

sans serif *(sans sayr-if)* A typeface that lacks *serifs,* which are tiny ornamental curves and such that appear at the edges of letters. Believe it or not, serifs actually make letters easier to read. Sans serif typefaces (*sans* from the French word for *without*) are harder to read, but better suited for titles. Times is an example of a serif font; Helvetica is sans serif. See also *serif.* "A simple desktop publishing rule is to use *sans serif fonts* for headlines or titles and serif fonts for the text."

SATAN *(say-tin)* Acronym for Security Administrator Tool for Analyzing Networks. SATAN is a database utility, though it gained popularity in the computer phobic media as yet another example that computers must certainly be evil.

save *(sayv)* 1. To store data in a permanent form, typically on a disk drive. 2. The command that saves data. Nearly every program has a Save command to store your work. "Use the *Save* command periodically to store your work."

save as *(sayv az)* To save a file to disk using a different name or format.

The Save As dialog box.

scalable font *(skay-lah-bul fawnt)* A type of font that can appear in different sizes and still look good. Nonscalable fonts can also appear in different sizes, but at certain sizes they look as horrible as seeing your skin pores through a magnifying glass. "I only use *scalable fonts* in my desktop publishing work, just in case some customer wants to change the type sizes at the last minute."

scan *(skan)* To read text, images, or bar codes into the computer. Accomplished by a device called a *scanner.* See also *scanner.*

ScanDisk *(skan disk)* A utility program that comes with DOS and Windows, which identifies and repairs problems on floppy or hard disks. ScanDisk is a more advanced and easier program to use than the ancient MS-DOS CHKDSK command.

scan line *(skan lien)* A horizontal row of dots produced an electron gun sweeping across the inside of the monitor. The number of scan lines determines the monitor's vertical resolution.

scanner *(skan-er)* 1. A device that can electronically "read" printed text or images into a computer. Scanners come in two sizes: flat-bed and handheld. *Flat-bed* scanners can scan an entire page at one time, and *handheld* scanners can scan in widths of approximately four inches. 2. In 1981, Hollywood released a bad horror movie called *Scanners,* where people could use mental powers to make other people's heads explode. See also *scan.* "While watching *Scanners* on TV and trying to concentrate hard

A generic, unimpressive scanner.

enough to make my dog's head explode, I decided to buy a *scanner* so that I wouldn't have to retype newspaper articles into my word processor."

scanning order *(skan-ing or-der)* The process in which a Macintosh searches all internal and connected devices for a start-up disk.

scan rate *(skan rayt)* The speed at which a monitor draws an image on-screen. Sometimes called the *refresh rate,* the scan rate is measured in hertz (Hz). The higher the scan rate, the more expensive your monitor. And, as anyone familiar with computers knows, the more you pay for it, the better it is. See also *refresh rate.* "My monitor has a *scan rate* of 72Hz. Most clerks in the grocery store have a scan rate of about 18 items a minute."

SCO UNIX *(es see oh yoo-niks)* A version of UNIX for PCs sold through the Santa Cruz Operation, which is coincidentally located in Santa Cruz, California.

scope *(skohp)* 1. A mouthwash typically not used by halitosis-happy computer programmers. 2. A term used by programmers to describe the area within a program in which a variable can be used. "While rinsing my mouth out with *Scope,* I noticed that the *scope* of my subprogram's variables actually included my own subprogram and those subprograms written by Bob. But that subject is really beyond the scope of this book."

Scrapbook *(skrap-book)* A desk accessory found on the Macintosh that stores frequently used graphics images or text for pasting into documents. See also *clipboard.*

S

scratch *(scratch)* A prefix used to describe temporary storage, as in scratch memory or scratch disk, for example.

screen blanker *(skreen blank-er)* See *screen saver.*

screen buffer *(skreen buf-fer)* An area of memory used to store the graphic or text image displayed on-screen. Also called *screen memory* or *video ram.* "And all this time I thought that a *screen buffer* was this thing from Ronco for only $19.95 that you use to clean your monitor."

screen dump *(skreen dump)* A printout of the image that appears on-screen. The unflattering term *dump* is often used in computer lingo to mean a wholesale copying of information from one place to another. We could dwell on this subject for a long time and get very descriptive, but the editorial matron at IDG Books, Diane Steele, would doubtless frown upon such verbosity. "Whenever my computer crashes for no apparent reason, I try to get a *screen dump* so that I can show the technician what happened and why his last solution didn't really work after all."

screen font *(skreen fawnt)* A bit-mapped font that mimics the appearance of printer fonts. Because printers often print with a resolution of 300 dots per inch or more, the fonts tend to look better printed than they do on-screen. As a result, the fonts that appear on-screen may look plain and simple compared to the fonts that appear on the printer, resulting in confusion when you try to figure out what you're doing. "I hate *screen fonts* because you can never tell what they'll look like until you print them out and waste paper in the process."

screen refresh *(screen ree-fresh)* See *refresh rate.*

screen saver *(skreen sayv-er)* A special program that periodically blanks out the screen and replaces it with utter darkness or often some form of graphic or enterainment. Screen savers prevent the same image from appearing on your screen and being "burned-in" permanently. For example, lots of older PCs have images of 1-2-3 or WordPerfect permanently etched into their monitors. Some screen savers can be quite creative. Rather than just blank the screen, they show images of some sort such as flying toasters, lightning flashes, or raindrops. See also *phosphor burn-in.* "If I don't touch my keyboard or mouse for five minutes, my *screen blanker* shuts off my screen and displays fish in an aquarium to protect my monitor from burn-in."

scripting language *(skrip-ting lang-gwaj)* A simple programming language designed to automate tasks but not really to build complete applications. Less than a programming language, scripting languages include AppleScript, the shell language in UNIX, MS-DOS batch files, and others.

scroll *(skrohl)* To move text or graphics vertically or horizontally on-screen as though your monitor were a porthole, looking at a much larger image a little bit at a time. "With a 250-page document, your monitor can show only half a page at any given time. To see the rest of your document, you have to *scroll* up or down. Then again, you can just pretend that you saw only part of the document so that you can't be held responsible for the rest of it."

S

scroll bar *(skrohl bar)* 1. Where Plato went for drinks with Aristotle. 2. A horizontal or vertical strip that appears at the right or bottom sides of a window and lets you use a mouse to scroll the image up and down or left and right. The scroll bar also shows you the approximate position of the current screen in relation to the beginning or end of the file.

scroll box *(skrol boks)* A rectangular control living on a scroll bar that allows you to scroll the image in a window. You can drag the scroll box up or down (or left or right) or click around it to scroll the image. "Don't waste time pressing the Page Up and Down keys. Move the *scroll box* wildly up and down in the scroll bar and pretend that there are people in there alternatively being slammed into the floor and ceiling."

Scroll Lock key *(skrohl lahk kee)* 1. A keyboard key that seems to do absolutely nothing when you press it. 2. In some (but not all) programs, a key that changes the mode of the cursor keys on your keyboard. Normally, pressing the up and down cursor keys causes the cursor to scroll up or down. But if you press the Scroll Lock key and then press the up or down cursor keys, the cursor remains fixed on-screen, and the text or graphics image appears to slide up or down underneath. If you try this with your program and nothing happens, you know that your program ignores the Scroll Lock key. "Sometimes I like to press the *Scroll Lock key* while using different programs just to see which programs actually use the Scroll Lock key."

SCSI *(scuz-zee)* 1. Acronym for Small Computer System Interface, which is yet another standard for connecting tape drives, hard disks, and scanners to computers. This is a truly whimsical and easily pronounceable acronym, like WYSIWYG, but not like GUI. With a SCSI interface in your PC, you can connect up to six peripherals, including: hard drives, CD-ROM drives, scanners, more hard drives, and more CD-ROM drives. See also *termination*. 2. A device that adheres to the SCSI standard. "This hard drive is a *SCSI* drive and so you need to spend *another* $120 for a *SCSI* card inside your PC for it to work."

SDRAM *(es dee ram)* Acronym for Synchronous DRAM, yet another type of DRAM. See also *DRAM*.

SDK *(es-dee-kay)* Acronym for Software Developers Kit, a suite of programs designed to help programmers create other programs. Usually includes a compiler, linker, plus tools, resources, and references required to build programs in that particular programming language.

SEA *(see)* Acronym that stands for Self-Extracting Archive, usually a Macintosh archive that was compressed using the StuffIt program. Files with the SEA extension can automatically uncompress themselves on a Macintosh floppy or hard disk. See also *StuffIt*. "Sometimes when I copy files from CompuServe, they come have the SIT or *SEA* file extension. If they have the SIT extension, I have to use StuffIt to uncompress them, but if they have the SEA extension, they uncompress themselves if I double-click on them."

S

search *(surch)* To scan through a document for a matching bit of data. See also *find.* "Because the board can't decide whom we should lay off, we're going to conduct a *search* of everyone's hard drive and fire all those who have the words *boss* and *toupee* in one or more of their files."

search and destroy *(surch and duh-stroy)* 1. A military term made popular during the Vietnam War, which is a nice way of saying to look for someone so that you can kill him. 2. A form of search and replace when you replace what you found with nothing. The proper term is really *search and delete,* but no one would turn to that entry. See also *find and replace.* "Someone told me that my computer program had bugs in it, so I spent the last few days on a *search and destroy* mission using pesticides long since outlawed by the government."

search and replace *(serch and ree-place)* To look for specific characters in a file and substitute them for another character or group of characters. See also *find and replace.*

 search engine *(surch in-jin)* A Web page designed to hunt down and locate information on the World Wide Web. There are several types of search engines: Yahoo is a catalog type of search engine. It contains lists of Web pages by category — like a library. WebCrawler is a robot type of search engine. It locates Web pages based on their *content,* the text or images that appear on the Web page. Excite is a content type of search engine. It examines the content of a Web page overall and matches that content with the searches you perform. The nifty thing about all this is that using a search engine on the World Wide Web is free. See also *World Wide Web.* "I was able to look up an old girlfriend on the Web using a *search engine.* She's making a million dollars a year selling pictures of her cats."

Some popular search engines are altavista.com, ask.com, dejanews.com, dogpile.com, excite.com, goto.com, hotbot.com, infoseek.com, lycos.com, search.com, webcrawler.com, and yahoo.com.

search path *(surch path)* See *path.*

search string *(surch string)* The group of characters that the computer looks for when given the Find or Find and Replace command. See also *string.*

sector *(sek-ter)* A unit of disk storage, the smallest unit into which information can be written. A formatting disk is divided into tracks and sectors. A track is a ring of information encoded on the disk. Each track is divided into sectors. On a PC, each sector holds 512 bytes of information. See also *cluster, track.* "The technician told my mother that her hard drive had a bad *sector,* so she took it home and scolded it."

secure browser *(seh-kyoor brow-ser)* A Web browser that is SSL-compliant, meaning that it can send and receive information and any eavesdroppers are unable to decipher it. Browsers from Netscape and Microsoft are considered secure browsers. Other browsers, who knows? See also *SSL, Web browser.* "Using *secure browsers*, all residents of the United States transferred their bank balances to off-shore accounts in 2006, rendering the IRS extremely frustrated."

S

Secure Sockets Layer See *SSL.*

Sed *(sed) S*tream *ed*itor, a UNIX program designed to manipulate text. Extremely cryptic but very powerful. See also *awk, Perl.*

seek *(seek)* To move the read/write heads of a disk drive so that information can be read from disk, in much the same way as you might move a needle over a record on your grandmother's old turntable. This is actually quite a religious term for a computer, don't you think? You'd expect a term like Go To or Find or Search. Seek, of course, always implies that there may be some chance at failure, which is probably why the computer gods selected it instead. See also *read/write head.* "I bought a Bible program and wanted to find the passage where 'Seek and ye shall find' occurs, but I got a *seek* error instead."

seek time *(seek tiem)* The amount of times, in milliseconds, that it takes a disk drive to move the read/write heads from one track to another. The *average seek time* value is used to compare different drives.

segment *(seg-ment)* A portion or part of something. With worms, a segment is like a new piece of the worm that makes it longer — a worm-slice, should the worm chance to crawl over an upended razor blade. In the PC, a *segment* refers to a 64K chunk of memory. "Programs generally run slow under DOS because they must fit their parts into puny little 64K memory *segments.*"

select *(seh-lekt)* To highlight and choose text or graphics that appear on-screen. A selected object can then be manipulated somehow by the program. Selected objects typically appear inversed (white on black) or inside a graphical outline. See also *cut, copy, paste.* "Before you can delete, copy, or cut anything off the screen, you have to *select* it first so that the computer knows what you want to delete, copy, or cut."

select all *(seh-lekt ahl)* To select everything in a document, all text and graphic images, at one time. This is a good command to use to erase everything at once, adjust everything on-screen, or copy everything at the same time. If used carelessly, this is also a good way to delete four years' worth of work at the touch of a button. "I chose the *Select All* command, and everything in my room became highlighted."

selected *(seh-lek-ted)* Highlighted text or graphics images that show you what objects will be affected by the next command you give (cut, copy, or delete, for example). "I told my grandfather that I had to click on the mouse to make objects *selected.* He thought that I joined a new cult or something."

self modifying *(self mod-ih-fie-ing)* When a program makes changes to itself while running. Many virus programs are self modifying (also called *mutating*) to prevent detection by antivirus software. Many artificial intelligence programs are also self modifying, to give the illusion of correcting themselves or adapting to outside stimuli like a living organism. "I wrote a chess program that's *self modifying.* It started out playing chess very well, but eventually rewrote itself into an accounting program."

semiconductor *(sem-ie-kon-duk-ter)* A material that is neither a good insulator nor a good conductor of electricity. Semiconductors are used to make transistors, diodes, integrated circuits, and

S

all the other neat stuff that make up the parts of a computer. Silicon and germanium are two popular materials used for semiconductors. See also *germanium, silicon.* "Before he got a job designing *semiconductors* in the electronics industry, George used to work part time as a conductor on Amtrak."

separator bar *(sep-uh-rayt-er bar)* A thin line on a pull-down menu that helps group related commands. See also *pull-down menu.* "The File menu of my word processor has a *separator bar* between the Church and State commands."

Separator bar divides the sections

A separator bar divides the sections.

sequential access *(see-kwen-shal ak-ses)* To scan information starting from the beginning, such as a tape backup or a cassette tape on your stereo. In comparison, random access lets you scan for information anywhere, such as on a CD-ROM disk. Sequential access is usually much slower than random access, although if you want to kill some time so that you can goof off for a while, it's a fine method for searching on your computer. See also *random access.* "Every time I want to play my favorite song stored on a tape cassette, I have to use *sequential access* by fast forwarding or rewinding. If I had the song stored on a CD-ROM disc, I could use random access and start playing the song immediately."

serial *(seer-ee-al)* To transmit data, one bit after another. Each byte is split up into bits and sent along in single file, usually through a single cable. This contrasts with *parallel*, which is where data is sent eight (or more) bits abreast — like marching in a parade. The advantage of serial is that the information can be sent over longer distances. See also *data word format, parallel.* "Talking is a *serial* activity because you have to speak the words one after another. Arguing is more parallel in nature because nobody bothers listening to what the other person has to say before he starts shouting right back."

serial communications *(seer-ee-al ka-myoo-nuh-kay-shens)* To transfer data one bit at a time through a single cable, usually through a modem. "Ted's our *serial communications* expert. He knows all about modems; transmission protocols, such as ZModem and Kermit; and who manufactured cereals such as Quisp and Quake."

serial mouse *(seer-ee-al mowse)* An input device (mouse) that plugs into a computer's serial port. This type of mouse is not as popular as it once was, because most PCs now come with special mouse ports. See also *bus mouse.* The serial mouse also tended to interfere with a computer's modem, which was another reason to hate them. "My *serial mouse* is doing 15-to-life for cheese theft."

serial port *(seer-ee-al port)* A connector on the back of a computer that allows data transfer, one bit at a time. Also known as a modem port, COM port, or RS-232 port. It comes in 9-pin and 25-pin sizes. See also *parallel port, RS-232C.*

S

"Lois bought a *serial port* for her PC, but was crushed to find out that no milk or sugar port was available."

serial printer *(seer-ee-al prin-ter)* An oddball printer that plugs into the serial port rather than a computer's parallel (or printer) port. Serial printers were popular in the early 1980s when some computers lacked parallel ports (or Centronics ports, as they were known then). Today, they're dinosaurs. "I decided to buy my boss the slowest printer possible, so I got him a *serial printer.*"

serif *(ser-if)* Tiny ornamental curves on letters to make them easier to read. Most typefaces have serifs. See also *sans serif.* "This book uses a typeface with *serifs* so that the printing won't strain your eyes and give you headaches while reading it. Too bad the same can't be said for legal documents, tax forms, or textbooks."

server *(sir-ver)* 1. Usually the most expensive computer that nobody can use because it's busy controlling the entire network. You would think that the server would be the "slave" on the network, but this isn't so. The server is really the "master computer," the one that all the other computers hook into and beg for the use of disk drives and printers. This is the same evil concept that dominated mainframe computing during the past three decades. See also *client/server network.* "If you want to sabotage a network, don't bother wrecking each computer. Just unplug the *server,* and then the whole network will sink like the Titanic." 2. A type of computer sold as a server, usually a powerful PC with lots of hard drive storage and maybe an extra microprocessor or

two. When the 486 was first introduced, it was sold as a "server" computer; today's high-end machines are also billed as servers. "Today's *server* is tomorrow's low-end entry machine."

session *(sesh-in)* 1. A 50-minute hour spent with a psychiatrist to help repair the mental trauma of having to use a computer. 2. An individual activity being carried out by a multitasking computer. See also *multitasking.* "Psychiatrists love multitasking computers. Since they charge $120 for an hour *session*, a computer running three sessions gets billed $360."

setting *(set-ing)* The configuration of a program that defines its appearance on-screen (color, window size, and memory usage, for example). "By the time the sun got done *setting* in the west, I had finished modifying the program's *settings* so that it wouldn't keep appearing as hot pink on purple every time you loaded it up."

setup *(set-up)* 1. The way a computer is configured. "Oops! Your computer doesn't know about your new hard drive. I guess you forgot that part of the setup process." 2. To install new software. 3. The name of the program used to install new software. See also *configure, install.*

sexadecimal *(seks-uh-des-uh-mal)* See *hexadecimal.*

 SGML *(es-jee-em-el)* Acronym for Standard Generalized Markup Language, a type of text formatting for Web page documents that stores several different ways to present the same information. See also *HTML, Web page.*

sh *(shel; es aych)* 1. The Korn shell in UNIX. An interface that lets you use UNIX, which was actually what Microsoft modeled DOS after (in case you didn't know). See *csh.* 2. The command you use to start the sh shell. "Dale uses UNIX all the time, and he thinks that the *sh* command is two letters too short."

shareware *(shayr-wayr)* Software that you can legally copy and give away but must pay for if you use it regularly. Many shareware programs often rival the features of commercial programs but cost far less. After you pay for shareware, you get a printed manual, telephone support, and notices of future upgrades. See also *public domain.* "*Shareware* programs let you try before you buy, which is like asking your local Ford dealer if you could drive around the latest Mustang for a few weeks before deciding whether you want to buy it."

sheet feeder *(sheet fee-der)* A tray that holds paper and gives up a page at a time to a printer. Sheet feeders let you use special stationery or letterhead that you may have lying around rather than use computer paper every time. "Every time my boss hands me a memo, I just flip it over, store it in my *sheet feeder,* and print on the other side, thereby saving valuable computer paper."

shell *(shel)* 1. An interface that's usually easier to use than the ugly program it's trying to cover for. For example, a DOS shell was a program that made DOS easier to use. Windows is a type of DOS shell, even though there are shells for Windows, such as the Norton Desktop, that supposedly make it easier to use. Actually, not all shells make things easier. Some shells make things more

complex, but if that's what the user wants, then it's still considered a shell. 2. The name given to any program that someone uses to control a computer. In DOS, the shell is really a program called COMMAND.COM. That program displays the DOS prompt, interprets your commands, and runs other programs. In UNIX, the shell is sh or csh. See *csh, sh.* 3. The name given to the command that runs another program from a first program. For example, the Shell command in WordPerfect allows you to run a second program without having to first quit WordPerfect. When you quit the second program, you're back in WordPerfect. "Sue sells csh (sea *shells*) by the sea shore, and she *shells* from csh (see *shells*) to see what she sells."

shielded *(shee-ul-ded)* A type of cable that's supposedly protected from radio frequency interference.

Shift key *(shift kee)* A modifier key primarily used to produce uppercase letters on the keyboard. Shift can also be used in combination with any key to generate a command or produce some wacky symbol. "Hold down the *Shift key* while tapping the F4 key once and then let both of them go. That's what Shift+F4 means when you see it printed in the manual. Shift+Tab means hold down the Shift key and press the Tab key."

Shift+arrow *(shift ayr-oh)* To hold down the Shift key, tap one of the arrow keys (up, down, left, right) and then let both of them go. This command is often used for moving the cursor to highlight text in a word processor. "Press *Shift+left arrow,* and the cursor highlights all the text you just wrote. Now if you press Del, you'll just wipe out all your valuable work in an instant."

S

Shift+click *(shift klik)* 1. To hold down the Shift key while clicking on the mouse button at the same time. Shift+clicking is used to select two or more objects on-screen. See also *click*. 2. On the Macintosh, any click of the mouse when used with any modifier key on the keyboard. In addition to Shift, you can use the Command (Apple) key, Option key, or a combination of them. "Ted Nelson, the developer of hypertext, claims that the Macintosh mouse actually has four buttons; three of which are on the keyboard."

 Shockwave *(shok-wayv)* An extension or plug-in for your Web browser that allows you to see animations or run programs over the Internet. See also *plug-in*.

shortcut *(short-kut)* A file alias, used in Microsoft Windows. The shortcut file is actually a representation (a link) to the original file.

shortcut keys *(short-kut kees)* A keyboard combination that serves the same function as a command on a pull-down menu. For example, Ctrl+S is the shortcut key for the Save command on the File menu.

 shortcut menu *(short-kut menyoo)* A pop-up menu associated with part of an application, icon, or window. The shortcut menu appears when you point the mouse at something and click the right mouse button. See also *right-click*. "Little Red Riding Hood clicked on Grandma's house to get the *shortcut menu,* but the wolf ate her."

shoulder surfing *(shohl-der sur-fing)* To look over another person's shoulder without being seen. Shoulder surfing is

often used to see which keys someone types for their password or to read someone's phone calling card numbers at a public phone. "Be careful for people *shoulder surfing* you whenever you use your calling card at a public phone. They may be trying to inhale your cologne or perfume, or they may be trying to read your phone calling card numbers."

Show Clipboard *(shoh klip-bord)* A command that lets you see what's being held in the clipboard, the last item that was cut or copied. By choosing the Show Clipboard command first, you can see what will appear on-screen if you choose the Paste command next.

shrink wrap *(shrink rap)* The clear, plastic covering on most computer software sold in the store, giving it the illusion that it hasn't been touched by the grubby little hands of other people before reaching your computer desk intact and pristine. Most software is sold in shrink-wrapped boxes for that sanitized look, much like finding a Sanitized For Your Protection paper loop covering the toilet seat at a motel. Most software stores do not accept returned software unless it's still shrink-wrapped, which makes you wonder how you would know to return it in the first place. "No, madam, *shrink wrap* will not make you thinner."

 SHTML *(es aych tee em el)* Acronym for Server-parsed HTML (Hypertext Markup Language), a type of Web page document that contains special commands to allow a Web page to do more, run faster, jump higher, and so on. See also *HTML*.

shut down *(shut down)* 1. To turn off a computer. 2. A series of commands executed when the computer is shut down. 3. The Windows command used to quit Windows and optionally turn the computer off. "No, sir, a brick tossed into the computer's hard drive is not a proper *shut down* command."

sidelit *(sied-lit)* Additional illumination from the side of a liquid crystal display (LCD) to make it easier to read. See also *backlight.* "If it weren't for my *sidelit* LCD, I wouldn't be able to use my laptop computer in a dark plane ride. I'd really miss all those 36,000-foot games of Solitaire."

Sieve of Eratosthenes *(seev ov eer-uh-tahs-thuh-neez)* A programming concept for finding prime numbers (any number that cannot be divided by anything other than 1 and itself), named after that ancient Greek guy. Used in benchmark testing.

SIG *(sig)* Acronym for *s*pecial *i*nterest *g*roup, which is a collection of people who share the same interest in computers such as using a specific computer like an Amiga, a type of program like dBASE IV, or a field such as artificial intelligence or desktop publishing. "Cool people say that they belong to a *SIG.* Uncool people say they belong to a special interest group because everyone knows that only cool computer people use acronyms whenever possible."

sign on *(sien on)* To call another computer, such as a local BBS, CompuServe, or Prodigy, and type your name and password so that you can start using the services. See also *logon.* "Before

breaking into the Pentagon's computers, we put the Do Not Disturb *sign on* the motel door and then plugged our portable computers into the phone jack so that we could dial out and *sign on* without anybody watching us."

signature *(sig-na-choor)* A file containing information to be appended

Sandra Hardin Gookin
Author, "Parenting For Dummies" and other such stuff
Visit our site for more Gookin Titles
http://www.wambooli.com/

My signature line.

to (put at the end of) an e-mail message or Usenet posting. These files typically contain your name, contact information, and, if you're a sophomore in college, about 4K of useless ASCII graphics and *Star Trek* quotes. "Howie was able to create a delightful *signature* using only three lines of text. Obviously, he's net-sensitive."

signal-to-noise *(sig-nul too noys)* The amount of information verses idle chatter in a newsgroup posting or e-mail message. Refers to posters who tend to gloop up their messages with unnecessary quotes or topics not relating to the subject. From a communications term referring to how much of the signal is disturbed by random noise on the line.

silicon *(sil-uh-kon)* 1. Sand. 2. An element that's used in making glass and the ceramic wafers out of which computer chips are punched. Do not pronounce this as "silly con." "The hors d'oeuvres wouldn't be complete at any computer party without a tray of *silicon* wafers."

Silicon Valley *(sil-uh-kon val-ee)* The place in Northern California that is world famous for making semiconductors, microprocessors, and other

S

computer electronic circuitry. It also has a few good pizza parlors and take-out Chinese restaurants. "We drove through *Silicon Valley* up El Camino Real to look for a job in the computer industry. But with computers so prevalent, we wound up getting a job with a computer company in Fresno instead."

SIMM *(sim)* Acronym for Single In-line Memory Module, which is a tiny circuit board that holds several memory chips. Several SIMMs plugged into a computer look like headless cockroaches stuck face-first in the surface of a Roach Motel. See also *SIP*. "*SIMMs* make it easier to install large amounts of memory. Rather than plug individual memory chips in your computer, you can just plug in a couple of SIMMs."

simulation *(sim-yoo-lay-shun)* A program or device that mimics the operation of something else, such as real life. A flight-simulation program mimics flying an airplane (although how many airplane cockpits do you know that use a keyboard to control the plane?), and a stock market simulation mimics the actual rise and fall of stocks on Wall Street. See also *emulation*. "To give my kids an idea what driving a real car is like, my computer has a driving *simulation* they can play with."

single-density *(sing-gul-den-suh-tee)* The earliest form of storage on magnetic media that has been replaced with double-density and quad, or high-density. A single-density 5¼-inch floppy disk can contain 180K of data, a double-density 5¼-inch floppy disk can contain 360K, and a high-density 5¼-inch floppy disk can hold 1.4MB. "Don't buy

single-density floppy disks because they're obsolete. Then again, so will everything else be in another month or two."

single-sided disk *(sing-gul sie-ded disk)* A floppy disk that stores data only on one side. Along with single-density, another antique.

single-user *(sing-gul yoo-zer)* Equipment that only one person can try to use at any given time. A laptop computer is a single-user computer because if two or more people try to type on the keyboard simultaneously, it may look obscene. Some database programs are single user, meaning that only one person at a time can use them. Multiuser database programs let two or more people use the program. See also *multiuser*. "Lots of companies want to eliminate *single-user* computers and connect everything in a network. That way, they can watch what everyone's doing and keep people from playing games on their computers at work."

SIP *(sip)* Acronym for Single In-line Processor, a type of memory expansion card similar to a SIMM. The difference between a SIP and a SIMM is that the SIP uses a row of tiny pins as a connector — like a cheap comb. SIPs aren't generally user-upgradable and are usually installed only at the factory. See also *SIMM*. "I need more *SIPs* because my PC gulps down memory."

SIT *(sit)* Extension given to a file that has been compressed using the StuffIt program. "If you have a *SIT* file, uncompress it using StuffIt."

site license *(siet lie-senz)* A software agreement that lets you legally use multiple copies of the same program on several computers at the same time. Site licenses are cheaper than buying multiple copies of the same program and legal in comparison to software piracy. "We have a *site license* for WordPerfect and DOS, but the folks who make the Space Zombies game want us to have a site license for 500 copies as well."

skipjack algorithm *(skip-jak al-gor-rithm)* The specific instructions for encrypting and decrypting files, used in the Clipper encryption chip that the government wants everyone to use so that they can read our mail. See also *Clipper chip.* "The Skipjack algorithm is classified as a government secret because if everyone knows how it works, they can figure out how to crack its code. If you want to learn how the Skipjack algorithm works, get a job with the government and then defect back to the people."

slave *(slayv)* A secondary device, usually connected to the computer after a master device. The master device could be a primary disk drive or some type of controller. The slave is merely a device attached and secondary to the master.

SLED *(sled)* Acronym for Single Large Expensive Disk, which is another way of putting all your eggs in one basket. Computers that use a SLED often have a multimegabyte hard disk that costs a fortune. "After we lost all our data because we bought lots of cheap hard disks, we decided to buy a *SLED* and get our money's worth. Then it failed anyway."

sleep *(sleep)* 1. A command used to suspend the computer's operation, to pause, for a given amount of time. 2. The ability of a computer to go into a low-power suspension mode.

Sleep button *(sleep but-un)* A switch on the computer that instantly activates sleep or suspend mode, powering down the system without actually turning it off. The sleep button generally has a crescent moon symbol on it, though this isn't consistent.

slimline case *(slim-lien kays)* A computer case that's short and narrow, perfectly suited for squeezing into tight spaces on desks that have no room. Slimline cases usually offer fewer expansion slots and disk drives than normal computer cases (referred to as desktop cases). If you have absolutely no plans to upgrade a computer in the future, get a slimline case. Otherwise, get a bigger computer case that offers more room for expansion. "I bought a slimline case because I didn't have much room on my desk to put a computer. Now I can't add a hard disk or another disk drive because the slimline case has no room. Wow, do I feel like I just got ripped off."

 SLIP *(slip)* Acronym for Serial Line Internet Protocol, a method of hooking your computer up to the Internet using a high-speed modem and standard phone line. See also *PPP.* "This is how we *SLIP* on the Net, SLIP on the Net, SLIP on the Net. This is how we SLIP on the Net, so early in the morning."

slot *(slawt)* A long, thin hole into which an expansion card is plugged. It's usually called an *expansion* slot, though in

S

advertising you may see that a PC comes with "eight slots," meaning that you can plug in up to eight expansion cards. The term *slot* is actually the easy term. Nerds call all the slots *the bus* and refer to it by terms such as MCA, ISA, EISA, and NuBus. See also *expansion slot*. "Plugging things into your PC's expansion *slot* makes upgrading your hardware Tinker Toy-simple. Only, remember to turn your computer off before you do this or else your PC's guts will smell like burnt toast."

small caps *(smal kaps)* A text attribute or style where lowercase letters are replaced by capital letters of a smaller size. For example, the following title is in small caps:

Bosco Slugworth Lances a Boil

The first letter of each word is capitalized. That's called *initial caps*. The subsequent letters are still uppercase, but in a smaller size than the other letters. That's *small caps*. If all the letters were capitalized, it would be called *all caps*. "These three charming old ladies came into the computer store looking for *small caps,* so I told them to go to the milliner instead."

Smalltalk *(smal-tok)* One of the first object-oriented programming languages in the world. Originally developed at the Xerox Palo Alto Research Center, the Smalltalk interface has been responsible for the graphical user interface ideas of the Macintosh and Microsoft Windows. So now you know who to blame. "Blake thinks he's cool because he programmers in a pure object-oriented program-

ming language like *Smalltalk* rather than C++. I'd think he was cool too if any of his programs ever worked the way they're supposed to."

smartcard *(smart-kard)* A type of credit card that contains a computer chip that remembers information. A special device can read the smartcard or write new information to it. This type of technology may one day replace the PCMCIA cards popular in laptops. Then again, it may not. See *also PCMCIA*.

Smartdrive *(smart-driev)* A disk caching program distributed by Microsoft with MS-DOS and Windows.

smart terminal *(smart ter-muh-nul)* A computer, connected to a network, that can function independently of the network. Smart terminals are usually just personal computers with their own hard disk, disk drive, and memory. In comparison, *dumb terminals* are usually nothing more than a monitor and a keyboard. See also *dumb terminal*. "*Smart terminals* scare most managers because they can't control them as easily. Who knows if that employee is working on a report or his résumé? Managers who distrust smart terminals are called 'dumb managers,' and managers who trust smart terminals are called 'smart managers.'"

smiley *(smie-lee)* An emoticon or ASCII "picture" that conveys a happy mood or something fun. It consists of a colon, hyphen and the right parenthesis, which looks like a face turned sideways:

:-)

People use e-mail use this symbol to denote a light mood because expressions are missed and jokes that would be taken as such in verbal communications often lose their meaning after they're written down. "I would have busted you in the chops for that message, had you not appended a *smiley*." See also *emoticon*.

SMM *(es em em)* Acronym for System Management Mode, a standard developed by Intel for automatically reducing energy consumption in its chips when the computer isn't being used. The idea behind SMM chips is that they conserve energy and prolong the batteries of laptop computers. "The latest Intel processors offer *SMM* to cut off power consumption by your computer if you're not using it. SMM is great for people too lazy to hit the on–off switch on their computers."

smoke and mirrors *(smohke and meerors)* Slang term describing special effects to make a product look and sound more enticing and powerful than it really is. Smoke-and-mirrors techniques are commonly used in advertising and sales. A great smoke-and-mirrors story has to do with the ancestor of the Macintosh, the ill-fated Lisa computer. (In many ways, the Lisa was the "father" [or is it "mother"?] of the Macintosh and Windows, but in a way it isn't because they stole the idea from elsewhere.) When the original Lisa was demonstrated for the computer industry, it wasn't a computer at all! Instead, under the table, the designers had rigged several Apple II computers, which actually controlled the Lisa. This is classic smoke and mirrors. "The product demo had us floored. But then a little dog pulled back the curtain on the

left and the computer said, 'Pay no attention to that nerd behind the curtain!' I suppose the whole thing was just *smoke and mirrors*."

 SMTP *(es em tee pee)* Acronym for Simple Mail Transfer Protocol, the basic way text messages are exchanged on the Internet. See also *POP2, POP3*.

snaf *(snaf)* The edges of tractor feed paper — the row of holes that the tractor mechanism grabs to push the paper through. Typically discarded after the paper has been printed on. Also called "chad."

Snappy *(snap-ee)* Short and sweet name for the Snappy Video Snapshot, a video image grabbing device for PCs, developed by Play, Inc.

sneaker net *(snee-ker net)* A non-network where information is exchanged between computers by copying files to a disk and then walking (in your sneakers) to another computer to use the disk. "Believe it or not, I once worked at a 'high tech' company that used *sneaker net* to transfer our files."

SNOBOL *(snoh-bal)* A specialized programming language for processing character strings (text). Developed at Bell Laboratories in 1962, SNOBOL is rarely used today, except as an answer for computer trivia questions. "*SNOBOL* isn't the Latin of ancient computer languages. No, it's more like Aramaic."

snow *(snoh)* Small flickering dots and specks that sometimes appear on certain monitors, caused when the screen image changes too fast for a lame monitor to handle. Usually found only on

CGA monitors or really bad VGA monitors. "Edna, this isn't *snow* on your monitor. I think we need to go to the pharmacy and get you some Head & Shoulders."

soft boot *(soft boot)* A reset that involves only part of the system. For example, quitting MS-DOS mode in Windows results in a soft boot where MS-DOS is unloaded and Windows is reloaded, which is not the same as restarting (rebooting) the entire computer.

soft hyphen *(soft hie-fen)* A word break in a word processing document that appears only when a word hangs precariously close to the right margin, in which case a hyphen hyphenates the word. At times, the term may also apply to any hyphen character, which is used to split a word. This contrasts with hard hyphens that are not supposed to split a word when that word is too close to the right margin, or when the hyphen is used as part of a phone number or other piece of text you don't want split. "No, if you poke a *soft hyphen,* you won't get gunk all over your fingers."

SoftModem *(soft-moh-dum)* A type of modem that is contained in RAM and controlled by a DSP. Essentially not a modem at all, but rather a simulated modem using other hardware.

software *(soft-wayr)* Computer programs. Applications. Software generally refers to any type of computer program, from an operating system such as DOS, to a utility to an application to a program stored on a ROM chip. This contrasts with *hardware,* which is the physical side of computing. It's the software that makes the hardware go. Without it, the hardware would be nothing but potential — like an uneducated

kid but minus the hyperactivity. See also *hardware.* "Og know difference between *software* and hardware. Hardware hard. Software soft."

software bloat *(soft-wayr bloht)* The tendency of computer programs to grow in features, complexity and disk size until the program's girth becomes more of a problem then the problem the software is trying to solve in the first place. "Microsoft is so embarrassed by the Excel software bloat that they won't divulge exactly how many lines of code are in the thing."

SoHo *(soh-hoh)* Acronym for Small Office/Home Office, which hardly anyone uses but computer magazines that are trying to create another acronym for everyone to remember. SOHO is often used to describe products that people think would be just perfect for a small office or home office, such as a computer desk that folds up into an aquarium or flower pot, or a portable lamp that doubles up as a food warmer. "If a big company buys a product, then it's not considered a *SOHO* product. If a big company wouldn't be interested in a product, then it's considered a *SOHO* product or something absolutely useless that nobody in their right mind would consider buying it in the first place."

sort *(sort)* To organize according to some pattern or rule. The typical sort is alphabetical, though you can also have numeric sorts. Sorts can also be ascending or descending. An ascending sort is from first to last, smallest to biggest, or A to Z. Descending goes the other way. "Kinkaid should be busy for a while. I just told him to *sort* our list of Japanese clients — in Japanese."

SoundBlaster *(sownd-blas-ter)* A type of music and sound expansion card for a PC. The SoundBlaster card has become something of a standard in all PCs. Most games are compatible with the SoundBlaster and many PCs even have SoundBlaster circuitry on their motherboard.

sound card *(sownd card)* A PC expansion card that adds sound and music abilities to the computer. See also *MIDI*.

source *(sohrs)* 1. The file being copied. 2. The location of the file being copied. The location of the copy is known as the target. "The first *source* for anything has to be your brain. Or it could be the devil, if you're possessed."

source code *(sohrs kohd)* Programming instructions. These are fed into a program called a compiler, which makes object code. A program called a linker then builds the final program out of the object code. Source code is created using a text editor. "Melvin is such a deft programmer that his *source code* reads like poetry. Okay, you have to be pretty weird to appreciate it."

space *(spays)* The character, or blank, produced by pressing the spacebar. ASCII code 32. Unlike the space made on a typewriter, with computers the space is actually a character on-screen, just like A or $ or the ~ thing. "I keep having to tell Tom that 'alot' is really two words. I told him to insert a *space* character and so he drew a picture of Captain Kirk."

spacebar *(spays-bar)* The biggest key on your keyboard, the one that produces the space character. "Is it called the

spacebar or the spacebar key? Is it a bar or a key? And, no, there will be no tired and obvious outer space cocktail lounge jokes here."

spaghetti code *(spuh-geh-tee kohd)* A program written so sloppily that it has no flow or logic to it. It's said of such a program that reading it is like following a noodle around a plate of spaghetti. Spaghetti code programs are typically written by those new to programming or by a programming committee. "Well, I guess if Sergio Leone wrote a program, it could be called *spaghetti code.*"

 spam *(spam)* (Often capitalized) 1. An annoying e-mail message or newsgroup post, typically one containing an advertisement. From Spam, a spiced ham meat kind of thing sold by Hormel. (Spam is short for spiced ham.) Also could be from a Monty Python sketch involving Spam. 2. A message sent to a group of people, via e-mail or on a newsgroup. The message typically isn't germane to the discussion topic, or is trying to sell something. 3. Unwanted e-mail. See also *e-mail, newsgroup, spew.* "The only way to fight *SPAM* is to not respond."

SPARC *(spark)* Acronym for Scalable Performance ARCHitecture, a RISC processor developed by Sun Microsystems for their line of workstations (SPARCstations). It must be cool; we've never seen one. See also *RISC.* "This Sun workstation is running kind of slowly. Maybe it needs another *SPARC* plug."

special character *(spesh-uhl kar-ek-ter)* 1. Any oddball or unusual character, one typically unavailable on the keyboard. For example, the trademark character

(™) is considered a special character because it's not found on the keyboard. 2. Characters that perform special functions, such as the * or ? characters used as wildcards to match filenames or text being searched for.

speed *(speed)* A measure of how fast something is. With microprocessors, the speed is measured in MHz (megahertz). Disk drive speed is measured in access time by the millisecond. Generally speaking, the larger the number, the faster the thing operates (and the faster the money comes out of your wallet). See also *MHz, millisecond.* "I wouldn't say this new printer is fast. Its *speed* is probably one notch above stop."

spell check *(spel chek)* To run a command that checks the spelling of text in a document. See also *spell checker.*

A common spell-check icon.

spell checker *(spel chek-er)* A program feature or command that looks for mispelled words and suggests corrections. This is only really necessary in English, where spelling still remains a mystery some 150 years after Webster made up the whole idea. While spell checkers do spot mangled English, they do not check the words in context: "Eye yam deer two ewe" is spelled correctly but makes no sense. "Now I never have to learn to spell because my computer *spell checker* does it for me."

spew *(spyoo)* A single message posted repeatedly to the same newsgroup. A spew can be spam, or it can be some doofus just reposting the same message over and over. Annoying. See also *spam.*

spike *(spiek)* A sudden, often lethal, increase in the power coming through the wall. Spikes are typically caused by lightning strikes nearby. They can potentially fry electronic equipment but more typically do nothing other than cause the screen to flicker momentarily. Look out your window. Find a tall tree. If a bolt of lightning hits that tree, it will send a power spike through all the circuits in the room you're sitting in, making your PC's guts go pop. See also *surge protector.* "I bought a surge protector to protect against power *spikes,* but I still unplug the computer during an electrical storm."

Spock *(spahk)* 1. The character Leonard Nimoy played on the original *Star Trek* television show. The computer-loving crowd admires Spock because he, too, enjoyed using computers. Some great Spock-computer *Star Trek* moments:

"This computer here is the key. Destroy this one and the whole planet goes."

"Computer? Compute to the last digit the value of pi." (The computer starts screaming here.)

"Landru is a computer."

"The computer lied."

See also *Vulcan.* "Okay, *Spock.* It's your turn to wear a red shirt and beam down to the planet." 2. A real doctor, well-known for his expert advice for caring for babies and for blocking trains carrying nuclear waste.

spoiler *(spoy-ler)* An e-mail message or newsgroup posting that contains information about an upcoming event, such as a long-awaited movie or TV show. The spoiler message would "spoil it" for someone who wants to see the show without knowing what's going to happen before hand. USENET posters are typically very nice about this, using the word *SPOILER* in the message subject to let others know they should skip the message if they don't want to know what's coming up.

spoiler space *(spoy-ler spays)* Several blank lines at the start of a message. These "push down" the bulk of the message, which contains a spoiler, so that if someone accidentally views the message they won't see something offending, like "Kosh is dead" or something like that. See also *spoiler*.

spool *(spool)* The process of sending tiny bits of information over a period of time, usually while the user is off doing something else. For example, a print spooler stores files to be printed, sending a little bit of each file to the printer every so often so that the computer is bogged down waiting for the printer. Spooling is a feature of the Windows and OS/2 operating systems.

spooler *(spoo-ler)* The device that spools. See also *spool*.

spreadsheet *(spred-sheet)*
1. A program that mimics a calculator with hundreds of displays all arranged in neat rows and columns. Each

An Excel spreadsheet.

display is really a "cell," which can store text, a value or a formula. The formulas are typical calculator formulas, often involving other cells. All this works together to create interactive numeric information, allowing you to examine data such as general ledgers, payroll accounts, loans and other types of financial and numeric data. Accountants love spreadsheets, as do scientists, mathematicians, and people with nothing better to do on a Saturday night. See also *macro, number crunching, template*. "I told my mother I'm learning *spreadsheets* at the office and she thought I was demoted to a maid." 2. The documents created by spreadsheet software. See also *worksheet*.

sprite *(spriet)* 1. A moving element in a graphic display, such as those found in video games. 2. (cap.) A sugar-flavored, carbonated beverage with exaggerated claims of refreshment that two out of three hard-core programmers and computer users prefer over Coke, Pepsi, or Kool-Aid. "Whenever I get tired of watching *sprites* on my computer, I drink a Sprite."

SRAM *(es-ram)* Acronym for Static Random Access Memory, which seems like an oxymoron, but the memory is still volatile like DRAM. SRAM is generally faster than DRAM, but also more expensive. See also *RAM*.

SS/DD *(es es / dee dee)* Acronym for Single-Sided/Double-Density, an obsolete floppy disk format that stored 180K of stuff on a 5¼-inch disk. "We found an old *SS/DD* disk in the storage room the other day. Stood around for about an hour marveling at such an antique."

SS/SD *(es es / es dee)* Acronym for Single-Sided/Single-Density, another obsolete floppy disk format that stored only 90K of data on a 5¼-inch floppy disk.

S

SSL *(es es el)* Acronym for Secure Sockets Layer, a protocol for sending and receiving information on the Internet in such as way that only authorized recipients can decode the information. See also *secure browser.*

stack *(stak)* A data structure that programmers use to store and remove data in a last-in, first-out (LIFO) order especially used in assembly language. Information is placed on the stack using a *push* command. Information is removed with a *pop* command (or a *pull* command). The most recent item pushed is the item popped, which is why the stack is known as a LIFO construction. Weird, but useful when programming. See also *LIFO, POP.* "Programmers who like pancakes prefer using *stacks.*"

Stacker *(stak-er)* One of the original disk compression utilities, designed to squeeze more life out of older computers by squeezing more stuff onto their hard drives. Eventually killed when Microsoft included disk compression "free" with MS-DOS and Windows.

standard *(stan-dard)* 1. A word that produces uncontrollable laughter from any engineer in the computer industry. Something management takes seriously (especially the marketing types). 2. A stubborn, mythical belief held by Computer Big Wigs that they can define specific methods, appearances, or equipment that everyone else in the world will voluntarily follow. See also *ANSI, ISO,* and any of the other number of standards defined by the computer industry that everyone either fiddles with or ignores. 3. A flag.

standard I/O *(stan-dard ei-oh)* Standard input and output. The keyboard usually provides standard input; standard output is usually sent to the screen.

star-dot-star *(star-dot-star)* See *.

star network *(star net-wurk)* 1. A network configuration where each computer (or node) has a direct connection to a central computer, hub or other device. The network map (topography) would resemble a star, with the big, hefty file server in the middle and piddly old PCs sitting around it. See also *server.* 2. CBS.

Start *(start)* The name given to the Start button on Windows' taskbar. See also *Start button.*

start bit *(start bit)* The tiny chunk of information that signals the beginning of data transfer. "Before my wife starts yelling at me for spending too much time at my computer, she starts wringing her hands. To me, that's a *start bit* signaling she's about to start nagging again."

Start button *(start but-ton)* A button on the far right side (or top) side of the taskbar in Windows, used to display the pop-up start menu to control various things in Windows 95 and later. The Start button can also be accessed by pressing the Ctrl+Esc key combination or the Windows key if your keyboard sports one.

The impressive Start button.

Star Trek *(star trek)* A science fiction TV show, with a rabid following among computer groupies. Star Trek tells the story of a spaceship sent from Earth to explore the galaxy so that its captain could find various women and have fisticuffs with strange, new aliens every week. Remarkably enough, the aliens all looked like human actors wearing lots of makeup and speaking perfect English. Known as ST:TOS on the Internet, for Star Trek: The Original Series. "I'm very thankful for _Star Trek._ Without it, we'd have to put up with lame _Voyage to the Bottom of the Sea_ computer humor."

Star Trek: The Next Generation _(star trek the nekst jen-er-ay-shin)_ The very popular sequel to _Star Trek, ST:TNG_ (as it's known on the Internet) has several beloved characters, including an android named Commander Data, a Klingon named Worf, and the very poised, sophisticated Captain Picard. Some two-year-olds know who these guys are before they even recognize Bert or Ernie (we're not even going to discuss Barney). "If you don't watch _Star Trek: The Next Generation,_ you may have trouble conversing with nerds, geeks, and gurus."

start-up disk _(start-up disk)_ The disk the computer's BIOS searches for an operating system. The operating system is loaded from the start-up disk. On a PC, this is the first floppy drive (A:) and then the first hard drive (C:). "My hard disk is my _start-up disk._ But when the hard disk starts acting flaky, I have a special floppy disk that I use for my start-up disk. If that floppy disk doesn't work, then I cry."

static _(staht-ik)_ 1. Random electrical noise that garbles voice and modem communication through the phone lines. "Every time I try to dial into NASA's computers, _static_ interferes and I have to hang up. Every time my mother-in-law calls, I make crackling noises with

my mouth and pretend that static is preventing me from hearing what she has to say." 2. Something that does not change.

stealth virus _(stelth vie-rus)_ A sneaky type of virus that tries to make itself invisible to anti-virus programs that may kill it. "I'm sorry, Jay, but pointing that expensive Air Force radar detector at your PC just won't work. It may be infected by a _stealth virus_ that our technology cannot detect."

stop bit _(stop bit)_ The tiny chunk of information that signals the end of successful data transfer. Hanging up the phone in the middle of a call is _not_ an example of a stop bit. "Some communications programs let you choose between one or two _stop bits._ Most of the time, one stop bit is fine, unless the other computer doesn't stop, in which case you'll need two stop bits."

storage _(stohr-edj)_ A place to put valuable information in the hopes you'll be able to find it again. Common storage devices are tape drives, floppy disks, hard disks, and CD-ROM discs. Memory (RAM) is also storage, though temporary. See also _RAM._ "We use a special optical disk for _storage._ That way, our data will survive a nuclear attack, even though we may not."

storage media _(stohr-edg mee-dee-ya)_ A disk on which you store information.

string _(string)_ 1. A group of letters. Humans call groups of letters _words,_ but computers call them _strings._ This is opposed to values or numbers. Strings are text. Strings can include letters, numbers, symbols, spaces and other

_S_

characters. Often strings are enclosed in double quotes. 2. A type of variable in a programming language which holds string information as opposed to a value. "I consider my name to be a representation of ancient history, but when I type it into my database, the computer just thinks of it as a *string* of meaningless characters."

string variable (*string var-ee-uh-bol*) A symbol that a program uses to represent a group of characters. Most databases use the string variable NAME to represent a person's name. "Yes, you should store the word 'yarn' in a *string variable*."

structured programming (*struk-sured pro-gram-ming*) 1. A method for writing programs in small subprograms or modules so they are easy to read and understand. Structured programming emphasizes that programs can be written using three types of statements: sequential, conditional, and loops. Sequential program statements run one after another. Conditional statements are IF-THEN or CASE statements. Loop statements are WHILE-DO, DO-WHILE, FOR-DO, and REPEAT-UNTIL statements. If you have no idea what this means, you probably don't need to know anything about structured programming, except for the fact that it rarely works and that's why programs today have so many bugs in them. "The closest I've come to *structured programming* is building a little house out of old issue of *TV Guide*." 2. A myth pursued by computer scientists with the same vigor that early Spanish explorers had when they searched the New World for the Fountain of Youth and the Seven Cities of Gold.

 StuffIt (*stuf-it*) A compression program for the Macintosh that can smash multiples files into a single file to take up less space. Most Mac shareware is distributed on-line in the StuffIt format. "My Boss asked me how to decompress the files he downloaded from CompuServe and I told him to StuffIt. Now I'm out of a job, but he still can't get to his files."

Sturgeon's law (*ster-jons law*) A truism from noted science fiction author Theodore Sturgeon: "Ninety percent of everything is crud."

style (*stiyel*) 1. Text formatting and character attributes all combined into one. Style refers to the way text looks. 2. The command used on some programs to format your text. The Style is a collection of formatting and character attributes that can be applied to text all at once. "I have two *styles* I use for my memoes: Fancy Sycophant, for writing letters to my boss, and Ugly Automaton, for writing letters to those who work for me."

stylus (*stie-les*) A long pointy thing, like a pencil. The stylus is a type of input device like a mouse. You use the stylus to draw on an electronic pad embedded with sensors. What you draw shows up on-screen. These things are more expensive than your typical computer mouse but offer a higher degree of control. See also *puck*. "If Baron Lytton had known computers, he may have said, 'The *stylus* is mightier than the mouse,' but he'd run the risk of being locked up for that."

su *(es yoo)* The UNIX command that allows any user to become the super user, or root account. This allows the user to make system modifications and run system commands without having to log in separately as root.

subdirectory *(sub-di-rek-tuh-ree)* The old term for a folder. A directory within or "under" the current directory. All disks have directories, in which they store files. The directories can also store other directories, which are then called subdirectories. Technically, the term applies only to directories "beneath" another directory. Generally, any directory on disk — save for the main or root directory — is called a subdirectory. See also *tree structure* for more confusion. "I'm sorry, Private, if you want to find a *subdirectory,* you'll have to look on the Navy's computers."

submenu *(sub-men-yoo)* A menu's menu. One menu contained inside another menu. For example, if you're presented with a menu of choices and selecting one of them displays another menu, you have a submenu. In a GUI, a submenu is often a secondary or tertiary menu that hangs on to the main menu like an ugly piece of gum. "Today's *submenu* offers several items: ham, pastrami, turkey, Provolone, Swiss, Cheddar, and a variety o' fixins."

subnotebook computer *(sub-noht-buk kom-pyoo-ter)* See *laptop.*

subroutine *(sub-roo-teen)* A miniprogram within a larger program. For example, a program may have a subroutine that displays text on-screen. The main program would "call" that subroutine any time it wanted to display text on-screen. "My son just can't seem to finish his homework. I think that his brain is missing some *subroutine.*"

 subscribe *(sub-skrieb)* 1. To sign up for a newsgroup. There is no real "sign up"; you merely tell your newsgroup reading software that you want to make one group part of your regularly visited places. That way the subscribed group always appears in the application, showing any new or unread messages. See also *newsgroup.* 2. To sign-up for a mailing list on the Internet. This one you must subscribe to by sending a mail message to a moderator or mailing list host.

subscript *(sub-skript)* Text that appears smaller and below the surrounding text. Subscript is a text formatting attribute available in word processors and other programs that let you manipulate text. The number 2 in H_2O is a subscript. See also *superscript.* "Jacob was trying to explain to me that the printer was broken, but it turned out he accidentally turned on *subscript* mode and didn't know it. Ah, the joys of WordPerfect. . . ."

suite *(sweet)* A collection of applications, usually major applications like a word processor, spreadsheet, database and others that would cost more separately. Theoretically, all programs in a suite are supposed to work together and use similar commands. Realistically, all programs in a suite are together simply because some company packaged them together in an effort to sell more programs (especially when it comes time to upgrade). Ideally, once you learn how to use one program in a suite, you can quickly learn the others. Also once you create data in one program, you can effortlessly (supposedly) share that data within other programs of the same suite. "An integrated program is one program that offers a word processor, spreadsheet, and database. A *suite* is a collection of three or more separate

S

programs that some marketing genius thought would look nice packaged together, regardless of whether they work alike or share data."

suits *(soots)* The people who run the computer company. Derogatory term used by engineers and low-level employees for those who wear suits all the time, claim to know a lot about computers, but are mostly MBA types who are just out for stock options and to play golf with the boss. The term suits comes in handy since their turnover rate is high and often it really doesn't matter who's wearing the suit.

Super VGA *(soo-per vee gee ay)* Faster than regular VGA. More powerful than EGA. Able to leap puny old CGAs in a single bound. Look, up on-screen, it's high resolution, it's colorful — yes! — it's SuperVGA. IBM introduced its best PC graphics standard in 1987, the VGA. Other manufacturers liked it, but offered an improvement called SuperVGA also known as SVGA. If you're buying a graphics card for your PC, Super VGA is the way to go. See also *VGA*. "*Super VGA* gives Phil the graphics horsepower he needs to see his naked lady GIF collection at full resolution."

supercomputer *(soo-per-kom-pyoo-ter)* Faster than a regular computer, a very large, powerful, and fast computer. Supercomputers are used for important things like drawing dinosaurs in *Jurassic Park*. Unlike a mainframe, the super computer has an interesting design that makes it very, very fast. That's about all you need to know because you can't have a supercomputer in your house; turning it on would dim all the lights in the neighborhood. "I hear the boys in the lab just love the new *supercomputer*. They bow to it each time they enter the room."

superscript *(soo-per-skript)* Text that appears smaller and above the surrounding text. Superscript is a text formatting attribute available in word processors and similar programs that manipulate text. The number 10 in 2^{10} is superscripted. See also *subscript,* unless you've already come here from there. "Simon Nathaniel the Fourth thinks it's really nifty if he prints his name with a *superscripted* four: Simon Nathaniel[4]."

Superstore *(soo-per-stor)* A large store that sells lots of different computer equipment, software, books, and furniture, except for the ones you really need. Most superstores give the illusion of offering the lowest prices for name brand equipment, but are often priced higher than competing stores that aren't part of a nationwide franchise. "Superman, Batman, Spiderman and Wonderwoman all bought their computers at a *superstore*."

supertwist *(soo-per-twist)* A type of laptop display that's much better than regular twist. "They call this a *supertwist* display because only SuperMan could twist the circuits that tight."

support *(suh-port)* 1. What you pay extra for when you pay extra. 2. What you don't get when you pay extra. 3. What you're supposed to get with each computer you buy, whether you pay extra or not. 4. Training or someone available for help with your new PC or a place to get it repaired. Support is the most important factor in buying a computer, one many people often neglect as a trade-off for a low price. Support includes service after the sale, as well as phone help, classroom help, and other assistance. Software vendors offer support in the form of phone lines, toll free or not, over which you can ask questions. Sometimes this actually works. "The only *support* that comes out of waiting on hold is support for the long distance Phone Company."

surfer *(sir-fer)* A slang term that describes someone who spends an inordinate amount of time exploring an electronic network, such as the Internet, CompuServe, or local electronic bulletin board systems. Often used with the slang term "Net," such as a "Net surfer." "If you have questions about using the Internet, ask Ted because he's the local Net *surfer* around here."

surge *(serge)* An increase in the power level coming through the wall socket. Surges are gradual and build to a point where they may do some damage to your PC's components. Usually this is prevented by a circuit breaker or — sometimes in an utterly unbelievable twist of altruism — the power supply may actually give up its life to save the rest of the PC's components. A surge is the opposite of a brownout, when the power drops to low levels and your PC may not even start at all. See also *spike, surge protector.* "Serge was expecting the power *surge* to make his computer run faster. However, the circuit breaker popped and, though he lost my data, his computer is once again saved from the perils of the electric company."

surge protector *(serj proh-tek-tor)* 1. A device that guards against power surges so that your computer doesn't blow up when the volts climb. See also *surge.* "Although a *surge protector* is a good thing to have for your PC, it won't protect your computer against other power line nasties, such as spikes, line noise, and people who trip over cords." 2. A device that protects you against Serge.

suspend *(sus-pend)* 1. To temporarily halt — not completely stop, more like freeze. "When I answer the phone, I must *suspend* my dot-matrix printer. Otherwise, I can't hear a darn thing." 2. A command in Windows 9x that puts the computer into an energy-saving sleep mode.

SVGA *(ess vee gee ay)* An acronym for Super VGA, a PC graphics adapter standard. See also *Super VGA.*

swap file *(swap fiel)* A chunk of your hard drive used to store information in memory. The operating system, in dire need of more RAM, simply copies a huge chunk of RAM to the swap file on disk. When it needs to access that memory again, it loads the swap file from disk into memory. This explains why PCs with not enough RAM in them work sluggishly under Windows; a lot of information is being copied back and forth to the swap file. See also *virtual memory.*

switch *(swich)* 1. A knob or lever that has two positions, usually On and Off. It can also be a graphical representation of a knob or button in a GUI. In IBM lingo, the Big Red *Switch* used to mean the on-off switch on the computer. "Back in the early PC days, the *switch* was really big and red. Today, on-off

S

switches are no longer red, nor are they necessarily big." 2. A command option or parameter. For example, the /F switch on the DOS FORMAT command is used to tell FORMAT how big of a disk to format. 3. To move from one program to another in a multitasking environment. See also *multitasking*.

SX *(es eks)* A suffix, added to older Intel microprocessor numbers, which indicated that the chip is something less than a DX model. The 386SX was crippled by running at half its bit-width internally. The 486SX was crippled by lacking a built-in math coprocessor.

synchronous *(sing-kroh-nus)* Happening at the same time, in synch. Usually this term applies to synchronous communications. In that mode, two computers communicate at a specific pace with each other, sending bits back and forth "on the beat." Microcomputer modems are asynchronous devices and do not send information at a specific pace. See also *asynchronous*. "No, Bob, *synchronous* communications doesn't mean we have to sing to each other."

syntax *(sin-taks)* 1. A tax on beer, alcohol, or cigarettes. 2. The rules regarding the way a language is put together. This applies to programming languages as well as human languages. "Computers are persnickety. Disobeying their laws of *syntax* is akin to telling your neighbor, 'Day nice outside hot not it is.'"

syntax error *(sin-taks er-or)* You have violated the rules of syntax. This usually happens when writing a computer program. If you flip-flop words or misspell something, the program compiler spits out a syntax error and then you're left

scratching your head to figure out what you did wrong. "Computers say Syntax Error because the people who programmed them are too lazy to make the message any more precise."

sysop *(sis-op)* Abbreviation of system operator, the head honcho in charge of the system. This term revolves primarily around computer bulletin boards (BBSs). The person who owns the computer and the BBS and in whose house it sits is the sysop. This is an exalted position among the modeming crowd. Everyone wants to be a sysop or be in the sysop's favor. See also *BBS*. "I begged the *sysop* for advanced access to his system; finally, he gave me level-six access. But the funny thing is, there's no one on level six."

SysRq key *(sis-tim ree-kwest kee)* A key added by IBM to its PC-AT keyboards that doesn't do squat. In fact, it's currently demoted to sharing the Print Screen key on most 101 keyboards. Back in the PC-AT days, IBM was rumored to be planning a use for the SysRq key in some newfangled operating system. But when OS/2 came out, it used the Ctrl+Esc key combination rather than SysRq. "About the only thing the *SysRq* key is useful for is seeing how people try to pronounce it."

system *(sis-tim)* 1. A way of doing things. 2. The program that controls the entire computer. See also *operating system*. 3. The whole computer. 4. The network. 5. The Powers That Be. 6. What you can't fight. "Something has to be in charge, and that's the *system*. It rules the computer. In real life, there's a system too, but it doesn't rule anything.

Instead, it's The Conspiracy who's in charge. And they watch everyone through cable TV and listen to our phone calls. And there's a helicopter over my head right now, and they're watching me type this. And that gnat is a spy for a terrorist group."

system clock *(sis-tim klawk)* An internal time clock maintained by the operating system. This clock is primarily used to record the time when files were saved to disk. "I once reset my PC's *system clock* wrong on purpose to prove to the boss that I was getting work done way ahead of the deadline."

system disk *(sis-tim disk)* A disk that contains all the programs required to start your computer. For most of us, the system disk is our hard drive, which starts the computer each time we turn it on. You can also start your computer from a floppy drive, which some people do just to kill time. "You can't start your PC without a *system disk.* Because of this, we recommend that everyone create an 'Emergency Boot Floppy' with which you can start your PC in times of woe."

System Folder *(sis-tim fol-der)* A special directory on a Macintosh computer that contains all the system files. This is roughly equivalent to the Windows directory on a PC. Into the System Folder you put (or have already installed) all the files necessary to make Mr. Mac boot up properly, special files and programs such as fonts, desk accessories, control panel thingies, and other stuff I can't think of. "The term *System Folder* makes it sound so neat and tidy. But the truth is that the System Folder is perhaps the junkiest folder on my disk."

system font *(sis-tim fahnt)* A typeface built into the operating system or GUI. System fonts are those fonts that *must* be there. Text on menus and in dialog boxes is usually composed using the system font. Yes, there can be more than one system font. "Truly, the *system font* is the most boring font you have. I recommend buying other, more exciting fonts and doing your documents with those instead."

system tray *(sis-tim tray)* An area on the far left side of the taskbar which contains the time, volume control and other tiny icons that control certain programs or control certain aspects of Windows 95 and later. Pointing the mouse at an item in the system tray often displays more information about that item. Clicking on an item activates it, usually displaying a dialog box or window offering more information. Items tend to come and go in the system tray; don't be alarmed if something disappears since it usually means you've stopped running a related program.

system unit *(sis-tim yoo-nit)* The IBM name for the computer box, also called the console. See also *console.* "Earl is such a card. He cleverly disguised his *system unit* in an old Philco TV box."

System V *(sis-tim vee)* A version of the UNIX operating system.

S

S

T

T: *(tee koh-lin)* The drive letter designation for what could be a network drive in your computer. You probably don't have a T:, but it could also be a hard drive, RAM drive, CD-ROM drive, removable drive, front-wheel drive, or any other type of drive in a C. Sheesh.

T1 *(tee won)* A high-speed communications line for Internet access, typically running at speeds up to 1.544 megabits per second. Only Internet providers, universities, and large companies typically have a T1 line, though that doesn't stop millions of Net surfers from dreaming about it.

T3 *(tee three)* A high-speed communications line for Internet access, providing speeds of 45 megabits per second.

tab *(tab)* 1. The character produced by pressing the Tab key. ASCII code 9. Also Ctrl+I. 2. A chunk of blank spaces created by pressing the Tab key. This chunk of spaces is treated as a unit so that if you wanted to delete the tab space, it would delete the whole thing, not one blank character at a time. "This is absolutely amazing. I pressed the *Tab* key, and this diet beverage rolled out of my disk drive slot."

Tab key *(tab kee)* The key on the keyboard that produces the tab character. In most programs, when you write something, pressing the Tab key moves you forward one tab stop, whether that's a chunk of spaces in word processing, a field in a database, or a cell in a spreadsheet. In a dialog box, pressing the Tab key moves you to the next input field or gizmo in the dialog box. You can move backward through the fields or cells by pressing the Shift key with the Tab key. This is known as a back tab. "On most PCs, the *Tab key* has two arrows pointing in opposite directions printed on it that leads me to believe that the key doesn't know which direction is which."

table *(tay-bul)* A way of organizing data or text into rows and columns, especially in a database context. You don't need a tablecloth for this kind of table, nor do you need good table manners. A data table is simply a way to store information or, in word processors, to present text in a neat and tidy manner. "Tax *tables* list income on the left side and tax categories along the top. In the middle, you can find out what outrageous amount the government wants you to pay."

table locking *(tay-bul lok-ing)* Used in database management systems where an entire table is locked while data is being updated.

tabulate *(tab-you-late)* 1. To arrange data or information in a column format. 2. To sum and print totals.

tag sort *(tag sort)* A sorting procedure where the key fields are sorted first to create the correct order and then the actual data records are placed into that order.

tagged queueing *(taygd kew-yoo-ing)* A method that enables a controller to process commands out of order that is typically received by a device driver.

tail circuit *(tayl sir-kut)* A circuit that connects the serial lines of two modems together.

Taiwanese *(tie-wah-neez)* Of or relating to the island of Taiwan; specifically, a computer or piece of hardware manufactured in Taiwan. Most no-name computers or hardware comes from Taiwan, where it can be reproduced reliably and at a reduced cost. Although sometimes used as a derogatory remark, some great innovations have come from Taiwan, particularly with regard to notebook computers.

TAL *(tee ay ell)* Acronym for Tandem Application Language. A programming language on Tandem computers that is a cross between C and Pascal.

Taligent *(tal-uh-jent)* An object-oriented operating system developed by Apple, IBM, and Hewlett-Packard in a desperate attempt to wrestle the operating system market away from Microsoft. Did it work? I don't know. You don't see anything called Taligent on your computer, do you?

tall card *(tall kard)* An expansion card for the IBM PC AT.

Tandem Computers A manufacturer of computers, founded in 1974. Tandem was acquired by Compaq in 1997.

Tandy *(tan-dee)* A manufacturer of PC's and electronics. It is also the parent company of Radio Shack and made the TRS-80, which was an early personal computer.

tape *(tayp)* A magnetic data storage medium (long, thin brown stuff), essentially the same material as audio- and videocassettes. Its advantages are its low cost and high density (ability to store lots of information). Its disadvantage is that it offers only linear or sequential access, which means that you have to rewind or fast forward through the whole tape to find what you're looking for. In contrast, disk drives offer random access so that you can get to any given point within a fraction of a second, with no rewinding or fast forwarding involved. You generally use tapes only to store backup copies of data. See also *sequential access.* "Okay. Who's the joker who put the Scotch tape into the *tape* backup unit?"

tape backup system *(tayp bak-up sis-tim)* A tape drive and software designed to back up files from your hard drive. See also *backup, tape drive.*

tape drive *(tayp driev)* A machine into which you insert a tape cassette that records data. The machine is like a tape recorder and player, reading and writing information to the tape. This process is how sophisticated PC users back up their data. They buy these backup tape cartridges, slam them into the tape drive, and then run special tape backup software. No swapping is involved (as long as the tapes can hold enough data), and the backup takes only a few minutes. Tape drives are about as expensive as new hard drives. Many formats are available: ¼-inch cartridge, 8mm VCR cartridge, 4mm audio, and

T

9-track. "I'm sorry about the demotion, Jason, but what you thought was a toaster oven was really our new $2,000 DAT *tape backup system*."

tape head *(tayp hed)* The electromagnetic component in a magnetic tape drive that reads and writes magnetic tape as the tape passes over it.

TAPI *(tee ay pee ie)* Acronym for Telephony Application Programming Interface. A Windows 95 application that enables Windows client applications to access voice services on a server. TAPI was designed to allow communication between PCs and telephone equipment.

tar *(tar)* Abbreviation of *tape-ar*chiver, a backup and archiving program used on UNIX computers. In addition to obviously copying files to a tape backup, tar can also be used to clump a bunch of files together and slap the TAR extension on them. Getting the files out again leads most people to madness (and, yes, if there were a simple solution, we'd offer it here). "Darryl was overjoyed to get FTP to work on the Internet, but getting his files out of the *tar* proved to be very messy."

target drive *(tar-get drive)* The drive containing the disk or tape on which data is recorded.

target journaling *(tar-get jur-nuh-ling)* The process of storing a copy of incoming messages.

task *(task)* A computer operation; something you do with a computer. For example, if you're word processing, the computer's task is word processing. This would be an utterly redundant

thing if it weren't for multitasking, which is the ability of a computer to do several things — several tasks — at the same time. "Most of the time, my computer's main *task* is to ignore me."

task bar *(task bar)* See *taskbar*.

task switching *(task swich-ing)* The art of switching between several programs running at one time. In Windows, you can do this by pressing Ctrl+Esc, Alt+Esc, or Alt+Tab or by clicking on a specific window that represents a program. When you move from one open application (task) to another, you are task switching. "The boss told me that I was *task switching* too often between Word and Solitaire."

 taskbar *(task-bar)* A strip of buttons along the bottom of the Windows desktop. Each button relates to a window or task on the screen, allowing you to switch between the tasks by clicking on the button. Also on the taskbar are the Start button and the system tray. (The taskbar can be moved to any side of the screen, but mostly it appears on the bottom.) "One of the most annoying things about Windows 95 is its disappearing *taskbar*."

A taskbar in use.

 TCP/IP *(tee see pee ie pee)* Acronym for Take Caffeine Periodically/Intravenously, Preferably. Har, har. Actually, it stands for Transfer Control Protocol/Internet Protocol, and it means that information can be shared between two strange networks. This is one of the ways in which information is sent back and forth over

T

the Internet. Nothing you need concern yourself with, really. "I went for a job interview that asked for *TCP/IP* knowledge. When I asked what it meant, they said 'We were hoping you knew!'"

TDD *(tee dee dee)* Acronym for Telecommunications Device for the Deaf. A device used by deaf people for text communication over the telephone lines.

TeachText *(teech-tekst)* A simple text-editing program that the Mac uses to read and display README files. "I don't think the *TeachText* program is teaching me anything."

tear-off menu *(tayr-off men-yoos)* A menu you can tear off the menu bar (symbolically, of course) and place at any convenient location on the screen. For example, you might press Ctrl while clicking on the File menu to tear it off. You can then drag it to any location on the screen. Tear-off menus are not widely used. "Baby Jonah accidentally got a hold of the computer. He found the *tear-off menus,* and now they're all over the floor."

technoweenie *(tek-noh-wee-nee)* Someone very, very into computers, often discussing them in cryptic and loving terms. The technoweenie may not lack social graces like a geek does, but he still tends to be overly absorbed by technology. See also *alpha geek.*

technology *(tek-nal-uh-jee)* A stone used to shape another stone (as in the Stone Age) could be considered technology. You could say, in the broad sense, that technology means the use of tools. Power tools. Big, anti-torque drills.

Large, dirt-moving vehicles. Ah, technology. More often, the word is used to refer to "high" technology, which is characterized by being abstract and not accessible to the naked eye. If you opened the hood of a vintage American car, you could tell exactly what was going on by seeing how the parts fit together and how they move. This is not-so-high tech. When you're talking about electronics, though, the relationships are not apparent. There could be millions of transistors on one silicon chip, and you would have no idea what the relationship of each was to its neighbors nor where to fit the crescent wrench. "*Technology* actually comes from the ancient Greek term that roughly translates as 'If your VCR is blinking 12:00 all the time, you probably won't get any of this stuff.'"

tech support *(tek suh-port)* Technical assistance for your computer. Tech support can come from the computer manufacturer, the computer store where you purchased your computer, or even from a computer-savvy friend.

Tech support after a long day.

tech writer *(tek rie-tur)* Someone who writes documentation for a hardware or software product.

telecom program *(tel-uh-kom pro-gram)* Communications software.

telecommunications *(tel-eh-kom-yoo-nuh-kay-shuns)* The field of technology dealing with communicating at a dis-

T

tance. It includes, but is not necessarily limited to, telephony, telegraphy, consumer radio, broadcast television, cable television, satellite television, radar, ham radio, CB radio, two tin cans connected by a string, and data transfer. "*Telecommunications* allows you to get confused at greater and greater distances."

telecommuting *(tel-eh-kom-yoo-ting)* The practice of working at home and communicating with the office. This communication is typically done through the phone, computer, and modem.

teleconferencing *(tel-eh-kon-fren-sing)* Communications by phone or computer, between groups that are in different locations.

telecopy *(tel-eh-kop-ee)* The formal term for a fax.

telematics *(tel-eh-mah-tiks)* The combination of telecommunications and computing.

telephony *(tel-i-fah-nee)* The art and science of making telephones happen. (Could just as well have been called "telephonology," but an editor was on the loose that day, and the word got cut short.) Essentially what happens in the telephony process is that the voice — and all embarrassing or annoying background noises — get converted into electrical signals that travel through the wires and then get reconverted to sound at the other end. All this, even though Alexander Graham Bell used only two ordinary cups and a length of wire to make the World's First Telephone happen.

Teletype *(tel-uh-tiep)* 1. The old clunky typewriter-like things that typed "by magic," thanks to remote wires that controlled the keyboard. In the early days of computing, Teletype machines were used to communicate with the behemoth computers of the time. You would type, klunka-wunka, and then the computer would type back at you, klunka-wunka-faster. All this would be transcribed on a long sheet of paper that fed into and out of the machine. 2. In these exciting, carefree computer days, Teletype is used to describe the dumbest and least sophisticated way to connect one computer to another. The Teletype is nothing more than a keyboard and monitor (also called a dumb terminal) that allows you to send and receive information from another computer. It's abbreviated TTY because most computer nerds can't remember whether Teletype has one or two *l*s in it. "In the early 1980s, I used to communicate with my friends on home computers using then-speedy 2400bps modems. At the same time, the hot line connecting the White House with the Kremlin was run on a sluggish old *Teletype* machine running at only 300bps. That meant that in the time Ronald Reagan could send 'Ivan, kiss your *@# goodbye,' I could have downloaded Tetris."

 telnet *(tel-net)* The closest thing UNIX has to a DOS modem program, it is a command you can use to dial up another UNIX computer, or really any computer on the Internet, and then log in and use that computer as though you were a terminal. "There is little you can do with *telnet* unless you understand UNIX."

template *(tem-playt)* A "master" document for a word processor, spreadsheet, or other application that is used as the starting point or rough draft for other documents. Generally, the template contains all the formatting, so all you have to do is fill in the blanks. Some software packages come with numerous templates so that you really don't even need to learn to use the software. You can create your own templates by performing the formatting and composing the text that will appear in every document of that type. Then, each time you need, say, an invoice, you open up the template file, fill in the blanks, and print the document. Then you can either save the additions to the file (as a new file now, so that you don't mess up the template) or not. "I'm going to use a *template* to write a letter to Santa Claus this year."

tendinitis *(ten-den-eye-tis)* Any tendon or muscle that is injured because of overuse. Tendinitis is a common injury for people who sit at the computer and type all day.

tera- *(tayr-uh)* A prefix meaning trillion (the same prefix from which we get the word *terrible,* by the way). Usually seen in computer use when talking about terabytes, which are pretty close to a trillion bytes (which is the same as 1,000 gigabytes, or a million megabytes). The actual measurement of a terabyte is 1,099,511,627,776 bytes. "If you had one dollar for each byte in a *tera*byte, it would take Bill Gates 134 years to catch up with you if he made 8 billion dollars a year (not including interest or subtracting taxes)."

teraFLOP *(tayr-uh-flop)* Acronym meaning one trillion floating-point operations (FLOPs) per second, a way to describe a very, very fast computer.

terminal *(tur-muh-nal)* A monitor hooked up to a mainframe computer. Terminal comes from the root of the Latin word for *death,* which makes you wonder why we board airplanes in terminals. Like people, terminals can either be smart or dumb, and the only way to find out how smart or dumb they are is to check how they relate to the computer. If a terminal has a mind of its own, it's a smart terminal. This means that it has some processors, maybe even a CPU, and maybe even a disk drive so that it can store its own data. With such capabilities, the terminal doesn't need to rely on the mainframe for all its operations. If all it has is a monitor and a keyboard (or similar peripherals), it's pretty dumb. "People can get terminally ill from sitting at *terminals* their whole lives."

terminal emulation *(ter-muh-nal em-yoo-lay-shun)* The ability of an average, run-of-the-mill desktop computer to cleverly disguise itself as a certain type of terminal hooked up to a mainframe computer. This can be done only with the right software, called terminal-emulation software. You need to worry about this only when you actually *want* to be hooked up to a mainframe computer — a rare circumstance for most of us mortals. "They've finally perfected Macintosh *terminal emulation* for the PC. Everything works really slowly, and the system crashes just before you save your file to disk. (You think we're kidding.)"

terminal session *(ter-mun-nal ses-shun)*
The time that a user is working at a terminal.

terminate-and-stay-resident program
(tur-muh-nayt and stay rez-uh-dent proh-gram) See *memory-resident program, TSR.*

termination *(tur-muh-nay-shun)*
A requirement of SCSI devices that one of them must be the last one in the chain. It works like stopping a leak; SCSI devices are all hooked together in a daisy chain. But the last device on the chain must be terminated (a special doohickey installed) to let the SCSI controller know that it's the last device. See also *daisy chain.* "If you don't do proper *termination,* your SCSI controller will appear dead to you."

text *(tekst)* Letters, numbers, and other characters or symbols on your keyboard. Just plain writing, no formatting or other fancy stuff. See also *ASCII.* "*Text* is boring."

text box *(tekst boks)* A box on the screen in which you can type text. Also called an input box. Oh, and you can edit text in the text box. What else? Nothing that we can think of right now. It's late, and *Star Trek* is on in three minutes. "Here's a good one: When you're searching for text, type 'my brain' in the *text box.* Then click the OK button. The computer won't find the text, and it will display a message that says 'Error: Can't find my brain.' Ha, ha."

text editor *(tekst ed-uh-ter)* A crude form of a word processor that lets you modify (edit) text files. Programmers use text editors to edit program source code files. This feature is handy because text editors don't use formatting or

graphics or anything fancy. Programmers just want something they can use to easily type their boring programming instructions without being bothered by the formatting. We mere mortal users can take advantage of text editors as well, even using them as a word processor if we like. They come in handy for working with small files. Indeed, this book was created using a text editor so that the authors had a common file format (plain text or ASCII files) in which to work. (Eventually, we all moved up to Microsoft Word for Windows because IDG Books told us that we were working too fast.) See also *editor.* "My award for the worst *text editor* ever goes to DOS's old crummy EDLIN."

text file *(tekst fiel)* A file that contains only text or ASCII characters. Many word processing, database, and spreadsheet programs give you the option of saving your stuff as "text only," or as a text file. This means that you lose all the formatting and special characters not associated with text files, but it also means the information can be easily digested by just about any other program on any other computer. See also *ASCII.* "*Text files* are the most common type of file format."

text mode *(tekst mohd)* The opposite of graphics mode. An operating mode where the PC displays text, not graphics, on the screen. "DOS used *text mode.* Windows uses slow mode."

thermal printer *(ther-mul prin-ter)*
A computer printer that creates an image by burning a sheet of wax paper in a neat and tidy fashion. Actually, "burning" is too harsh of a word. The wax paper is merely darkened by the printing mechanism, creating text and

T

graphics in a smooth, quiet fashion without wasting any ink. Unless your fax machine uses plain paper, it contains a thermal printing mechanism. Thermal paper is often waxy and will turn all black if you leave it out in the sun. "My *thermal printer* has a reputation for having a smell as bad as a dot-matrix printer's noise."

thesaurus *(the-saw-rus)* 1. A collection of words and other words with the same meaning. 2. The capability of a word processing program to come up with synonyms to match a word you've chosen. You can highlight a word and ask the thesaurus for some synonyms, and the software generates a list of alternatives or suggestions. There is a Murphy's law of thesauruses: The more certain you are that a synonym with exactly the right flavor exists, the more certain your thesaurus is not to even list the word you're referencing, let alone its synonyms. "What would the *thesaurus* offer if you looked up synonyms for molecular beam epitaxy?"

three-dimensional spreadsheet *(three-duh-men-shun-el spred-sheet)* In spreadsheet technology, the practice of creating a group of spreadsheets and organizing them like pages of a book. Thus, they have depth, besides the usual rows and columns. Depth is the third dimension of the spreadsheet. "I started to learn how to work on a *three-dimensional spreadsheet,* but I got lost because I had only a two-dimensional brain."

thumbnail *(thum-nale)* A small depiction of a page or image.

tick *(tik)* 1. Another name for the apostrophe character; see ' (apostrophe). 2. A notch on the axis of a chart that denotes an increment. For example, if the Y axis represents Dollars, every tick mark might represent $100. 3. A beat in your computer's internal clock-ticking, time-keeping thingamabob. PC computers generate 18.5 ticks per second. So, if you hear some nerd say "How many clock ticks was that interrupt?" you know that a clock tick is just about $\frac{1}{18}$th of a second and can nod your head knowingly. "There was this German POW camp in World War II. And one summer day, the kommandant assembled all the prisoners out under the hot sun. He said, 'Today, we will do special exercises. I want you to tilt your heads left to right, left to right. When you tilt your head to the left, you will say *tick!* When you tilt your head to the right, you will say toc! Everyone!' So all the prisoners started tilting their heads, tick-toc, tick-toc, out under the hot sun — with sweat just pouring from their faces. Everyone did this except for one prisoner. He just tilted his head to the left over and over, going 'tick, tick, tick.' The kommandant walked up to the man, looked him over, and said, 'We have ways to make you toc.'"

TIFF *(tif)* Acronym for Tagged Image File Format, a bitmapped graphics file format used frequently for images that are read in by using a scanner. TIFF files are high-resolution dot images. "No, we don't support that graphics standard here. We support PCX, GIF, *TIFF,* and anything painted by Lichtenstein or Klee."

tilde *(til-dee)* See ~.

T

tiling *(tie-ling)* A technique for arranging various windows in a graphical user interface so that they're all nicely sized and organized like a mosaic, without overlapping each other. The key here is "without overlapping." Another arrangement possibility is "cascading." See also *cascade*. "*Tiling* is a good choice when it doesn't matter whether the images in each window are chopped off and difficult to read."

time sharing *(tiem shayr-ing)* A strategic use of resources (microprocessor, printer, disk drives) with mainframe or networked computers. The time that is being shared is the computer's processing time. Typically, it's being shared among several users and also may be shared among several programs. In a time-sharing situation, the computer is programmed to know how to use its processing resources to attend to a hierarchy of priorities. "Because our computer knows how to manage *time sharing* so well, I think that I should have my own time-sharing program so that my time will get divided properly among my kids, my spouse, and my job."

time slice *(tiem slies)* The amount of processor time allocated to an application, usually measured in milliseconds. For example, if you're running several programs at once in Windows, each program gets a "slice" of the computer's time. The size of the slice can be adjusted, allowing some important programs to use up more time than other not-so-important ones. See also *multitasking*. "Roy found this old film from the 1940s. It shows Albert Einstein creating *time slices* with a Ginsu knife."

title bar *(tie-tel bar)* In a GUI like Windows or the Mac system, this is the, well, title that is prominently displayed on a long bar that stretches across the whole window. It is an especially effective invention because you always know where you are and don't need to call customer service to get you unlost. It typically includes the name of both the application you're using and the document you're working on. Even when you haven't named the new file yet, the program provisionally calls the document something like Untitled or Document, until you come up with your own name for it. "I was hopelessly lost until I looked up at the *title bar,* which said that I was working in Microsoft Word on the T.DOC document."

TLA *(tee el ay)* Acronym for three-letter acronym. The computer industry — and the government — are fond of these. "Nope, our manual just makes too much sense. Why not fill it with more *TLAs* and have Mr. Fujimori stick some raw Japanese in there, too."

 toaster *(toh-stur)* 1. A computer device that's so homegrown, so user friendly, and so intuitive that it's almost like the toaster you use to toast bread. The original Macintosh design was fondly called the "toaster" by its fans. "The original Macintosh was fondly called the *toaster* at the height of its popularity. Now it's often called the footstool." 2. A device called the Video Toaster is used in the Amiga computer to allow you to create studio-quality videos in your own home.

toggle *(taw-gul)* 1. A type of switch that alternates between two modes, on or off, typically. An example is the button on your TV that turns it both on and off. When the TV is off, the button turns it on, and vice versa. In a computer program, a toggle may be a graphical button or some other option that can be either on or off. Selecting the button once turns it on; pressing the button again turns it off. "I keep *toggling* between slow and slower mode on my PC. I don't think I paid enough money for this thing." 2. An option for a command or program that can be either on or off.

token ring network *(toh-ken ring net-werk)* A networking format in which PCs are connected in some way. They use this token thing, passed between the computers on the network hose, to decide who's on first. That's the most we can make out of this definition. This is heady IBM stuff. Most people use Ethernet networks because they are easier to understand. We always think of bus tokens when we see token ring network in print. See also *network*. "No, sir, I don't think you'll find a book on the *token ring network* in the Fantasy section."

toner *(toh-ner)* The black, icky stuff laser printers print with. Technically, toner consists of highly carcinogenic, electronically charged ink particles, just like a photocopier. It's used to form the image on paper. Actually, the laser printer "welds" the toner to the paper using heat and tiny laser beams manned by elves. "Marcia was changing the *toner* when it broke open. Now she looks like she works in a coal mine."

toner cartridge *(toh-ner kar-trij)* The box containing toner for a laser printer (or other type of machine, like a copier or fax machine). This technology makes an unbearable job simply horrible. In older machines, you would have to fill the toner container with powdered toner, which had the advantage of allowing you to approximate the effects of six years' worth of cigarette smoking in a mere ten minutes. Today, toners equate themselves to just about a pack of cigarettes. "I told Phil about having his old toner cartridges recharged, but he misunderstood and tried to plug one into the wall."

tongue depressors *(tong dee-press-ers)* Paper or plastic inserts for floppy disk drives, designed to protect them from damage during transport. Most of today's floppy drives are quite robust and no longer require the tongue depressors.

toolbox *(tool-boks)* 1. For software developers, a set of programs that can be used as building blocks for creating applications so that they can avoid the need for reinventing the wheel every time they write a program. "Using a *toolbox*, anyone can create a cool-looking program with only several weeks of intensive training." 2. For software users, a collection of tools that serve a common purpose. See also *tools*.

tool palette *(tool pal-et)* A collection of buttons that provide a way to select functions available in drawing programs or image editors.

tools *(toolz)* A set of programs you can use within a given software application that have effects like the real-life tools they're named after. Bear with us on this one. As an example, in a paint program you might have "brushes" of different

A tool palette.

diameters, a roller, and a spray can. These are tools you can use in the program to get a specific job done. "I'm having such a good time playing with all these *tools* that I don't know when I'll get around to actually painting a picture."

top-down programming *(tahp-down proh-gram-ing)* Writing the larger parts of a program first and filling in the details later. "*Top-down programming* doesn't mean that you build the program's roof and then the foundation later. It's more along the lines of you write the overall feeling for the program first and then fill in the holes later."

topology *(toh-pahl-uh-jee)* 1. The configuration of a Local Area Network — how the network is physically laid out. The basic types are centralized and decentralized; the basic formats are the star topology (centralized) and the bus and ring topologies (decentralized). Understand this concept and you too can make massive sums working as a network coordinator. 2. The study of the actor Topol.

touch pad *(tahch pad)* An input device for which all you need to do is touch a spot and it will register as a signal to the computer. The "spots" are actually cleverly disguised keys or buttons, and the whole front of the touch pad display is a layer of soft plastic.

tower PC *(tow-er pee see)* A desktop computer on its side, but really a computer that was made to stand vertically (up and down). This type of computer usually has more room and tends to be more powerful than mere mortal desktop models. "Since Kevin lives by an airport, the FAA told him to put little red lights on top of his tower PC."

TPI *(tee pee eye)* Acronym for *tracks per inch*, the amount of information that can be stored on a disk. The more tracks per inch on the disk, the higher the disk's "density" and the more data it can store. It's also a good way to tell some high-density disks from low-density ones. The lower-density disks use 40 or 80 TPI. High-density disks use 135 TPI. "I've been using computers for over 12 years now, and no one I know uses the term *TPI* when they talk about a floppy disk."

track *(trak)* A "ring" of information on a disk. Most disks record information on disks by storing that information on several concentric rings, or "tracks," recorded on the disk's surface. This is complex, disk-formatting stuff. The track contains sectors that each contain 512 bytes of information — the stuff you save on the disk. Knowing about tracks and sectors isn't important in using a disk. The information may come up only when you use special disk utilities (disk repair and diagnosis programs) or when formatting the disk. The term *cylinder* may also be used to refer to a track of information on a disk. "This disk is no good. I guess my AMTRAK file keeps jumping the *tracks*."

trackball *(trak-bahl)* An input device that operates very similarly to a mouse. Whereas a mouse has a ball you roll on your tabletop, in the case of the trackball, the ball part is on top and you rotate it using your fingers. Trackballs are very popular with artists,

A trackball, ready to roll.

who find the large ball easier to manipulate than the clumsy soap-on-a-rope-like mouse. They're also common on notebook computers because then you don't have to have this device hanging outside the case, nor do you have to roll it around on a flat surface, such as on your thigh. "Not only is this *trackball* easier to use than a mouse, but it also doesn't have a tendency to roll itself off the desk as much."

TrackPoint II *(trak-poynt too)* A tiny knob, embedded between the G and H keys on the keyboard, developed by IBM as an alternative pointing device that substitutes for a mouse. The TrackPoint II looks and feels like the red tip of a rubber eraser and is actually easy to use once you get the hang of it and realize that it won't rub pink stuff off all over your fingertips. "Tim tried to yank out the *TrackPoint II* in his laptop with a pair of pliers. That was until I told him that it was supposed to be there and that he could use it like a mouse."

tractor feed *(trak-ter feed)* A mechanism for feeding paper through dot-matrix printers. This kind of paper is what is commonly known as "computer paper," the stuff with the holes on either side. See also *snaf.* "I always have trouble lining up the little holes so that the paper will go through the *tractor feed* without getting overly perfed."

tractor food *(trak-ter food)* Your most valued documents, caught in the jaws of a tractor-feed mechanism. "I watched as my precious annual report became *tractor food* in a matter of seconds."

transfer-load files *(tranz-fer-lohd fiels)* The hilarious name of the command used to open files in early Microsoft applications. Obviously, they stole the term "Open" from somewhere else.

transparent *(tranz-pehr-ent)* 1. A computer function that's pretty close to invisible in its action. 2. Anything that happens without your being directly involved or requiring your input or attention is transparent. For instance, a fax being sent while you continue to work on another document is a transparent operation. "My communications software sends documents to other users *transparently.* They don't even see the document on the other end."

trash *(trash)* A special place to put unwanted documents and files. The trash icon on the Mac desktop looks just like a trash can, and all you have to do to dispose of your unwanted stuff is to click on the item in question with the mouse and drag it to the trash can. A handy feature of the Mac trash can is that its sides bulge out when it has discarded files in it, and it doesn't ultimately dump the stuff until you give it the command to Empty Trash — just like in real life! "The nicest thing about the Mac *trash* can is that the dogs don't knock it over every Thursday night."

The Trash icon found on the Mac.

tree structure *(tree struk-chur)* One of the more visual concepts in organizing files on a hard drive. Files are stored in directories, each of which is connected to other directories like branches in a tree. The main directory on every disk is called the root directory. Other directories branch from the root, and still other directories branch from them, making the thing look like an electronic family tree. See also *path.* "I almost had a heart attack when Earl walked by with the pruning shears, claiming he was going to fix his hard drive's *tree structure.*"

trigonometry *(trig-uh-nom-uh-tree)*
A branch of mathematics having to do with relationships of parts of a triangle. If you hear terms like sine, cosine, and tangent, you can nod wisely and say, "Ah, trigonometry!" Trigonometry helps you figure out unknown measurements of a triangle (such as an angle or a side) based on known elements. "You could use *trigonometry* to figure out the height of a distant mountain, if you know how far it is to the mountain and what the angle of view to the peak is, and also if someone whispers its height in your ear."

trinary *(trie-nayr-ee)* 1. Three. For example, a solar system with three suns. 2. The name for the base three counting system. Supposedly, they're working on *trinary* computers, which will eventually supplant binary computers. See also *binary, trit.* "Boy, if you thought that binary was rough, wait until you have to count in *trinary!*"

triple-click *(trih-pel-clik)* To click the mouse button three times in rapid succession to access very weird and arcane functions. Triple-clicking is uncommon and is used only in programs whose designers could not figure out more effective means of accessing features. "When I *triple-click* on this icon, I get a message telling me to stop drinking so much coffee."

trit *(trit)* A trinary digit. A trit can be 0, 1, or 2. "Binary is to bits as trinary is to *trits.*"

troglodyte *(trog-luh-diet)* From the Greek word meaning "cave dweller," a special class of nerd that prefers to work in the dark recesses of computer rooms.

People who have developed nocturnal feeding habits like bats and moles. See also *Morlock.* "The university cafeteria is keeping special hours — not to mention a special diet — for the *troglodytes* on campus."

Trojan horse *(troh-jen hors)* A nasty computer program cleverly hidden inside a legitimate program. It comes from a strategy used in the Trojan War, where the Greeks pretended to give the gift of a huge wooden horse as a peace offering to the city of Troy. As Troy slept, the many soldiers hidden inside the horse clambered out and attacked the city, which most historians agree was a sneaky thing to do. Sneaky computer programs that pretend to do one thing but yet disguise a more nefarious deed are called Trojan horses. You are more likely to find a Trojan horse packaged inside shareware or freeware than in off-the-shelf commercial software. "There is argument behind the notion that Microsoft Windows is a *Trojan horse.*"

TRON *(tron)* 1. A BASIC programming language command, a conjunction of *tr*ace and *on*. The TRON command displays information about the program as it runs, allowing the programmer to examine what's going on and hunt for errors. 2. A 1982 Disney film, most of which was created inside a computer — the first time that was ever done. Had there been a better script, *TRON* might have amounted to something nifty. See also *Cray.*

troubleshooting *(truh-bul-shoo-ting)* The process of tracking down an error or glitch, often through a process of elimination. "*Troubleshooting* is easy if all you ever do is blame the computer."

T

true *(troo)* The opposite of false. Or, it can also mean "yes" or "on." In binary math (also called Boolean math), true means 1 or positive, and false means a 0 or negative. "Believing that a computer would save me time and effort proved too good to be *true*."

TrueType *(troo-tiep)* A category of fonts created jointly by Apple Computer and Microsoft that bypasses the need for a page description language or utility that enables fonts to be displayed on-screen. Instead, the smarts that translate the font to the screen or to the printer are kept inside the font itself. In the olden days, you had to pay dearly for computer programs and printers that understood a multitude of fonts and displayed and printed them well. TrueType fonts take care of the details, making everything look and print swell. TrueType fonts are also called scalable fonts, which means that you can select any type size without having to worry about distortions. See also *PDL, scalable font.* "Using these widely available and inexpensive *TrueType fonts,* I've been able to design a document that looks just as bad as my handwriting."

TSR *(tee es ar)* Acronym for *terminate-and-stay-resident* program, a special type of program that always stays in RAM and can be easily activated by a keystroke or hot key. Also known as a memory-resident program, which is a better term, but TSR is the name the programmers called it (after the name of the internal DOS function), so the marketing department (which loves three-letter acronyms anyway) just followed suit. These programs became popular when Borland SideKick was introduced in the mid-1980s. SideKick gave you instant access to a slew of interesting little programs, all by pressing the Ctrl+Alt keys at the same time. SideKick would "pop up" right on top of whatever other program you were running. At the time, this feature proved immensely handy. Other programmers learned the SideKick secret, and soon dozens of TSRs and pop-up programs appeared. The problem was that because Borland cheated to get the pop-up effect, none of the TSRs would cooperate with each other. A TSR-laden PC would often crash, and the programs would conflict. The pop-up type of TSR program isn't popular anymore, thanks to multitasking programs such as Windows. Popular TSRs include the mouse driver, CD-ROM driver, DOSKEY keyboard enhancer, and certain file-undeleting utilities. "Please, Mr. Cooper, don't get all upset just because the old folks' home has adopted *terminate-and-stay-resident* software."

TSTN *(tee ess tee en)* Acronym for Triple-SuperTwist Nematic display, a type of screen found on high-end laptops.

TTFN *(tee tee ef en)* Online acronym for *ta-ta* for now. Another way to say good-bye in an e-mail message or newsgroup posting. "I was worried when Ryan always signed his electronic epistles *TTFN,* until I found out it wasn't anything dirty."

TTL *(tee tee el)* Acronym for Transistor-to-Transistor Logic. What is it? Who knows, who cares, why bother. TTL was listed as a type of computer monitor, typically the old-style monochrome monitors, and the acronym really bugged most PC users. Everyone always asked "What's TTL stand for?" Now you know. "I feel so culturally enriched now that I finally know what *TTL* stands for."

tty *(tee tee wie)* 1. A UNIX command that tells you which terminal you're using. "I typed *tty* on my laptop, and the computer told me that I was about to land at O'Hare." 2. Abbreviation of teletype. 3. A type of terminal emulation, usually meaning (and this is a secret) "absolutely no emulation whatsoever." See also *terminal emulation.*

Turing machine *(toor-ing ma-sheen)* A simple computer developed by A. M. Turing in the 1930s. It was supposed to be able to diagnose which problems were solvable by machines. It did this by reading a piece of paper tape. Turing's machine could only move the tape forward, put a mark on it, erase the mark, or stop it in its tracks. Turing claimed that the machine could solve any problem that could be expressed as an algorithm. See also *algorithm.* "I don't think I'd have a use for a *Turing machine.* I just want to solve the problems; I don't care whether they *can* be solved."

turnkey system *(turn-kee sis-tem)* A computer system all packaged and ready to go for a specific task. The system is complete with computer, monitor, keyboard, disk drives, software, and other peripherals. The term comes from the automotive industry — where you can put a key into your car, turn it, and operate the vehicle without anything else to buy, install, set up, or learn. "I always thought that *turnkey* had something to do with sardines."

tutorial *(too-tor-ee-el)* A training session that guides the student step-by-step through a procedure. Of particular interest are the tutorials that are packaged with many contemporary software programs. Generally, they are interactive so that you can play along and push keys to get the program to continue. "The *tutorial* for my accounting package comes with instructions for loading a gun."

TWAIN *(twayn)* Acronym for Technology Without An Important Name, a standard for acquiring graphics, such as input from a scanner, computer video, or something else that brings graphics into the computer. "Since Adobe Photoshop can gobble up a *TWAIN* image, we should buy a TWAIN scanner."

tweak *(tweek)* To customize, tailor, adjust, rearrange, cajole, or otherwise mess with. More specifically, it means changing settings on a piece of hardware or software so that your needs are more closely attended to. "I want to *tweak* my word processing program so that it stops beeping when I misspell a word."

Twinkie *(twink-ee)* A staple in the diet of computer programmers and other nerds. Fits into most of the four basic food groups. Also, the consumption of Twinkies has been used as a defense in the most egregious crimes. Thus, if you need a scapegoat, invoke the Twinkie defense. See also *M&Ms.* "Because I had some heavy-duty programming to do, I had some *Twinkies* for a power breakfast."

T

twisted pair *(twist-ed payr)* One wire that's secretly a pair of wires wrapped around each other. It is the kind of wire typically used in commercial telephone systems. The wire is "twisted" because you talk into the mouthpiece and it's heard in the earpiece. If the wire weren't twisted, you would talk in the mouthpiece and the sound would come out the mouthpiece. The term is also used in Local Area Networks, especially those that use common phone wiring to connect the computers. (Common phone wiring is the same thing as "twisted pair.") The good thing about twisted pair is that it's cheap and ubiquitous; the drawback is that it doesn't carry nearly as much information as the thicker coaxial cable (the stuff cable TV comes over). "Here come our network guru and his female companion. Jeez. Aren't they a *twisted pair?*"

TXT *(tee ecks tee)* 1. Abbreviation for *text.* 2. A file extension used for text files, generally in DOS-based computing. Examples include LETTER.TXT and GOFISH.TXT. "When I tell my word processor to save my files as 'text only,' it automatically slaps the *.TXT* extension to the filename."

type-ahead *(tiep-uh-hed)* A term for a buffer (a part of memory) that allows you to continue typing while the computer is busy doing something else; you type ahead of what you see on the screen. The stuff you type appears as soon as the computer is unbusy. "Because of the *type-ahead* buffer in Windows, I can enter several commands and wait for the computer to catch up. I seem to do that a lot."

typeface *(tiep-fays)* The design of characters in a font. Typeface refers to the physical characteristics of a family of letters and numbers. Typesetting has grown into a major art form, and the number of available typefaces — even to personal computer users — is almost endless. The main division between the categories of typefaces lies in their use of serifs — the little hooky things at the ends of the letters. Thus, they are called either serif typefaces or sans serif (without serif) typefaces. Other categories include display faces and decorative faces. "One of my favorite *typefaces* is Omar Serif."

typewriter *(tiep-rie-ter)* 1. A mechanical device used to print images on paper. Considered obsolete in the era of the computer. Heck, even IBM sold off its typewriter division years ago. 2. A typeface that resembles typewriter output (so much for advances in technology!). 3. Of or referring to the layout of keys on a computer keyboard. The computer keyboard (the alphabet keys, at least) is laid out just like a typewriter keyboard. There is no reason for this layout. See also *QWERTY.*

T

U: *(yoo koh-lin)* Oh, no! It's drive U on a PC! Run for the hills!

UART *(yoo-art)* Acronym for Universal Asynchronous Receiver/Transmitter, the gizmo — actually, the integrated circuit — in a computer that changes the parallel data stream inside the computer into the serial data stream. It takes the bits marching eight abreast inside your computer and lines them up single file for the serial port. This is required for devices that use the serial port, such as a modem. See also *bit, modem, parallel port, serial port.* "Oh, my serial port, UART the port of my dreams!"

UCB *(yoo see bee)* Acronym for the University of California at Berkeley. A place where many interesting things happen, some of which deal with computers.

Ultra-ATA *(ul-truh ay tee ay)* Another version of the ATA standard, an interface for storage devices. See also *ATA.*

Ultra-SCSI *(ul-truh skuz-see)* A version of the SCSI standard that's twice as fast as Fast-SCSI. See also *SCSI.*

UMB *(yoo em bee)* Acronym for *u*pper *m*emory *b*lock, an area of upper memory on a PC that can be "filled in" with real memory using some sort of memory-management magic that only the eggheads can comprehend. A memory device driver, such as the DOS EMM386.EXE, is required in order to create UMBs. Then, using other memory-management magic too mental to mention here, programs can be *loaded high* into those UMBs, which makes more memory available to your programs. It's magic! See also *conventional memory, high memory, memory, terminate-and-stay-resident program.*

unary *(yoo-nu-ree)* 1. Base 1, as opposed to base 2 binary. 2. In programming languages, an operation that takes only one argument, such as the – sign in front of a number to make it negative.

unbundle *(un-bun-duhl)* To sell components in a system separately, as opposed to bundle.

undelete *(un-duh-leet)* To put something back the way it was before you deleted it. To restore a file after you have deleted it; to resuscitate it; to resurrect it. See also *restore, unerase.* "Just because there is an *undelete* command doesn't mean that you should be careless with the delete command."

underline *(un-der-lien)* 1. In word processing or desktop publishing, the attribute applied to ▬▬▬▬▬ text that makes it look *Underline character.* underlined. Underlined text was once used in typed manuscripts to indicate that the typesetter should use italics. 2. The underline character on your keyboard. See _ (underscore). "I knew a guy who tried to underline things by typing a word, backspacing (which erased the word), and then typing the *underline* character. Although that would work on a type-writer, with a computer you must use a special command that underlines the text for you."

underscore *(un-der-skor)* Another term for underline, probably introduced by the more musical-minded among computer users. See _ (underline). "Now that you're a power user, Michael, you'll need to stop saying underline. It's *underscore*."

undo *(un-doo)* 1. To put the situation back to the way it was before you messed it up. 2. A command in most applications that enables you to cancel the effects of whatever you just did. You can undo typing and formatting commands, but don't get careless about your work because you can't undo everything. "I just hope that when I die and get to Heaven, God offers me an *undo* command."

undocumented *(un-dok-yoo-men-ted)* A feature of your hardware or software that is not explained in the user manual. This happens either because the manu-facturer forgot, didn't think it was important, hasn't figured out itself how the feature works, or wants to keep it a secret from you or its competition. Computer book authors love to find undocumented features in software products; it's their life! "I stumbled upon an *undocumented* feature that makes Windows run 100 times faster."

unerase *(un-ee-rays)* Just like undelete; however, this term was coined by DOS utility guru Peter Norton when he first came upon the idea of undeleting files in the early 1980s. Norton created a program called UnErase — the first of its kind — that recovered deleted files. He made tons of money and founded a complete category of computer soft-ware called *utility programs*. See also *guru, undelete, utility.* "All praise be to Peter Norton on high! Thank you, O Peter, for thy grace and thine *UnErase*."

unformat *(un-for-mat)* 1. A command that undoes the damage when you acci-dentally reformat a disk. This was wholly necessary in the early days of hard drives; the FORMAT C: command, which formatted hard drives, offered no warning! The unformat command allowed such a boneheaded maneuver to easily be repaired. 2. To restore a disk that has been accidentally reformatted.

Unicode *(yoo-nuh-kohd)* A new "univer-sal" standard for sharing information between different programs and com-puters. Unicode is meant to replace the ancient ASCII standard and includes all the characters represented by the ASCII standard as well as additional charac-ters for displaying languages such as Greek, Hebrew, Arabic, Russian (which uses Cyrillic), Chinese, Japanese, and Korean. See also *ASCII*. "Now that com-puters are being used all over the world, computer companies want to adopt the *Unicode* standard for sharing docu-ments because that means more market share for them in countries like Taiwan, Pakistan, and Greece."

u

Unicorn *(yoo-nuh-korn)* A mythical creature that looks like a horse with a single spiral horn jutting out from its forehead. According to legend, only a pure virgin maiden, who could tempt the unicorn to lay its head and horn in her lap, could tame a unicorn. Obviously, the origin of this legend has sexual overtones that aren't polite to discuss in public. "Many girls love unicorns when they're growing up. Then, when they get older and start dating men, they realize that mythical creatures really have lots more to offer than real-life human beings."

unidirectional *(yoo-nuh-dee-rek-shun-uhl)* The transfer or transmission of data in a channel in one direction only.

Uniform Resource Locator *(yoo-nee-form ree-sors loh-kay-tor)* See *URL*.

Uniform Naming Convention *(yoo-nee-form nay-ming kon-ven-shun)* The method PCs use to specify a remote directory or resource on a local area network. The UNC has the format *\\computer\resource,* where *computer* is the computer's network name and *resource* is the name of the shared disk drive, folder, or printer.

uninstall *(un-en-stall)* To remove hardware or software from a computer system.

union *(yoon-yun)* In a relational database, the joining of two files.

universal client *(yoo-nuh-ver-sal klie-ent)* A computer that can access a wide variety of application on the network, such as a mail program (an e-mail, for example) that can access multiple messaging systems.

Universal Serial Bus *(yoo-nuh-ver-sal seer-ee-al bahs)* A new serial port standard that allows as many as 127 different devices to be connected to a single port. Known by its acronym, USB. The speed of the Universal Serial Bus is relatively slow, which limits the type of devices that can be connected. For most users, however, it provides an excellent solution for a PC that's running out of slots, interrupts, or DMAs. See also *DMA, expansion slot, FireWire, IRQ.*

UNIX *(yoo-niks)* An operating system developed at Bell Labs in the late 1960s and refined throughout the '70s and '80s. Written in the C language (which was developed by the same folks at the same time), UNIX is a multiuser operating system, often found running on minicomputers and workstations, though versions for the PC have existed since the early '80s. You also can install UNIX on personal computers and mainframes. UNIX is very popular on college campuses and in scientific communities. All of the Internet has its roots in UNIX. The advantages of UNIX lie in its portability from one system to another and in its support of a wealth of applications programs, many programmer's utilities, and programming languages, making it popular among the wizard and geek factions. Primarily, UNIX is a command-line operating system, very similar to DOS but much more crude and cryptic. Several GUIs are available for UNIX, including X Window, Open Look, NeXTStep, and others. Incidentally, the name UNIX is a pun of sorts; It's a take-off on an operating system named Multics. Multi, Uni — get it? See also *C, DOS, Linux, operating system.* "When a programmer must protect his harem of PCs, he gets some *UNIX.*"

u

unload *(un-lohd)* To remove a program from memory or take a tape or disk out of its drive.

unmark *(un-mark)* To deselect a block of text, which removes its highlighting.

 unsubscribe *(un-sub-skribe-eeng)* To remove your subscription to a newsgroup or mailing list. The opposite of subscribe. See also *subscribe*.

unzip *(un-zip)* 1. To remove files from a ZIP archive. See also *archive, ZIP.* 2. (cap.) The name of the program that unzips.

up *(up)* In the general direction of the sky or ceiling, unless you're in Australia (just checking to see whether you were paying attention). "Up" is used to refer to the direction of the top of the document, even if the top is nowhere on the screen and is in fact just another happy electronic memory to your computer. See also *up arrow.* "To scroll *up,* keep jabbing at the up-arrow key."

up arrow *(up ayr-oh)* 1. An arrow pointing upward, as found on one of your cursor keys. Pushing the up-arrow key moves the cursor up in the document by one line of text. "You won't believe this: I pressed the *up arrow,* and my computer levitated." 2. A control at the top end of a vertical scroll bar in most graphical applications. Clicking the up arrow in graphical applications with the mouse usually moves the contents of the window down a line or so. Yes, the up arrow moves the contents down, but that's so that you can see "up" to the preceding line on the screen. Weird, backward, hard-to-understand — yes, this is how a computer makes life easier for everyone. If only the steering wheel on your car worked that way. . . .

update *(up-dayt)* To change data in a file or database. The terms *update* and *edit* are often used for the same meaning.

upgrade *(up-grayd)* 1. To improve on an existing piece of hardware or software program, adding new features or abilities that make it just like new. An upgrade could also imply a full replacement. "We upgraded our computers from old Macintoshes to old PCs." 2. A new software program that requires the presence of an older version of the computer before the new one can be installed. Such software upgrades are usually cheaper than buying all new versions.

uplink *(up-leenk)* The communication channel from a station to a satellite.

upload *(up-lohd)* To transmit a file from your computer to another computer. If you're sending a file to another computer, you're uploading. That computer, on the other hand, is downloading the file from you. It doesn't matter who started the file transmission or which computer you're using. If you're sending a file, you're uploading it. See also *download.* "I often *upload* my word processing files onto CompuServe to send to publishers in remote parts of the world, such as Indiana."

uppercase *(up-er kays)* Capital letters. The terminology comes from the earliest days of typesetting, when the individual metal letters mounted on blocks were stored in trays. The typesetter would pick out the letters that were needed for the job and arrange them on a plate. The capital letters would be stored in the top (or upper) case, and the small letters would be stored in the bottom (or lower) case. See also *case sensitive, lowercase.* "Text typed in all

u

uppercase letters is hard to read. In fact, it almost seems as if the writer is SHOUTING AT YOU."

upper memory *(up-er mem-oh-ree)* Memory on a PC between the 640K mark and one megabyte — a 384K chunk. Upper memory was marked "reserved" by IBM in the original PC design. Items such as video memory, expansion cards, and the BIOS were placed there, but the memory could not be used for running programs. (DOS runs programs in the first 640K of memory, called conventional memory.) See also *conventional memory, high memory, UMB.* "Every time Phil gets a haircut he loses some *upper memory.*"

UPS *(yoo pee ess)* 1. Acronym for Uninterruptible Power Supply, a fancy term for battery backup — an emergency supply of power in case the power coming out of the wall suddenly stops or when Jim, the dork from marketing, trips over the PC's cord. Having a UPS often means that you have just enough time to save your stuff and turn off the computer while you're in the dark. You can't really work from the backup battery in the UPS. "This blackout is horrible, but there's Jim, sitting in his office with the only working PC hooked to a *UPS.* Let's unplug him and run something useful instead, like the Nintendo." 2. Acronym for United Parcel Service, a delivery firm that brings you computer goodies you order through the mail.

uptime *(up-tiem)* 1. The time that the computer is actually working and you can get stuff done, as opposed to downtime, when the computer isn't feeling well and nothing works. "The dog is pretty lethargic, Doctor. How can we

increase his *uptime?*" 2. A UNIX command that reports statistics on how long the computer has been running.

upward compatible *(up-werd kom-pat-uh-bol)* Something designed with the future in mind. The item in question, usually a document or file created by some application or piece of hardware, will work with the next version of the product or with components that are not on the market yet. Generally, software is downward compatible only, meaning that the newest versions of the application will work with files generated from previous versions, but the previous versions will not work with files created with the new version. See *downward compatible.* "Wow! This new computer is really designed for *upward compatibility.* There's a plug in the back marked R2-D2 Connection."

urban legend *(ur-bun lej-und)* A cultural myth propagated as true, usually via e-mail on the Internet. Such stories seem plausible, but cannot be verified and eventually turn out to be utterly false. The dead giveaway is usually that the story was related by a "friend of a friend" who swears it happened to them or their cousin. When the person is tracked down, they further claim that it was a "friend of a friend," and so on. Common urban legends spread through e-mail include the famous Post Office Internet Tax; the FCC's imminent ban on all religious programming; the $250 cookie recipe; and the belief that various large companies are owned by the Church of Satan. It's all bunk.

 URL *(yoo ar el)* Acronym for Uniform Resource Locator, a type of command that can fetch a variety of types of information from various corners of the Internet.

u

Common URLs are http, for Web pages; ftp, for File Transfer Protocol sites; gopher, for gopher servers; mailto, for sending e-mail; and news, for accessing newsgroups. See also *Web browser.* "They'll think that you're a Net weenie if you pronounce *URL* like 'Earl.'"

Uruguay *(yoor-uh-gway)* The second smallest country in South America. Mostly agricultural, Uruguay exports meat and textile products. Its capital is Montevideo, which has some lovely museums. See also *Montevideo.* "Our sojourn to South America just wouldn't be complete without a trip to *Uruguay.*"

usability *(yooz-uh-bil-uh-tee)* Various aspects of software or hardware that make it easy to understand and use.

USB *(yoo ess bee)* Acronym for Universal Serial Bus. See also *Universal Serial Bus.*

 USENET *(yooz-net)* 1. Contraction of *user network*, a facility of the Internet that offers a wide variety of newsgroups, bulletin boards, and public forums. 2. The same thing as a newsgroup, or the entire group of newsgroups. See also *Internet, newsgroup.* "Old-timers know Internet newsgroups as *USENET.*"

user *(yoo-zer)* The person using the computer and software as a tool, as opposed to the programmer or hardware engineers. The term has nothing to do with the skill level of the person at the keyboard. Even nerds of the high programming priesthood are mere users when they sit at a computer. See also *user friendly, user group, user hostile.* "The computer industry is the only legitimate industry that calls its customers *users.*"

user base *(yoo-zer bays)* The number of people using a particular piece of hardware or software. "The larger the user base, the more successful the product, which is like saying the larger the user base, the larger the user base."

user friendly *(yoo-zer frend-lee)* 1. A system or program that is easy to learn and use. 2. Supposedly implying that the software or hardware is easy enough for even you or me to understand. Also called intuitive or idiotproof. It means that you can easily figure out what to do without having to look it up in the manual or the online help. Yeah, right! See also *user, user hostile.* "You know, the computer industry must figure that *user-friendly* means slow and plodding."

user group *(yoo-zer groop)* A club or gathering of computer users devoted to the study of a particular piece of software or hardware. There are user groups for the Macintosh, Adobe Photoshop, DOS, and many, many more. See also *SIG.* "*User groups* are a great source of information and a good place to ask questions about your computer or a software package. But if you show up late, stick around and listen to the conversation. You might have accidentally stumbled upon a meeting of the Older Guys with Pen Packs and Pot Bellies Society."

user hostile *(yoo-zer hos-tiel)* The opposite of user friendly. No matter how well you treat your computer and the software installed in it, they never lift a finger to make your life any easier. The epitome of user hostility is a cursor blinking on an otherwise blank screen — the DOS prompt. "I worked on a computer that made me enter the code <pil4,69> whenever I wanted to print a plus sign. Now *that* was a *user-hostile* machine."

u

user ID *(yoo-zer ie dee)* Yes, you can get "carded" by your computer. This number or code word is assigned to you by the system administrator or is one you make up yourself. It's used to tell the computer who you are, often in place of your name. For example, Bill Gate's ID on the Microsoft internal mail system is billg. Don't confuse the user ID with the password. The ID is something that identifies who you are to other people using the computer. In contrast, the password is secret and proves to the computer that the guy who logs in as billg is really Bill Gates and not some joker from the competition who's trying to learn all Microsoft's secrets. See also *password, user.* Recently overheard in the system administrator's office at a major software vendor: "No, I'm sorry, the *user ID* god is already taken. You'll have to think of something else."

user interface *(yoo-zer in-ter-fays)* What you see when you turn on the computer. The set of prompts, cursors, and software devices with which you interact to get something done in a program. The interface is what you see — in your face — and how you communicate with the computer and (hopefully) get things done. See also *DOS, GUI, interface, Windows.* "The best *user interface* is on *Star Trek,* where they actually tell the computer what to do. Did you ever hear the Enterprise's computer say 'Bad command or file name'?"

username *(yoo-zer naym)* The same thing as a user ID. See also *user ID.*

user profile *(yoo-zer proh-fiel)* A little blurb about a member or user of a network that others can access so that they have a better sense of whom they're talking to. Users write their own blurbs that might include their name, age, geographic location, the kind of computer they're using, and their interests as they relate to that specific bulletin board. "Fortunately, my *user profile* didn't include the fact that I have twelve designer pocket protectors."

utility *(yoo-til-i-tee)* Software intended to help you fix, tweak, or enhance your system. Unlike a true application, a utility generally doesn't produce any output or documents. Instead, utilities are designed to make working with the computer or your operating system easier. Utilities were once called software tools, and they were intended for use primarily by programmers to help ease programming drudgery. See also *backup, debugger, file compression, undelete, unerase, virus.* "At the time of the Michelangelo virus scare, sales of computer antivirus *utilities* went way up. It makes you wonder who thought up that Michelangelo thing."

UUCP *(yoo yoo see pee)* Acronym for the UNIX-to-UNIX Copy Program, an international Wide Area Network of all sorts of UNIX computers, all interconnected á la the Tholian Web. UUCP is a program used to copy information from one UNIX computer to another, which is sort of a backbone of the whole Internet system. "We've hooked up our top security project on a computer with *UUCP.* It allows us to exchange mail with other UNIX sites and read USENET user groups, and it allows hackers to try to crack into the computer."

u

u

V: *(vee koh-lin)* The drive letter designation for what's most likely a network drive on a PC. See also *C:, D:, E:, F:, G:, H:, I:, J:, K:, L:, M:, N:, O:, P:, Q:, R:, S:, T:, U:, W:, X:, Y:, Z:*.

V.Fast *(vee-fast)* A (once) fast modem standard, set up according to the CCITT V standards (and there are lots of them). These standards all start with V followed by a dot and a number. The number indicates how fast the modem can go (though there is no relation between the number and the modem's speed), and other modems that share the standard can communicate with each other. Supposedly a V.Fast modem toots along at 14,000+ bps — maybe even 28,000 bps. "After the *V.Fast* standard proves too slow, will there be V.Faster and V.Fastest standards?"

vaccine *(vak-seen)* A utility that helps your computer fight computer viruses. It works by looking for the symptoms of virus activity, such as suspicious attempts to infiltrate relatively secluded areas of the hard drive, drowsiness, and high fever. The vaccine then removes the virus, making your PC infection free. See also *virus.* "So let me get this straight — you tried to cure your PC of any possible virus by sticking a moldy orange into your disk drive? Why not just try a *vaccine* next time?"

vacuum tube *(vak-yoom toob)* An old-fashioned technology used in early computers. This device transmits information by controlling the flow of electrons, as semiconductor diodes and transistors do in modern computers. "A *vacuum tube* is something you can look for in a computer museum, such as the marvelous Boston Computer Museum, which, incidentally, is in Boston."

value *(val-yoo)* 1. The content of a field or variable. 2. In spreadsheets, the numeric data within the cell.

value-added network *(val-yoo-ad-ed net-wurk)* A communications network that provides extra services (read: value added). Examples of extra services are message sorting and forwarding and error detection and correction.

vandal *(van-dols)* 1. A type of Internet virus that visits unsuspecting Web page browsers. Using Java or ActiveX, it invades a computer and can either destroy files or send sensitive information back to the host over the Internet. This is not the same thing as a cookie, which is passive. See also *cookie, virus.* 2. (cap.) A member of the Idaho state football team, which usually gets chomped on by the Montana Grizzlies.

V

vaporware *(vay-por-wayr)* Products, whether hardware or software, that have yet to materialize on the market but are promoted as though they were about to revolutionize the computer industry. In many cases, there is plenty of good reason to believe that the product will never even make it to the market, at least not in the lifetime of its purveyors. See also *Microsoft*. "Anything you've read about or heard about in the computer industry but have yet to see in a store is *vaporware*."

VAR *(vahr)* Acronym for *value-added reseller,* an individual or business that integrates components provided by an original equipment manufacturer *(OEM)* and gets them properly packaged and documented for end users who usually need all the bells and whistles. VARs often package hardware, software, training, documentation, and even custom software services for specialized industries. See also *bells and whistles, end user, OEM.* "We purchased a large medical system from a *VAR.* The advantage is that we can complain to one source for all our problems."

variable *(vayr-ee-uh-bol)* In programming, a symbol that represents a numerical value or string of text used in the program. Using variables gives the programmer the flexibility of changing the value at any point in the program, even if there seems to be no need for that kind of flexibility at the outset. See also *wildcard.* "The content of a *variable* can change at any time. This leads me to believe that Bill Clinton's brain contains way too many variables."

VAX *(vaks)* A line of computers produced by Digital Equipment Corporation (DEC). In the olden days, the term VAX was often used to mean a large, cumbersome yet highly capable and powerful computer. The notion of "a VAX on your desktop" used to be thought of in science-fiction terms. In 1988 or thereabouts, it became a reality as the microcomputers of the time reached the processing capabilities of the early VAX computers. "No, it's not true that the first Apple computer was the result of the engineers leaving a Mommy *VAX* and Daddy *VAX* alone overnight."

VBA *(vee bee ay)* Acronym for Visual Basic for Applications. A subset of Visual Basic that provides a common macro language for Microsoft applications. VBA lets users and programmers extend the function of programs such as Word, Excel, and Access.

VB Script *(vee bee skript)* Acronym for Visual Vasic Script. A programming language from Microsoft for Web applications. It is an extension of the Microsoft Visual Basic language.

VBX *(vee bee eks)* Acronym for Visual Basic eXtension, but often just called a Visual Basic custom control. VBXes are reusable programs, written by other people, that you can add to your own Visual Basic or C++ programs so that you don't waste time writing part of a program somebody has already written. VBXes first appeared in Visual Basic, and just as their popularity has peaked, Microsoft plans to make them obsolete and make everyone use instead a new standard named OCX. See also *OCX.* "Visual Basic is so popular is because you can buy loads of *VBXes,* paste them together, and make powerful programs quickly with almost no effort besides shelling out lots of money to buy VBXes from different companies."

V-chip *(vee-chip)* A chip that blocks TV programs deemed inappropriate for the viewing audience; namely, children.

VCR *(vee see ar)* Acronym for *videocassette recorder*. A machine that records and plays back videotapes.

VDISK *(vee-disk)* A DOS device driver used to create a RAM drive. See also *RAM disk, virtual disk*.

VDT *(vee dee tee)* Acronym for video display terminal, otherwise known as a monitor (with a keyboard). The term VDT, however, is more apt to be used when talking about the negative health effects of these machines, which have been implicated in everything from eyestrain to birth defects. They produce a substantial amount of electromagnetic radiation, which may or may not be enough to cause the various maladies that monitors have been accused of causing. For protection, it is possible to get screens that filter out these electromagnetic fields. Screens that polarize the visual output so as to avoid glare are even more widely available. See also *radiation*. "I like my *VDT,* but I'm worried about the EMFs it produces. I'm worried that I might get RSI or CTS from all that typing, too. It's that dangerous side of computing that gives me so many of life's thrills."

vector graphics *(vek-tor graf-iks)* Graphics that are drawn using lines. The that starts at a certain point and goes off in a certain direction for a certain distance. (Certainly, you knew that.) Vector graphics are fine for CAD programs, though don't expect to see many flower vases done that way. See also *bitmap, graphics*. "Victor loves *vector* graphics over bitmaps."

verify *(ver-uh-fie)* To confirm the existence of something. In computing, often refers to the double-checking that takes place after a file is copied. You verify that the duplicate is identical to the original. This makes the copy process take a bit longer because the computer has to double-check, but it ensures that no errors were produced during the duplication process. "Because disk media is much more reliable than in the old days, most DOS users don't bother to *verify* file copies."

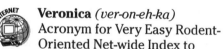 **Veronica** *(ver-on-eh-ka)* Acronym for Very Easy Rodent-Oriented Net-wide Index to Computerized Archives, which is a program developed at the University of Nevada to help you search through various Internet Gopher servers to find the information you need. Veronica, like her pals Archie and Jughead, were made obsolete by the World Wide Web. "The real *Veronica* would probably have nothing to do with any Gopher."

version *(ver-zhun)* An edition of a product. Versions are usually designated with a number, such as "SlothCom 2.0 for Windows," in which 2.0 is the version number, second version, first release. You can't count on the numbers being in numerical order (we don't know why this is so), but typically 1 comes before 2, 2 comes before 3, and so on. The decimal portion of a version number generally represents a small enhancement or bug fix to the initial version release so that Version 2.1 is always more reliable than 2.0. Intermediary releases have more digits following the decimal, such as Windows 3.1.1, which is really just Microsoft's way of avoiding the fiasco caused by releasing a whole new version. "*Version* 1.0 of any product — the first one out the chute — is generally the worst. Of course, the computer industry knows that we know that, so we can't recommend Version 1.1 either."

vertical *(ver-tuh-kal)* Relating to the up-and-down direction. In computers, we can talk about vertical markets, vertical centering, vertical columns, vertical justification, and vertical scrolling, all of which apply in some way to up-and-down-ness. "Charlie told me he was feeling *vertical* today."

vertical market *(ver-tuh-kal mar-kit)* Relatively few consumers who desire specific software. Most programmers who don't work for major software vendors create programs for the vertical market. For example, real estate agencies are a vertical market that needs specific software written for it — stuff you can't find on the shelf in the Software-o-Rama. "Elevator software is a *vertical* market."

vertical scan frequency *(ver-tuh-kal skan free-kwen-see)* Also called refresh rate. The number of times a display screen is refreshed per second.

vertical scroll bar *(ver-tuh-kal skrohl bar)* The gizmo on the right side of a window in a graphical application and used to scroll the document up or down. By clicking the scroll bar with your mouse or using the arrow keys, you can move the contents of the window up or down in various increments. The little marker that travels along the bar, the *elevator box,* shows you how far along you are in the document. See also *horizontal scroll bar.* "To get to the end of my document, I put these little people in the *vertical scroll bar's* elevator box. Then I say 'Free fall!'

and drag the elevator box quickly to the bottom of the scroll bar. It may scare the little people, but I get to the bottom of my document quickly."

VESA *(vee-za)* Acronym for Video Electronics Standards Association, an organization devoting its existence to setting video standards for computers. The most prominent standard set by VESA has been the development of the VESA local bus, which was designed to make IBM computers run graphics faster. The VESA bus was replaced by the PCI bus, which does the same thing and more. See also *PCI.*

VGA *(vee jee ay)* Acronym for Video Graphics Array or Video Gate Array, a color graphics display standard that was an improvement over its predecessors in terms of color selection, resolution, and accuracy of image. A VGA monitor can display as many as 256 colors at one time. The resolution measures image sharpness; with VGA, that's 640 pixels horizontally by 480 lines vertically. Super VGA monitors are even more impressive, with resolutions reaching 1,024 x 768. See also *CGA, EGA, graphics, monitor, resolution, SVGA.*

video *(vid-ee-oh)* Anything visual in a computer. More specifically, it can refer to the display function of your computer (that is, video display) or the act of incorporating video devices (VCRs and video recording equipment) with computer technology. Video standards established by the Video Electronics Standards Association help to ensure that your computer components work together in such a way that you can actually see something on the screen (which is nice). That's the kind of video that's common to all computers. "I got my father *video* software for his birthday. Now he sits around all day in dark glasses in front of his computer yelling, 'Cut!' into a megaphone."

video accelerator *(vid-ee-oh ak-sell-er-ay-tur)* A hardware component on a display adapter that speeds up full-motion video.

video adapter *(vid-ee-oh uh-dap-ter)* An expansion card allows your software and your PC's monitor to talk with each other. Also called a *video card.* See also *CGA, EGA, expansion slot, SVGA, VGA.* "The graphics on your PC consist of two elements: the monitor and the *video adapter.* The monitor you see. The video adapter lurks inside your PC's guts."

video board *(vid-ee-oh bord)* See *video adapter.*

video card *(vid-ee-oh kard)* See *video adapter.*

videoconferencing *(vid-ee-oh-kon-fren-seeng)* A communications setting where two groups of people in different locations can see and hear each other using electronic communications.

video memory *(vid-ee-oh mem-oh-ree)* A special part of the computer's RAM in which images displayed on the screen are stored. "Fran must have lots of *video memory.* He remembers seeing the old *Gary Moore Show* live on TV."

video mode *(vid-ee-oh mohd)* The various resolutions and number of colors available for the different types of graphics adapters used by IBM-compatible computers. Twenty video modes are now used, ranging from 0 to 19. Characteristics include whether they display graphics or text only, color or monochrome, the number of colors, the

resolution (height and width in pixels), and, in text-only mode, the number of columns (or the number of characters you can fit on a line). See also *mode.* "Jane pasted some flowers on her monitor to help cheer up its *video mode.*"

video RAM *(vid-ee-oh ram)* The chips used to make up video memory. These are built into high-end video adapter boards. "The Megalons used a *video RAM* to break into Captain Video's secret fortress."

videotext *(vid-ee-oh-tekst)* Words and numbers that come to your computer (or your TV, for that matter) over the wires. Types of videotext that are commonly transmitted include news, weather information, and stock quotes. In Europe, a videotext system was designed for use with their cable television. Using a special type of computer, you can hook into the system and access information right at home on your TV. Americans must have thought this was too dumb because we never bothered with it. "*Videotext* is an appropriate format for up-to-the-minute news that must be transmitted quickly to be valuable — stuff such as 'Hey! Some guy just broke into your house. Go check the bedroom window.'"

virtual disk *(vur-choo-uhl disk)* A make-believe disk that doesn't exist in reality, like most flying saucers. Actually, a virtual disk is a fancy term for a RAM disk, a disk created from the computer's memory. See also *RAM disk.* "Father Matthew wants to put all his sermons on a *virtual disk.*"

virtual machine *(vur-choo-uhl mah-sheen)* 1. A software simulation of another computer. A virtual machine is useful for testing software on large

v

computers, such as mainframes. For example, a group of engineers typically creates a new computer on a larger mainframe and then runs tests to see how the computer performs. All this is done before the first real machine is created, primarily to work out the bugs. New microprocessors are created in a similar manner. 2. On 386 and later PCs, a special operating mode, V86 mode, in which the microprocessor can pretend that it's actually several 8088 computers all running at the same time. This is how operating systems such as Windows and OS/2 can *multitask* (run more than one program at a time).

virtual memory *(vur-choo-uhl mem-oh-ree)* Using disk drive storage to simulate RAM. Some operating systems borrow parts of the disk drive and swap out massive chunks of memory to a file — a *swap file* — on disk. That way, true memory (RAM) is made available for programs that need it. The memory saved on disk can be put back into real memory when it's needed later. See also *hard disk, memory, RAM.* "You can tell when your computer uses *virtual memory;* your system slows w-a-y d-o-w-n."

virtual reality *(vur-choo-uhl ree-al-uh-tee)* An oxymoron that describes a brave new world of computer technology that creates a simulated multidimensional environment. The user is actually encased in the environment, or can be, with paraphernalia that can include a helmet, goggles, gloves, and a belt, all used as input devices. Getting "inside the space" makes you feel as though you're trapped in a dream world. Within a virtual reality environment, you can see, hear, and feel your way around a software application. The main uses of virtual reality now are

games and design and engineering. Already, game arcades offer virtual reality setups where you can hunt down and kill your opponent in a place called cyberspace, which is not far from downtown L.A. More significantly, virtual reality is used for engineering because it allows the engineer or designer to simulate any view of the product being worked on. For instance, in designing a car, you can actually simulate being inside the engine. See also *artificial intelligence, expert system, knowledge base.* "Sometimes I think my whole life is one big *virtual reality* machine — especially when the cat talks to me."

virus *(vie-ruhs)* 1. A nasty type of program created by nasty people. The virus is capable of replicating itself and doing severe damage to the contents of other users' systems. To protect your

A computer virus is a nasty thing.

system against viruses, you should 1) get your software only from reputable places; 2) run an antivirus utility; 3) religiously back up your hard drive so that lost data can be quickly and reliably replaced. See also *vaccine.* "If you can't cure your computer of a *virus* it's caught, you should at least let it rest and feed it plenty of chicken soup." 2. Another term for a Trojan horse, though it's inaccurate. See also *Trojan horse.*

VIS *(vee eye ess)* Acronym for *voice information service.* A variety of voice processing service applications.

visible bell *(viz-uh-bul bell)* A program option that has a visual signal, such as a flashing status bar or menu bar.

VisiCalc *(viz-uh-kalk)* Trademarked name for the first spreadsheet software, originally developed for CP/M and the Apple II computers. VisiCalc means "visible calculator," which is how its designer envisioned it: a grid of cells, each of which worked like a calculator. The concept was refined by Lotus in its 1-2-3 application. Microsoft Excel now dominates the spreadsheet market. Even so, a VisiCalc user would feel right at home using 1-2-3 or Excel.

VisiCorp *(viz-uh-korp)* The company that developed the once-popular VisiCalc program. VisiCorp died the painful death of many early computer software developers: It announced a wonderful new program that took just too long to develop. People grew old waiting for VisiCorp's much praised VisiOn (Vizee-On, though I always pronounced it "vision") software. Besides, at that point, Lotus was winning over the IBM world with its easy-as 1-2-3 spreadsheet.

Visual Basic *(vizh-yoo-el bay-sik)* A Microsoft dialect of the BASIC language that lets you create programs by drawing your user interface on the screen and then writing BASIC commands to make the program actually do something worthwhile. Microsoft also uses Visual Basic as a common language for all its business applications, such as Excel, Word, and Access. Theoretically, in the future you will be able to write Visual Basic commands to make Excel or Access easier to use. Realistically, most people will probably never attempt this feat unless they want to drive themselves crazy. "*Visual Basic* is so popular because it makes programming a whole lot easier than using an arcane language like C++ or Pascal. The only thing Visual Basic doesn't make easier is figuring out why you want to write a program in the first place."

visual programming *(vizh-yoo-el prohgram-eeng)* A way of creating software by making menu choices with the mouse and cutting and pasting items so that actual typing and linear thought are minimized. The plus side is that you don't have to know much about programming to be able to work with this technology and produce results. The minus side is that many of your choices are made for you and you often have no way to customize certain options. See also *program*. "*Visual programming* makes it possible for someone such as Uncle Ralph to create custom applications. Remember his spice rack? Doesn't the thought of Ralph programming make you cringe?"

VLAN *(vir-choo-ul loh-kul ayr-ee-uh netwerk)* A group of two or more hosts that are not necessarily on the same physical network but share the same network address.

VLB *(vee ell bee)* Acronym for VESA Local Bus. See also *VESA*.

VL-Bus *(vee el-bahs)* Yet another term for a VESA Local Bus. See also *VESA*. "Boy, my computer has VESA, VLB, and *VL-Bus,* and it has only one slot!"

VLSI *(vee el es ie)* Acronym for *Very Large Scale Integration,* a technology that refers to semiconductor chips. The chip is engineered so that it can accommodate a large number of transistors and can do more. See also *CMOS, MOS, semiconductor*. "*VLSI* circuits are not larger than other chips; they just contain more information."

VMM *(vee em em)* Acronym for Virtual Memory Management, a hardware or software device that controls virtual memory. See also *virtual memory*.

VOD *(vee oh dee)* Acronym for *v*ideo *on d*emand. The ability to deliver a movie or other video program to an individual Web browser or TV whenever the user requests it.

voice mail *(voys mayl)* Any system for sending, storing, and retrieving audio messages, like an answering machine.

voice processing *(voys pros-ess-eeng)* The computerized handling of the voice.

voice recognition *(voys rek-uhg-ni-shun)* Technology that can recognize and work with the spoken word. It translates sound signals into digital signals that can be processed and analyzed by a computer. The prospect offers a whole new world of opportunity for computers: being able to talk to your computer as you talk to your friends (or, more appropriately, to your children) and being able to repot your plants or remodel your kitchen while you're doing your computer work. Voice-recognition technology is in a constant primitive state. See also *voice synthesis*. "The first thing I'd do with *voice recognition* technology is tell Windows exactly what it can do with the General Protection Fault error message."

voice synthesis *(voys sin-thuh-sis)* The opposite of voice recognition. Here, the computer can create something that sounds like speech from text that it reads from a hard or floppy disk. Voice synthesis is much easier to create than voice recognition, which is why computers talk like computers. "I had always imagined my computer was female. But when I plugged in that *voice synthesis* expansion unit, it sounded like Arnold Schwarzenegger on a slow day."

volatile memory *(vol-uh-tiel mem-oh-ree)* Another term for RAM. Computer memory is often called volatile because it requires a constant flow of electrons to maintain its contents. Turn the power off and — poof! — there goes memory. See also *RAM*. "Walk gingerly around the computer. You don't want its *volatile memory* to go off."

volume *(vahl-yoom)* 1. Another name for a disk, whether hard or floppy. Comes from the old computer days when instead of your having a disk inside your computer, the lab technicians mounted a tape volume on a high-speed tape machine. The term works for computer storage the same way that a volume is a single book in a larger collection of works. See also *disk, floppy disk, hard disk*. "I got an error message that said "No volume in drive A," so I turned up my stereo." 2. The control in Windows that sets how loud the computer's speakers play.

volume label *(vahl-yoom lay-bol)* A disk's name. See *label*.

von Neumann *(vahn noy-man)* The father of all modern computers. John von Neumann invented an architecture that created a data bottleneck named for him. Basically, it involves a very fast CPU and fast storage, but the processing is slowed down to the rate of the transmission of the data from one place to another. Yes, his name is von Neumann, but you pronounce it "von Noy-man." "Yes, Dr. *von Neumann* and not two guys named Steve really started this computer revolution."

V

voodoo *(voo-doo)* Tried-and-true technology to apply when all else fails. Rather than press keys and click a mouse, you can chant invocations, do ritual dances, or feed weird concoctions of exotic herbs to your computer in an effort to get it to cooperate. "If your PC worked fine yesterday and for some reason it won't today — even though you didn't change a thing — it's *voodoo.*"

VRAM *(vee-ram)* Another term for video memory, often applied to the actual RAM chips. See also *video memory.*

VRML *(vurm-uhl)* Acronym for Virtual Reality Modeling Language, a 3-D version of the standard HTML Web page document. "To see a *VRML* document on the Web, you need a Web browser that understands *VRML.*"

Vulcan *(vol-kan)* 1. A planet in Epsilon Eridana. 2. Name for a person from the planet Vulcan. From *Star Trek*'s Mr. Spock. 3. A computer wizard, like *Star Trek*'s Mr. Spock. See also *Spock.*

Vulcan nerve pinch *(vol-kan nurv peench)* 1. A manipulation of the neck or shoulder that renders someone blissfully unconscious. Used by Mr. Spock on *Star Trek* to contrast with Captain Kirk's coldcocking some alien. 2. Nickname for the Ctrl+Atl+Delete key combination that renders a PC unconscious (actually reboots it). See also *Ctrl+Alt+Delete.*

V

W: *(dub-ohl-yoo koh-lin)* A disk drive letter designation, probably representing some disk drive on the network as opposed to a disk drive in your system. Really, it would have to be your 21st hard drive, your 20th CD-ROM drive, your 14th removable drive, or 19th RAM drive, or something else so utterly nuts that it doesn't deserve mentioning here. (Honestly, most high-letter drives are network drives.)

W2K Windows 2000 An operating system by Microsoft designed to be the successor to Windows NT 4.0.

Wabi *(wah-bee)* Acronym for Windows Application Binary Interface, a Windows emulator for the X Window system.

 WAIS *(ways)* Acronym that stands for Wide Area Information Server, which is a valiant attempt by the Internet to make it easy to search for specific types of information. Made obsolete by the World Wide Web.

wait state *(wayt stayt)* A short delay that occurs when a microprocessor accesses data from memory. Because the microprocessor is generally faster than the memory chips, it waits for the memory chips to "catch up" by sitting around and having a cup of coffee for the duration of one wait state each time it accesses the memory. A *zero wait state processor* is much faster and takes advantage of faster memory chips. How long is a wait state? It depends on how fast the processor is. In any case, it's a slice of time way too fast for a human to experience. See also *zero wait state.* "I had to call tech support yesterday about my laptop. They said it had only one *wait state,* but when I took it to the post office, it suddenly gained about 40 wait states!"

A cloudy wallpaper.

wallpaper *(wahl-pay-per)* A graphics image placed on the desktop, or background, of your GUI. If you close all windows in your GUI, you see the wallpaper underneath. Computer wallpaper serves no particular purpose, but it can be interesting and amusing to your friends. "My favorite *wallpaper* is the Nagel painting called *Sushi.*"

Wambooli protocol *(wom-boo-lee proh-toh-kahl)* A complex algorithm for data transmission that means nothing whatsoever. From the nonsense word *Wambooli* and the nonsense term *protocol.* "Yup, I'd bet that new *Wambooli protocol* will smoke out that RARP thing Karl's working on." See the Wambooli Web page at http://www.wambooli.com/.

W

WAN *(wan)* Acronym for Wide Area Network. See also *Wide Area Network*.

Wang *(wayng)* A computer manufacturer, Wang Laboratories.

wapro *(wah-proh)* The Japanese term for word processor. We just thought we'd throw it in here because it's one of those terms you usually don't see in computer dictionaries. "The proper response to the question *'Wapro?'* is 'Wa-kari-mas-en,' or 'I don't understand.'"

warez *(wayrz)* Pirated software. A term used by online pirates to refer to the program they've stolen or hacked into.

War Games *(woor gayms)* A 1983 film starring Matthew Broderick about a teenage hacker who gains access to a top secret military computer. As is always the case in such situations, the computer attempts to initiate World War III. Yet another example of Hollywood's fascination with modems and nuclear weapons.

warm boot *(warm boot)* The process of restarting your computer by pressing Ctrl+Alt+Del or an equivalent reset button. A warm boot occurs when you restart the computer without turning it off. Warm booting is much faster than cold booting, which occurs when you turn the computer off and then back on. See also *cold boot, Ctrl+Alt+Del, reboot.* "After installing certain software on my

Another type of warm boot.

hard disk, the programs tell me to restart the computer by pressing Ctrl+Alt+Del, which *warm boots* it. That seems so much cozier than the cold boot approach."

Warp *(warp)* A processor developed at Carnegie-Mellon University that was the predecessor of iWARP. See also *OS/2*.

warp coils *(warp koy-els)* 1. The magic that allows a starship to glide through space at high speeds without any chiropractic injuries to the crew. 2. Any sufficiently advanced or mysterious thing inside a computer that you don't understand. "The PC won't boot! Why doesn't someone check the innertubular couplers, quantum phase adjustment wing nuts, or the *warp coils?*"

watch icon *(watch ie-kon)* A mouse pointer that looks like a tiny little watch. The watch icon, indigenous to the Macintosh computer, tells you that the computer is thinking and that you have to wait. In the early days of the Macintosh, the watch's little hands did not move. Today's watch icons are much more sophisticated. See also *beachball pointer, hourglass icon.* "Spacelab, this is Houston. You'll have to wait on that emergency meteor collision avoidance program. We're still getting the *watch icon* here."

watt *(wot)* A unit of measure for power consumption. Watts equals volts times amperes. Hence, a 10-volt, 10-amp power source puts out 100 watts of power. It helps if you think of watts in terms of a lightbulb. A 100W lightbulb is much brighter than a 60W bulb. TV studios use 1000K bulbs to light their sets, which are terribly bright. The typical PC uses 250W of power, just like a 250W lightbulb. See also *amp.* "I use 50-*watt* lightbulbs in my computer room, so I don't get too much glare on the screen. Also, I'm a troglodyte, so it reminds me of my cave-dwelling forefathers."

 WAV *(wayve)* 1. A type of sound file in Windows. 2. The extension of a file that contains a WAV sound.

WD *(dub-ohl-yoo dee)* Acronym for Western Digital, a manufacturer of computer equipment, most famously hard drives. The WD acronym is often included in the drive's model number

 Web *(web)* 1. Nickname for the World Wide Web. See also *World Wide Web.* 2. Prefix for any of a number of things having to do with the World Wide Web.

 Web-based application *(web-bayst app-lee-kay-shun)* Software that runs on or interacts with a Web site on the Internet.

Web browser *(web brow-zer)* Software designed to view documents written in HTML, which includes all pages on the World Wide Web. There are two popular Web browers, one from Netscape and the other from Microsoft. Web browsers display information on the Internet using text, graphics, sounds, and all sorts of interesting distractions. They can also display gopher, ftp, and newsgroup information. See also *plug-in, World Wide Web.* "The spider asked if I was going to kill her, and I said that I was just a *Web browser.*"

 Webcam *(web-kam)* A videocamera, attached to the Internet, that uploads images to the

Internet either at intervals or in realtime. Popular webcam images have shown college dorm rooms or someone's driveway. Imagine that!

 Webcast *(web kast)* To send live video programming to the Internet.

 Web catalog *(web kat-uh-logs)* A page on the World Wide Web that contains a listing of other Web pages, organized by topic or subject. A Web catalog is like a library card catalog, listing Web pages by subject or topic. See also *search engine.* "The most popular *Web catalog* is Yahoo."

 WebCrawler *(web-crah-lur)* A robot designed for searching the World Wide Web. WebCrawler displays its results based on how many Web pages contain words similar to those you're searching for. See also *robot.*

 Web folder *(web fohl-dur)* A folder on a Web server. You can view files and folders on a Web server just as you would on any computer system. However, when you save a file to a Web folder, the file is saved on that Web server and not on your computer's hard disk.

 Webmaster *(web mass-tur)* A person responsible for a Web page or Web site.

 Web page *(web payj)* A document on the World Wide Web. A page has nothing to do with the length of the document; some pages are short, and some are very long. But any single document is still merely a page.

w

 Web search site *(web surch site)* See *search engine.*

 Web server *(web sir-ver)* A computer or a software program running on a computer that answers requests for Web pages on the World Wide Web. Web servers are usually part of your Internet Service Provider's array of computers. Or your business may have a computer that works as a Web server, answering HTTP requests from the Internet and sending Web page information to other computers.

 Web site *(web siet)* A collection of Web pages closely linked to each other. A company's presence on the World Wide Web. A Web site is merely the entire collection of Web pages relating to a specific topic or owned by a business, group, or individual. For example, you have your own, personal Web site, which consists of several Web pages dedicated to your cat's recovery from chemotherapy. A Web site is not the same thing as a Web server. See also *Web server.*

 Web space *(web spays)* Disk storage space that can be used to hold Web pages. Typically offered as a service of an Internet Service Provider, your Web space can store your HTML documents, which makes them available to anyone on the Internet. Of course, you have to follow rules about filenames and locations in your Web space, and, for a hefty fee, you can get someone to actually tell you what they are. "Every Internet provider should offer you some *Web space* as part of its monthly fees."

 Web TV *(web tee vee)* Another stupid attempt to get computer users to watch TV. Seriously, a type of computer that uses the TV as an output device for viewing information on the World Wide Web. But computer owners from way back know that TV sets make for lousy computer monitors. So while you're viewing the Web TV stuff, it looks okay, but if you visit anywhere else on the Web, you suffer the perils of eyeball frazzle. See also *eyeball frazzle.*

Webzine *(web-zeen)* A magazine published on the World Wide Web.

wedged *(wejd)* A device that fails to operate or slows down because of an overflow of information. A wedged device doesn't necessarily crash the system; the computer may still work for a while, for example, but the modem remains wedged.

wetware *(wet-wayr)* The human brain.

WFWG *(win-dohz for werk-groops)* Acronym for Windows for Workgroups; one that's very hard to say as an acronym, so no one does anyway. See also *Windows for Workgroups.* "I told my Mom I was working on *WFWG,* and she thought I'd become a professional wrestler."

what-if *(wot-if)* A term used for testing a spreadsheet with various values, generating different results for analysis. Like, "If I made a gazillion dollars, what percentage would my house payment be?" And then you can enter another value: "Now what if I worked at McDonalds? Hey, can this thing deal with negative numbers?" What-if testing is commonly used in spreadsheets, in which you can enter different values into cells of the spreadsheet and the formulas recalculate their results based on the different scenarios. See also *spreadsheet.* "Jimmy used a spreadsheet to calculate various *what-ifs* for the money he embezzled. Now he's doing 5 to 10 but is trying to get the judge to work out a what-if for good behavior."

wheel mouse *(weel mowse)* Another name for the Microsoft IntelliMouse. It's like a regular mouse but with a wheel-like button between the two standard PC mouse buttons. See also *IntelliMouse.*

A wheel mouse.

Whetstone *(wet-stohn)* The name of a program used for testing the speed of a microprocessor. The Whetstone is used as a standard test for microprocessor speed. See also *microprocessor, MIPS.* "Hey, my computer can do 1,500 *Whetstones* — and that's with one cable tied behind its back!"

whitespace *(wiet-spays)* Tabs, spaces, blank lines, and other padding around text in a document, but refers specifically to formatting source code for computer programming. "Your code is too hard to read! Try adding some whitespace in there to break it up!"

Wide Area Network *(wied ayr-ee-uh net-werk)* A network of computers that spans a large distance, as opposed to a Local Area Network, which involves computers in the same building. See also *LAN, network, network operating system, node.* "Realtors can access a

Wide Area Network that provides multiple listings and other services for your computer. That way, they can send messages such as 'Hey! Mr. and Mrs. Turkey looking for duplex — completely real estate ignorant. Be on the lookout!'"

widow *(wid-oh)* 1. The last line of a paragraph abandoned at the top of the next page while the rest of the paragraph sits at the bottom of the previous page. See also *orphan.* "Sometimes, if your document is full of *widows,* simply writing about a bunch of elderly bachelors makes the widows disappear." 2. A female spouse who is abandoned by her husband who spends far too much of his time in front of his computer.

widower *(wid-oh-er)* The male version of a computer widow. See also *widow.*

wildcards *(wihld-kahrds)* Characters or symbols used in place of a number of possible combinations. Wildcards represent one or more characters that "could be anything" in a search or command. For example, if the * symbol is a wildcard, the search text *s*ing* matches any word or item that starts with an *s* and ends in *ing.* See also **, ?.* "*Wildcards* come in handy when you search for text and don't know how to spell, when you search for files and don't know their whole names, or when you play Shanghai with the in-laws and have a lousy hand."

WIMP *(wimp)* A disparaging acronym for *w*indows, *i*cons, *m*enus, *p*ointing device. It's the wimpy GUI way of using a computer as opposed to using the command line. See also *command line, icon, menu, mouse, window.* "Don't show me that *WIMP* interface! I'm a real man! Give me the DOS prompt any day!"

W

Win *(win)* 1. A prefix applied to any product, device, or program that has anything remotely to do with Microsoft Windows. 2. The old DOS command used to start Windows. "Is it a coincidence that Windows starts with *'win'?"*

Win32 *(win-thur-tee-too)* A program that's compatible with the 32-bit version of Microsoft Windows. Includes Windows 9x, Windows NT, and Windows 2000.

WinCIM *(win-sim)* Acronym for Windows CompuServe Information Manager, a graphics front end for using CompuServe in Windows. Believe it or not, CompuServe is a text-based online service. However, by using a front end like WinCIM, you can use your pull-down menus and mouse to wade through all the various menus. See also *CompuServe, front end.*

WIN.INI *(win in-ee)* The configuration file for Windows, though its importance is diminished under Windows 95 and later. This file contains commands that determine how Microsoft Windows looks and behaves on your computer. The WIN.INI file is an ASCII file, so you can edit it using a text editor. If you ever lose or modify your WIN.INI file, Windows may not work properly on your computer. "Every time you install a new program, it automatically updates your *WIN.INI* file. For the fun of it, I copied my WIN.INI file to my boss's computer, so now his computer refuses to work properly."

Winchester disk *(win-ches-ter disk)* A hard disk. For years, hard drives were called Winchester disks. This had nothing to do with any company named Winchester that made hard drives. Instead, it referred to the first IBM hard drive that stored 30 megabytes of information on each side. Because the drive was a 30-30, people dubbed it a Winchester disk after the famous Winchester rifle. Until the mid-1980s, hard drives were often called Winchester disks. This drove everyone nuts because they assumed that some person or some company named Winchester made the disks. It just wasn't so. Today they're called hard disks, plain and simple. See also *hard disk.* "Yes, ma'am, our hard disks come in three sizes: *Winchester,* Colt, and Daisy."

window *(win-doh)* An area on the screen that displays data, programs, or information. A window can be moved, resized, opened, and closed, allowing you to organize the data on your computer screen. In most GUIs, you can open numerous windows at the same time and juggle information on the screen. You can switch between windows by simply clicking the window you want. However, you can work in only one window — called the *active window* — at a time. See also *active window, GUI.* "Sometimes I get carried away and open 20 or 30 *windows* at the same time. This usually results in the building inspector coming in with a worried look on his face and muttering something about earthquakes."

Windows *(win-dohs)* Short for *Microsoft Windows,* the most widely used operating system for PCs. Windows began its life in 1983 as a shell (graphical user interface) for DOS computers. Windows/386 was a custom version of Windows for the 386 computer that had more power than the original version. And Windows 3.0, which appeared in 1990, became a rival to DOS with advanced applications and programs that made it almost an out-right replacement. Finally, Windows did become its own operating system in 1996 with Windows 95.

Windows 98 was the upgrade to Windows 95. The code name was Memphis. Windows 98 fixed many bugs in Windows, enhanced performance, and had better support for more hard-ware. It also supported the use of two monitors.

Windows NT was introduced in 1993. Windows NT is a 32-bit operating system that boots directly and includes built-in networking. Windows NT comes in ver-sions for the desktop (NT Workstation) and the server (NT Server).

Windows 2000 Professional and Windows Millenium both have been released in the year 2000. Windows 2000 Professional is a friendlier version of Windows NT, and Windows Millennium Edition is more of an upgrade to Windows 98.

Today, every PC sold comes with a copy of Windows on it. This may have more to do with sneaky Microsoft licensing habits than any desire on behalf of the computer-using community. Even so, Windows is nice because it provides a common way of using programs, making them easier to learn. Plus, Windows manages the way your PC works and takes care of common chores, such as working with the printer and disk drive. For example, when you set up a printer in Windows, that printer is automati-cally available in all your Windows pro-grams. This lets us poor users concen-trate on our work rather than on fussing with the computer and printer drivers or some such. See also *GUI, Microsoft.*

 Windows/286 *(win-dohs too-ay-tee-siks)* The second edition of Windows, specifically designed for the 80286 or PC/AT computer environment.

Windows 3.x *(win-dohs three-poynt-eks)* The successor to Windows/386 and the direct ancestor of Windows 95. Still technically a DOS shell, this program was the first popular graphical DOS shell and one of the first programs to take full advantage of the 80386 microprocessor. Two ver-sions were released: Windows 3.0 in 1990 and Windows 3.1 in 1992. Windows for Workgroups is also considered a Windows 3.x product.

Windows/386 *(win-dohs three-ay-tee-siks)* Similar to Windows/286, but customized for the special operating modes of the Intel 80386 microprocessor. The direct ancestor of Windows 3.x, which is the ancestor of Windows 95.

 Windows 9x *(win-dohs nien-eks)* A generic term for Windows 95, Windows 98, and Windows Me. See also *Windows.*

Windows CE *(win-dohs see-ee)* A version of Microsoft Windows designed to run on handheld computers. A failure because Microsoft attempted to put everything from the desktop version of Windows into Windows CE, which made the operating system too cumbersome for the hand-held computer motif.

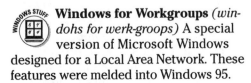 **Windows for Workgroups** *(win-dohs for werk-groops)* A special version of Microsoft Windows designed for a Local Area Network. These features were melded into Windows 95.

W

Windows keys *(win-dohs kees)* Two special keys on a 101-key keyboard (which actually makes it a 104-key keyboard) that perform special functions in Windows. The Windows key pops up the Start menu (the same as pressing Ctrl+Esc). The shortcut menu key displays the shortcut menu for whichever item is highlighted on the screen — the same as pointing the mouse at that item and right-clicking. "No, you don't need *Windows keys* to use Windows."

Windows Me *(win-dohs em-ee; win-dohs mee)* Officially called Windows Millennium, the "final" version of Windows 95. Introduced in 2000, this is the consumer version of Windows. (Windows 2000 is the business version.)

Windows Messaging *(win-dohs mes-uh-jeeng)* The new name for Microsoft Exchange, which was the old name for the Microsoft e-mail program.

Windows Millennium Edition *(win-dohs mel-en-ee-um)* See *Windows Me.*

Windows NT *(win-dohs en-tee)* The business edition of Windows. Replaced by Windows 2000. See also *Windows.*

Windoze *(win-dohz)* Slang for Windows. "I'd use Linux any day over Microsloth Windoze."

WinMark *(win-marks)* A measurement unit used to determine the speed of a computer when it's running Windows-based programs. The two most common WinMark measurements are the Graphics WinMark

(which measures the speed of displaying graphics) and the Disk WinMark (which measures the speed of accessing a hard disk). The higher the WinMark value, the faster the computer. "My computer is better than your computer because *PC* magazine rated mine as scoring 21.8 on its Graphics WinMark test and your computer only scored 17.4. Nya, nya, nya."

WINS *(wins)* Acronym for Windows Internet Naming Service, a part of Windows networking that allows NetBIOS names to be translated into IP addresses. Not worth messing with, unless you're in a big company that needs such a thing, in which case someone else will mess with it for you.

winsock *(win-sock)* Short for *Windows sock*ets, a set of programs designed to help Internet software access and use the Internet on a Windows PC. Essentially, the winsock is included with your Internet dialer program. It makes the connection to the Internet and activates the winsock software. Other Internet programs you run then use winsock to access the Internet. "Nope, unless your flight simulator program is on the Internet, you won't need a *winsock* to fly."

winsock2 *(win-sock-too)* The latest, wizbang version of the winsock standard. See also *winsock.*

Winstones *(win-stones)* A benchmark test of a computer's ability to run Windows. See also *benchmark.* "*Winstones!* Meet the *Winstones!* They're a way to measure your PC! When you're running Windows, it will see just how fast fast can be!"

Wintel *(win-tel)* An adjective describing a computer with an Intel processor that is capable of running Windows. Wintel essentially describes what's commonly called a PC. Same thing. "I assume that if we renamed *PCs For Dummies* to *Wintel For Dummies,* few people would buy it."

WinZip *(win-zip)* A version of the popular ZIP file archiving and compression utility specific to Windows.

wireless *(wy-er-less)* Anything without wires. The future trend is not to use wires in communications. So, supposedly, computer networks, telephones, modems, and other types of communications will all be transmitted through the air digitally. Eventually, power supplies could be wireless too, if the power companies could ever figure out how to meter wireless power.

wiz *(wiz)* A computer user who is sharp and fast and looks good at the computer. A wiz is not quite as adept as a wizard. See also *guru, hacker, wizard.* "Thank you for writing and calling me a computer *wiz.* Please note that wiz does not contain an *h.* That means something else entirely."

wizard *(wiz-erd)* 1. A computer user of high caliber. Not quite a guru, a computer wizard can solve most problems in most cases without assistance of any kind. See also *guru, hacker, wiz.* 2. Instructional blueprint that guides the user through a series of steps to accomplish a task, such as the PageWizard in Microsoft Publisher.

WMF *(dub-ohl-yoo em ef)* Acronym for Windows MetaFile, which is a special graphics file that was once used in earlier versions of Microsoft Windows. It was yet another attempt at a common file format. "Any time you see a graphics file with the *.WMF* file extension, it's either really old or was created by someone who doesn't know that the .WMF file format is obsolete."

Word *(wurd)* Slang for Microsoft Word for Windows (or Macintosh), a word processor from Microsoft.

word *(wurd)* 1. A chunk of information. A collection of data bits that are processed as a unit. On the PC and with most microcomputers, a word is 2 bytes of data, 16 bits "wide." Sometimes a word is as little as a byte (8 bits). The size varies, which is why we're being vague here. 2. A unit of the English language, such as *duh.* "Yes, Microsoft *Word* can write whole documents, which makes us wonder why they didn't call it Microsoft Document."

WordPerfect *(wurd-pur-fekt)* A word processor originally from WordPerfect Corporation, which has been bought and sold and, as this book goes to press, is owned by Corel Corporation.

Word Pro *(wurd proh)* A word processing program from Lotus.

word processing *(wurd prah-ses-eeng)* The act of using a word processor. Writing.

word processor *(wurd prah-ses-er)* An application that lets you write and edit documents. Word processors generally include the capability to copy and move text (by individual words, phrases, or paragraphs), search for specific words or phrases, insert and delete text, format the document (including margin settings, fonts, and character styles), and, of course, print the document. Popular word processors include

Microsoft Word and WordPerfect. See also *text editor*. "My *word processor* has features that let me create tables and columns. Hey, you'd almost think this was a construction project instead of a memo."

word separator *(wurd sep-er-ay-tor)* A character, such as a blank space, comma, or period, that separates a word.

word size *(wurd siez)* See *word*.

WordStar *(wurd-star)* One of the first word processors ever sold and also one of the first to lose its dominance in the market through mismanagement and the failure to upgrade the program for three years. WordStar existed in the days when computer keyboards lacked function keys and cursor (arrow) keys. WordStar defined certain keystrokes that are still used by many programs today. These keystrokes are usually referred to as "WordStar commands."

WordStar Keystroke	*What It Does*
Ctrl+S	Moves cursor one character to the left
Ctrl+D	Moves cursor one character to the right
Ctrl+E	Moves cursor one line up
Ctrl+X	Moves cursor one line down
Ctrl+A	Moves cursor one word to the left
Ctrl+F	Moves cursor one word to the right
Ctrl+Y	Deletes a line

"Although hardly anyone uses *WordStar* anymore, lots of programs still use WordStar commands because they're based on ancient computer history. With Windows becoming more popular, WordStar commands may finally fade from memory like a bad dream."

word wrap *(wurd rap)* The way a word processor automatically determines whether the word you are typing will fit within the right margin, and, if not, places that word on the next line. With word wrap, you don't have to press the Enter key at the end of each line, as you once had to do with a typewriter. You continue typing. Text editors do not have word wrap; you have to press Enter at the end of each line. See also *hyphenation*. "*Word wrap* used to be considered a bonus feature for early word processors. Today, a bonus feature is the built-in space shuttle simulator and advanced physics calculation module."

workgroup *(wurk-groop)* A collection of computers on a network. All the computers in Sales, for example, could be in the "Sales" workgroup, which is a small part of the entire company's network. For example, e-mail could be sent only to computers in a certain workgroup.

worksheet *(wurk-sheet)* A document created by a spreadsheet program. Not all spreadsheet programs refer to their data files as worksheets; some call them spreadsheets, others call them pages or sheets, and some even call them documents. In any event, a worksheet can be saved as a file on disk. See also *document, spreadsheet*. "I saved my Budget *worksheet* on disk as BUDGET-A and then saved the budget I show to the IRS as BUDGET-B."

workstation *(wurk-stay-shun)* A nebulous term used to describe a powerful computer generally used for scientific or engineering applications, such as CAD. A workstation usually has tons of RAM, gobs of disk storage space, a high-resolution graphics adapter and monitor, and a powerful microprocessor. Workstations often use the UNIX operating system, but some high-end Macintosh, DOS, and OS/2 machines qualify as workstations. See also *mainframe, network, PC*. "At work I have a Pentium Pro *workstation,* and at home I have a Pentium MMX playstation."

 World Wide Web *(wurld wied web)* The fun part of the Internet, often abbreviated WWW or just Web. The World Wide Web is a way to access the information on the Internet for both text and graphics, like you'd read in a magazine. Each document on the World Wide Web — a Web page — can contain links to other Web pages displaying additional information. It's those links that make the Web like a giant spider's web; all Web pages are interlinked and related to each other somehow. The Web is now the "hot topic" or "next big thing" to hit computerdom. Because of that, and because the computer industry is so into the Internet, the Web is given lots more attention than it deserves. See also *Internet, Web browser*. "The *World Wide Web* is just another valiant attempt to make the Internet easier to use and navigate."

WORM *(wurm)* Acronym for *Write Once Read Many,* a disk medium to which you can write data only once but read the data as often as you like. Most optical disks are WORM media: MO disks, DVDs, and CD-Rs, for example. Plain CD-ROM disks, however, are not WORM media because only the manufacturer can supply the information on the disk. There is no "writing to" a CD-ROM; they have read-only memory (ROM). See also *CD-R, DVD, MO, ROM*. "The best two acronyms in all computing are SCSI and *WORM*. It's entirely possible to have a SCSI WORM drive, and, if you do, constantly refer to it as that. It's bound to upset someone somewhere."

worm *(wurm)* A type of virus that infects system after system, like a worm chewing through soft earth. The most famous WORM virus was the one released by a college student that shut down the entire Internet in only three hours. (He expected that it would take 24 hours and was rather surprised at what he'd done.) See also *virus*.

WPG *(dub-ohl-yoo pee jee)* Acronym for WordPerfect Graphic, a special graphics file format that gives WordPerfect the ability to display pictures in your documents. WordPerfect comes with several .WPG files for you to play with, although none of them are useful when you want to get some real work done. "If you're going to draw a picture of me with a clueless look on my face, at least store the graphic as a .*WPG* file so that I can display it in my WordPerfect document."

wristpad *(rist-pad)* A foam-rubber pad fitting in front of the keyboard and designed to elevate your wrists as you type. Supposedly. this cuts down on some nasty injuries that can take place if you type with your wrists slouched down below the keyboard, which is the way we all type anyway. "Since Mrs. Levitt isn't around to whack your wrists with a ruler, like she did in typing class, you'd better get a *wristpad*."

wrist rest *(rist rest)* A platform used to raise the wrist to keyboard level for typing. Very similar to a wristpad.

wristwatch pointer *(rist-wach poyn-ter)* See *watch icon.*

write error *(riet ayr-or)* An error that occurs when you attempt to save data to a disk. Write errors can occur because of glitches on the disk surface, not enough space on the disk, or when trying to save to a write-protected disk. A good user interface "traps" the write error, gives you some clue about the exact problem that occurred, and, maybe, if the computer's in a good mood, tells you how to fix it. Otherwise, the system might crash. "Nothing induces computer panic like having a beautiful document created in memory but not being able to save it to disk, thanks to a *write error.* Try another disk."

write protect *(riet proh-tekt)* To modify a disk or file so that others are unable to edit or erase its data. You can write-protect a disk by activating the write-protect tab, a doohickey that makes the disk unwriteable. On 3½-inch disks, you flip the write-protect tab so that it exposes (or opens) the hole in the disk. On ancient 5¼-inch disks, you placed a piece of opaque tape over the write-protect notch on the side of the disk. Write protection is useful when you are copying disks and want to protect the originals. "When I gave my files to a coworker to examine, I *write-protected* the disk so that she couldn't change the files. But just in case, I also made a backup copy. And I'm holding her husband and children hostage."

WWW *(dub-ohl-yoo dub-ohl-yoo dub-ohl-yoo)* Acronym for World Wide Web. See also *World Wide Web.*

WYSIWYG *(wiz-ee-weeg)* Acronym for What You See Is What You Get, the ability to view information on the screen as it should appear when printed. There are degrees of WYSIWYG in computer-dom, but most people agree that the Macintosh and Windows environments offer true WYSIWYG. In fact, WYSIWYG is so common now that the term is quickly falling out of common use. "If this page layout program offers a *WYSIWYG* display, why does it need a Print Preview command?"

X

x *(eks)* 1. Something that is unknown. 2. A placeholder for what could be any other number. For example, MS-DOS 6.*x* refers to all the releases of MS-DOS Version 6: 6.0, 6.1, 6.2, 6.22, and so on.

X: *(eks koh-lin)* A disk drive letter for some type of disk drive in a PC. Actually, "drive X" sounds kind of mysterious. *Viruses from Drive X* would be a great title for a creepy David Cronenberg movie. Most likely, drive X: would be a network drive. See *map*.

x86 *(eks-ay-tee-siks)* A designation for the Intel family of microprocessors used in the IBM PC and its ilk. "The *x86* designation replaced 80x86 probably because it's easier to type."

X.25 *(eks twen-tee-fiev)* A communications protocol for arranging data in packets that includes identification of both the recipient and sender of the data. This is mostly advanced network stuff, not required knowledge unless you plan on someday bringing in the big bucks by being a network guru. See also *network*.

xBase *(eks-base)* A generic term for any program that can read, write, edit, modify, and otherwise totally destroy database files compatible with the dBASE program. Some popular xBase programs are Microsoft FoxPro, CA-Clipper, and Alpha Four.

 XCMD *(eks-see-em-dee)* External command available for the Macintosh HyperCard programming language. Accessing the XCMDs means that a HyperCard programmer has more functions and pizzazz available than when using HyperCard alone. See also *HyperCard.* "Josh used a bunch of cool *XCMDs* to spice up his fungi HyperCard database."

Xcopy *(eks-cah-pee)* A DOS and OS/2 utility that copies files and subdirectories.

XENIX *(zee-niks)* A version of the UNIX operating system that was adapted by Microsoft to run on personal computers. In the old days, you couldn't "buy" a copy of UNIX like you could buy DOS or System 7 or OS/2. So Microsoft packaged its own version of UNIX, which it called XENIX. Now people use SCO XENIX or SCO UNIX from the Santa Cruz Operation, Inc. See also *Linux, UNIX.* "Lauren had the computer science club rolling with her repertoire of archaic *XENIX* puns."

XGA *(eks jee aye)* Acronym for *Extended Graphics Array*, a type of video adapter that provided a higher resolution than previous adapters. Utterly failed as a standard; like PGA, it was too expensive and not enough software supported it. "When a computer acronym contains the letter X, as in *XGA* graphics, it typically means the marketing department has already used the II, Turbo, Pro, Gold, and 2000 monikers."

Xjack *(eks-jak)* A registered trademark for a pop-out phone chord connector typically found on laptop computers. Also written in all caps: XJACK. "Most of the better PCMCIA modem cards have an Xjack connector on them, which makes hooking up a phone line easier than some of the dorky methods of the past."

XMODEM *(eks-moh-dum)* 1. A communications protocol for transferring files between computers (often across phone lines) and catching errors that occur during transfer. This ensures that the file sent is identical to the file received. See also *checksum, CRC, Kermit, YMODEM.* 2. The name of a program that included the XMODEM file-transfer protocol. XMODEM, written by Ward Christensen, is often called "the Christensen protocol" by some old-timers. "Oh, Charles, darling, get with the times! No one uses plain old boring *XMODEM* anymore."

XMODEM-1K *(eks-moh-dum won-kay)* A variation on the XMODEM protocol where 1-kilobyte packages were sent instead of 128-byte packages. It was faster than plain old XMODEM.

XMS *(eks-em-ess)* Abbreviation for *Extended Memory Specification*, a memory-management standard for allowing DOS applications to access extended memory. XMS memory-management software provides access to the extended memory through the XMS standard, a set of rules developed by Microsoft and other industry bigwigs. Windows 95 uses an XMS memory manager named HIMEM.SYS. See also *expanded memory, extended memory, extended memory specification.* "I'm going to need a new *XMS* manager on my PC. All my extended memory is threatening to go on strike."

XON/XOFF *(eks-on / eks-awf)* Signals for stopping and starting the flow of data during transmission between computers. XON/XOFF lets the receiving computer stop the flow of information so that it can be processed as it comes in. The XON character is actually Ctrl+S. That stops data from being sent and also allows you to catch up and read the screen. The XOFF character is Ctrl+Q. On some systems, only the Ctrl+Q character gets things moving after being frozen by a Ctrl+S. See also *flow control, Pause key.* "We used *XON/XOFF* signals with our walkie-talkies."

XOR *(zor)* A logical operation, otherwise known as *exclusive OR* or sometimes an EOR. See also *exclusive OR.*

xref *(kros ref-rens)* To cross-reference something.

XT *(eks-tee)* Acronym for *Extended Technology,* a model of the IBM PC computer that extended the architecture of the original 8080; extra expansion slots and a hard drive were added.

X Window *(eks win-doh)* A windowing system, developed at MIT, that runs under UNIX and was originally released in May 1994. Called simply X, it is has been described as oversized, overengineered, and extremely complicated. X Window enables users to run applications on other computers in a network and then to view the output on their own screen.

x-y matrix *(eks-wie may-tricks)* A group of rows and columns where the x-axis is the horizontal row and the y-axis is the vertical column.

89	59
Y	
y	
121	79

Y: *(wie koh-lin)* The drive letter name for some disk drive in your PC, one you probably don't have, but because a PC is capable of having a Y: drive, it has to be in here in this dictionary. Most likely, a Y: on your computer would be a network drive. I'm serious: It's a network drive. See also *network drive*.

Y2K *(wie too kay)* Acronym for the Year 2000 problem, where 2000 is 2K. Back in the 1970s and 1980s, memory was so precious that programmers stored only the last two digits of the year, such as 92 for the year 1992. They didn't predict the results of the clock's turning over from 1999 to the year 2000. Panic and mayhem happened, and everyone started looking for solutions. As it turned out, there were no real problems when the clock rolled over to the year 2000. Some computers were affected, but most were fixed so that all the major comforts of life still existed: Planes flew and the television continued to work.

yacc *(yak)* Acronym for *Yet Another Compiler Compiler,* a UNIX tool used to create other languages and compilers. See also *UNIX*. "I know the letters are *cc*, but does *yacc* have to really stand for *Yet Another Compiler Compiler?*"

Y adapter *(wie uh-dap-ter)* A cable with one end on one end and two ends on the other end — like the letter *Y.* This setup allows two devices to be connected to a single port; however, only certain kinds of devices allow Y adapters.

 Yahoo! *(yah-hoo)* A large catalog of information stored on the World Wide Web, at www. yahoo.com. See also *Web catalog*.

The Yahoo Web site.

Yamaha *(yaw-maw-haw)* A Japanese company known for its production of electronics and motorcycles. It now makes CD-ROM writers and music synthesizers.

Year 2000 bug *(yeer too-thow-sand buhg)* See *Y2K*.

yiblette *(yib-let)* A small piece of something, usually a long skinny piece. A wee little chunk of cable. The plural is yiblettes. "One piece of spaghetti is a yiblette, not enough to get fat on."

YMODEM *(wie moh-dum)* A communications protocol based on the XMODEM standard. YMODEM allows faster data transmission than XMODEM, but was soon eclipsed by ZMODEM. See also *protocol, XMODEM, ZMODEM.*

y

Z

Z: *(zee-koh-lin)* Name for the last disk drive in a PC. Whew!

Z80 *(zee ay-tee)* The name of an old, 8-bit microprocessor used in the days of CP/M; developed by an ex-Intel employee to mimic the Intel 8080. See also *CP/M*. "Nary 20 years ago, the *Z80* was considered the cutting edge of technology. Today, that and $2.25 will buy you a tall, double, latté."

Zamboni *(zam-boh-nee)* 1. The machine used to clean the ice in an ice skating rink. This machine was developed in the early 1940s by Frank Zamboni. 2. The act of cleaning the ice using a Zamboni machine. "Our hockey team is so bad that the best part of the game is watching the Zamboni."

A real Zamboni!

zap *(zap)* 1. To remove a file permanently from the disk. Unlike deleting a file, zapping a file removes it without the possibility of its being undeleted. See

also *undelete*. "The first thing any 3-year-old learns how to do on any PC is to *zap*." 2. To zero out the contents of memory; to write the value zero (or some other value) to every location in memory, perfectly erasing whatever was there before. 3. To accidentally erase a disk drive. "Oops! Nothing on this disk. You must have accidentally *zapped* it." 4. To touch something and experience a static electrical discharge.

Zephram Cochrane *(zef-ram kahk-ran)* The man who invented the *warp drive*. He was lost in deep space and ended up on a remote planet where a feminine energy force was keeping him alive, young, and virile for centuries — like an outer space *Sunset Boulevard*. Of course, Captain Kirk stumbled upon him and rescued him by letting the energy force inhabit the body of Betty from *Father Knows Best*. Zephram and Betty lived happily ever after on that planet. "In the future, *Zephram Cochrane* will have colleges, universities, cities, and spelling bees named after him."

zero wait state *(zeer-oh wayt stayt)* A condition where the microprocessor does not have to wait before it can read information from RAM. See also *wait state*.

ZIF *(zif)* Acronym for *zero insertion force*, a type of socket for plugging in chips, usually the CPU, such as the

Pentium. Unlike other types of chip sockets that force you to push a chip into place, a ZIF socket lets you blithely drop the chip in the socket and then close a lever to cinch the chip securely in place. "If it weren't for the *ZIF* socket, we'd be putting microprocessor chips into our motherboards with the same force and zeal that a toddler shoves a building block into the VCR."

zip *(zip)* 1. A suffix applied to files that have been compressed with the PKZIP utility. A zip file may be anywhere from 5 percent to 95 percent smaller than the original file (or group of files, if more than one was compressed at a time). This process is useful for transferring files over a modem or for saving disk space. 2. The act of creating a zip file. "Dolores always *zipped* her files twice. She was afraid that they might accidentally become unzipped on the hard drive and embarrass themselves." 3. (all caps) A type of removable disk (and drive) — like a super floppy drive. ZIP disks can store 100 megabytes of information, and they're fast, like a hard drive. These disks are actually descendants of the old Bernoulli box (made by the same company, in fact). See also *Bernoulli box.*

ZMODEM *(zee-moh-dum)* The most popular and efficient communications protocol, used by nearly every communications program to send files back and forth. A successor to the XMODEM, YMODEM line (so ZMODEM was the obvious name for it), this file-transfer protocol allows information to be sent over the phone lines quickly and reliably. Also, ZMODEM sends the file's name and other information, automatically saving the file to disk for you. This

strategy was a massive leap in convenience over the clumsy, older XMODEM method of doing things. See also *XMODEM, YMODEM*. "When I asked Klaus how he wanted me to send the file, he kept saying "*ZMODEM, ZMODEM*." I thought he was saying "the modem, the modem," so I kept asking over and over."

 zone *(zohn)* A group of network devices on AppleTalk. See also *AppleTalk*.

zoom *(zoom)* 1. To enlarge or reduce an image, typically a document displayed in a window. You zoom in to enlarge the image. You zoom out to reduce the image. This is a boon to some users with large monitors, allowing them to display information large enough to be seen by the naked eye. 2. The command that zooms in or out, changing the way a document appears in a window. "I tried using the *Zoom* command to make my computer go faster, but it made my text bigger instead."

zoom box *(zoom boks)* An area or button on a window that increases the window size to full-screen proportions. "Arny, get your ear away from the monitor; it's a *zoom box,* not a boom box."

The Zoom box in Microsoft Word.

Ten Computer Terms That Don't Mean Squat

client: As the individual computer was forced into being part of a network, the role of *client* came into play, as in client/server. That means that your computer, once robust and capable on its own, became a mere cog in the network machine — a client — while the server (the master) sat fat and in charge elsewhere. The term *client* is now used to refer to anything that happens on your computer, as opposed to elsewhere. Huh? Does *everything* happen on your computer anyway? Why would "e-mail client program" be necessary? Even though the term is correct, on your computer you run an e-mail program. Unless you're sitting in the network room actually using the server as your PC, there's no other term you can use for it.

e-: The *e* prefix can be applied to any current term to make it sound new and cool. The trend branched from e-mail, which originated in the 1970s and is an abbreviation for *electronic mail*. *E* is now prefixed to anything to give it a new, modern sheen — despite whether the *e*-whatever is actually an improvement over the original, as e-mail was and is.

fast: Everything is relative. To label something as fast merely means that it's "fast now." Later, like in two weeks, what you think is fast now will be slow. To call something "fast" in the computer industry only shows that you haven't been around long.

i-: See *e-*.

microcomputer: When minicomputers and mainframes were popular, the term *minicomputer* meant something. Today, it's obsolete. Microcomputers are now merely computers. Even mainframes and supercomputers are now merely computers because many use the same hardware and the same components as desktop computers. *Everything* now is a computer.

microfloppy: Once, there were 8-inch floppy disks. Then came the 5 ¼-inch minifloppy disk. Then, along came the 3 ½-inch microfloppy. Because the older types of disks are now as rare as volleyball in a snowstorm, the term *floppy disk* now applies primarily to microfloppies.

multimedia: Combining graphics and sound. Back in the early 1990s, the craze was multimedia. You may still see the term bandied about today, but with *everything* technically qualifying as multimedia, the term holds no meaning. In fact, if someone were so foolish as to create some form of monomedia, it might actually make headlines.

new: Nothing is new in the computer industry. There's merely old hardware made smaller and faster and new software made larger and slower. The truly new stuff never gets noticed.

standard: The computer industry is full of standards, like a barnyard is full of you-know-what. Most standards are declared by groups or committees, published, and then ignored. Some standards are announced by big companies that tell other companies to follow the standards and then pay a licensing fee. The result is that nothing is standard and variations proliferate.

workstation: If you're serious about using a computer, then that computer is a workstation. If you want to sell a plain PC for more money, call it a workstation. If a company is too cheap to buy a computer for every worker, then it sets up generic computers called workstations. What is a workstation? It's a redundant word for *computer.*

Ten Mispronounced Computer Words

/etc: The proper pronunciation of the /etc subdirectory in UNIX and Linux is "ET-see." Saying "et-SET-er-uh" or "ee tee see" will get you strange looks from UNIX lovers.

ASCII: It's properly pronounced "AS-kee" not "ASK-two." (See *ASCII*.)

DOS: It rhymes with *boss,* not *dose*.

Ethernet: The starting *e* is a long *e:* "EE-ther-net," and not a short *e* (as in *men*). It comes from the word *ether,* which is pronounced "EE-ther." But there's also the word *ethereal,* which is pronounced "uh-THEER-ee-al," and that confuses people.

GIF: Most people say "jiff," like the peanut butter. A small but stubborn contingent claims that it's "GIF," as written.

GNU: It's "noo." Some people have a tendency to say "gah-NOO," but the *g* is silent, just as in *gnu* (which is an African antelope).

GUI: Pronounced "GOO-ee" or often by letters, as in "jee-yoo-eye." Try to avoid saying "gwie" or "gwee" as in *Guido*.

Linux: The only official source on this pronunciation is Linus Torvalds himself, who says "LEE-nooks." The natural tendency of American English readers is to say "LIE-nuks." The presumptuous and those-who-pretend-like-they're-hot-stuff crowd says "LIN-uks."

queue: Say "kyoo." It means "a line" in all English-speaking countries, except America. As an interesting side note, the American computer book publisher QUE once began life as Queue, named after a printing queue. The name was shortened to just QUE after it was found that most people could not pronounce *queue*.

vi: The UNIX people argue back and forth about whether it's pronounced "vee-ie" or "vie," but they all agree that you should never call this text editor "six."

Ten Old-Timer Computer User Words

ARPANET: Before the Internet, there was the ARPANET. Although some, having been on the Net since 1991 or so, will claim to be Internet old-timers, the true grizzled computer veteran would have had an ARPANET account way back in the 1970s.

BBS: Long before the Internet became popular (and because few had ARPANET access, or even wanted it), people with computers and modems communicated using bulletin-board systems. These computers, often sponsored by individuals with a spare computer and a phone line, were the sole means of e-mail, communication, news, and software for a decade or so before the World Wide Web took over. You may still find BBSs operating in your area; a computer users' group, club, or local computer store may run one.

code: Used as a noun, refers to the instructions contained inside a program. Whenever old-timers would talk about a crummy program, they would mumble "Bad code." It was like they didn't see the program as an individual thing, but rather as lines of computer code. As a verb, code means " to write programs," so a high compliment might be "Man, can you code!"

CRT: It isn't a monitor. It isn't a screen. And it's definitely not "that TV-set-like thing on top of the keyboard." No, it's a CRT (cathode ray tube).

DOS: Although this term is not as venerated as other terms, a growing portion of the computer-using community claims a certain status because they had to "put up with" DOS. Or maybe they mastered DOS or merely just miss DOS.

foo: A term commonly used by UNIX lovers that can mean just about anything. In a way, it is the John Doe of UNIX filenames. It's also found in various programming books, where it's overused to the point of nausea.

hack: A prestigious and worthy occupation, hacking was often a necessity in the old days, when programs required modification in order to work on different equipment. Believe it or not, there was a time when a floppy disk formatted on one computer was utterly unreadable by any other computer. A hack, which was a noble attempt to get something to work properly, was required in order to make things work together. Conversely, it could also be a sloppy-yet-effective attempt, requiring even more hacks to get things right.

terminal: Before microcomputers came along in the late 1970s, all computers were massive things too important to be used by just one person at a time. So all the computers had terminals attached, though which you could use the thing. Even today, many old-timers refer to PCs as terminals.

VAX: Perhaps the most common yet unpopular type of minicomputer ever. Because most universities had a VAX, many of today's old-timers were weaned on it. Having used or — better still — programmed on a VAX is a real sign that someone is an old-timer.

zap: A common term for old-timers to use, probably because it has so many confusing uses. You can *zap* (copy) a file. You can also *zap* (delete) a file. The hardware could be *zapped* (destroyed) by a power surge. In most other cases, the definition of *zap* was always left up to the speaker, which made the term confusing but still highly useful.

Ten Words Tech Support Doesn't Want to Hear

computer genius: Whether you call yourself one ("I don't want to mess around with baby things — I'm a computer genius, so will you just tell me. . . .") or you confess that your friend is one, tech support couldn't really care less. If someone really were a computer genius, he probably wouldn't call tech support in the first place, right?

crunch: A sound made when two things that prefer to live apart are suddenly, through a means unnatural to them, live closer together; implies pain. Crunch is not a good thing to happen to any part of a computer.

hose: You use a hose to water your lawn; computers use cables. Yeah, we know, we know — we often use the term *hose* to describe the cable that connects computers on a network. We're being cute. It's a cable. It's plastic with one or more metal wires down the middle. It's not a hose.

idiot: Refers to someone who's a few kilobytes short of a megabyte, sometimes used in a self-deprecating way — which is okay for tech support. But when you call the tech support person an idiot, you don't get much tech support.

OEM: Acronym for original equipment manufacturer and inserted into the serial number of any Microsoft product pre-installed on your computer. Whenever you phone Microsoft for tech support, it hears "OEM" and immediately redirects you to Dell or Gateway or whomever made the computer. Dell or Gateway (or whoever) then replies that it doesn't support software it didn't write and re-directs you to Microsoft — and on and on. "OEM is quickly replacing *Catch-22* as a phrase for 21st century frustration."

shrink wrap: The clear, plastic material used to enclose new computer stuff. Tech-support people prefer that you give it the Old College Try before you phone up and have them assist you. "Back in the early 1990s, WordPerfect technical support claimed that 40 percent of its first-time callers still had the software in its shrink-wrapped box."

sizzle: See *crunch*.

thing: A name used to describe that with which the caller is unfamiliar. A thing could be software, hardware, something on the screen, a switch, a knob, a button, a graphic, an icon, a window, a dialog box, a connector, a jack, a disk, or anything the caller wants it to be. In most cases, "thing" probably refers to the computer, as in "This thing doesn't work."

IDG BOOKS BOOK REGISTRATION

Register This Book and Win!

We want to hear from you!

Visit **http://my2cents.dummies.com** to register this book and tell us how you liked it!

- Get entered in our monthly prize giveaway.

- Give us feedback about this book — tell us what you like best, what you like least, or maybe what you'd like to ask the author and us to change!

- Let us know any other *For Dummies*® topics that interest you.

Your feedback helps us determine what books to publish, tells us what coverage to add as we revise our books, and lets us know whether we're meeting your needs as a *For Dummies* reader. You're our most valuable resource, and what you have to say is important to us!

Not on the Web yet? It's easy to get started with *Dummies 101*®: *The Internet For Windows*® *98* or *The Internet For Dummies*® at local retailers everywhere.

Or let us know what you think by sending us a letter at the following address:

For Dummies Book Registration
Dummies Press
10475 Crosspoint Blvd.
Indianapolis, IN 46256

...FOR DUMMIES™

BESTSELLING BOOK SERIES